Luminos is the Open Access monograph publishing program from UC Press. Luminos provides a framework for preserving and reinvigorating monograph publishing for the future and increases the reach and visibility of important scholarly work. Titles published in the UC Press Luminos model are published with the same high standards for selection, peer review, production, and marketing as those in our traditional program. www.luminosoa.org

BERKELEY SERIES IN POSTCLASSICAL ISLAMIC SCHOLARSHIP

Series Editors: Asad Q. Ahmed and Margaret Larkin

1. *The Light of the World: Astronomy in al-Andalus,* by Joseph ibn Naḥmias; edited, translated, and with a commentary by Robert G. Morrison
2. *Language between God and the Poets: Maʿnā in the Eleventh Century,* by Alexander Key

Language between God and the Poets

Language between God and the Poets

Maʿnā in the Eleventh Century

Alexander Key

UNIVERSITY OF CALIFORNIA PRESS

University of California Press, one of the most distinguished university presses in the United States, enriches lives around the world by advancing scholarship in the humanities, social sciences, and natural sciences. Its activities are supported by the UC Press Foundation and by philanthropic contributions from individuals and institutions. For more information, visit www.ucpress.edu.

University of California Press
Oakland, California

Suggested citation: Key, A. *Language between God and the Poets: Maʿnā in the Eleventh Century.* Oakland: University of California Press, 2018.
DOI: https://doi.org/10.1525/luminos.54

Library of Congress Cataloging-in-Publication Data

Names: Key, Alexander (Alexander Matthew), author.
Title: Language between God and the poets : maʿnā in the eleventh century / Alexander Key.
Description: Oakland, California : University of California Press, [2018] | Series: Berkeley series in postclassical islamic scholarship ; 2 | Includes bibliographical references and index. | Key, Alexander 2018
Identifiers: LCCN 2018009383 (print) | LCCN 2018013953 (ebook) | ISBN 9780520970144 | ISBN 9780520298019 (pbk. : alk. paper)
Subjects: LCSH: Islamic philosophy—11th century. | Islamic poetry—11th century. | Arabic language—Religious aspects—Islam.
Classification: LCC B741 (ebook) | LCC B741 .K4338 2018 (print) | DDC 181/.92—dc23
LC record available at https://lccn.loc.gov/2018009383

25 24 23 22 21 20 19 18 17
10 9 8 7 6 5 4 3 2 1

In Memoriam
Wolfhart P. Heinrichs, 1941–2014
James Richard Jewett Professor of Arabic, Harvard University

CONTENTS

ACKNOWLEDGMENTS

This is a book that remains imperfect but that has nevertheless been rescued by many of my colleagues. Geert Jan van Gelder reminded me with painstaking and patient corrections how Arabic morphology and poetry work; Ulrich Rudolph reminded me that Richard Frank wrote more than two articles; David Vishanoff reminded me how to write a book; Beatrice Gruendler reminded me to look at Abū Hilāl al-ʿAskarī again; Gabriella Safran reminded me that Gilles Deleuze is not everything; Roland Greene reminded me not to write backwards; Sepp Gumbrecht reminded me what theory does; Rebecca Gould reminded me that translation is a universal claim; Indra Levy reminded me that this book is an experiment; Michelle Karnes and Robert Gleave both reminded me that there are readers out there who care; Toril Moi reminded me that Wittgenstein could work for them; Vincent Barletta reminded me that critics did read Wittgenstein; Shahzad Bashir reminded me that dates have meaning; James Weaver reminded me about Manfred Ullman; Dafna Zur and Alvan Ikoku reminded me that writing is hard; and Lara Harb (both in her published work and in generous comments on drafts of this book) reminded me what scholarship on Classical Arabic is. Behnam Sadeghi provided an unsolicited, detailed correction of a passage that didn't make it into the book, but he reminded me about the stakes and scope of accurate philology. My department of Comparative Literature and my Division of Literatures, Cultures, and Languages showed me that Arabic doesn't have to exist in a vacuum. The Division's Poetics Focal Group taught me about poetics and listened with patience to me trying to explain al-Ǧurǧānī on more than one occasion. The Stanford Humanities Center helped me bring together some of the names above to improve the manuscript and then gave me a place to finish the revisions. Stanford Libraries provided me with a faculty study next to the PJ classification in the Cecil H. Green Library, and Bob Gregg stopped by to remind me the book would get finished. At the beginning of the writing process, Felicitas Opwis invited me to give a lecture in the Islamic Studies Lecture Series at Georgetown University and forgave (I hope) my failure to submit the lecture to *Mélanges de l'Université Saint-Joseph*. Closer to the end, Mohammad Salama invited me to give a lecture at SFSU. Ghufran Alkhamis provided her superlative words-per-minute typing rate in Arabic at a crucial moment. Khalil Barhoum offered to proofread the Arabic text and did so with patience and aplomb. Yusuf Mullick proofread the Arabic indexes after my last minute call for help on Twitter. The University of California Press, and the series edited by Asad Q. Ahmed and Margaret Larkin, agreed to publish the book, and the reviewers provided support. One anonymous reviewer's reading of the theology chapter was particularly important and rescued me from a damaging misrepresentation of my own ideas. Rodrigo Adem provided some very helpful comments late in the revision of that same chapter. Elias Muhanna read a nearly final version and put his finger right on a major problem while saying, "Don't change a word." My father, Geoffrey Key, read all the drafts, agreed with Geert Jan van Gelder about "baptism" being a bad translation of *waḍ*ʿ, located innumerable moments of incoherence, and provided useful rewordings. Finally, I am excited for Johanna Soon-Young Key and Ruby Soo-Jin Key to pick up this book; they have seen plenty of drafts lying around their childhoods. Joyce Jieun Song, my partner and their mother, has been the source of all my inspiration ever since we met, sixteen years ago in Nazareth.

NOTE ON TRANSLATION PRACTICE, TRANSLITERATIONS, AND FOOTNOTES

My treatment of *maʿnā* and *ḥaqīqah* is consistent throughout: whenever I say, "mental content" in English, the Arabic word is *maʿnā*, and whenever I say, "accurate," "accuracy," or "accurately" in English, the Arabic word is *ḥaqīqah*. This applies in all contexts. In order to make arguments about translation, I sometimes (as here) use the Arabic words themselves in transliteration.

The full Arabic text for a direct quotation is always given in a footnote. All direct translations are mine and are marked by the presence of quotation marks. Paraphrases are also furnished with the Arabic text in a footnote, a practice that makes the relationship between my periphrastic explanations and the original words of the scholars themselves available for interrogation by readers who know Arabic. For readers who do not know Arabic, the boundaries between paraphrase, interpretation, and explanation will be somewhat blurry. This is an acceptable and inevitable part of any translation process. The inclusion of the original Arabic texts in the footnotes has also allowed me to be more idiomatic in translation, and to more frequently use paraphrase, than might otherwise have been the case. This is particularly true in the translations of poetry, where I have struggled toward a goal of aesthetic impact in English, often at the cost of accuracy, by manipulating the lineation and enjambment.

In all the footnotes, I have provided the page number and line number of Arabic and Persian texts. I have added critical voweling to the Arabic footnotes and removed any editorial punctuation. Interpolations in square brackets within the Arabic footnote text are my own, unless attributed in parentheses to the editor of the text in question.

There is a general English index, an Arabic index for the text in the footnotes, and a pair of short Arabic indexes for the quotations of poetry.

The transliteration or romanization system used is known colloquially as "ZDMG" and officially as DIN 31635 from the Deutsches Institut für Normung. While this system is heavy on the non-English diacritical marks, it has the advantage of replacing one Arabic letter with one English letter in all cases. Readers who do not know Arabic and are interested in pronouncing these foreign words may like to know that *ḫ* stands for a guttural *kh*, *š* for *sh*, and that both ʿ and ʾ are variants on the glottal stop. The remainder of the diacritical marks are only really important for those who study Arabic and its dialects.

Dates are given in the Gregorian solar calendar, and I have a discussion of this choice in the section of chapter 1, "Contexts," titled "The Eleventh Century."

OPENING STATEMENT

What is language? How does language work? Scholars writing in Arabic in the eleventh century had good answers to these two questions. Their theories of language, mind, and reality—of words, ideas, and things—appear in books about how to describe God, how to interpret scripture, how to solve logical problems, and how to criticize poetry. They used a conceptual vocabulary very different from the Anglophone or European toolbox that academia provides for us today. This book is a study of their Arabic intellectual world and a translation of their approaches to questions that still concern us a millennium later. It is a book about these scholars' analyses of how their minds worked, and of the role language played when they turned those minds to the world outside.

My methodological principle in this research has been to follow eleventh-century Arabic scholars' conceptual vocabulary into their areas of concern. This is consequently a book about *maʿnā* (their word for mental content) and about *ḥaqīqah* (their word for accuracy). It is very much a work of philology. But a tantalizing prospect has persistently intervened, the prospect of finding theories about aspects of human experience that are universally applicable. We share with these eleventh-century scholars the experience of having a mind, using language, and enjoying poetry, but this shared experience is impaired by the absence of shared vocabulary. So this is a book of philology and translation, in which I write about how *maʿnā* did not play a role in their conceptual vocabularies that is at all equivalent to the role "mental content" plays for us today. *Maʿnā* was an omnipresent, useful, and stable word that enabled eleventh-century scholars to explain a great deal, whereas my invariable translation, "mental content," is an uneasy academic neologism with a highly uncertain reception and different implications in different scholarly disciplines. I use it to mean the stuff of cognition. The benefit of "mental content" is its strangeness in ordinary English: while it can cover an appropriate range of cognitive items and processes, its awkwardness reminds us that we are dealing with a conceptual vocabulary that is not our own. *Ḥaqīqah* was equally omnipresent, and I suggest in this book that it was always used to describe something claimed to be accurate. My argument is not that we should always translate *maʿnā* as "mental content" and *ḥaqīqah* as "accuracy" or "accurate account" (although I have done so in this book) but rather that it is useful to always think of *maʿnā* as mental content and *ḥaqīqah* as the process of getting something right. My decision in this book to persist invariably with a single translation for *maʿnā* and *ḥaqīqah* is a practical tactic to make that thought experiment easier. Translation in this book is an experimental process and not a conclusion.

I engage in the translation struggle because of the tantalizing prospect outlined above: that eleventh-century Arabic scholarship contains observations of interest to twenty-first-century academics who work on language, translation, or literary criticism but do not read Arabic. I also engage because philology is "the discipline of making sense of texts" (Sheldon Pollock),[1] and I think that my experimental translations of *maʿnā* and *ḥaqīqah* have produced answers that help us further understand the theological, lexicographical, logical, and literary-critical work of the scholars studied in this book. I show how a curated Arabic lexicon interacted with pragmatics and was fundamental to all other scholarly disciplines, how Islamic theology was both about naming and about science, how logic was built with both Greek and Arabic, and how this new Arabic logic combined with old Arabic grammar to produce literary criticism. These are all eleventh-century Arabic accounts of what language is and how it works.

These Arabic accounts used *maʿnā* in descriptions of both the connections between mind and language, and the connections between mind and reality. The meaning of a word was a *maʿnā,* and the attribute, quality, or essence of an extramental thing was a *maʿnā.* The word *ḥaqīqah* could then be used to describe any of these connections as accurate. If language pointed accurately at mental content it was *ḥaqīqah,* and if mental content accurately reflected extramental reality it was *ḥaqīqah.* Cognition took place in and with *maʿnā;* mental content was the stuff of cognition. When words aligned accurately with mental contents, they were *ḥaqīqah.* When mental contents were an accurate account of the real world, they were *ḥaqīqah.* Eleventh-century scholars writing in Arabic all thought about cognition and language in similar ways, using a single vocabulary. We do not have parallel concepts or practices in English or other European

1. Pollock (2014, 22).

languages. On the contrary, we have vocabularies with genealogies entirely unconnected to this Arabic conceptual vocabulary. This is why it is difficult for us to see how lexicographers could have been so influential in the creation of theory, how theologians could have thought that arguing about naming was rational and ontologically salient, how a logician could have used the vocabulary of Arabic grammar and theology to explain mental existence, and how a literary critic could have described literary beauty as produced by grammar and logic. My book tries to explain these positions.

At every step in their intricate theorizing, the eleventh-century scholars were negotiating the relationships between words, ideas, and things using an autochthonous vocabulary based around *maʿnā*. But they were not negotiating our sensitivities to the boundaries between these three categories, nor were they struggling to explain the meaning of the words *maʿnā* and *ḥaqīqah*. These were just words that they used as part of their core conceptual vocabulary. They did not care about the fault lines of a European history of ideas that was still several centuries in the future. They were sensitive to different things; they cared more about hermeneutics, for example, than about the threat of linguistic relativism, and this makes their solutions to questions of language reference and accuracy all the more interesting. The problems are the same: we still have minds and use words like they did, but the contours of debate have changed along with the vocabulary. In certain areas, this is an advantage: an intellectual culture obsessed with hermeneutics, suffused with bilingualism, and in possession of both a vast canon of classical poetry and a carefully curated lexicon was arguably in a better position to produce theories of language than we are today.

I have chosen to focus on four scholars who lived and worked in what is now Iran and Iraq. All four men would prove hugely influential in the centuries to come, although, as the remarks above may lead one to expect, not all of them would be as famous in Europe as they were in the Arabic, Persian, and Turkic worlds. The one man whose fame and theories crossed north into Europe was the Aristotelian philosopher Ibn Sīnā (Avicenna), whom I use to investigate a discipline he played an oversized role in creating: Arabic logic. The other three were less translated. Ibn Fūrak was a theologian, exegete, and legal theorist whose reworking of the Ašʿarī theological school's doctrines remains a reference point today. Ar-Rāġib al-Iṣfahānī was a contemporary of both men and a lexicographer who wrote exegesis, creed, literary compendia, and literary criticism, and who provided much of the synthesis between Neoplatonic and Perseo-Arabic ethics that Abū Ḥāmid al-Ġazālī (d. 1111) would make famous a century later. Finally, ʿAbd al-Qāhir al-Ǧurǧānī was a grammarian who wrote two works of literary criticism that changed the field for ever.

Al-Ǧurǧānī's poetics, his account of the aesthetics of language in both the Quran and Classical Arabic poetry, is the subject of my seventh chapter, "Poetics."

His theories cannot be understood, nor could they have come into being, without the Arabic lexicography that ar-Rāġib exemplifies, the Islamic theology that Ibn Fūrak represents, or the Aristotelian logic developed by Ibn Sīnā. But to make lexicography, theology, and logic the servants of literary criticism would be unfair to the scholars who worked in those fields. Ar-Rāġib had his own ideas about poetics; Ibn Fūrak, his own perspective on the Quran's language; and Ibn Sīnā, his own clear sense of a philosophical mission. I do not want to present these genres, or these scholars, in a story of chronological progression or influence. I would like them to be test cases through which I advocate for a philological focus on *maʿnā*. If I can demonstrate that reading for *maʿnā* helps us understand ar-Rāġib, Ibn Fūrak, Ibn Sīnā, and al-Ǧurǧānī, then readers may be tempted to use the same strategy for reading the work of other scholars from other genres in other centuries. This hope is also a deliberate rejection of disciplinary and genre boundaries. These scholars knew that exegesis was different from legal theory, and that ethics was different from poetics, but that did not stop them writing books in both or all fields, nor did it stop them from writing what we may consider philosophy in their exegesis or poetics in their ethics. Most important for my methodology, these discipline-conscious scholars, who never missed an opportunity to delineate the terminological and conceptual differences between the genres of scholarship they covered, used a stable conceptual vocabulary with *maʿnā* at its core across all their books without distinction. That is my contention, and its translation my task.

In chapter 2, I work through the precedents for the use of *maʿnā* that were available to scholars in the eleventh century. *Maʿnā* was a word that had already done a great deal of work in translations from Greek, in literary criticism, in grammar, and in theology. With that terrain laid out, chapter 3 pauses to establish a methodology for translation with the help of Wittgenstein, Kuhn, and secondary scholarship on Arabic. Then, in chapter 4, I start to lay out eleventh-century epistemology. It begins with the lexicon. I use ar-Rāġib's works to describe the basic set of eleventh-century assumptions about what language was, how reference and intent worked, and what *maʿnā* and *ḥaqīqah* meant. Ibn Fūrak shared these assumptions, and with his theology I show how reading for *maʿnā* reveals how epistemology (his account of how we know) could bleed into ontology (his account of what there is) and vice versa. It is here that we see some of the fruits of what was for eleventh-century authors an unproblematic slippage between language and cognition, and between the mind and the world. *Maʿnā* was undoubtedly cognitive, but it was also linguistically determined, just as while it was clearly in the mind, it was also out there in the extramental world as well. Neither slippage was as problematic for Ibn Fūrak and ar-Rāġib as it is for us. Their understanding of cognition was almost entirely linguistic, and it was anchored by the lexicon. Their understanding of God allowed him, using a single mechanism consisting of *maʿnā,* to control both the qualities of extramental things and the cognitive representations of those qualities and things in human minds.

From Arabic lexicography and Islamic theology I move to Aristotelian logic with Ibn Sīnā. Here, reading for *maʿnā* shows how this move is not as great a conceptual leap as one may expect. Greek logic turned into Arabic logic when it started working with *maʿnā,* and reading logic through this lens reveals the connections between Greek structures and the linguistic, literary, and theological discussions of the Arabic eleventh century. Ibn Sīnā also provides some clarity on whether logic is about cognition or about language, clearing up a millennium-old commentary *quaestio* about the relationship of the linguistic opening passages of *De Interpretatione* to logic. *Maʿnā* was the item of autochthonous Arabic core conceptual vocabulary that enabled this move and several of Ibn Sīnā's other core philosophical contributions. His account of logical cognition also provided al-Ǧurǧānī, a few decades later, with a conceptual vocabulary that could be turned to aesthetics. *Maʿnā* is the conceptual vehicle by which Arabic grammar entered al-Ǧurǧānī's poetics. I argue that it is only by focusing on *maʿnā* that we can clearly see these connections. In the final translation problem of the book, I aim to explain how a literary critic located lyric eloquence in grammar itself. Al-Ǧurǧānī did this by using an account of cognitive process that explained how the *maʿnā* in our heads is manipulated by the words we hear and read. Those words come to us in syntactic, grammatically governed, order. The beauty lies in this sequencing and in the associated adjustments that the poet makes. Poetics becomes grammar; grammar becomes logic; and poetic genius is the unexpected in syntax. Accuracy becomes dynamic. The contents of our heads are where the magic happens. With al-Ǧurǧānī we have a model in which new mental content is created, content that never had and never will have a referent in language or in the world outside. Literature uses grammar, logic, and even theology, but it goes beyond them to create something new. The achievement of al-Ǧurǧānī's criticism was to explain, using *maʿnā,* how this worked.

From Greek, to Arabic and Persian, and then to English (via Latin), this is a book about translation. The eleventh-century scholars who wrote Arabic also spoke (and in some cases wrote) Persian. They read Greek in translation. Today, I write in English, a language with a European history stretching back through Latin, into which I am trying to transpose the Arabic writings of native speakers of Persian. The critical extra element that makes the translation process so problematic and so important is that I am translating theories. Or, as Thomas Kuhn would put it, I am translating core conceptual vocabulary that helps shape the theories it constitutes. This circular process makes it hard to jump from an eleventh-century Arabo-Persian space into a twenty-first-century Anglo-European one. It is worth restating that there is no word in English that does the work done by *maʿnā* in Arabic. My choice in this book, "mental content," does a job as a placeholder, but that is all. In chapter 3 I will delve into these methodological questions of translation in more detail. I will defend my experimental attempt to replace a single theoretical term with a single theoretical translation, arguing that the resultant dissonance in the English target language reminds us that we do not have a core conceptual vocabulary in which epistemology and ontology bleed into each other. On the contrary, we have a conceptual vocabulary that separates them into "epistemology" and "ontology." There was no word for either in eleventh-century Arabic.

1

Contexts

This is a book about four eleventh-century scholars who lived a millennium ago. But it is also a book about ideas that took shape as if the world outside did not exist. The authors involved conceived their accounts of language, divinity, reason, and metaphor as universal accounts of the human condition. They did not see their Muslim, Arabic, Persian, medieval, context as a determining factor in these universal accounts, and neither should we. To claim that eleventh-century Muslim scholars, writing in Arabic, expressed a universal human spirit with just as much purchase on language, mind, and reality as we achieve today is an endorsement of the position in the history of thought made famous by Leo Strauss.[1] However, in order to make sense of eleventh-century texts we need to explore the books their authors had read, the debates in which they were taking part, and the *a priori* commitments they held: this is the methodology for the history of thought advocated by Quentin Skinner.[2]

THE ELEVENTH CENTURY

What can we say about the eleventh century? It was known, in its own calendar, as the fifth century of the Islamic era that started in 622 A.D. with Muḥammad's emigration from Mecca to Medina (*al-hiǧrah;* hence the name of that calendar: Hiǧrī) and was counted in lunar years thereafter. The different calendars are, of course, a translation problem. The boundaries of the eleventh-century that I am using (1000

1. Strauss (1989).

2. Skinner (2002).

and 1100) are not just artificial; they were wholly absent from the imaginations of the scholars who lived between them, for whom those same years were numbered 390 and 493. I have chosen to provide dates in just one calendar, the Gregorian solar calendar dominant in my target language, English. This entails a slight loss of exactness: lunar-solar conversion is only accurate when one is in possession of the day and month in the source calendar, and so dates in this book should be regarded as approximate, plus or minus one year. My excuse for this loss of exactness is that the sources do not always provide the day and month for events such as births and deaths, which means that imprecision is found on both sides of the translation process (when the day and month is known in Arabic, I do of course ensure that the English date is accurate). The boundaries of the eleventh century also cut off differing amounts of the early lives of my four authors, as well as awkwardly forcing famous later scholars such as al-Ġazālī (who was born in 1058) into an imagined "eleventh-century" picture. I would therefore like to say at this early point in the book that I use the phrase "eleventh-century" simply as shorthand for the period of time in which the four scholars in whom I am interested worked. With "eleventh-century," I am not trying to make my English translation sound awkward in order to highlight a gap in conceptual vocabulary, as is the case with "mental content." On the contrary, I am aiming for an idiomatic English phrase that can indicate the years with which I am concerned. Another way to look at the utility of this flawed chronological label is that it enables me to avoid many other types of labels that are arguably more problematic (classical, postclassical, late Abbasid, Būyid, renaissance, medieval, Islamic, Islamicate, Arab, Persian, etc.).

What else can we say about the eleventh century? Although we do not give our years the same numerical labels, or determine them with the help of the same celestial body, we do share the chronological unit of a calendar year with Ibn Fūrak, ar-Rāġib, Ibn Sīnā, and al-Ǧurǧānī. Like them, we record our family histories in generations, and count time in years. This means that we can try to imagine what the weight of scholarly and linguistic precedent felt like to them. The civilization in which they wrote was an established one. Its first written text, the Quran, was understood to have been gathered by the prophet's followers in the 640s and 650s, and the foundational grammar of Sībawayh (d. ca. 796) was written in the 790s. So for our four authors, their particular confessional community and its concern with language was over 350 years old, and some of the scholarly texts they read were over 200 years old. As for the Arabic language itself, it was well over a millennium old; the "first clear attestation of an Arabic word occurs in the Kurkh monolith inscription of the neo-Assyrian monarch Shalmaneser III (853 B.C.E.)."[3] Transposing this chronology onto my own Californian situation at the beginning

3. Al-Jallad (2018, 315).

of the twenty-first century, 350 years ago European colonialists were still failing to establish a foothold on the eastern seaboard of what is now the United States, and 200 years ago those colonists (now a state) were fighting the Anglo-American War while California had become part of the First Mexican Empire. Readers of this book in the Europe where I grew up are in the same chronological relationship to Galileo, Hobbes, and Descartes as Ibn Fūrak and his contemporaries were to Sībawayh. When we users of English on either continent rewind an equivalent distance to the reign of Shalmaneser and his use of Arabic, there are no early attestations of our language (at what was the time of Tacitus we are scarcely aware of a language related to English among the Germanic peoples). One may therefore say about the Arabic eleventh century that its scholarly pursuits were as old as California and its language as ancient as Latin. When they read Greek philosophy, Aristotle (d. 322 B.C.) was as far removed from them as Muḥammad is from us.

THE FOUR SCHOLARS

In the world of Classical Arabic scholarship it is easy to forget that we know of our authors' lives only through their appearances in the biographical literature or from their own works. Although we share with them the contours of a human life and a life spent reading books, we do not have access to much information about how their lives looked or felt. Their published works usually provide little of the information that a biographer may look for today, and autobiographical writing was rare. This leaves us with the innumerable biographical dictionaries produced across all disciplines and confessional identities from the early ninth century onward, scaled up by their authors for detail or down for concision, with lax and catholic attitudes to inclusion or with rigorously policed boundaries. These collections of biographies constitute a massive self-referential and self-disciplining archive, produced contention and invention, and are now all that we have. In this archive, our four authors fared quite differently.

The archive reminds us of its own scale. To read it for the biographies of these four men is to be confronted with the depth and breadth of the intellectual conversations in which they were engaged: a great number of scholars across a large geographical space, working on a broad range of topics. Much of this information is now lost to the vicissitudes of time and the difficulties of preserving manuscripts across a millennium, but a great deal is still available in printed editions (relatively few) and unedited manuscripts (vast in number), and I have not read all of it by any means. My primary methodological response to the scale of the archive has been to privilege depth of reading over breadth. I chose to select four scholars for this book because this choice has enabled me to read sufficient amounts of their work. Extending my scope to more authors would, within the inevitable constraints, have led me to read less of each author's work, and perhaps most problematic, to read selections and passages rather than complete books. The kind of argument that I am making, one in which I take a commonplace word that occurs almost everywhere and show how it reveals a functioning conceptual vocabulary that helps us understand theories about language, is the kind of argument that necessitates reading books from start to finish. As a result, I have read Ibn Fūrak's *Muǧarrad*, al-Ǧurǧānī's *Asrār* and *Dalāʾil*, and ar-Rāġib's *al-Iʿtiqādāt*, *aḏ-Ḏarīʿah*, *Muqaddimah fī t-Tafsīr*, *Tafṣīl*, and *Rasāʾil* in their entireties. I have read around widely in the same authors' other works, and in those of Ibn Sīnā, in whose case I have also relied on secondary scholarship to supplement my reading of the first seven chapters of his *Eisagoge*, the first two chapters of his *Categories*, and the first chapter of his *De Interpretatione*. (Work on Ibn Sīnā's *Sophistical Refutations* remains a desideratum.)

In this book, major eleventh-century authors other than the four selected appear occasionally. They include al-Qāḍī ʿAbd al-Ǧabbār al-Asadābādī (d. 1025; see J. R. T. M. Peters on his theories about language)[4] and the equally well-known theologian and legal theorist Abū Bakr al-Bāqillānī (d. 1013, the subject of a recent dissertation by Rachel Friedman).[5] Others do not appear at all, for example the important Andalusian literary theorist Ibn Rašīq (d. ca. 1064). A great theologian and legal scholar, Ibn Ḥazm (d. 1064), appears only in the biographical review of Ibn Fūrak. The absence of these latter two men could possibly be excused by their geographical distance from the conversations that are the subject matter of this book. But spending as much time in the archive as I have over the last eight years has led to the emergence of personal predilections and judgments, and this has particularly been the case in my preference for Ibn Fūrak over al-Bāqillānī. I judge the former to have published more intellectually cohesive works than the latter, to little fanfare in Anglophone and European-language scholarship. That scholarship has, however, made great strides in recent decades when it comes to language theory, and this is particularly true in an area that I only touch on in passing in this book: legal theory. (See inter alia my review of a recent important work on legal theory and literalism by Robert Gleave.)[6]

Ar-Rāġib

Ar-Rāġib is the first of our four men. They are all men; the eleventh century was patriarchal, and while women wrote poetry, took part in Hadith transmission, and created identity (on which see Nadia El Cheikh),[7] they were excluded from the production of the extant theory, whether lexicographical, theological, logical, or

4. Peters (1976).

5. Friedman (2015).

6. Key (2015). Cf. Ali (2000), Gleave (2012), Lowry (2004), Vishanoff (2011), Zysow (2013).

7. El-Cheikh (2002), (2005), (2015).

literary-critical. Abū al-Qāsim al-Ḥusayn b. Muḥammad b. al-Mufaḍḍal ar-Rāġib al-Iṣfahānī was the author of a hugely influential glossary of Quranic and scholarly vocabulary, a thinker whose approach to problems of theology, ethics, politics, and poetry was invariably linguistic. He never met an academic problem that he could not reduce to a matter of signification and therefore to the lexicography he had mastered. Ar-Rāġib was the subject of my doctoral dissertation, and consequently the first eleventh-century scholar in whom I noticed the attitudes to language that are the subject matter of this book. I do not intend to repeat here the detailed intellectual biography of ar-Rāġib that I have provided elsewhere; instead I will provide a brief survey that touches on his sectarian affiliation and the confusion over his death date. Both questions are, appropriately enough, problems of translation: ar-Rāġib did not himself have any confusion about the dates of his own lifetime, nor did he exhibit any uncertainty as to his own sectarian positions and beliefs. These questions have arisen only in the biographical archive over the millennium that separates him from us.

As we will shortly see with Ibn Fūrak, the biographical archive produced lists and compendia of scholarly biographies according to theological and legal schools of thought, as well as of scholars according to birthplace and date. Ar-Rāġib appears in no such collections until a century after his death (al-Bayhaqī),[8] and even thereafter the notices are short on biographical detail or concerned with confusion about his theological affiliations (as-Suyūṭī).[9] From the twelfth to the twentieth century, notices in both Arabic and European languages have provided a variety of incorrect death dates (aḏ-Ḏahabī, al-Ḫwānsārī, Brockelmann, etc.),[10] and it is only through recent research (including my own) that we have been able to ascertain from the oldest manuscript witness to his Quranic glossary that ar-Rāġib was alive in or before 1018.[11] It is quite possible that ar-Rāġib's internally consistent but confessionally diverse set of doctrinal positions kept him out of biographical dictionaries that were in the process of delineating rival orthodoxies. The madrasa taxonomical process had little motivation to engage with the biography of a scholar who had combined ideas from schools of thought and creedal identities that were, in hindsight, in conflict with each other. And yet we just don't know enough about Iran in the eleventh century to be confident ascribing an iconoclastic or even catholic selection of doctrinal solutions to ar-Rāġib. In his community, he may well have been representative and uncontroversial. He

8. Al-Bayhaqī (1946, 112); Key (2011), (2012, 40–41); Meyerhof (1948, ##131, 132).

9. Key (2012, 83), as-Suyūṭī (1979, 2:297).

10. Brockelmann (1996a, 1:289), (1996b, 1:505), aḏ-Ḏahabī (1985, 18:120–21), al-Ḫwānsārī (1991, 216), Key (2012, 39).

11. Al-Ǧawharǧī (1986), Key (2012, 32f), ar-Rāġib (409/1018).

could not have known that in the future it would be the Aš'arī creedal synthesis of Ibn Fūrak, rather than his own, that would contribute to what would be known as Sunni Islam. It is unlikely that he combined figurative interpretation of the Quran (a technique associated with the Mu'tazilī School of theology) with a refusal to deviate in any way from divine precedent in the description of God (a position associated with the rival Ḥanbalī School) because of a wish to be uninfluential or idiosyncratic.[12]

The best way to bring some concrete philological fact to ar-Rāġib's biography is to examine his published work. This will also help orient us in the scholarly world of the eleventh century. Ar-Rāġib was an exegete as well as a man of letters and an aesthete. Apart from the glossary of the Quran mentioned above, his most popular work was a literary anthology of prose and poetry, and beyond that he wrote both ethics in a Neoplatonic and post-Aristotelian vein, and poetics that foreshadowed al-Ǧurǧānī's advances in understanding eloquence (albeit his authorship of the poetics work has not been established beyond all doubt).[13] Ar-Rāġib's literary anthology, Quranic glossary, and ethical treatises proved most popular in the madrasa marketplace, as can be seen from the distribution and transmission of their manuscript copies around the world. His creedal work was only just preserved, and the same is true of his poetics; it seems that the creedal work was too idiosyncratic and the poetics quickly overshadowed by al-Ǧurǧānī. Today, almost every Arabic library in the world has a copy of ar-Rāġib's glossary of the Quran, and the text is virtually unchanged from its earliest manuscript witness. His literary anthology remains a popular source of scatological data about sexuality for researchers, and his ethicopolitical works are the subject of twenty-first-century commentary in North Africa.[14] One reason for the popularity of his ethics is the influence he had on the much more famous al-Ġazālī, an influence that took the form of al-Ġazālī's large-scale and unattributed copying, as demonstrated by Wilferd Madelung.[15]

The catholic synthesis that characterizes ar-Rāġib's positions places him, despite *ex post facto* uncertainty about his sectarian affiliations, at what may be called the center ground of Islamic theology and politics. This is certainly true when we compare him to Ibn Fūrak and Ibn Sīnā. As we will see below, the former was a proud theologian whose careful parsing of words and reality would leave

12. Key (2011), (2012, 80–85).

13. Key (2012, 53, 259), ar-Rāġib (ca. 14th century). Cf. al-Andalusī (1987). My thanks to 'Umar as-Sanawī al-Ḫālidī for his identification of ar-Rāġib's ms. with the *Mi'yār*; further work will be forthcoming from us both.

14. Key (2011), (2012).

15. Madelung (1974).

him open to the criticism of later taxonomizers such as Šams ad-Dīn aḏ-Ḏahabī (d. 1348), and the latter was a proud Aristotelian who would be thus excoriated by al-Ġazālī. Ar-Rāġib, on the other hand, espoused at different times all three of the major trends in Arabic intellectual thought through the eleventh century and beyond. At times he hewed close to the first school of Islamic theology, the Muʿtazilah; at others, he was sympathetic to their opponents and the school of Ibn Fūrak, the Ašʿarīyah, and yet he often claimed to be part of the stream that cried a pious plague on both their houses and rejected the process of theology itself. His was a synthesis of Islamic intellectual history, for as Sabine Schmidtke writes: "Within the Sunni realm at least, Ashʿarism proved more successful and enjoyed a longer life than Muʿtazilism, yet, like Muʿtazilism, Ashʿarism was constantly challenged by traditionalist opponents rejecting any kind of rationalism."[16] Ar-Rāġib played all three roles and espoused Shia ideas and slogans, to the chagrin of each school and sect's madrasa taxonomizers. The name he gave to his own preferred affiliation, "traditionists, senior sufis, and wise philosophers,"[17] does not to the best of my knowledge appear anywhere else. And yet it combined three major streams of theological and ethical thought and practice: traditionist piety and rejection of complex dialectical theology, the mystical approach to epistemology that has been called "Sufism," and the Aristotelian and Neoplatonic ethical heritage that proved so attractive to later synthesizers such as al-Ġazālī.[18] Ar-Rāġib then allowed this combination to seep, however subtly, into his glossary of the Quran, a work that would become an irreproachably orthodox and popular reference work across the coming millennium. This centrality allows me, in chapter four, to use ar-Rāġib to establish eleventh-century assumptions about language and the lexicon.

Ibn Fūrak

Abū Bakr Muḥammad b. al-Ḥasan b. Fūrak enjoyed a decorated career teaching and debating theology across what is now Iraq, Iran, and Afghanistan until his death by poisoning in 1015, when he was around seventy-five years old. His biography therefore sounds very different from that of ar-Rāġib. Rather than dealing with a catholic synthesis of contested mainstreams, we meet the school synthesizer himself. As we will see, Ibn Fūrak was so fundamental in constructing the doctrine of the Ašʿarī School of theology that he appears today in the footnotes of Arabic and European-language scholarship as the citation that establishes an Ašʿarī position. His controversial death provides an incontrovertible *terminus post quem* for his eleventh-century life. His biography will also read differently from that of

16. Schmidtke (2008, 19).

17. Ar-Rāġib (1988a, 252.16). مذهب أهل الأثر ومحصّلي الصوفية والحكماء.

18. Key (2012, 73–97).

ar-Rāġib because there is a great deal more material available to us. Conversely, while ar-Rāġib's biography can easily be found elsewhere,[19] a detailed synthesis of the biographical material on Ibn Fūrak is less immediately available. I will attempt to provide a synthesis here. It is a short review of Ibn Fūrak's biography, and it will tip the reader headlong into a maelstrom of creedal positioning, archival parsing, and theological controversy. The topics and allusions may seem abstruse, but careers and even lives were at stake.

In the extant bibliographical tradition, Ibn Fūrak first appeared in the work of his pupil, the well-known Sufi exegete Abū al-Qāsim al-Qušayrī (d. 1072). In his influential monograph *ar-Risālah* (*The Epistle*), al-Qušayrī mentioned Ibn Fūrak with veneration on multiple occasions. It is clear that Ibn Fūrak was a source of historical knowledge, spiritual guidance, and creedal principle; an authority whose presence in the text would make al-Qušayrī's case for his beliefs more persuasive.[20] Ibn Fūrak was also an acknowledged source of wisdom, so when al-Qušayrī wrote about the need for devotees to be patient with the blandishments of fellow mystics more advanced on the Sufi path, he called on an anecdote from his teacher: "I heard Ibn Fūrak saying, 'There is a proverb: if you cannot bear the blacksmith's hammer then why be his anvil?'"[21] Ibn Fūrak was also a moral and scholarly paradigm, so in the creedal apologetic for his Aš'arī School of theology written by the Damascene historian Ibn 'Asākir (d. 1176), we learn of Ibn Fūrak's charitable work for the sick, tireless rate of publication, and service in the structures of his Sufi order. Ibn 'Asākir also reports (on the authority of al-Qušayrī) that Ibn Fūrak told a story of having been taken in chains to Shiraz after an accusation of creedal error only to catch sight at daybreak on arrival of a mosque inscription "God takes care of his servants," (Quran 39:36, az-Zumar) and to know in his heart he would soon be released.

According to Ibn 'Asākir, Ibn Fūrak taught first in Iraq, then moved to Rayy, where he was involved in theological disputes. He next received a commission to Nishapur, where the authorities built him both a madrasa and an infirmary, and then when his published works in theology and law had reached almost one hundred, he was summoned to Ghazna. In Ghazna, which lies in what is now eastern Afghanistan, Maḥmūd b. Sebüktigin (r. 998–1030) was leading an empire he had created that stretched from Iran to India. Maḥmūd was engaged in a political process of policing theological disputes in the emerging consensus that would in later centuries become Sunni Islam. According to Ibn 'Asākir, Ibn Fūrak engaged

19. Key (2011), (2012).

20. Al-Qušayrī (1966, 1:22). Translation: al-Qušayrī (2007).

21. Al-Qušayrī (1966, 2:749; cf. 2:536f).

in intense dispute with the followers of a rival school of theology (al-Karrāmīyah), and on his return journey to Nishapur "was poisoned" and died.[22]

The biographical tradition we have access to today does not produce just cross-references that enable us to fill in the gaps. It also reports from sources that are lost. Ibn ʿAsākir's work on Ibn Fūrak used a biographical dictionary that Ibn Fūrak himself had written, which is now lost: *Ṭabaqāt al-Mutakallimīn.*[23] In his dictionary of adherents to the Šāfiʿī legal school, the Hadith scholar Ibn aṣ-Ṣalāḥ (d. 1245) reported a biography of Ibn Fūrak that he attributed to the now-lost history of al-Ḥākim an-Nīsāpūrī (d. 1014). This biography confirms the information in Ibn ʿAsākir and may well have been its source. To add extra color, al-Ḥākim via Ibn aṣ-Ṣalāḥ also reported that Ibn Fūrak attributed his study of theology to the moment when a legal scholar whom he was frequenting was stumped by one of Ibn Fūrak's hermeneutical questions. The scholar covered up his ignorance with bluster and was corrected by another authority, and that second authority was subsequently recommended to Ibn Fūrak. Ibn Fūrak decided he had to study this discipline for himself.[24]

Thus far, we have dealt with hagiography. Ibn Fūrak has appeared as an admired and influential figure whose achievements and movements are reported in multiple sources. But he did not die peacefully in his bed, and the theological controversy that (may have) killed him reverberated across the Islamic world. It reverberates in the biographical tradition. Writing in the thirteenth century, Ibn aṣ-Ṣalāḥ alerts us to a near-contemporary of Ibn Fūrak, albeit from thousands of miles to the west. The famous Andalusian legal scholar Ibn Ḥazm celebrated what he claimed was the execution of Ibn Fūrak by Maḥmūd of Ghazna as punishment for an alleged speech crime: Ibn Fūrak had maintained that the prophet Muḥammad was a "messenger" during his lifetime and then just a "prophet" thereafter (the title, "messenger" was usually reserved for prophets who brought divine scripture, making "prophet" a broader and less prestigious category). Ibn Ḥazm held that Ibn Fūrak had contradicted the plain statements in the Quran and elsewhere that "Muḥammad is the messenger of God," statements that occur without explicit temporal restrictions on their reference.[25] The legal school that Ibn Ḥazm played a large part in creating (*aẓ-Ẓāhirīyah*) was, after all, founded on exactly this sort of methodology, antithetical to the careful ontological parsing

22. Ibn ʿAsākir (1928, 232–33). Cf. Allard (1965, 321–29). Allard's study predates the availability of most of the sources I have used.

23. Ibn ʿAsākir (1928, 125.1). Thanks to Rodrigo Adem, who is working on a study and translation of Ibn Fūrak, for this reference.

24. Ibn aṣ-Ṣalāḥ (1992, 1:136–38).

25. Ibn Ḥazm (1899–1903, 4:215). Cf. Massignon (1982, 3:199).

of Ibn Fūrak. For Ibn Ḥazm, if the Quran said Muḥammad "is" the messenger of God, then Ibn Fūrak was not allowed to restrict that "is" by saying Muḥammad was first a messenger and then a prophet. To give a brief preview of my arguments in chapter 5, Ibn Ḥazm and Ibn Fūrak shared a belief that names and naming mattered, and that what one called God had a direct connection to one's salvation. But they disagreed about how accuracy was determined. For Ibn Ḥazm, *ḥaqīqah* was literal word use in divine revelation, a precedent that had to be followed. For Ibn Fūrak, *ḥaqīqah* was cognitive accuracy: the ability of human language to get at the truth about God.

Ibn aṣ-Ṣalāḥ was, like al-Qušayrī, Ibn ʿAsākir, and al-Ḥākim, sympathetic to Ibn Fūrak. He denied that Ibn Fūrak had ever actually taken such a position about the use of the term "messenger." Ibn aṣ-Ṣalāḥ attributed Ibn Ḥazm's accusation to a slander against Ibn Fūrak's Ašʿarī theological school by their rivals in Ghazna, the Karrāmīyah. Ibn Fūrak's own work appears to bear out this defense; he wrote that God can, if he wants, make a single messenger serve for every nation on earth (thus implying that the category is not necessarily bound by time and place),[26] and in this discussion of controversies concerning the category of "messenger," he was silent on the question of whether "once a messenger always a messenger" was true for Muḥammad.[27]

Ibn aṣ-Ṣalāḥ was actively engaged in policing the boundaries of creedal positioning, which required clear determinations of which scholars fall where in the biographical taxonomies. He was keen to give his readers in the madrasa an explanation for Ibn Ḥazm's attack. He explained that the Karrāmīyah slander reported by Ibn Ḥazm in fact stemmed from their misreading of a different theological controversy, that of whether a saint knew he was a saint. Ibn aṣ-Ṣalāḥ directed his readers to al-Qušayrī, who had indeed reported that Ibn Fūrak maintained in the face of opposition (including al-Qušayrī himself) that the saint was unaware of his sainthood, because were he to be confident in it, he would no longer fear God. Ibn aṣ-Ṣalāḥ also wrote that al-Qušayrī explained Ibn Fūrak's position further (I have not been able to find the text in al-Qušayrī's published works) as referring to the feeling of being a saint, not the statement of whether or not one is a saint.[28] This extra statement functions, in this biographical entry, as a gloss on Ibn Fūrak's position, allowing the reader to understand that the saint may well not feel like a saint (and thereby still be afraid of God) but would still be able to say he was a saint (and thereby perform as a Sufi in the order). The move is typical of the archive; its goal is the stability and integrity of the archive itself.

26. Ibn Fūrak (1987, 175.16).

27. Ibn Fūrak (1987, 174–76), (1999, 128–29).

28. Ibn aṣ-Ṣalāḥ (1992, 1:138), al-Qušayrī (1966, 2:662).

As the centuries passed, the bibliographers of the madrasa continued to place Ibn Fūrak in the mainstream, either by repeating and synthesizing the early accounts discussed above, as Ibn Ḫallikān (d. 1282) did,[29] or by including extra detail that would be significant to their readership, as did Taqī ad-Dīn aṣ-Ṣarīfīnī (d. 1244) and aḏ-Ḏahabī. Aṣ-Ṣarīfīnī, for whom Ibn Fūrak was the first entry in his biographical dictionary of Hadith transmitters who worked in the city of Nishapur, wrote that Ibn Fūrak was a transmitter of the Hadith collection of the ninth-century Abū Dāwūd, which in aṣ-Ṣarīfīnī's thirteenth century was becoming one of the six canonical Sunni collections.[30] Aḏ-Ḏahabī repeats that information in his biographical dictionary,[31] and in his even more voluminous history he also takes the time to enumerate the controversy with Ibn Ḥazm discussed above. There, aḏ-Ḏahabī criticizes Ibn Fūrak, nevertheless prefers Ibn Fūrak to Ibn Ḥazm, and overall sides with Maḥmūd of Ghazna, whose empire must have looked in hindsight like a great moment for Sunni Islam.[32] Then, in the entry on Maḥmūd himself, aḏ-Ḏahabī relates a suggestive anecdote in which Ibn Fūrak appears to represent theology's potential to lead people astray. Ibn Fūrak was telling the ruler that God should not be described as being high, because that would open the door to God being described as low, when Maḥmūd exclaimed: "I wasn't going to describe him at all until you started pressuring me!" Ibn Fūrak is rendered speechless and dies shortly thereafter, galled [literally! "They say his gall bladder split."][33] The implication in the anecdote is that the two events are connected, and that Maḥmūd is right to distrust the complicated theories of the scholars. This is the traditionist attitude to theology that we encountered with ar-Rāġib, who wrote: "The discussions about whether God wills for himself, or whether he wills with an eternal will, or with a created will, and if with a created will is the will in a specific place or not in a specific place—God has protected us from needing to deal with these matters!"[34]

Tāǧ ad-Dīn as-Subkī (d. 1368) has perhaps the longest biographical entry on Ibn Fūrak. He includes a complete review of the sources reviewed above with his critical commentary, extra hagiographic anecdotes such as the claim that Ibn Fūrak would stay up all night reading the Quran in any house he visited if there were one available, and an explicit justification of the need to revisit the question

29. Ibn Ḫallikān (1948, 3:402).

30. Aṣ-Ṣarīfīnī (1989, 15–16).

31. Aḏ-Ḏahabī (2004, 11:109–110).

32. Aḏ-Ḏahabī (1990–2001, 28:147–49).

33. Aḏ-Ḏahabī (1990–2001, 29:73).

34. والكلامُ في أنَّ الله تعالى هو مريدٌ لنفسه أو بإرادة قديمة أو مُحْدَثة وأنه وإنْ كان مريداً بإرادة مُحْدَثة فهلْ هي في محل أو لا في محل مما كفانا الله أَمْرَه. Key (2012, 81), ar-Rāġib (1988a, 270).

of his controversial death. As-Subkī does not blame Maḥmūd of Ghazna but rather calls the scene before the ruler fake news and the poisoning a response by the Karrāmīyah to their failure to convince Maḥmūd to execute Ibn Fūrak on false charges. As-Subkī sides with aḏ-Ḏahabī against Ibn Ḥazm; Ibn Fūrak, against aḏ-Ḏahabī; and al-Qušayrī, against Ibn Fūrak. The entry is an exercise in theological defense of Ibn Fūrak, preservation of the reputations of the ruler Maḥmūd and the mystic al-Qušayrī, and professional self-promotion vis-à-vis his slightly older contemporary aḏ-Ḏahabī.[35]

Apart from providing a fascinating window into the biographical and taxonomical processes of Islamic scholarship, what this complicated accounting of theological controversies shows us is that Ibn Fūrak was widely read among the great scholars of his time, famous in the century of his death as far afield as Islamic Spain, and while he was controversial in terms of what he said about God, he was not tangential to the conversation. It is worth stressing again that the point of contention between Ibn Fūrak and Maḥmūd was linguistic; it was an argument about what to say, and how to talk about God. Ibn Fūrak had wanted to police Maḥmūd's speech according to the logic that he had developed, but Maḥmūd resisted. At the interface between politics and theology, everyone was focused on language.

For the purposes of this book, I have used Ibn Fūrak's survey of the creedal positions of al-Ašʿarī, *Muǧarrad Maqālāt al-Ašʿarī* (*An Abstraction from the Statements of al-Ašʿarī*), in Daniel Gimaret's exemplary edition. I will also make some use of Ibn Fūrak's legal and hermeneutical work.[36] The *Muǧarrad* is, however, much more than a survey. Abū Ḥasan al-Ašʿarī (d. 935) was the eponymous figure around whose ideas the Ašʿarī School of theological doctrine was founded. It was this Ašʿarī School that provided a set of dialectically established creedal positions that self-identified as universally Muslim and around which Sunni Islam would coalesce in a process of distinguishing itself from its opponents.[37] Ibn Fūrak studied in Baghdad at the beginning of his career with one of al-Ašʿarī's students, Abū al-Ḥasan al-Bāhilī, and then wrote at the beginning of the *Muǧarrad* that the work was designed to meet an express need for knowledge of the principles that governed al-Ašʿarī's theories and upon which al-Ašʿarī's dialectical successes against his opponents had been built. It was a matter of gathering "both that for which there is textual evidence and that for which there is no textual evidence, in which latter case I have answered according to what is appropriate for al-Ašʿarī's principles and rules. I will also tell you where there are internal inconsistencies in al-Ašʿarī, where there are consistent doctrines, and where we have resolved

35. As-Subkī (1964–, 4:127–35).

36. Ibn Fūrak (1906), (1999), (2003).

37. For a concise review: Heinen (2011).

inconsistency by selecting what is closest to his schools of thought and most suited to his principles."[38] A principle was "that upon which knowledge of other things is built." Ibn Fūrak thought that if he laid out al-Ašʿarī's principles, he would need to give fewer examples.[39] Ibn Fūrak did indeed then explicitly disagree with al-Ašʿarī's positions. Al-Ašʿarī thought that holy men who were not prophets or messengers could be completely immune from sin, but Ibn Fūrak wrote that "nothing like that is said by us."[40] Ibn Fūrak highlighted inconsistencies between al-Ašʿarī's published works on, for example, the question of whether or not God's eternality is in his self, and confidently decided that, according to "our community of skilled theologians," it is.[41] He wrote that al-Ašʿarī's followers were largely ignorant of some of the contradictions within his oeuvre, and that this may have been due to inconsistent distribution of al-Ašʿarī's published works.[42]

In his book's closing paragraph, Ibn Fūrak was confident that he had achieved the goal he set himself.[43] A diffuse and sometimes contradictory set of dialectical debates had become a single, internally consistent, ordered and referenced manual of creedal positioning. The logic to which it adhered was that of Ibn Fūrak, even if he couched his statements in language that attributed the theology to al-Ašʿarī. Al-Ašʿarī's own debates, and by extension the teaching of al-Bāhilī, had failed to produce an account of al-Ašʿarī's governing principles, so Ibn Fūrak had taken on the task and then used the rules and principles identified to tidy up the doctrine. What better place could there be for us to look for the conceptual vocabulary of the eleventh century than a work self-conceived as the imposition of a consistent eleventh-century epistemology (Ibn Fūrak's) on a diffuse tenth-century theology (al-Ašʿarī's)?

Scholarship on Islamic theology has already made good use of Ibn Fūrak's work as a source for al-Ašʿarī's ideas, an approach of which he would have approved. This is a fair caricature of Ibn Fūrak in the work of A.I. Sabra, Daniel Gimaret,

38. وأنْ أَجمع لكم منها مُتفرّقها في كتبه ما يوجد منها منصوصاً له وما لا يوجد منصوصاً له أَجَبْنا فيه على حَسَب ما يليق بأصوله وقواعده وأُعرّفكم مع ذلك ما اختَلف قولُه فيه في كتبه وما قَطَع به منهما وما لم يَقطع بأحدهما ورأينا أنَّ أحدهما أَولى بمذاهبه وألْيَق بأصوله فنبّهنا عليه. Ibn Fūrak (1987, 9.5–8).

39. حدُّ الأصل هو ما يُبنى عِلْمُ غيره عليه. Ibn Fūrak (1999, 146). والإبانةُ عن كشْف أصوله في هذا الباب تُغني عن الجواب في تفريع المسائل التي تتفرّع عن هذا الأصل. Ibn Fūrak (1987, 134.19–20).

40. ولا يقال مِثْلُ ذلك عندنا. Ibn Fūrak (1987, 126.16).

41. وعليه الحذّاقُ من أصحابنا المناظرين عنه. Ibn Fūrak (1987, 326.7–12).

42. وهذا [الخلافُ] غيرُ معروف عند أصحابه لعزّة وجود هذا الكتاب عند أكثرهم وبعضه لقلّة عِنايتهم بتدبرّها [لعل الصواب: بتدبرّه (جيماريه)]. Ibn Fūrak (1987, 165.11–12).

43. Ibn Fūrak (1987, 338.24–339.2).

and Louis Massignon. (Cf. Jan Thiele.)[44] Ibn Fūrak will instead appear in this book *qua* Ibn Fūrak, an experiment in reading him that permits his authorial voice to come through, both in the criticism of al-Ašʿarī detailed above and, more engagingly, in his remarks about the state of the eleventh-century field. Expressing sentiments familiar to an academic seeking to publish in any age, Ibn Fūrak wrote that a monograph on al-Ašʿarī's doctrine already existed, that it was full of errors and mistakes, and, most damaging, that it had already "spread throughout the lands!"[45] Comfortingly, perhaps, posterity was kind to Ibn Fūrak's work, which survives in print today while that of his rival, Muḥammad b. Muṭarraf aḍ-Ḍabbī al-Astarābāḏī, is lost.[46]

Ibn Sīnā

When we come to review the biography of our third scholar, Abū ʿAlī Ḥusayn Ibn Sīnā (d. 1037), the situation is completely different. Rather than trawling through the untranslated Arabic and Persian biographical and bibliographical archive, we are dealing with a philosopher whose Latinized name, Avicenna, is familiar to all students of European Scholasticism and Humanism, and whose cultural ubiquity is revealed by, inter alia, the appearance of his portrait in medical-facility waiting rooms across the Middle East. He was a successful politician in a turbulent period of history, a logician and philosopher whose work reshaping the Aristotelian and Neoplatonic traditions transformed the subsequent millennium of Arabic intellectual endeavor, and the doctor who took over from Galen as the standard reference in Europe until the seventeenth century. We are also in an entirely different situation when it comes to European-language scholarship. From his autobiography, and from the many accounts of his contemporaries, we know about his life and how he imagined it. In Dimitri Gutas's *Avicenna and the Aristotelian Tradition,* we have a primer and reference to this information and, more important, an analytical map of Ibn Sīnā's works and their engagement with the Arabic Aristotle of the eleventh century.[47] Much of Ibn Sīnā has been translated into English (long after it was translated into Latin), and monographs and collections on various aspects of his philosophy and legacy abound.[48] Less work has been done on Ibn Sīnā's philosophy of language, and it is here that I will focus my attention. Ibn Sīnā will

44. Gimaret (1988), (1990); Massignon (1982); Sabra (2006), (2009); Thiele (2016a, 229–30).

45. اعلمْ أنه قد انتشر هذا الكتاب في البلدان. Ibn Fūrak (1987, 323.14).

46. Gimaret (1985, 198–201).

47. Gutas (1988).

48. Good starting points: Adamson (2013), McGinnis and Reisman (2004), Reisman and al-Rahim (2003).

also represent, for my purposes, the discipline of Arabic logic that was proving so attractive and productive in the eleventh century.

There is a famous and possibly apocryphal anecdote from the beginning of the thirteenth century that during a discussion of lexicography at the court of ʿAlāʾ ad-Dawlah Muḥammad, the ruler and patron/employer of Ibn Sīnā (r. ca. 1007–41 in Isfahan and beyond), the prominent lexicographer Abū Manṣūr al-Ǧabbān said to Ibn Sīnā that he did not care to compete with a logician: "We do not approve of your statements about the Arabic lexicon." Ibn Sīnā was reportedly embarrassed, and the criticism stung him into writing a series of epistles on lexical niceties (including a lexicon or glossary, *The Language of the Arabs*).[49] Sure enough, when ʿAlāʾ ad-Dawlah tested Abū Manṣūr on a later court occasion, Ibn Sīnā was prepared to jump in and demonstrate a command of Arabic lexical rarities and provenances that shamed his opponent and led to a prolonged apology.[50] Ibn Sīnā clearly represented the discipline of logic for his contemporaries. This anecdote shows us not only that in the Arabic eleventh century there were charged discussions about lexicography at court but also that the totemic status of the study of word meanings was such that a scholar whose power spanned academia and politics could be stung into writing a dictionary. Ibn Sīnā's eleventh-century desire to perform literary expertise in addition to medicine and philosophy would be reflected in the archive of subsequent centuries: the twenty-page biographical entry on Ibn Sīnā in Ibn Abī Uṣaybiʿah's (d. 1270) history of medicine includes eight solid pages of complex poetry composed by the logician on subjects including old age, the soul, and love ("It is as if I am magnetic, and she is iron.")[51]

Al-Ǧurǧānī

Al-Ǧurǧānī's reputation as the greatest theorist of Arabic poetics is a reputation cemented in the madrasa system, largely through the efforts of the great polymath Faḫr ad-Dīn ar-Rāzī (d. 1209), who wrote a systematized madrasa-ready version of al-Ǧurǧānī's theories.[52] Abū Bakr ʿAbd al-Qāhir b. ʿAbd ar-Raḥmān al-Ǧurǧānī died in 1078 or 1081 after a life spent writing and teaching in his native town of Gorgan at the southeastern tip of the Caspian Sea, in what is now Iran. This is about as much as we know of his biography; in stark contrast to Ibn Sīnā and Ibn Fūrak he maintained a stellar reputation unadorned by biographical (or indeed autobiographical) information. (See Lara Harb in 2016 and, from 1944,

49. Gutas (1988, 216, 442–44).

50. أنت منطقيٌّ ما نُعارضك وكلامُك في لغة العرب ما نَرضاه. Al-Qifṭī (2009, 4:176–77).

51. فكَأَنَّني | قَدْ صِرْتُ مَغْناطِيسَ وَهِيَ حَدِيدُ . . . Ibn Abī Uṣaybiʿah (1884, 2:16.7). But cf. Gutas (1988, 511).

52. Ar-Rāzī (1992).

Muḥammad Ḫalafallāh's review of the scholarship in Arabic up to that point.)[53] We know almost as little about his life as we do about ar-Rāġib's, the difference between the two being largely that al-Ǧurǧānī's name would be associated with his ideas throughout the millennium after his death, whereas ar-Rāġib's theories were either submerged in the facticity of his lexicography or appropriated by the more famous al-Ġazālī.

Al-Ǧurǧānī's efforts in teaching (or the success of his pupils) meant that when the madrasa bibliographers came to review his career they had plenty of evidence of other scholars studying with him or commenting on his works.[54] But al-Ǧurǧānī first appears in extant surveys as a poet, in the collection of contemporaneous poetry gathered by his slightly younger contemporary and Baghdadi bureaucrat ʿAlī b. Ḥasan al-Bāḫarzī (d. 1075). Al-Ǧurǧānī's entry is ten lines of poetry in praise of the dominant politician of the day, the founder of the madrasa Niẓām al-Mulk (on whom more below).[55] Then a century later, in his biographical dictionary of literary figures, Ibn al-Anbārī (d. 1181) tells us that al-Ǧurǧānī was one of the greatest grammarians of the age, and that his teacher Ibn ʿAbd al-Wāriṯ was, atypically for this period, the only teacher that al-Ǧurǧānī ever had, because he never left Gorgan.[56] Ibn ʿAbd al-Wāriṯ (d. 1030) was the maternal nephew of the great grammarian Abū ʿAlī al-Fārisī (d. 987),[57] on whose studies of morphology and syntax al-Ǧurǧānī wrote voluminous commentaries,[58] which are extant (and have been studied by Antonella Ghersetti) along with his shorter pedagogical grammar books.[59] Even in the thirteenth century with Ibn al-Qifṭī (d. 1248 and one source of the Ibn Sīnā anecdote above), al-Ǧurǧānī remains largely a grammarian notable for not leaving Gorgan. Beyond grammar, al-Qifṭī mentions al-Ǧurǧānī's work on Quranic inimitability, which "showed his knowledge of the principles of eloquence and the path of concision,"[60] and "a number of scattered discussions that he fixed in a volume, which was like a notebook for him."[61]

53. Ḫalafallāh (1944, 14–23), Harb (2017). See also Harb and Key forthcoming in the *Journal of Abbasid Studies* 5(1–2), a special issue on al-Ǧurǧānī.

54. Ibn al-Anbārī (1970, 274), al-Qifṭī (2009, 1:222, 223, 343; 2:100, 248, 306, 355; 3:118).

55. Al-Bāḫarzī (1993, 1:499–500).

56. Ibn al-Anbārī (1970, 264–65).

57. Ibn al-Anbārī (1970, 251), al-Qifṭī (2009, 3:116–18).

58. On morphology: al-Ǧurǧānī (2007). On syntax: al-Ǧurǧānī (1982).

59. Ghersetti (2011), al-Ǧurǧānī (196–), (1972), (1987 (1988), (1990).

60. وله إعجازُ القرآن دلَّ على معرفته بأصول البلاغة ومَجاز الإيجاز. This book is al-Ǧurǧānī's *Ar-Risālah aš-Šāfiyah fī Wuǧūh al-Iʿǧāz*, printed in al-Ǧurǧānī (1992a, 573f). Also al-Ǧurǧānī (1959b).

61. وله مسائلُ مَنثورةٌ أثبتها في مجلد هو كالتذكرة له. Al-Qifṭī (2009, 2:188–90).

The key moment for al-Ǧurǧānī's reputation came slightly later in the thirteenth century with the great polymath Faḫr ad-Dīn ar-Rāzī. His reading of al-Ǧurǧānī (although not unprecedented; see Noy)[62] would dominate the madrasa and consequently dominate intellectual history. The works of al-Ǧurǧānī that ar-Rāzī synthesized in his concise textbook were not the works of grammar noted by the biographers. He wrote that the most important knowledge, the noblest discipline, was that of language, without which nothing else could be known. But people were confused about how language worked and about its principles until al-Ǧurǧānī, "the Glory of Islam," came and laid out those principles. Ar-Rāzī wrote that al-Ǧurǧānī "wrote two books in this field, the first of which he called *Dalāʾil al-Iʿǧāz* [*Indications of Quranic Inimitability*] and the second of which he called *Asrār al-Balāġah* [*Secrets of Eloquence*]."[63] These two books are the subject of significant English-language scholarship by Margaret Larkin and Kamal Abu Deeb,[64] and are the texts I focus on in my final chapter. They are also the subject of a forthcoming special issue of the *Journal of Abbasid Studies,* in which Avigail Noy and Matthew Keegan successfully expand the story of al-Ǧurǧānī's reception beyond ar-Rāzī, and Harb and I briefly review the secondary scholarship.[65] The *Asrār* and *Dalāʾil* were a singular event in the history of Arabic language theory. But they required reading, and here ar-Rāzī started a trope for al-Ǧurǧānī's biography: that his works were disorganized: "But al-Ǧurǧānī, may God have mercy on him, because he was bringing out the principles and divisions of this science, its requirements and rules, neglected to take care of arrangement into sections and chapters, and was also exceedingly prolix."[66] I will discuss the accuracy of this characterization and its theoretical implications in the chapter on al-Ǧurǧānī. Ar-Rāzī felt that he needed to rewrite al-Ǧurǧānī for the madrasa, although the chronological gap between them was less than two hundred years and the language, Arabic, was the same.

THE MADRASA

Looking through the archive for the biographies of these four scholars does not just remind us how dependent we are on its taxonomies, heresiographies, biographical

62. Noy (2016, 140–44).

63. Al-Ǧurǧānī (1954), (1992a); ar-Rāzī (1992, 50–51).

64. Abu Deeb (1979), Larkin (1995).

65. Avigail Noy, Matthew Keegan, and Harb and Key: all forthcoming in the *Journal of Abbasid Studies* 5(1–2), a special issue on al-Ǧurǧānī.

66. ولكنه رحمه الله لكونه مستخرجاً لأصول هذا العلم وأقسامه وشرائطه وأحكامه أَهْمَلَ رعايةَ ترتيب الفصول والأبواب وأَطْنَبَ في الكلام كل الإطناب. ar-Rāzī (1992, 51).

dictionaries, and syntheses. The archive also reminds us that the story of their works was written in institutional settings they could not have foreseen. It cannot have been apparent to al-Ǧurǧānī, writing his long iterative notebooks of theory, that there would be a pressing institutional need for his ideas to be turned into textbooks less than two hundred years after his death. The creation of that need is the story of an educational institution: the madrasa. It can only now be written with hindsight by historians for whom the eleventh century appears as a turning point for intellectual history. The madrasa was the Islamic educational structure that came out of the mosque, turned into something like a university, and would go on to dominate the next millennium.

With several centuries of intellectual production across a range of confessional, professional, and aesthetic disciplines behind them, tenth- and eleventh-century Arabic-language scholars were engaged in complex theoretical debates. The debates associated with language were the most advanced, not least because they had started first. For example, the glossary of the Quran written by ar-Rāġib at the start of the 1000s came more than two hundred years after the first extant dictionary had been written by al-Ḫalīl b. Aḥmad (d. ca. 786), the teacher of Sībawayh.[67] But while these disciplines have been shown to be mature by the tenth and eleventh centuries,[68] they had not yet been significantly impacted by institutional structures. Scholarship had been taking place in homes, courts, mosques, and in a wide variety of structures with variant relationships to the state (a state that tended, as a gross generalization, to restrict itself to the military and fiscal aspects of politics, leaving sociocultural hegemony to be negotiated by the scholars). While the madrasa that made its appearance in the eleventh century did not necessarily change the balance of power between society and state in the way its founders may have intended, it did change the venue of scholarship. Nor did the madrasa necessarily change the content of scholarship. But what it did do was slowly change the form, giving impetus to existing trends toward the solidification of genre and disciplinary boundaries, and increasing the degree of specialization and professionalization among scholars, whether they were professional bureaucrats (*kuttāb*, on whom in this period see Andrew Peacock),[69] teachers, authors, or any combinations thereof.

With hindsight, scholarship does look different in the centuries following the famous eleventh-century madrasas founded across what is now Iraq, Iran, Afghanistan, and Turkmenistan (in Baghdad, Balkh, Nishapur, Herat, Isfahan, Basra, Merv, Amol, and Mosul) by the Persian vizier of the Turkish Seljuk dynasty,

67. Al-Ḫalīl b. Aḥmad (1980), ar-Rāġib (1992).

68. Heinrichs (1995).

69. Peacock (2015, 189–215, esp. 208f).

Niẓām al-Mulk (d. 1092).[70] If we look only at theories of language, many of the new ideas that I deal with in this book as cross-genre conversations become in the twelfth, thirteenth, and fourteenth centuries disciplines of their own, with textbooks, manuals, and disciplinary identities to be taxonomized. The structured education that took place in madrasas needed curricula, and the formal consequences were inevitable. This does not in any way imply that there was change in the degree of innovation, creativity, or theoretical complexity across Arabic scholarship. (Some final rebuttals of that old trope have been provided by Robert Wisnovsky and Khaled El-Rouayheb.)[71] What it does mean is that while in the eleventh century we have to skip across genres and disciplines to establish the usage of *maʿnā,* in the fourteenth and fifteenth centuries we can look at two disciplines with their own textbooks and rules (*ʿilm al-maʿānī,* "the science of *maʿānī* [the plural of *maʿnā*]" and *ʿilm al-waḍʿ*, "the science of word coinage"). But these new disciplines cannot be understood without their eleventh-century heritage, and the clarity they provide is illusory. There is little to be gained from our reading a textbook in either field without an understanding of the conceptual vocabulary that informed it; it would be like trying to comprehend the theory of relativity without knowing what Einstein and his contemporaries meant when they used the word "gravity."[72] Furthermore, these two disciplines do not by any means represent the full breadth of usage of *maʿnā* after the eleventh century. *ʿIlm al-maʿānī* was the label for a subsection of the new "Science of Eloquence," one of the branches of formal literary study developed from al-Ǧurǧānī's work. But at the same time, the word *maʿnā* was being used to write and develop theories in all the other literary subsections, as well as outside the study of poetry and poetics altogether. And just as in the eleventh century, this apparent terminological confusion does not appear to have been a problem for the scholars actually doing the work. It becomes a problem only when we come to translation. I think that we have to look at the eleventh century in order to understand how *maʿnā* worked in the madrasa centuries. The purpose of this book is to engage with the interacting genres that preceded the influential madrasa textbooks and their associated disciplinary identities.

It is my hope that this book on the eleventh century will help scholars of Arabic poetics, logic, and intellectual history more broadly deal with occurrences of *maʿnā* and *ḥaqīqah* in the thirteenth through the nineteenth centuries. My reading of *ḥaqīqah* as a label for accurate processes from the early periods onward could productively connect with Khaled El-Rouayheb's analyses of fifteenth- and sixteenth-century scholarship as "suffused with the rhetoric of *taḥqīq,* that is, of the need to

70. Melchert (2011).

71. El-Rouayheb (2006), (2015); Wisnovsky (2004a).

72. Cf. Kuhn (2000, 231).

critically assess received scholarly propositions."[73] My experiment of reading *maʿnā* as "mental content" could help scholars of the later *ʿilm al-maʿānī* understand how *maʿnā* was both the label for a formal subsection of a discipline and also used across that whole discipline and beyond without contradiction. My experiment could also help scholars of *ʿilm al-waḍʿ* understand exactly what the object of the process of word coinage was and where that object was located. For the object of concern in ʿAḍud ad-Dīn al-Īǧī's (d. 1355) *Risālat al-Waḍʿ* was *maʿnā*, and the separate linguistic discipline created by al-Īǧī and his commentators on this foundational two-page treatise was concerned with mapping the ways that vocal forms (*alfāẓ*) indicated mental contents. It did so through a taxonomy that combined grammatical parts of speech (such as noun, verb, and proper noun) with the logical categories of universal and particular to create a complete linguistic map of word coinage. Al-Īǧī used *maʿnā* both to talk about the mental content of other scholars ("the *maʿnā* of the statement of the grammarians that . . .") and to construct his own theories about the functioning of prepositions and relative particles.[74]

The *ʿilm al-maʿānī* created by as-Sakkākī (d. 1229) and al-Ḫaṭīb al-Qazwīnī (d. 1338) in *Miftāh al-ʿUlūm* (*The Key to the Sciences*) and *Talḫīṣ al-Miftāḥ* (*Condensed Version of the Key*) was the study of syntax, inspired by the work of al-Ǧurǧānī himself. This disciplinary area of study excluded the consideration of, inter alia, comparison (*tašbīh*), language that went beyond the lexicon (*maǧāz*), antithesis (*muṭābaqah*), and paronomasia (*taǧnīs*), all of which still inevitably consisted of analysis of the poetic manipulation of *maʿānī* and were dealt with in *ʿilm al-bayan* and *ʿilm al-badīʿ*. (See Noy, Harb, and William E. Smyth.)[75] After the eleventh century *maʿnā* was used both as a disciplinary label and to do theoretical work across multiple disciplines. Scholars writing in Arabic across the madrasa centuries continued to use the word *maʿnā* to develop and to name their studies of what language was and how language worked. *Maʿnā* remained core conceptual vocabulary for many centuries after our four scholars' deaths.

73. El-Rouayheb (2015, 32), Ibrahim (2013, 396).

74. . . . أنَّ معنى قول النحاة . . . فإنَّ الحرف يدل على معنى في غيره وتحصُّلُهُ بما هو معنى فيه والموصولُ أمرٌ مُبْهَمٌ يتعيَّن عنده بمعنى فيه. Al-Īǧī (2010, 10.14, 21–22), as-Samarqandī (2010, 29.13–19). For more on *ʿilm al-waḍʿ*, see Weiss (2014).

75. Harb (2013, 84f), (2015, 302); Noy (2016); Smyth (1986).

2

Precedents

Let us now rewind from the madrasa centuries back through the eleventh century, and into the first three hundred years of extant Arabic scholarly output. Language use is first and foremost the use of precedent according to rules, and it is the past that determines how a word is deployed and then accepted. *Maʿnā* was an established and oft-used word that had formed part of scholars' conceptual vocabularies for several hundred years by the time our four scholars were at work. When we try to map this history of usage we notice that this single word, *maʿnā,* had been used to translate multiple Greek words into Arabic, was present as a label in the names of specific genres and groups, and was used to build and explain theories about both words and things. We have no word in English or European languages that plays the same roles, so let us therefore start to get acquainted with *maʿnā* as it would have appeared to our four scholars. In the course of this survey, we will encounter the word *ḥaqīqah* at several key points. This will also be our first encounter with the grinding complexity of some of the semantic, epistemological, and theological debates that had the use of *maʿnā* at their core. A non-Arabist reader in a hurry may wish to skip ahead to the translation theory in chapter 3.

IN TRANSLATION FROM GREEK

Texts in Greek were a major source of theoretical discussions, and I will discuss the details of that integration in more detail in the chapters on Ibn Sīnā and al-Ǧurǧānī. Here, in this chapter on the precedents for use of the word *maʿnā,* I would like to turn briefly to ninth-century translations of Greek, and to a representative genre of scholarship: medicine. We are lucky to have Manfred Ullmann's magisterial (and hand-written) dictionary of translations, which primarily surveys Arabic interaction with the work of Galen (d. 216) and Aristotle. It quickly becomes apparent that *maʿnā* was a word used to translate a number of quite different Greek words into Arabic. This tells us that ninth-century Arabic translators were in the same position with regard to Greek as we twenty-first century translators into English are with regard to Arabic. In the absence of a shared conceptual vocabulary, translation has work to do.

Ullmann documents moments when *maʿnā* was used to translate *theōria, pragma, sēmainō,* and *tropos,* and also in phrases that translated the adjectives *paraphoros* and *presbutikos.*[1] Let us address these moments with some more detail. In Athens in the fourth-century B.C., Aristotle remarked that the methodology he was using to understand "the good" (begin at an accepted starting point and fill in the detail later) was one that should be followed "in other areas too" (*ton auton dē tropon*). The ninth-century Arabic translator, most likely Isḥāq b. Ḥunayn (d. 911),[2] translated this phrase as "according to this *maʿnā.*"[3] *Maʿnā* was a fundamental concept for the translators. The Baghdadi Christian Aristotelian al-Ḥasan Ibn Suwār (d. 1020), whom we will meet again in the chapter on Ibn Sīnā, explained that translators needed to conceive a *maʿnā* in the same way as the original author, and that he had produced a critical, comparative, multi-manuscript edition of Aristotle's *Sophistical Refutations* in order to "get the *maʿnā.*"[4] Four hundred years after Aristotle, in second-century-A.D. Rome, Galen wrote that a large book on anatomy by his predecessor Marinus (of Alexandria, fl. 100) was marred by omissions. In ninth-century Baghdad, Ḥunayn b. Isḥāq (d. 873, father of the aforementioned Isḥāq and author of a treatise on these Galenic translations characterized by what Uwe Vagelpohl calls "vigorous pragmatism")[5] translated the phrase about the omissions, *ellipes de tēn theōrian,* as "you find his *maʿānī* to be inadequate."[6] Galen also used the adjective *paraphoros* to describe

1. *Theōria* ("theory," "speculative practice"), *pragma* ("matter," affair"), *sēmainō* ("signify"), *tropos* ("mode, manner"), *paraphoros* ("having deviated from the course," "incorrect"), and *presbutikos* ("like an old man"). Ullmann (2002–7, 1:865, 3:886). Translations selected from Liddell and Scott (1968).

2. Aristotle et al. (2005, 27).

3. Arist. *Eth. Nic.* 1098a33. Arabic: وعلى هذا المعنى. Ullmann (2002–7, 3:492). English translation from Aristotle (2002, 102).

4. لمّا كان الناقِلُ يحتاج في تأدية المعنى إلى فهمه باللغة التي إليها يُنقَل إلى أنْ يكون متصوَّراً له كتصوُّرِ قائله . . . فلأنّا أحْببنا الوقوفَ على ما وقع لكلّ واحدٍ منهم كتبنا جميعَ النقول التي وقعتْ إلينا ليقع التامل بكلّ واحدٍ منها ويُستعان ببعضها على بعضٍ في إدراك المعنى. Georr (1948, 198), via Vagelpohl (2010, 254).

5. Vagelpohl (2010), 248.

6. Gal. *Anat. Admin.* 4:10. Ḥunayn:

the incorrect speech of other authorities about inflammation in the eyes, and Ḥunayn chose to describe such speech as having "no *maʿnā* to it."[7]

In all these examples, the word *maʿnā* would seem to be roughly equivalent to the English "meaning." But in his work on medicines, Galen warned that confusion about the names "dry" and "wet" would lead to uncertain knowledge of the *pragmata,* and then both names and knowledge of *pragmata* would become confused. (We will return to *pragmata* in chapter 6 below.) Ḥunayn translated this as "when the labels indicating them become confused, then so does knowledge of the *maʿānī* and the actual things."[8] Galen had used a standard Greek binary of *onoma* and *pragmata,* a pairing we could map onto the English pairing of "words/names" versus "things." Galen had warned that labeling confusion leads to confusion about what things actually are. When Ḥunayn wanted to say this in Arabic, he moved to an epistemological structure with three components. He made a specific distinction between the labels of the medicines on the one hand, and then both their *maʿānī* and their *umūr* on the other. The word *umūr* here stands for the actual physical medicines themselves. The *maʿānī* are Ḥunayn's third category: they are not the labels (the words are the labels), and they are not the actual medicines either. They are *maʿānī,* a core conceptual category not found in Greek or English without recourse to neologism.

In his work on body parts affected by disease, in a typological discussion of changes to organs, Galen again stressed the importance of consistent use of medical terminology, and he remarked how, "what speech signifies" has confused both junior physicians and philosophers (*tōn sēmainomenōn ho logos*). The translator, either Ḥunayn or his nephew Ḥubayš b. al-Ḥasan al-Aʿṣam (fl. ninth century),[9] rendered this phrase as "the *maʿānī* that are indicated by names."[10] The Arabic

وَجَدْتَهُ في معانيه ناقصاً. Ullmann (2002–7, 1:295–96).

7. Gal. *De Pulsibus Libellus ad Tirones.* Galen (1821–33, 8:484). Ḥunayn: لا معنى له. Ullmann (2002–7, 2:31–33, 3:55–56).

8. *Ex oun toutōn tōn prophaseōn hē tōn onomatōn chrēsis tarachtheisa kai tēn tōn pragmatōn epitarattei gnōsin. Hōsautōs de kai peri xērou kai hugrou tōn onomatōn sugxuthentōn kai hē tōn pragmatōn gnōsis sunexuthē.* Ḥunayn:

لمّا تشوّشتْ الألقابُ الدالة عليها تشوّش بذلك العلمُ بالمعاني والأُمور. Gal. *De Simplicium Medicamentorum Temperamentis ac Facultatibus* 3.12. Galen (1821–33, 11:569), Ullmann (2002–7, 3:176).

9. Garofalo (1997, 15).

10. *Anamnēsthōmen d' eis ta paronia chrēsimōs kai tōn en tēi peri iatrikōn onomatōn pragmateia lelegmenōn, entha peri tōn sēmainomenōn ho logos ēn, ha kakōs sugcheousin ouk oligoi tōn neōterōn iatrōn te kai philosophōn.* Arabic [starting at *entha*]:

حيث ذكرتُ المعانيَ اللتي تدل عليها الأسماء. Rudolph E. Siegel's English translation says simply "where I discussed the signs." Gal. *De Locis Affectis* 1.3. Galen (1821–33, 8:32), (1976, 28); Ullmann (2002–7, 3:274).

conceptual vocabulary revealed by this translation choice matches the three-part division that we encountered in the previous example. There are words and things, and then there are those mental contents that result from the input provided by language. Ḥunayn or his nephew read the Greek and then wrote *maʿānī*. They read a combination of Greek words that Liddell and Scott tell us is also found in Sophocles (d. 406 B.C.): *chō logos sēmainetō* (translated variously as "now let your speech signal your meaning" or "you may tell your story") and that is clearly about forming a speech act to communicate one's meaning.[11] Galen had certainly read Sophocles, and it is possible that Ḥunayn or his nephew had too. (Maria Mavroudi has shown that Sophocles was read by Ḥunayn's fellow Christians in ninth-century Iraq.)[12] What is interesting for us is that in Sophocles' literary moment he seems to want to stress the process by which ideas are consciously turned into words (facts, lies, and silence are in play; Deianeira is telling the Messenger he can now speak freely). It is fun to imagine that this line was on Ḥunayn's mind when he used the Arabic word *maʿānī* for Galen's dry injunction about the same process of turning ideas into words. In a more prosaic final example, when the Archbishop of Constantinople Gregory of Nazianzus (d. 390) proscribed that his order wear shoes and crutches like old men, the tenth-century Christian Arabic translator rendered *presbutikos baktēreuontes* as "crutches according to the *maʿnā* of an old man."[13] In the mind of the translator, this was an idiomatic and appropriate Arabic phrase that could do the work done in English by "like": think of an old man, and then you will know what kind of crutches we are talking about.

These six Greek words (*theōria, pragma, sēmainō, tropos, paraphoros,* and *presbutikos*) were all translated (or in the case of *paraphoros* and *presbutikos,* translated in part) by *maʿnā*. The choice we have now is whether to shoehorn these *maʿānī* into a word such as "meanings," or to force them into a neologism such as "mental contents." The decision to make six different words into one single word has already been made by the ninth- and tenth-century translators; the question before us now is how to do justice to that Classical Arabic choice. Our primary task in this book is the translation of the Classical Arabic conceptual vocabulary, not the Greek one. Greek simply helps us see what Arabic was doing. Translation will be the subject of the next chapter. Here, I would just like to note that if we were to choose "meanings," then these six Greek words would represent a set of usages that does not match how we use the word "meaning" in English. The advantage

11. Soph. *Trachiniae* 345. Translations: Richard Jebb and Robert Torrance via Perseus Digital Library.

12. Mavroudi (2015, 329–30).

13. Gregory of Nazianzus (2001, 136). Arabic:
والعُكّازاتُ على معنى الشيخ. Ullmann (2002–7, 3:182).

of “mental content” is that it is an awkward neologism that makes us ask exactly what the Arabic word *maʿnā* was doing. It also helps us identify that some sort of content is in play, and provisionally locate that content in the mind.

IN BOOK TITLES

Some usages of *maʿnā* and its plural *maʿānī* were so well-established by the eleventh century that they appeared in the titles of books and the slogans of polemicists. They fit the same patterns of usage we have encountered in the translations from Greek, and could just as well be rendered in English as “mental content.” Once again, the awkward nature of the resultant translations will remind us that these are genres and controversies that we just do not have in the histories of Anglophone or European theology, literary criticism, or grammar. And yet they were fundamental to the conceptual vocabulary of eleventh-century Arabic, and therefore to the theoretical discussions that are the subject matter of this book. Eleventh-century scholars would have read a great many books that dealt with *maʿānī al-Qurʾān* (“the *maʿānī* of the Quran”) or *maʿānī aš-šiʿr* (“the *maʿānī* of poetry”), and they would have studied *maʿānī an-naḥw* (“the *maʿānī* of grammar/syntax”) at school.

Let us start with the foundational text of the Quran, over three centuries distant when our four authors heard and read it but pedagogically, linguistically, epistemologically, and rhetorically omnipresent in their intellectual lives. The idea that the Quran had contents, *maʿānī,* was uncontroversial. And these contents were assumed to be located in the mind; they were mental contents. Unsurprisingly, the question of whose mind the contents of the Quran were in was theologically problematic, and we will confront it in chapters 4 and 5. But no one would have disagreed with the statement that the Quran was full of *maʿnā.* Perhaps the most famous book to enshrine this principle in a title was Abū Zakarīyah al-Farrāʾ’s (d. 822) *Maʿānī al-Qurʾān.* As we have the text today, al-Farrāʾ’s work starts with a transmission note from one of his students, who wrote that this was “a book containing the *maʿānī* of the Quran” that al-Farrāʾ had dictated from memory starting in the early Tuesday and Friday mornings of the month of Ramadan in the year 818. The teacher’s opening words were: “Exegesis of the problematic desinential inflections of the Quran and its *maʿānī* begins with the transmission consensus that the *alif* in the *basmalah* is elided.” This is an orthographic statement about the opening phrase of the Quran known as the *basmalah* (*bi-smillāhi r-raḥmāni r-raḥīm,* “In the name of God, the merciful, the beneficent”) and how it is written down. According to al-Farrāʾ, the reason that Quranic orthography omitted the upright stroke of the letter *alif* was that the *basmalah* was a place in the Quran so well known that a reader would never be “ignorant of the *maʿnā* of the *alif.*” It was, after all, a customary linguistic trait among the Arabs to whom the Quran was revealed that abbreviation and elision were practiced “when the *maʿnā* was known."[14] There is no doubt here that *maʿnā* is the mental content of speech, nor that this mental content is what is at stake when questions of orthography or grammar are under consideration. The single letter *alif* has a *maʿnā* so well known in a certain phrase that its physical representation on the page may be omitted. A book such as that of al-Farrāʾ, largely concerned with the accurate reading of the Quranic text and the discussion of dialectical variations therein, would therefore accurately be given the title "Mental Contents of the Quranic Text." The word *maʿnā* appears a great deal in the book; the lessons al-Farrāʾ dictated often consist of a paraphrase of the mental content of a certain word, or a statement that two words have the same or different mental contents, all backed up with evidence from sources including Arab poets, lexicographers of Arabic, and his own authorial judgment. And it was not just single words and letters that had mental contents; whole phrases or verses did too. The phrase "If God willed it, he would depart with their hearing" (Quran 2:20, al-Baqarah) is therefore explained by al-Farrāʾ as "the mental content, and God knows best, is that if God willed it he would make their hearing go away." The rhetorical thrust of the verse stays the same; the mental content is stable (albeit al-Farrāʾ piously eschews confidence in his interpretation), and only the syntax changes. We will return to syntax and *maʿānī* with a vengeance in chapter 7.

If the *maʿānī* of the Quran could be the mental contents occasioned by both letters and whole verses, so a book on "the mental contents of the Quran" could include more than the lexicographical and orthographical notes of al-Farrāʾ. Writing in tenth-century Egypt, Abū Ǧaʿfar Muḥammad an-Naḥḥās (d. 950) started his *Maʿānī al-Qurʾān* by saying that the book would also include explanation of the Quran's rare words, juridical prescriptions, and verses that abrogated other verses, all based on scholarly precedent from religious and lexicographical authority. But what was at stake in all these subgenres of Quranic study was the *maʿānī* of the Quran—the mental contents it contained. An-Naḥḥās was interested in desinential inflections only insofar as they were needed to grasp the *maʿnā*, and when he wanted (taking part in a long-standing debate)[15] to stress the Arabness of the Quranic language, he wrote that "the mental contents of the Quran are found only through the Arabic lexicon."[16]

14. لأنها وقعت في موضع معروف لايجهل القارئُ معناه ولا يحتاج إلى قراءته فاستُخفّ طرحُها لأنَّ مِن شأن العرب الإيجازَ وتقليل الكثير إذا عُرف معناه. Al-Farrāʾ (1960, 1:2.2–4).

15. Rippin (2016).

16. فدلّ على أن معانيه إنما وَرَدتْ من اللغة العربية . . . فقصدتُ في هذا الكتاب تفسيرَ المعاني والغريبَ وأحكامَ القرآن والناسخَ والمنسوخَ . . . وآتي مِن القراءات بما يَحتاج إلى تفسير معناه وما احتاج إليه المعنى من الإعراب. An-Naḥḥās (1988, 1:42.1–43.1).

After this Quranic introduction (more valuable detail and references can be found in Andrew Rippin),[17] it makes sense that multiple genres of pre-eleventh-century scholarship would produce books that dealt with the range of mental contents, *ma'ānī,* occasioned in authors' and readers' minds when each genre of text was read. And while a comprehensive survey is beyond our scope here, a cursory review of the lists of book titles in Fuat Sezgin's bibliographic survey of pre-eleventh-century works bears out this conclusion. Sezgin's volumes dealing with Quranic sciences, Hadith, poetry, grammar, and lexicography list nearly a hundred books with *ma'nā* in their title. Their contents are of course not all the same: the mental content produced by poetry is not the same as the mental content produced by prophetic Hadith, nor are all the disciplines identical in their preoccupations. But they are all using *ma'nā* in the same stable way. So when Abū Ǧa'far Muḥammad at-Ṭaḥāwī (d. 933) wrote, in response to requests from his companions, a substantial collection of Hadith designed to defend that corpus from its critics, it became known as *Kitāb Ma'ānī al-Āṯār—The Book of the Mental Contents of Prophetic Traditions.*[18] When Ibn Qutaybah (d. 889) wrote his *Kitāb al-Ma'ānī al-Kabīr fī Abyāt al-Ma'ānī* (*The Big Book of Ma'ānī Dealing with Ma'ānī Verses*), which is also known as *Ma'ānī aš-Ši'r* (*The Ma'ānī of Poetry*), he was producing a set of explanations of selected verses from the canon of Arabic poetry, the words of which might not have been familiar to his urban Baghdadi audience.[19] He spent a great deal of time explaining the *ma'nā* of descriptive terms used by poets from previous centuries, so the chapter on "Lines with *Ma'ānī* about the Hyena" starts with a single line from al-Kumayt b. Zayd al-Asadī (d. 743):[20]

> *Like the mother of 'Āmir hiding away in her den, but the hunter has the rope.*
> *The wolf will provide for her family.*

One can imagine that this line was as obscure to a ninth-century Baghdadi bureaucrat as it may be to us. Ibn Qutaybah provides the mental content in a concise paragraph: the mother of 'Āmir is an alternative name for the hyena, an animal known for its stupidity, which is evinced by its habit of sticking to its den until its hind legs can be snared by the rope of a hunter who pretends to have abandoned the chase. Wolves have been known to raise the children of hyenas after the parents were hunted, and in some cases interbreed. Provided with this account of the

17. Rippin (2015).

18. Sezgīn (1967–, 1:437–38), aṭ-Ṭaḥāwī (1994, 1:11).

19. Cf. Harb (2013, 146 n. 463).

20. كَما خامَرَتْ في حِضْنِها أُمُّ عامِرٍ | لَدَى ٱلحَبْلِ حَتَّى عالَ أَوْسٌ عِيالَها. Ibn Qutaybah (1984, 1:212).

maʿnā, the reader of Ibn Qutaybah is now equipped to use the line as an apt quotation in a literary performance (the process known as *adab*).

The Quran, Hadith, and profane poetry all had *maʿānī* that could be recaptured and paraphrased by the scholars who worked to interpret them. Language was the interface between the mental contents of authors and readers. It is therefore unsurprising that language itself was analyzed using *maʿnā* as a label for the functions and meanings behind the words themselves. Any discussion of the function of a certain particle in syntax, or the import of a certain tense or mood of a verb, or indeed the type of illocutionary force intended by a speaker would be a matter of *maʿnā*. As we will see, al-Ǧurǧānī's poetics was at heart a theory of syntax, and the ingredients of syntax were *maʿānī*. This was not a controversial terminological assumption. For example, when al-Ǧurǧānī's predecessor in the canon of great grammarians, Abū al-Qāsim az-Zaǧǧāǧī (d. ca. 949), wrote a book about the grammatical functions of particles, he called it *Maʿānī al-Ḥurūf* (*The Maʿānī of Particles*). The first four particles dealt with were "at," "all," "some," and "like," and az-Zaǧǧāǧī then continued for another 133 Arabic words, explaining the semantic load of each word and how it functioned in Arabic syntax.[21]

Maʿnā was the word used to describe what happened in people's heads when they were faced with language. And seeing as the Quran, Hadith, and poetry were all made up of language, *maʿnā* was also the word used to describe what happened in people's heads when they interacted with those texts.

IN THE ARABIC DICTIONARY

The Arabic lexicographical tradition, as we will see in chapter 4, was itself a map of usage and precedent. What did the authors of dictionaries say about *maʿnā?* As was the case with all the words that existed in Arabic, a lexicon became firmly established during the first four centuries of Arabic scholarship, and the etymological relationships between words were delineated and argued over with reference both to the canon of pre-Islamic poetry and to anthropological lexical fieldwork among nomadic Arabic tribes. The word *maʿnā* was no exception. The lexicographers went to work on it just as they went to work on every other Arabic word in their vast, ever-expanding, mutually referencing dictionaries and manuals of morphology. And in David Larsen's recent article, we have a comprehensive engagement with both the lexicographers' work and the uses of *maʿnā* in early poetry on

21. عندَ, كلّ, بعض, and مِثل. az-Zaǧǧāǧī (1984, 1–3).

which they drew. He concludes, inter alia, that "outward exposure of inner content is one of *maʿnā*'s master metaphors."[22]

The first lexical question was what part of speech, what type of noun, *maʿnā* was. On the face of it, *maʿnā* could be either a *maṣdar* (a quasi-verbal event noun) or a noun of place. These two parts of speech are in the case of the word *maʿnā* indistinguishable, so one could choose to read *maʿnā* as either the act of aiming or the place of aiming. Larsen and I might be tempted to prefer the latter, but al-Ǧurǧānī, himself a grammarian, wrote a voluminous commentary on his teacher's study of morphology, in which he concluded that in such cases the *maṣdar* is the starting point from which the noun of place derives. (The *maṣdar* was also, according to Gerhard Endress, the morphological form used most often to translate abstract and universal concepts from Greek.)[23] Al-Ǧurǧānī's general statement is backed up in the specific case of the word *maʿnā* by a scholar specializing in fine-grained lexical distinctions, Abū Hilāl al-ʿAskarī (d. ca. 1010), who confirmed that while *maʿnā* looked like it could be a noun of place, it was indeed a *maṣdar*.[24]

But what did the lexicographers say that verb from which *maʿnā* derived meant? One of their traditional etymological starting points, the Quran, provided little assistance. Neither the word *maʿnā*, nor the root from which it is derived (*ʿ-n-y*) appears in the Quran, although Larsen has interrogated the appearance of the related root *ʿ-n-w* at Quran 20:111 (Ṭā Hā), noted the appearance of *ʿ-n-y* in a variant reading of Quran 80:37 (ʿAbasa), and supplied the word's Hebrew cognate (*ma'neh* from the same *ʿ-n-y* root.)[25] The word *ḥaqīqah* does not appear either, although the root *ḥ-q-q* is used by the Quran to talk about truth a great deal.

In the work of Abū al-Ḥusayn Aḥmad Ibn Fāris (d. 1004) we read a synthesis of the work of the previous four centuries of lexicographers that tells us that the *maʿnā* of a thing is what you get when that thing is tested, or the basic default state of a thing (via al-Ḫalīl b. Aḥmad, d. 786),[26] or the purpose of a thing that is revealed when you look for it (via Abū ʿAbdallāh Muḥammad b. Ziyād Ibn al-Aʿrābī, d. ca. 846). In the absence of Quranic precedent, the sources adduced by Ibn Fāris to prove his reading are nomadic Arabic prose and poetry, in which the verb from which *maʿnā* derives (*ʿanā*) is used for the putting forth of plants (by the earth) or

22. David Larsen, "Captivity and Meaning in Classical Arabic Philology," forthcoming in the *Journal of Abbasid Studies*.

23. The *maṣdar mīmī* of a form I third radical weak verb is identical to the *ism aẓ-ẓarf or ism al-makān*. Endress (1987, 19), (2002, 236); al-Ǧurǧānī (2007, 2:1057), Kouloughli (2016b), Larsen (2007, 158f), Wright (1898, 1:128).

24. والمفعولُ يكون مصدراً ومكانًا وهو هاهنا مصدر. Abū Hilāl (2006, 45.12).

25. Larsen (2007, 163–67, 194).

26. ولم يزدْ الخليلُ على أن قال معنى كلّ شيءٍ محنته وحاله التي يصير إليها أمره. Ibn Fāris (1946–52, 4:148).

water (by a waterskin). In a representative piece of eleventh-century lexicon construction, Ibn Fāris used the Umayyad poetry of Ḏu ar-Rummah (d. 735) to claim this etymological origin for *maʿnā:* what the land would produce.[27] An origin that would give land content, just as language has content.

IN THE OPENING SENTENCE OF THE FIRST ARABIC BOOK

Let us leave the accounts of the lexicographers here. We will return to the conceptual importance of the lexicon in chapter 4, and here I would like to turn back to usage. I do not want to cede control of the game to the lexicographers in the first innings! The first complete extant book we have in Arabic, a book given simply the name *al-Kitāb* (*The Book*), uses the word *maʿnā* in its very first sentence. The author of this foundational study of grammar was Sībawayh, a Persian speaker working in Basra, in southern Iraq, and the opening statement of his book was that "language is the noun, the verb, and the particle that comes for a *maʿnā,* neither noun nor verb."[28] It is highly instructive to note that the commentary tradition's response to this somewhat gnomic statement was not to ask what *maʿnā* meant; it was rather to ask exactly what this category of "particle" was and then use *maʿnā* to explain the different theoretical options.[29] The commentators also asked exactly what the word I have translated as "language" meant; *al-kalim* was a rare plural of *al-kalimah,* "word," and they disagreed about the significance of Sībawayh's word choice (in English we tend to say "language" at times like this, but "language" is an English word not exactly replicable in Arabic, where we find the words *lisān* ("tongue"), *kalām* ("speech"), *luġah* ("lexicon"), *qawl* ("speech act/statement"), and more.[30]

The word *maʿnā* was in play during Sībawayh's foundational Arabic answer to the question I am phrasing as "What is language?" And as he tried to explain what Sībawayh had meant, Abū Saʿīd as-Sīrāfī (d. 979) asked himself how one would answer this question: "Why did Sībawayh say, 'and the particle that comes for a *maʿnā,*' when we know that nouns and verbs also come for *maʿānī?*" The assumption in this short snatch of dialectic is clear: as-Sīrāfī's readers are already familiar with the word *maʿnā;* everyone knows how to use it. Nouns, verbs, and particles

27. Ibn Fāris (1946–52, 4:146–49). See also Larsen's "Captivity and Meaning in Classical Arabic Philology," forthcoming in the *Journal of Abbasid Studies.*

28. فالكَلِمُ اسمٌ وفِعْلٌ وحَرْفٌ جاءَ لمعنىً ليس باسمٍ ولا فِعْل. Sībawayh (1966, 1:12.2).

29. Ar-Rummānī (1993–94, 109), as-Sīrāfī (2008, 13–14.) Cf. Bernards (1997, 3f).

30. Cf. Gilliot and Larcher (2016).

all have *maʿānī*. It is the word to use when talking in Arabic about what language is and how language works. It is core conceptual vocabulary.

What was as-Sīrāfī's answer to his own question, and how did he explain Sībawayh's use of the word *maʿnā?* It should come as no surprise that an answer to a question about *maʿnā,* posed in terms of the functioning of *maʿnā,* should itself consist of a statement about how *maʿnā* worked. As-Sīrāfī said that the *maʿānī* of particles (which we encountered with az-Zağğāğī above) consisted only of acts of negation, affirmation, and connection between nouns and verbs, both of which had their own *maʿānī.* These *maʿānī* in nouns and verbs were different, existed integrally to each such word, and could be recaptured through paraphrase in answer to the question "What is . . . ?" The function of particles could also, of course, be recaptured through paraphrase, but the *maʿānī* of particles could be reasoned only alongside the *maʿānī* of the nouns or verbs to which they referred, whereas the *maʿānī* of nouns or verbs stood on their own and could be used as the basis for further reasoning. As-Sīrāfī's explanation of Sībawayh's gnomic reference to a mental content on account of which particles are used was that, for example, the conjunction "from" is used for a mental content that could be defined as "dividing a part from a whole" and that relied on the mental content of the noun or verb being divided. One couldn't reason the mental content of "from" without reasoning the mental content of what it was from.[31] What we can see here is some of the contours of a grammatical-logical framework that has one foot in Aristotelian logic and the other in Sībawayh's descriptive linguistics. This is a combination that was born out of polemical struggles between logicians and grammarians in the tenth century (see Peter Adamson and Key),[32] and it would be finally resolved in the eleventh century, as we will see in chapters 6 and 7. At this stage in the book I wish only to highlight the centrality of *maʿnā* to the discussion and its stability as an item of conceptual vocabulary in constant and widespread use.

IN A WORK OF LEXICAL THEORY

Abū Hilāl al-ʿAskarī (d. ca. 1010, on whom see George Kanazi and Beatrice Gruendler)[33] was a lexicographer and literary critic who wrote a book of lexical

31. وإنْ سأل سائلٌ فقال لِمَ قال وحرفٌ جاء لمعنىً وقد علمنا أنّ الأسماء والأفعال جِئن لمعانٍ قيل له . . . أنّ الحروف إنما تجيء للتأكيد .. وللنفي .. وللعطف .. والأسماءُ والأفعالُ معانيها في أنفسها قائمةٌ صحيحة ودليلٌ على ذلك أنه إذا قيل ما الإنسانُ كان الجواب عن ذلك أنْ يقال الذي يكون حيّاً ناطقاً كاتباً .. وإذا قيل ما معنى قام قيل وقوعُ قيامٍ في زمانٍ ماضٍ فعُقِلَ معناه في نفسه قبلَ أنْ يتجاوز به إلى غيره وليس كذلك الحروف .. فعلمنا أنها تؤثر في المعاني ولا يُعقَل معناها إلا بغيرها. As-Sīrāfī (2008, 1:13.25–14.13).

32. Key and Adamson (2015).

33. Azarnoosh and Negahban (2008); Gruendler (2005), (2007); Kanazi (1989).

definitions. The stated aim of that work was to clarify the differences between *maʿānī* that were close to each other and thereby dismantle the concept of synonymy.[34] It was a work of fine semantic distinctions that dealt with both the inherited lexicon of classical and scriptural precedent and with the living scholarly and ordinary language of the late tenth and early eleventh century: "the vocal forms of the jurists, the theologians, and all the rest of people's conversations."[35] He gave an account of how around twelve hundred pairs of words each differed in their meaning: "the difference between mental contents that are close to each other."[36] One such pair of words was, happily for us, *maʿnā* and *ḥaqīqah*.

Before we come to Abū Hilāl's detailed discussion of *maʿnā* and *ḥaqīqah* we need to explain what he meant by "vocal forms." *Maʿnā* was an established and commonplace word for the mental content that could be accessed and expressed through language. It was primarily cognitive and resided in people's minds. The linguistic expression of these mental contents was then a separate category, *lafẓ* (plural *alfāẓ*), and the two terms very often sat in opposition to each other. *Lafẓ* can be translated as "vocal form," "verbal form," "vocal/verbal expression," or "utterance." I have invariably chosen "vocal form" to avoid confusion in English with the grammatical category of "verb," and as a nudge toward the omnipresence of the binary—vocal form / mental content—even when only one side of it is mentioned: vocal form / mental content. *Lafẓ* also tended to stand, in theoretical discussions about language, for both spoken and written expression.

Lafẓ was the real-world extramental existence of language, whether the vibration of the air produced by human vocal cords or the marks on the page produced by humans' pens. This notion of physical impact matches the standard definitions of *lafẓ* in the Arabic lexicon: a *lafẓ* is literally the act of ejecting something from one's mouth. The additional distinction between word and script was also available when necessary, laid out, for example, in the ninth century by al-Ǧāḥiẓ (Abū ʿUṯmān ʿAmr b. Baḥr, d. 868 and a dominant literary voice of the ninth century and beyond). His taxonomy of communication famously identified five forms that could accurately indicate mental contents: vocal form, physical gesture, dactylonomy, writing, and context/performance (this last category reflected the way we may say that the presence of a corpse, or a building, "speaks volumes").[37]

34. Abū Hilāl (2006, 29, 33).

35. وما يجري في ألفاظ الفقهاء والمتكلمين وسائر محاورات الناس. Abū Hilāl (2006, 30.2–3).

36. Abū Hilāl (2006, 29.8).

37. وجميعُ أصناف الدلالات على المعاني من لفظ وغير لفظ خمسةُ أشياء لا تنقص ولا تزيد أولها اللفظ ثم الإشارة ثم العَقد ثم الخط ثم الحال التي تُسمّى نِصبة والنصبةُ هي الحال الدالة . . . ولكل واحد من هذه الخمسة صورةٌ بائنةٌ من صورة صاحبها . . . وهي التي تَكشِف لك عن أعيان المعاني في الجملة ثم

Abū Hilāl started his 232-word entry on *maʿnā* and *ḥaqīqah* with the statement that "*maʿnā* is intent, the specific intent with which a speech act happens (the lexical *maʿnā* of the word 'speech' may be: 'that to which intent attaches itself.') *Ḥaqīqah,* on the other hand, is a speech act that is lexically placed according to its assigned place in the lexicon."[38] This is Abū Hilāl saying that *maʿnā* and *ḥaqīqah* are linguistic categories: the intent behind a speech act and the lexical accuracy of a speech act. I will return to the lexicon and these categories in chapter 4. Abū Hilāl then provides the morphology: *maʿnā* is a *maṣdar* from the root *ʿ-n-y.* Next, he turns to theology to make the argument that *maʿnā* is a word for a human linguistic category, albeit one that can point toward God: "*maʿnā* is our hearts' intending what we intend to say. And what we intend is the *maʿnā.* God is therefore [if we intend him] the *maʿnā.*" Abū Hilāl understood *maʿnā* as an internal human process of intent, one that had its fulfillment in a speech act. If a human being wanted to talk about God, then God would be the *maʿnā* of the resultant speech act. But Abū Hilāl acknowledged that there was a theological problem here, one that had been identified by the oft-cited and foundational early Basran Muʿtazilī theologian Abū ʿAlī al-Ǧubbāʾī (d. 915): "God cannot be described as 'a *maʿnā.*'"[39] God may have been what people wanted to talk about, but he could not actually be in people's hearts, subject to their intentions. He could be the *maʿnīy* ("the thing intended," a passive participle of the same *ʿ-n-y* root, less commonly used) but not a *maʿnā.*[40] An accurate account of the situation would recognize that the *maʿnā* was the human being's intent, not the divinity itself. After all, wrote Abū Hilāl, were one to say, "I intend to say, 'Zayd'" or "I wanted to talk about him," then one would not actually be conjuring up Zayd's presence. Mental content is not the same thing as extramental existence.[41]

عن حقائقها في التفسير Al-Ǧāḥiẓ (1960, 1:76.10f, 78.1f). Cf. Behzadi (2009, 62f), Miller (forthcoming). Dactylonomy is the practice of counting on the fingers.

38. الفرق بين الحقيقة والمعنى أنّ المعنى هو القصد الذي يقع به القولُ على وجهٍ دون وجهٍ وقد يكون معنى الكلام في اللغة ما تعلَّقَ به القصدُ والحقيقةُ ما وُضِع من القول موضوعَه [في أصل اللغة] على ما ذكرنا. Abū Hilāl (2006, 45.9–11).

39. ولهذا قال أبو علي رحمة الله عليه إن المعنى هو القصد إلى ما يُقصَد إليه من القول فجَعَلَ المعنى القصدَ لأنه مصدرٌ قال ولا يوصَف اللهُ تعالى بأنه معنى لأن المعنى هو قصدُ قلوبِنا إلى ما نقصِد إليه من القول والمقصود هو المعنى. Abū Hilāl (2006, 45.13–16).

40. واللهُ تعالى هو المَعْنِيُّ وليس بمعنىً. Abū Hilāl (2006, 45.16). See ويقال إنه عزّ وجلّ مَعْنِيٌّ بالتشديد لأنه المقصود بالكلام والإخبار فيصح ذلك فيه. Al-Qāḍī ʿAbd al-Ǧabbār (1965–74, 5:253.7–8). Cf. note 47 below.

41. وحقيقةُ هذا الكلام أنْ يكون ذكرُ الله هو المعنى والقصدُ إليه هو المعنى إذا كان المقصودُ في الحقيقة حادثاً وقولُهم عنيتُ بكلامي زيداً كقولك أردتُه بكلامي ولا يجوز أنْ يكون زيدٌ في الحقيقة مراداً مع وجوده فدلّ ذلك على أنّه عُنِيَ ذِكرُه وأُريدَ الخبرُ عنه دونَ نفسه. Abū Hilāl (2006, 45.16–19).

By this point, Abū Hilāl has used the words *maʿnā* and *ḥaqīqah* to make statements in two different ways. He used them as subjects in definitional statements: "*maʿnā* is intent" and "*ḥaqīqah* is use according to lexical precedent." But he has also used the same two words as tools to explain how his language is working. When he said that the dictionary definition of "speech" can be "that to which intent attaches itself," he said, "the *maʿnā* of speech is that . . ." ("the mental content of the word 'speech' is that . . .") And when he explained al-Ǧubbāʾī's theological statement, he said that "the *ḥaqīqah* of this speech is that . . ." ("an accurate account of this speech is that . . .") These two words, *maʿnā* and *ḥaqīqah,* are so omnipresent in any discussion about semantics that they do double work: they are used to explain themselves.

After using al-Ǧubbāʾī and theology to clarify the boundary between the epistemological and the ontological, Abū Hilāl went on to consider examples from ordinary language usage of *maʿnā* and *ḥaqīqah.* First of all, while people do say, "the *maʿnā* of your speech is . . ." they do not say, "the *maʿnā* of your movement is . . ." People don't talk about gestures as having *maʿnā,* but they do talk about words as having *maʿnā.* Abū Hilāl's conscientious survey of ordinary language then led him to report that people do sometimes use *maʿnā* to talk about nonlinguistic events, for example in the phrase "your being admitted to see that person has no *maʿnā.*" This is found elsewhere—for example, in his history of Baghdad Ibn Abī Ṭāhir Tayfūr (d. 893, on whom see Shawkat Toorawa)[42] reports a ninth-century insult: "You have no *maʿnā* in the palace of the caliph!" (Josef van Ess translates *maʿnā* here as "function.")[43] In order to negotiate the range of usages of the word *maʿnā,* Abū Hilāl used the Arabic linguistic concept of semantic extension (*tawassuʿ*). Words have *maʿnā,* and by a process of semantic extension, actions such as admittance into a powerful person's presence may, or may not, have *maʿnā.* This extension works because the phrase "your being admitted to see that person has no *maʿnā*" can be reconstructed as "your being admitted to see that person has no benefit that is worth mentioning in a speech act."[44] Having established the principle of semantic extension, Abū Hilāl chose to make a distinction between the way it applied to *maʿnā* and the way it applied to *ḥaqīqah.* He thought that ordinary language exhibited more semantic extension for *ḥaqīqah* than it did for *maʿnā.*[45] Both categories were primarily used for language: speech

42. Toorawa (2005).

43. Ibn Abī Ṭāhir Ṭayfūr (1949, 125), van Ess (1991–95, 3:159).

44. والمعنى مقصورٌ على القول دون ما يُقصَد ألا ترى أنك تقول معنى قولك كذا ولا تقول معنى حركتِكَ كذا ثم تُوسّع فيه فقيل ليس لدخولك إلى فلان معنى والمرادُ أنه ليس له فائدة تُقصَد ذكرَها بالقول. Abū Hilāl (2006, 45.20–22).

45. وتُوُسِّعَ في الحقيقة ما لم يُتَوَسَّعْ في المعنى. Abū Hilāl (2006, 45.22–23).

has cognitive mental content (*maʿnā*) and things have lexically accurate accounts (*ḥaqīqah*) given of them. But whereas the use of *maʿnā* was largely restricted to cognition connected to language, the usage of *ḥaqīqah* could slip further away from language into the description of things.

Abū Hilāl's final remark in the entry is directed with an admirable frankness toward the most liminal case of the usage of *maʿnā:* the qualities of things in what we may call theological physics. This is a usage that I address in detail at the end of this chapter, in the sections "Theology" and "Theologians (Muʿammar)." What led Abū Hilāl to consider this theological usage, despite his clear preference for making *maʿnā* be only about language, was his report that in ordinary language we say, "the *ḥaqīqah* of the movement is . . . ," but we do not say, "the *maʿnā* of the movement is . . ." The reason that we do not talk about movements as having *maʿānī* is, for Abū Hilāl, that people have already called the movements themselves *maʿānī:* "They call the bodies and the accidents *maʿānī.*" The people he was talking about were the theologians, and "accident" is an Aristotelian word for a nonessential quality or property of a thing. Abū Hilāl thought that the reason movements were called *maʿānī* was, again, the process of semantic extension, and he ended the entry with a reminder that such semantic extension is not an open-ended process: it cleaves to precedent.[46]

Al-Qāḍī ʿAbd al-Ǧabbār had used *maʿnā* in a very similar way when discussing a theological question related to Abū Hilāl's: the legitimacy of describing God as a "thing." Where Abū Hilāl had used *maʿnā* for the prelinguistic (or pre- and postlinguistic, in the case of an ongoing conversation between two people) cognition of speech acts, and of bodies, and of the accidental qualities of bodies, ʿAbd al-Ǧabbār described how *maʿnā* could be used for the prelinguistic cognition of speech acts, and of things, and of actions undertaken by those things. ʿAbd al-Ǧabbār wrote that "it is possible one could say about a fixed thing that it is a *maʿnā,* just as we say that the act of combining things is a *maʿnā.* According to this usage, it would be necessary to say that God is a *maʿnā.*" Furthermore, just as Abū Hilāl had explained the relationship between the speech-act usage of *maʿnā* and the things/qualities-of-things usage as being one of semantic extension, so ʿAbd al-Ǧabbār explained the relationship between the intent-of-speech-act usage and the things/actions-of-things usage as being a different kind of semantic extension (in his case "going beyond the lexicon," *maǧāz,* on which more below).

ʿAbd al-Ǧabbār wrote, and here I am paraphrasing, that we can talk about both things and the act of combining things in the same way—as mental

46. فقيل لا شيء إلا وله حقيقةٌ ولا يقال لا شيء إلا وله معنى ويقولون حقيقةُ الحركة كذا ولا يقولون معنى الحركة كذا هذا على أنهم سمّوا الأجسامَ والأعراضَ معانيَ إلا أنّ ذلك تَوسُّعٌ والتَوسُّعُ يلزم موضعَه المستعملَ فيه ولا يتعداه. Abū Hilāl (2006, 22–25).

content—because both are objects of thought about which we intend to talk. Furthermore, the word *maʿnā* is used for the intent (*qaṣd*) behind speech acts, but it is also used, by a process of semantic assimilation, for the target of those speech acts (*maqṣad*). But this does not work for God, and he cannot be called a mental content, although he can be the target of a speech act.[47] ʿAbd al-Ǧabbār left it to his reader to infer the reason for this final step in the reasoning: God is an object of thought for whom no comparisons or connections are possible or permissible. We can hypothetically consider the logic of a statement that God is a mental content, but the theological ramifications are too problematic. This is exactly what happened with Abū Hilāl. The linguistic description of God was carefully policed by theologians of all stripes. What Abū Hilāl and ʿAbd al-Ǧabbār confirm here is that *maʿnā* was used as a label for mental contents, for the things we hold in our minds and for the things to which we give names. The only limit on its usage and on its broad applicability to the things we think about was that it could not be easily used for the creator himself.

ADHERENTS OF *LAFẒ*, ADHERENTS OF *MAʿNĀ*, AND THE PURSUIT OF *ḤAQĪQAH*

Lafẓ and *maʿnā*, vocal form and mental content, were the primary categories for discussions of language and mind. They were not theories but, rather, core conceptual vocabulary items that contained shared assumptions about what mind and language were. No one disagreed with their existence; no one denied that *lafẓ* or *maʿnā* existed. How, then, could these basic conceptual categories have supporters or be associated with controversies? How do we explain the existence of "adherents of mental contents" or "adherents of vocal forms" (*aṣḥāb al-maʿānī* and *aṣḥāb al-lafẓ*)? The answer is that *maʿnā* had been used to do more than just theorize linguistic or hermeneutic processes. Al-Ǧāḥiẓ, while engaged in an argument with Aristotle about frogs and fish and bemoaning the loss of knowledge to the vicissitudes of time, exclaimed that "it all comes down to the process of understanding *maʿānī*, not vocal forms, and to the *ḥaqāʾiq*, not to the expressions used to describe them."[48] This is equivalent to us saying about Aristotle today, "It's the ideas and getting them right that matters!" The pairing of *maʿnā* and *lafẓ* was characterized by opposition: an adherent of *maʿnā* would by definition be opposed to

47. وربّما يقال في الشيءِ المثبَت إنه معنىً كما نقول إنّ التأليف معنىً فعلى هذا الوجه يجب أنْ يقال فيه تعالى إنه معنىً لكنّ ذلك إنما يُستعمل في هذا الوجه على هذا المجاز والتشبيه بالمقصَد لأنّ ما يصح أنْ يُقصَد إليه أُجرِي عليه الاسمُ الذي يتعلّق بالقصد فلذلك لا يُستعمل فيه جلَّ وعز. Al-Qāḍī ʿAbd al-Ǧabbār (1965–74, 5:253.12–15).

48. ومدارُ الأمر على فهم المعاني لا الألفاظ والحقائق لا العبارات. Al-Ǧāḥiẓ (1966–69, 5:542.6).

an adherent of *lafẓ*, just as the *maʿnā* of a sentence was by definition not the same as its *lafẓ*. The utility of the distinction between mental content and vocal form was that it was a binary.

The other word that al-Ǧāḥiẓ used, *ḥaqīqah*, was not on either side of this binary, but rather described the nature of the relationship between the two. Let us briefly address it here. *Ḥaqīqah* was used to denote the accuracy of a mental content, whether with regard to a vocal form in language, or with regard to extra-mental reality. Its plural form, *ḥaqāʾiq*, was therefore "accuracies" or "accurate accounts." In al-Ǧāḥiẓ's exclamation, this "getting it right" was exactly what mattered. This usage was common across all disciplines, and having access to *ḥaqīqah* or the *ḥaqāʾiq* was universally understood as a good thing. Ar-Rāġib used the plural form in this way in his exegesis, as did Ibn Fūrak's pupil al-Qušayrī some decades later. Ar-Rāġib: "This is the interpretation of the righteous forefathers, and of the owners of the *ḥaqāʾiq* who know the *ḥaqīqah* of the soul referred to in this Hadith and its corporeal substance, but as for the later Muʿtazilah . . ." We are not concerned here with ar-Rāġib's subsequent take on Muʿtazilī interpretations of Hadith and Quran, but rather the way he uses *ḥaqīqah* and *ḥaqāʾiq* for accuracy and truth in this quotation.[49] The phrase "accurate accounts of things" (*ḥaqāʾiq al-umūr* or *ḥaqāʾiq al-ašyāʾ*) was a common description of the target of philhellenic philosophy, and "accuracies" were the divine truths available through Sufism: *les réalités spirituelles* (Paul Nwyia translating Abū al-Ḥusayn an-Nūrī, d. 907).[50] In a recent and posthumously published article, Heinrichs identified the same constellation of usage for *ḥaqīqah* across early theology and Sufism, as well as the way *ḥaqīqah* functioned in a pairing with *maǧāz*.[51] In the tenth-century diagrammatic classification of the sciences by Ibn Farīġūn, knowledge itself is defined as being "of things and their *ḥaqāʾiq*."[52] The phrase *ḥaqāʾiq al-umūr* could be successfully rendered in English as "the essential nature of things" (Gutas) or "the profound realities" (Mohamed Arkoun, both translating Abū ʿAlī Miskawayh, d. 1030).[53] But when Arabic scholars in and before the eleventh century wanted to talk about truth and reality, they did not reach for a Latinate word meaning "deep" or for a logical category ("profound" and "essential," respectively). Instead they reached for the conceptual vocabulary that is the subject of this book: it was mental contents

49. وهذا قولُ السلف وأصحاب الحقائق الذين عَرفوا حقيقة الروح المُعيَّنة هاهنا وكونه جوهراً له بذاته قَوامٌ . . . وأما متأخرو المعتزلة Ar-Rāġib (2003, 980.3–81.1). Cf. al-Qušayrī (2000, 2:75.10).

50. Nwyia (1970, 324; cf. 272, 368).

51. Heinrichs (2016, 256).

52. العلمُ معرفةُ الأشياء وحقايقها [كذا]. Biesterfeldt (2017), Ibn Farīʿūn (1985, 133).

53. Arkoun and eds. (2009), Gutas (1983, 232). Cf. Wakelnig (2014, 326.8).

that mattered, and accurate accounts of them that needed to be pursued: *maʿānī* and *ḥaqāʾiq*, respectively.

Maʿnā and *ḥaqīqah* were used to describe and dignify the pursuit of truth, and this is how, as terms that could bear such value, they were used to structure controversies and hierarchies across many genres of scholarship. They were key components of a conceptual vocabulary that we can throw into relief by comparing it with how we use words like "meaning" in English. We use the phrase "theory of meaning" for a linguistic and philosophical account of reference and the connections between language and mind. But we also use "meaning" as a term laden with value: "a personal search for meaning in life" or, conversely, "a meaningless pursuit." This combination is comparable to the Arabic use of *maʿnā* and *ḥaqīqah* in both accounts of reference and in the pursuit of broad philosophical and divine truths.

But we do not, in English, have "adherents of meaning." In Arabic, that label did exist: *aṣḥāb al-maʿānī.* Who were they? In the sections that follow, I review the major debates and controversies that took *maʿānī* and *alfāẓ* as their labels. In literary criticism and theology the binary opposition of *lafẓ* and *maʿnā* came to stand for both positions and methodological approaches. This was a scholarly tradition that often turned to the vocabulary of linguistic structures in order to explain all kinds of epistemological and ontological debates, and that loved nothing more than to schematize and curate its own disagreements. There were adherents of *lafẓ* and *maʿnā* in arguments about the methodology of literary criticism, in debates about society that used *lafẓ* and *maʿnā* to label variant political philosophies, in analyses of syntax, in theological-hermeneutical arguments, and in dialectics on the philosophy of action that used *maʿnā* to explain cognition and physics. I will very briefly deal with each of these in turn, dipping into debates across a range of disciplines in order to highlight representative uses of the word *maʿnā.*

Literary Criticism

When eleventh-century literary critics argued about sound versus meaning in Arabic, they used the vocabulary of *lafẓ* and *maʿnā* as a way to draw distinctions between words and ideas. They were the primary vocabulary used to discuss how language worked. This does not mean that these arguments resulted in complete agreement about whether a certain poetic technique should be associated with *lafẓ* or with *maʿnā;* the matter of paronomasia, for example, could be considered a question of *lafẓ,* since the sound of the words was the location of the assonance or alliteration, but it could also be considered a matter of *maʿnā.* This was because when the mental contents associated with those vocal forms did not align and interact, the paronomasia would be to little effect (for reviews of such disagreements and the usage of the terms, see Iḥsān ʿAbbāṣ, Lidia Bettini, Kamal Abu Deeb, Wolfhart Heinrichs, Djamel Eddine Kouloughli, and, from the eleventh-century itself, Abū ʿAlī Aḥmad al-Marzūqī, d. 1030).[54] But however much literary critics disagreed, the same core conceptual vocabulary of *lafẓ* and *maʿnā* was in play. The two terms were always in the same relationship to each other, and they can always be translated as "vocal form" and "mental content." The conversation about form and content is not, of course, unique to Classical Arabic. To take an example almost at random, Susan Sontag advocated in the late twentieth century for "essays which reveal the sensuous surface of art without mucking about in it." Was she calling for a focus on *lafẓ* as opposed to *maʿnā?* The problem is that the binary was constituted differently in her Anglophone theory and in al-Ǧāḥiẓ or al-Ǧurǧānī's Classical Arabic theory. Sontag wanted to "cut back content" because the mechanical drive to retrieve it leads us to ignore the sensory, and sensual, experience of form.[55] Some Arabic theory did use *maʿnā* in this way: the Quran was on some accounts inimitable because it communicated mental content, subject matter, known only to God. Others argued that such a position missed the unique beauty of the Quran's linguistic structure, its form. But here the two genealogically unconnected theories part ways: Sontag invested her form with erotics, whereas Arabic read its form as grammar. (In chapter 7 we will see how grammar, just like erotics, could lead to beauty.)

Politics and Society

The relationship between vocal form and mental content was often, in the ninth and tenth centuries, a proxy for broader critical discussions of the nature and purpose of literature. Perhaps the most famous moment came when al-Ǧāḥiẓ cited the opinion that mental contents were merely strewn in the street and accessible to the masses and foreigners, whereas vocal forms were the true site of eloquence and linguistic skill. When it came to assessing Arabic eloquence, word choice and poetic meter reigned supreme.[56] This passage was so famous that al-Ǧurǧānī included an extended reading of it in the opening discussions of the *Asrār,* a reading that showed al-Ǧāḥiẓ to be privileging the interaction of mental contents over the interactions of a rhyme scheme (cf. Jeannie Miller).[57] Elsewhere, however, al-Ǧāḥiẓ presented his readers with a conflicting opinion, arguing that true elo-

54. ʿAbbās (1971, 140, 370–71, 403–4, 422–25); Abu Deeb (1979, 50–52), (1990, 354–55); Bettini (2011, 110f), Heinrichs (1998); Kouloughli (2016a), (2016b); al-Marzūqī and Abū Tammām (1991).

55. Sontag (1966, 13, 14).

56. وذهب الشيخ إلى استحسان المعنى والمعاني مطروحةٌ في الطريق يَعرفها العجميُّ والعربيُّ والبدويُّ والقرويُّ وإنما الشأن في إقامة الوزن وتحيُّز اللفظ وسهولة المخرج في صحة الطبع وجودة السبك. Al-Ǧāḥiẓ (1966–69, 3:131.9–132.1). Cf. Miller (2016b).

57. لأنه رأى التوفيقَ بين المعاني أحقَّ والموازنةَ فيها أحسن. Al-Ǧurǧānī (1954, 10.5). Jeannie Miller forthcoming in the *Journal of Abbasid Studies.*

quence was effective communication. The ultimate test of communication was to communicate elite mental contents to the masses, clothing them along the way with the intermediaries of correct vocal forms. He wrote that a noble mental content simply deserved a noble vocal form.[58] In these contradictory positions, ethical and political arguments about literature and eloquence were at stake. Mental content was either tarred by its association with the street or reified as elite truth. In these passages, al-Ǧāḥiẓ was not concerned with the structure of language, nor with mechanisms of signification or reference; rather, he was using the words *lafẓ* and *maʿnā* as labels for vectors of concern to him in ninth-century Iraq, and he was not alone in doing so. The question as to whether Arabic eloquence should enable elites to communicate with the masses or whether in fact it enabled elites to separate themselves from the masses was a political issue.

The Iḫwān aṣ-Ṣafāʾ (a mysterious group of tenth-century authors)[59] took the pairing in a slightly different direction. For them, the inarticulate masses and eloquent elites both understood mental contents (equivalent to al-Ǧāḥiẓ's "strewn in the street"). However, women, children, and the masses then falsely located eloquence in the sweet and pure sounds of words. The Iḫwān considered such popular assumptions to be false, and thought that not everything that sounded nice was eloquent. Bawdy songs, for example, were mental contents with no accuracy: *maʿānī* with no *ḥaqīqah* sung by drunkards and children. The mental contents that the Iḫwān did care about were *ḥaqīqah:* accurate praise that was actually deserved by its recipient, balanced on a happy medium by equally legitimate criticism. The language they valued communicated these *maʿānī* effectively, and effective communication was important because the stakes were high: *maʿānī* were principles first conceived in the soul with precision, but *alfāẓ* (vocal forms) were for the Iḫwān base matter; *maʿānī* were like souls and *alfāẓ* like bodies. What troubled the Iḫwān here was not the relationship between language and mind, nor indeed the question of how to determine eloquence. When they thought about mental content they felt threatened by women and children having access to mental content in the same way as they did, because everybody used speech to communicate. For elitists with a spiritual and emancipatory project this was a problem, and the Iḫwān solved it by using *ḥaqīqah* as a claim of accuracy that separated their own true, accurate, spiritually achieved *maʿānī* from the base ideas expressed by their inferiors in drunken song. When the Iḫwān spoke, they described the result with the words *maʿnā* and *ḥaqīqah,* loading both words

58. فإنَّ حق المعنى الشريف اللفظ الشريف .. إلى أنْ تُفهِم العامةَ معاني الخاصة وتَكسُوَها الألفاظَ الوسيطة التي لا تلطُف عن الدهماء ولا تجفو عن الأكفاء فأنتَ البليغُ التام. Al-Ǧāḥiẓ (1960, 1:136.6, 136.15–16). Cf. Key (2012, 172–75), Thomas (2000, 112f).

59. Callataÿ (2005), Iḫwān aṣ-Ṣafāʾ (2010–), Netton (2002).

with ethical and political values. Their speech was accurate communication of a mental content. When everyone else spoke, it was the noise of animals, madmen, drunkards, children, and women.[60]

Linguistics

Al-Ǧāḥiẓ used the pairing of *lafẓ* and *maʿnā* to discuss the position of Arabic eloquence between elites and masses, and the Iḫwān used the same pairing to reinforce their own elite status. These ethical and political polemics about literature and society proved frustrating for scholars who wanted to focus on the mechanics of how language worked. If language itself was the subject of inquiry, it was painfully obvious that vocal form and mental content worked together and that they were only separated and given priority over each other in the service of polemic. Ibn Ǧinnī (Abū al-Fatḥ ʿUṯmān, d. 1002) wrote against the idea that the *lafẓ-maʿnā* pairing could be meaningfully separated. The fact that vocal forms were important did not mean that the mental content being communicated was irrelevant. Vocal forms were simply the way to get a point across. For example, one might make a proverb rhyme so it could be remembered, in which case the vocal form of the proverb would impact the reception of its mental content.[61] Al-Ǧurǧānī was frustrated by these discussions too, and by the imprecision of the trope, invoked by even Ibn Ǧinnī, that vocal forms were the servants of mental contents. Al-Ǧurǧānī wanted to map the connections between language and cognition but was forced to deal with ethical polemics and metaphorical or theologically motivated explanations that he thought were subject to misinterpretation. I do not mean to imply that al-Ǧurǧānī's frustration is evidence of any inconsistency between the polemical use of *lafẓ* and *maʿnā* in al-Ǧāḥiẓ or the Iḫwān and the linguistic use of *lafẓ* and *maʿnā* in Ibn Ǧinnī and al-Ǧurǧānī. In all cases the pairing referred to the same two levels of physical linguistic vocal form and cognitive mental content. But Ibn Ǧinnī and al-Ǧurǧānī were more concerned with how the levels interacted than with one level being "better" than the other. From this perspective the very opposition of the two levels was unproductive: both were *prima facie* involved in language.

Ibn Ǧinnī and al-Ǧurǧānī used the pairing of *lafẓ* and *maʿnā* to explain syntax. Al-Ǧāḥiẓ and the Iḫwān used the same pairing to label political dynamics, in effect thinking of language politics in terms of language itself. To understand this difference, we may imagine an author using "signifier" and "signified" in an article on

60. Iḫwān aṣ-Ṣafāʾ (1957, 3:119.7–122.3).

61. فإنها [الألفاظَ] عنوانُ معانيها وطريقاً إلى إظهار أغراضها ومَرامِيها . . . ألا ترى أنَّ المَثل إذا كان مَسجوعاً لذَّ لِسامعه فَحَفِظَه . . . فإذا رأيتَ العربَ قد أصلحوا ألفاظاً وحسَّنوها .. فلا ترينّ أن العنايةَ إذ ذاك إنما هي بالألفاظ بل هي عندنا خدمةٌ منهم للمعاني. Ibn Ǧinnī (1952–56, 1:215.15–16, 216.1–2, 217.5–7).

how good Barack Obama's rhetoric was. I use this thought experiment to suggest three things: that the use of linguistic categories outside linguistic disciplines was more prevalent in pre-eleventh-century Arabic than it is in twenty-first-century English, that this breadth of usage does not imply any dissonance in meaning, and that this breadth of usage could give a literary-critical flavor to conversations about politics, society, and more.

Theology

My next example of precedent comes from theology and the definition of "monotheism" (*tawḥīd*). A famous late-tenth-century scholar, Abū Ḥayyān at-Tawḥīdī (d. 1023), was reviewing definitions of core conceptual vocabulary that had been provided by his teacher Abū Sulaymān as-Siǧistānī (d. ca. 985, on whom see Joel Kraemer).[62] The definition comprised a belief in God's oneness together with a verbal profession of God's oneness. At-Tawḥīdī reported that as-Siǧistānī, after this definition, had gone on to explain that when he said, "a person professed God's unity," he was referring not to a simple verbal profession, but to a thoroughgoing conception of the unity of God that went beyond denials of polytheism to conceive of an unblemished, unqualified, and indescribable essence captured by the phrase "he is one alone; he alone is one." That essence was a *maʿnā,* and as mental content the power of the phrase should not, as-Siǧistānī said, be located in its syntactic symmetry, "as is the habit of the adherents of *lafẓ*."[63] The words "he is one alone; he alone is one" are not theologically salient because of their repetition and inversion (an antimetabole), but rather because of the deep mental content they convey. What we have here is the use of the pairing of vocal form and mental content to privilege mental content and denigrate critical focus on the level of vocal form. It seems that the methodology from which as-Siǧistānī and at-Tawḥīdī wanted to distinguish themselves was a literary-critical approach to theology: the adherents of *lafẓ* are accused of having located the theological force of "he is one alone; he alone is one" in the antimetabole itself.

Just like the Iḫwān, as-Siǧistānī used the pairing of vocal form and mental content to privilege the latter. When he said "adherents of *lafẓ*," he meant people whose readings were not to be trusted. What then might it mean to have adherents

62. Kraemer (1986).

63. وليس معنى قولنا وَحَّدَ فلانٌ أنه قال هو واحِدٌ هذا مفهومُ العامة لا معقولُ الخاصة بل معنى قولنا وَحَّدَ أي عرَفه واحِداً وعَلِمَ واحداً وأثبَت واحِداً ووجَد واحِداً [ذكر المحقق حسين أنَّ في التحقيق السابق للسندوبي: عَلِمه و أَثبته ووَجده] لا لأنه نَفَى عنه الثانيَ والثالثَ فصاعداً وكيف ذلك ولا ثانيَ له فيُنفَى ولكنْ لأنه واحدٌ وحْدُه بل هو وحْدُه واحِدٌ لا على سبيل نَسْقٍ في عادة أصحاب اللفظ ولا على تعقيبٍ يَقتضيه أَلْفُ أكثرِ الخلْق بل على لحْظِ ذاتٍ لا شَوْبَ فيها. At-Tawḥīdī (1970, 457.5–9).

of *maʿnā?* What implications might such a phrase convey? On the one hand it could be used to describe interpretation (whether criticism of poetry or exegesis of scripture) that focused on the meaning behind the words. It could also be used for poets who aimed primarily at complex metaphor (Ibn Ṭabāṭabā, d. 815, quoted by al-Marzūqī).[64] But the phrase "adherents of *maʿnā*" had a specific theological history. It was perhaps first used to refer to a group of theologians who subscribed to a doctrine proposed by the ninth-century theologian Muʿammar b. ʿAbbād (d. 830) about the functioning of things he called *maʿānī*. This is a doctrine that deserves its own special section, which is up next. I have deliberately left it to the end of my survey of precedents despite the inversion of chronology this involves: Muʿammar's *maʿānī* need to be read in the context of everyone else's.

Let us return to al-Ǧāḥiẓ. His work engaged with theology on such a deep and systematic level as to make the distinction between literature and theology meaningless (see Miller's review of James Montgomery),[65] and he wrote that the Quranic statement "God taught Adam all the names" meant that God taught Adam "all the *maʿānī*" (Quran 2:31, al-Baqarah, on which see further below). But al-Ǧāḥiẓ then went on to say that by *maʿānī* he did not mean "the constitution of colors, tastes, and smells, or the multiplications of finite and infinite numbers." He was clearly sensitive to the fact that *maʿnā* was used both for the mental contents connected to words and for the mental contents that result from cognition of either the qualities of physical bodies or the components of arithmetic. Al-Ǧāḥiẓ then wrote: "The only way to name those mental contents that exceed the bounds of what is required or go beyond the limit of a description is to enter them into the sphere of knowledge and say, 'a thing and a *maʿnā*.'"[66] Al-Ǧāḥiẓ knew that mental content *in toto* was a broader category than the mental content connected to names by the lexicon. The way to deal with arithmetic or the cognition of physical bodies and their qualities was therefore to *name* a thing and then also voice the extra bit of mental content required to specify what one is talking about. One could think, for example, about a camel that smelt of lemons and thereby one would have a mental content of "camel smelling of lemons." But there is no name in the lexicon for a package thus constituted. One would have to say "a camel smelling of lemons" and thereby (in al-Ǧāḥiẓ's vocabulary) name both a thing and a *maʿnā*. This is why

64. وهم أصحابُ المعاني فطلبوا المعانيَ المُعْجِبة . . . وجَعلوا رُسومَها أن تكون قريبةَ التشبيه لائقة الاستعارة. ʿAbbās (1971, 404), al-Marzūqī and Abū Tammām (1991, 7.7–10).

65. Miller (2016a).

66. وقولُه جلّ ذكره ﴿وَعَلَّمَ آدَمَ الأَسْماءَ كُلَّها﴾ إخبارٌ أنه قد علّمه المعانيَ كلها ولسْنا نَعني معانيَ تركيب الألوان والطعوم والأراييح وتضاعيف الأعداد التي لا تنتهي ولا تتناهى وليس لِما فضَل عن مقدار المصلحة ونهاية الرسم اسمٌ إلا أن تدخُله في باب العلم فتقول شيءٌ ومعنى. Al-Ǧāḥiẓ (1965b, 1:262.12–15). Cf. translation and analysis in Miller (2016b, 68).

when al-Ǧāḥiẓ said that God taught Adam all the *maʿānī*, al-Ǧāḥiẓ did not mean that God taught Adam every possible mental content. God did not teach Adam the composition "camel plus lemon smell"; rather, he taught Adam the mental content "camel" and the mental content "lemon smell," just as he taught Adam the mental content of each number but not the mental content of every possible arithmetical composition. In any case, color, taste, and smell were *maʿānī*.

This same assumption can also be read outside Islamic theology. A century later in Baghdad, the Jewish theologian Saadiya Gaon (d. 942) was engaged in refuting the belief that all composite bodies were created from eternal spiritual beings. One of his objections to this theory was that such spiritual beings would have to have heat, cold, moistness, and dryness in order to be the source of those same four attributes in physical bodies, as was claimed by his opponents. Equally, he could not accept that the posited spiritual beings had color, taste, limit, dimension, quantity, place, or time, because "all these *maʿānī* were attributes of bodies," and the spiritual beings were claimed to be prior to bodies.[67] Gaon's argument was that the theory was incoherent. On the one hand it implied that the spiritual beings needed heat and cold in order to be the source of heat and cold in bodies. On the other hand, it implied that because the spiritual beings were prior to bodies, they could not have color or quantity. The Arabic word that Gaon used for all these different attributes of physical bodies was *maʿnā*. Heat, cold, dimension, and quantity were all *maʿānī*. If we translate *maʿānī* as "mental contents," then Saadiya was assuming that hot, cold, and all the other attributes of physical bodies were cognitive judgments: things that we judge, in our minds, other things to have.

THEOLOGIANS (MUʿAMMAR)

The theological discussions that used *maʿnā* are dominated by Muʿammar, whose ninth-century claim about what we now call physics, the study of the basic principles that govern the physical world around us, used *maʿnā* as its central concept. As we saw from Abū Hilāl, this usage of *maʿnā* was noticed by his contemporaries, who worked to explain it, just as scholarship would work to explain it again in German, English, and French over a millennium later. Let us start with the presentation of the theory by Abū al-Ḥusayn al-Ḫayyāṭ (d. ca. 913) in his *Kitāb al-Intiṣār*. "Chapter 34: Muʿammar's statements on generation and on *maʿānī*."[68] Al-Ḫayyāṭ

67. أرى أن هذه الأشياء التي ادّعَوها لا يجوز أن تكون لا حارةً ولا باردةً ولا رطبةً ولا يابسةً إذ عندهم أنّ هذه الأربع منها خُلقتْ وأرى أيضاً أنها لا يجوز أن يكون لها لونٌ ولا طعمٌ ولا رائحةٌ ولا حدٌّ ولا مِقدارٌ ولا كَثرةٌ ولا قلّةٌ ولا في مكان ولا في زمان لأن هذه المعاني كلها هي صفات الأجسام وتلك الأشياءُ هي عندهم قبل الجسم. Gaon (1880, 42.12–17), (1948, 52); Wolfson (1976, 117 n. 29).

68. قوله في التولُّد وفي المعاني. Al-Ḫayyāṭ (1957, 46.10). Cf. van Ess (1991–95, 5:264–65).

starts the chapter with a review of what appears to be a self-evidently unlikely theory: Muʿammar's claim that every single action in the world is actually accompanied by thousands and thousands of other actions stretching to infinity. Every act of every actor, whether God or human, is actually an infinite number of acts that occur at the same time. Al-Ḫayyāṭ then works to reduce the counterintuitiveness of this theory, first by explaining that Muʿammar was in fact responding to another early theologian, Abū Isḥāq an-Naẓẓām (d. ca. 840), who held that when God acts he does so in a single state but on an infinite number of bodies. Now, it may seem that Muʿammar was claiming that if each action has infinite objects then it must in fact be an infinite number of actions. But this is not the case, and here al-Ḫayyāṭ makes an important statement about *maʿnā:* "You should know that this school of thought that I am describing from the statements of Muʿammar is in fact a statement about *maʿānī.*" Al-Ḫayyāṭ explains that Muʿammar claimed that when there are two motionless bodies next to each other, and then one of them moves and the other doesn't, then there must have been a *maʿnā* subsisting in the one that moved, on account of which it moved, and no such *maʿnā* in the other. Otherwise, it could not have moved before the other one.[69] So for Muʿammar, on al-Ḫayyāṭ's reading, *maʿnā* is something that a body has on account of which it moves. But where does that *maʿnā* come from? Al-Ḫayyāṭ tells us that Muʿammar's answer was that there was another *maʿnā* that caused the first *maʿnā* to be there, and so on.[70] Perhaps a decade or so later, Abū Qāsim al-Kaʿbī (d. 931) wrote that Muʿammar was the only person to have such a theory, and paraphrased it thus: every instance of motion is only at variance from a state of rest because of a *maʿnā* separate from that motion, and vice versa. Each of those *maʿānī* is then only at variance from the other because of another *maʿnā,* and so on to infinity.[71]

Muʿammar's claim also appears in the *Maqālāt al-Islāmīyīn* of al-Ašʿarī, a foundational text of Arabic theology. Al-Ašʿarī's description of Muʿammar's position

69. اعلمْ علَّمك اللهُ الخيرَ أنّ هذا المذهب الذي وصَفه صاحبُ الكتاب [ابن الراوندي] من قول معمَّر هو القول بالمعاني وتفسيرُه أنّ معمَّراً زعم أنه لمّا وجد جسمين ساكنين أحدُهما يلي الآخر ثم وجد أحدَهما قد تحرّك دون صاحبه كان لا بد عنده من معنى حَلَّه دون صاحبه من أجله تحرَّكَ وإلا لم يكن بالتحرك أَولى من صاحبه. Al-Ḫayyāṭ (1957, 46.16–19).

70. فإذا كان هذا حُكماً صحيحاً فلا بد أيضاً من معنى حدثٍ له حلَّت [من أجله (نادر)] الحركةُ في أحدهما دون صاحبه وإلا لم يكن حلولُها في أحدهما أولى من حلولها في الآخر وكذلك أيضاً إنْ سُئلتُ عن ذلك المعنى لِما كان علَّةً لِحلول الحركة في أحدهما دون صاحبه قُلتُ لمعنى آخر وكذلك أيضاً إنْ سُئلتُ عن ذلك المعنى كان جوابي فيه كجوابي فيما قبله. Al-Ḫayyāṭ (1957, 46.20–24).

71. والذي تفرَّد به [معمَّرٌ] القولُ بالمعاني وتفسيرُها أنّ الحركة إنما خالفتْ السكونَ لمعنى هو غيرها وكذلك السكونُ إنما خالفَ الحركةَ بمعنى هو غيره وأنّ ذَينكَ المعنيين إنما اختلفا أيضاً بمعنى هو غيرهما ثم كذلك كل معنيين اختلفا بمعنيين غيرهما إلى ما لا نهاية له. Al-Kaʿbī (1974, 71.6–9). Cf. Ibn Ḥazm (1899–1903, 5:46.14–24), van Ess (1991–95, 5:265–66).

(for we are always dependent on the reports of others when it comes to Muʿammar, none of whose work has been preserved)[72] reads: "Some say that the body, if at rest, is only at rest because of a *maʿnā* that is movement. Without that *maʿnā* of movement the body would not, back in the time when it was the first to move, have been the first to move."[73] According to al-Ašʿarī, Muʿammar even explained the state of rest as being the result of a prior *maʿnā*-driven movement. This is a theory in which it is assumed that things have *maʿānī* that make them do things, or give them color, or make them alive, and so on. Each *maʿnā* is then dependent on a further *maʿnā*, and that *maʿnā* on a further *maʿnā*, in an infinite chain of dependence. At every stage, the *maʿnā* of movement is the only thing that makes the previous *maʿnā* of movement move. These *maʿānī* depend on each other, but "they do not have a sum total, and they cannot be gathered together. They all occur in the same instant."[74] According to this theory, there is no other explanation for why some things are black and others white, some things moving and others not, some things alive and others not. The *maʿānī* are "actions of the place in which they inhere."[75] This is a conceptual vocabulary for a physics that has no correlate in English. Muʿammar's theory, according to al-Ašʿarī, is that if something is white, black, moving, or alive, then something must make it white, black, moving, or alive. The *maʿānī* that do this then need to be made what they are by other *maʿānī*, and so on to infinite regress.

What are these *maʿānī*, and where are they? As Abū Hilāl noted, this is a theological usage of the word that is connected with what he believed was its core meaning: prelinguistic cognition or mental content. The clue that we get in the theological texts themselves is that *maʿnā* was a broad category, from which one could distinguish more technical categories such as the accidental quality or attribute (*ʿaraḍ*). As al-Ašʿarī says, theologians "disagreed about why the *maʿānī* that inhered in bodies were called 'accidents.'"[76] Furthermore, on the page directly preceding his discussion of that disagreement about why a *maʿnā* might be called an accident, al-Ašʿarī used the very same word to talk about language, reference, and

72. Daiber (2015).

73. واختلفَ الناسُ في المعاني فقال قائلون إنّ الجسم إذا سَكَن فإنما يَسكُن لمعنى هو الحركةُ لولاه لم يكن بأنْ يكون متحرّكاً أُوْلى من غيره ولم يكن بأنْ يتحرّك في الوقت الذي يتحرك [فيه (ريتر)] أَوْلى منه بالحركة قبل ذلك. Al-Ašʿarī (1929–33), 372.2–5). Cf. translations and analysis in Sabra (2006, 241–42), van Ess (1991–95, 3:74–83, 5:266–67).

74. وإذا كان ذلك كذلك فذلك الحركةُ لو لا معنى له [كذا] كانت حركةً للمتحرّك لم تكن بأنْ تكون حركةً أُوْلى منها أنْ تكون حركةً لغيره وذلك المعنى كان معنى لأنْ كانت الحركةُ حركةً للمتحرك لمعنى آخر وليس للمعاني كلٌّ ولا جميعٌ وإنها تَحدُث في وقت واحد. Al-Ašʿarī (1929–33, 372.5–8). Cf. translations and analysis in Sabra (2006, 241–42), van Ess (1991–95, 3:74–83, 5:266–67).

75. المعاني التي لا كُلَّ لها فِعلٌ للمكان الذي حلّته. Al-Ašʿarī (1929–33, 372.13–14).

76. Al-Ašʿarī (1929–33, 369). For translations: Dhanani (1994, 38–39), Sabra (2006, 240–42).

meaning: "Al-Iskāfī was one of those who said that the *maʿnā* of the statement with regard to the created thing was that it . . ."[77] These are the two usages that Abū Hilāl identified, working together unmarked and unremarked upon. *Maʿnā* was both prelinguistic cognition and cognition of physical forces, what Hans Daiber calls "ein Relationsbegriff von ontischer Qualität."[78]

In his section on theological disagreements about movement and rest, al-Ašʿarī cited the opinion of al-Ǧubbāʾī that movement and rest are ways of being in a place, and that: "the *maʿnā* of movement is the *maʿnā* of passing away; every movement is a passing away. But the *maʿnā* of movement is not the *maʿnā* of changing position; the nonexistent movement is called passing away before it comes to be. It is not called changing position."[79] Al-Ǧubbāʾī was making a distinction between three related technical concepts: "movement," "passing away," and "changing position." In physics today we may call these "forces" or "interactions." Whatever the translation, we are talking about principles that govern the physical world. Al-Ǧubbāʾī was using a vocabulary based around *maʿnā,* and from our perspective today, it looks as if he is saying two things at the same time: that the Arabic word for movement did not mean the same thing as the word for passing away or the word for changing position, but also that the quality or force of "movement," when present in an object in extramental reality, was not the same quality or force as "passing away" or "changing position." This was both lexicography and theological physics. In English, we tend to use different phrases for each of these. We may therefore say either that "'normal force' *does not mean the same thing* as 'applied force,' or that: "normal force *is not the same thing* as applied force." When Arabic theorists, whether lexicographers like Abū Hilāl or theologians like ʿAbd al-Ǧabbār, wanted to make the same distinction they did so using different conceptual vocabulary with an equivalent degree of clarity. Abū Hilal described the difference between "does not mean" and "is not" as being a difference between a process of intent on the one hand, and a target of intention on the other. He said that the phrase "*maʿnā* of . . ." was used for both statements, in the former case with accuracy and in the latter case by a process of semantic extension. ʿAbd al-Ǧabbār agreed, and his name for the process of semantic extension was *maǧāz.* In English, we use quotation marks and the phrases "means" and "is" to make the distinction. In Arabic, theorists used a core conceptual vocabulary based around language and reference to do the same job. For al-Ǧubbāʾī, of course, the distinction did not matter. He

77. Al-Ašʿarī (1929–33, 368).

78. "A relational concept of ontological quality": Daiber (1975, 82).

79. وكان الجبائي يزعم أنّ الحركة والسكون أكوان وأنّ معنى الحركة معنى الزوال فلا حركة إلا وهي زوال وأنه ليس معنى الحركة معنى الانتقال وأنّ الحركة المعدومة تُسمّى زوالاً قبل كونها ولا تُسمّى انتقالاً. Al-Ašʿarī (1929–33, 355.12–14). Thanks to David Bennett for the reference.

was talking about both the meaning of the word "movement" and the extramental reality of the physical interaction of objects that was movement.

Another way we can think about the usage of *maʿnā* in theology is to notice that it was often used to talk about things one could think about but not see. If something was a body (and therefore both extramental and able to be seen), then it would not be *maʿnā.* So for the early and influential Shia theologian Hišām b. al-Ḥakam (d. ca. 803), human qualities were *maʿānī.* They could not be things or bodies, so they had to be *maʿānī,* what we can think about and talk about but not see. (In Hišām's theology, "things" were what al-Ašʿarī tended to call "bodies.")[80] Along the same lines, al-Ašʿarī also reports that Ǧaʿfar b. al-Mubaššir (d. 849) said that the soul was not a body, nor in a body, but rather a *maʿnā* between the atom and the body.[81] David Bennett has raised the further question of whether the word *maʿnā* was used for not doing something or for the absence of movement: al-Ašarī records disagreements about whether not acting was a *maʿnā* separate from the person (not) doing it,[82] and that Hišām and others considered movement to be a *maʿnā* whereas being at rest was not.[83]

The potential limit on this use of *maʿnā* for the cogitated unseen was, as we saw above with Abū Hilāl and ʿAbd al-Ǧabbār, whether it could be used for God. Abū al-Ḥasan al-ʿĀmirī (d. 992) was prepared to connect a Neoplatonic rational soul to what he called "the divine *maʿnā,*" but theologians avoided such locutions.[84] In another report in *Maqālāt al-Islāmīyīn,* Ibn Kullāb (d. ca. 855) had said that while God was unlike any other he could not be said to be a *maʿnā.*[85] This seems to make sense; one could describe the soul as a *maʿnā,* or attributes and qualities as *maʿānī,* or explain physical forces and their absence with *maʿānī,* because all these were in effect mental content; they were human cognitions that could be subsequently communicated in language. Even al-ʿĀmirī's divine *maʿnā* can be fitted into this account, for when he talks elsewhere of *maʿānī ilāhīyah,* in the plural, he is dealing with the divine matters that pious human beings pursue and seek to apprehend. Everett Rowson's translation of this process is "determining divine concepts."[86]

80. وحُكي عن هشام أنه كان يزعم أن صِفات الإنسان أشياءُ لأنّ الأشياء هي الأجسامُ عنده وكان يزعم أنها معانٍ وليست بأشياء. Al-Ašʿarī (1929–33, 344.15–345.1). Thanks to David Bennett for the reference.

81. Al-Ašʿarī (1929–33, 337.2–3), Gimaret (1988, 155).

82. واختلف المتكلمون في الترك للشيء والكفّ هل هو معنىً غير التارك. Al-Ašʿarī (1929–33, 378.13–14), Bennett (2017).

83. وحَكى زرقانُ عن هشام بن الحكم أنه كان يزعم أن الحركة معنىً وأنّ السكون ليس بمعنى . . . حكاه أبو عيسى عن أصحاب الطبائع. Al-Ašʿarī (1929–33, 345.2–5), Bennett (2017).

84. فقد ظهر إذاً أنّ النفس النطقية بِقِنْياتها الأبدية وصُوَرها العقلية أشْبَهُ شيءٍ بالمعنى الإلهي. Al-ʿĀmirī and Rowson (1988, 106.9).

85. Al-Ašʿarī (1929–33, 496.9), Frank (1999, 216 n. 115).

86. تقرير المعاني الإلهية. Al-ʿĀmirī and Rowson (1988, 128–32).

Calling God a *maʿnā*, however, was not permissible for ʿAbd al-Ǧabbār: "God cannot be described as a *maʿnā*, because *maʿnā* is the intent of the heart to speak about what it wants. This is why we say, 'The *maʿnā* of this speech is such and such,' and 'My *maʿnā* in this discourse is this and that,' and why someone may ask their companion, 'What is your *maʿnā* in that speech?'"[87] ʿAbd al-Ǧabbār was citing examples from ordinary language to show that *maʿnā* is prelinguistic intent. He then went on to note, just as Abū Hilāl had, the usage made famous by Muʿammar: "The theologians have acquainted each other with the use of this vocal form for causes, so they say that 'the moving thing moves because of a *maʿnā*.' They use that statement in place of the statement 'It is moving because of a cause.'"[88] ʿAbd al-Ǧabbār did not distinguish at all between the *maʿānī* that were prelinguistic mental contents and the *maʿānī* that Muʿammar believed were an infinite series of causes: if we allow Muʿammar's infinite causal *maʿānī*, then "this will lead to an inability to put faith in accurate accounts of names."[89] The *maʿnā* that Muʿammar used to explain causality and physical forces was the same *maʿnā* that lay behind names in language.

Maʿnā was a word that was available for Muʿammar to pick up and use. He used it in a way consistent with his peers. What theories may have influenced him, and how he may have been inspired by reading the work of others, are questions of translation. We can speculate as to what foreign concepts may have influenced Muʿammar as he thought about causality. Harry Austryn Wolfson suggested that Muʿammar was translating the Aristotelian term *phusis* and that his theory of *maʿānī* "represents his theory of nature [*phusis*] as the cause of motion and rest."[90] This is quite possible, for the *phusis* Aristotle discussed at the beginning of Book Two of his *Physics* was described there as existing, and just like *maʿnā* it was also only conceptually separable from the thing in question.[91] But Aristotle's conceptual vocabulary was not the same as Muʿammar's, and we cannot easily map *phusis* onto *maʿnā*. For example, the distinction Aristotle draws between natural materials (where *phusis* is found) and man-made objects (where *phusis* is not found) is central to his theory,[92] but to the

87. Al-ʿĀmirī and Rowson (1988).

ولا يوصَف [اللهُ] بأنه معنىً قال شيخُنا أبو علي لأنّ المعنى هو قصدُ القلب بالكلام إلى المراد ولذلك يقال إنّ معنى هذا الكلام كَيْتَ وكَيْتَ وإنّ معنايَ بهذا الخطاب كذا وكذا ويقول القائلُ لصاحبه ما معناكَ في هذا الكلام. Al-Qāḍī ʿAbd al-Ǧabbār (1965–74, 5:253.4–7).

88. وقد تعرف المتكلمون استعمالَ هذه اللفظة في العِلَل فيقولون إنّ المتحرّك متحرّكٌ لمعنىً ويُقيمونه مقامَ قَولِهم إنه متحرّكٌ لِعِلّة. Al-Qāḍī ʿAbd al-Ǧabbār (1965–74, 5:253.9–10).

89. وهذا يؤدّي إلى ألّا نَثِقُ بحقائق الأسماء. Al-Qāḍī ʿAbd al-Ǧabbār (1965–74, 7.9–13, 18). Cf. Miller (2016b, 69).

90. Kelsey (2015, 44); Wolfson (1965, 684), (1976, 147f).

91. Arist. *Ph.* 193b5.

92. Arist. *Ph.* 192b.

best of my knowledge it is extraneous to Muʿammar's. There is also the evidence from the contemporaneous translation movement: when Isḥāq came to translate Aristotle's *Physics,* he did not use *maʿnā* for either Aristotle's *phusis* ("nature") or his *archēn kinēseōs* ("starting principle of motion"), but rather *ṭabīʿah* ("nature," a word indeed later used for causation and as such summarily dismissed by Ibn Fūrak)[93] and *mabdaʾ li-l-ḥarakah* ("starting point of motion"), respectively.[94] Wolfson's other suggestion, that Muʿammar's *maʿnā* comes from the reports of Christian theologians describing the Trinity as an eternal *maʿnā,* is equally possible.[95] It is not impossible that theologians were responding to Christian uses of *maʿnā* to describe the divine, but we are engaging in guesswork here at the remove of more than a millennium. Many scholars have been down this path and suggested a range of origins that includes, inter alia, Classical Indian philosophy. (The scholarship has been reviewed by Daiber.)[96]

I think, however, that Muʿammar's *maʿānī* theory, a staple of ninth-century theology/philosophy/physics, makes sense within the bounds set by the literary critic and lexicographer Abū Hilāl. In the seventh through tenth centuries, the conceptual vocabulary of *maʿnā, lafẓ,* and *ḥaqīqah* was everywhere. It was not omnipresent: the confluence of language, mind, and reality was sometimes confronted with other words, as we will see below with the discussion of name, naming, and named, and as Fritz Zimmermann has documented in the work of Abū Naṣr al-Fārābī (d. 950).[97] But this chapter has demonstrated that *maʿnā, lafẓ,* and *ḥaqīqah* were stable and available words from the eighth century onward. When scholars thought about the principles, natures, and qualities of things around them they did so, inescapably, with the stuff of cognition: mental content that they could later put into words. They usually called this mental content *maʿnā.* This is why I juxtapose theology, logic, and poetics in this book: because I am convinced that the language game being played by scholars in each of these disciplines, on each of these fields, was the same. It is as if, on one of those vast expanses of adjacent sports pitches that one finds in parts of the United Kingdom, multiple games were being played next to one another, each with different players and their own ball but all returning to the same changing rooms and all identifying themselves as doing the same thing: playing amateur football.

93. مَن قال بالطبيعة المجيبة والطبعِ المولّدِ مُخطئٌ .. لا يصحّ أنْ يكون مِن جنسِ الجواهر [أوْ] الأعراضِ .. . . . [الطبيعةُ والطبعُ] لفظ فارغ مِن معنىً معقولٍ Ibn Fūrak (1987, 131.16–132.1).

94. Aristotle (1964, 1:78f), van Ess (1991–95, 2:40). Cf. Ibn Fūrak's dismissal of the idea that "nature" could explain generation: Ibn Fūrak (1987, 131.16).

95. Wolfson (1956, 3f), (1976, 112f, 115, 147–67).

96. Daiber (1975, 82).

97. Zimmermann (1981, cxxix–cxxxvii).

3

Translation

Thus far I have endeavored to present my reading of *maʿnā* as a word with a single meaning as relatively uncontroversial. I believe that this is an accurate reflection of the word's status for those who used it in the eleventh century and before. Only someone writing a book that sought to expose minute semantic differences where they had been previously denied or ignored would notice, as we have seen Abū Hilāl notice, any dissonance in the use of the word. But my approach stands in stark contrast to the consensus in much of the secondary literature, where *maʿnā* is either discussed as vague and imprecise, or else is divided up into separate and mutually incompatible meanings. My core criticism of both of these approaches is that they rest on vectors of *maʿnā* that are unmarked in the original texts, and unremarked upon by the scholars who wrote those texts. I think that the only way that we can read *maʿnā* as vague or imprecise is to think likewise that a word in English such as "play" is also vague and imprecise because it can be put to so many different uses; one can play tag in the morning and then watch someone else play Hamlet in the evening.

I accept that dividing *maʿnā* up into separate meanings is a legitimate translation methodology, but while I have learned a great deal from scholars who have done just that, it is a methodology that has risks. If what we are trying to understand is a conceptual vocabulary that we do not share, any translation technique that slices up the original vocabulary into new divisions risks domesticating that alien conceptual vocabulary to our own. Concepts with which we are not familiar thereby appear familiar, but as they do so they change, and a gap appears between us and the use that the original authors made of their words. It is true that this gap is an inevitable part of translation, but I think that it is our job to minimize it.

Philology should be aware of the challenges (which means basically being aware that time travel is impossible), but it should also be committed to playing, as well as we possibly can, the language games of the past.

LANGUAGE USE (WITTGENSTEIN)

The idea of language as a game that is played comes from the later work of the twentieth-century philosopher Ludwig Wittgenstein. I have found his ideas about how language works to be very helpful in the struggle to translate. At the heart of his account lies the conviction that what matters most for language is usage. This means that the answer to the question, "What is language?" is that a language (in our case the Arabic language used by eleventh-century scholars) is the use that people make of it, not some set of fixed or fluid meanings. If we choose to agree with Wittgenstein, we should no longer say, "*Maʿnā* means one thing" or "*Maʿnā* has two or more meanings." Instead we only ask, How did these people use the word *maʿnā?* At stake here is the question of whether or not one subscribes to a theory of language in which meanings exist outside the context of their use. Wittgenstein did not. However, if we say, "*Maʿnā* means one thing" or "*Maʿnā* has two or more meanings," then we are subscribing to such a theory: for these statements to make sense, meanings need to have an existence separate from their ordinary usage, an existence that we can map and thereby determine. In the years since Wittgenstein's death and the posthumous publication of *Philosophical Investigations,* his theory of language, and his denial that meanings have any such existence, has not met with universal acceptance. Nevertheless, I think that it provides a good methodology for making sense of *maʿnā* in Classical Arabic.

This is why, in the preceding chapter on precedents for the use of *maʿnā,* I spent little time on the Arabic lexicographical tradition. I did not want that kind of picture of language to dominate the reader's understanding of *maʿnā*. I did not want the reader to think that there was some truth in the etymology of *maʿnā,* or in the Semitic root of *ʿ-n-y,* or in a dictionary definition, that may have guided all the uses scholars made of that popular vocabulary item. Instead, what I wanted to do was lay out a roughly representative selection of those uses in order that it may act as an orientation to the subject matter of this book: the theories of ar-Rāġib, Ibn Fūrak, Ibn Sīnā, and al-Ǧurǧānī about how language worked. These theories about language consisted of a great deal of use of the word *maʿnā* in serious and complex games played in the spaces between God and the poets.

There is a double irony in my use of theory here: Wittgenstein would have hated the Arabic assumptions about *maʿnā;* they represent exactly the kind of stable structure that he thought did not exist. The Arabic lexicographers, for their part, would no doubt reject my attempt to abandon their dictionary etymologies in favour of Wittgenstein's focus on usage. But I think we do need a theory of language, a tentative universal diagnosis of what linguistic reality is, before we start to translate. Wittgenstein provides that for me; his theory of language supports my philological practice.

For Wittgenstein in *Philosophical Investigations,* use is all that matters. Use is the only part of language that can be shown to actually exist. This is the central conclusion of Wittgenstein's late work, and it has guided my reading of the work of Arabic theorists who used the word *maʿnā* unmarked, over and over again, in a series of ways that I consider to be stable, rigorous, and cohesive. This is exactly how Wittgenstein thinks language works. He does not think that language consists of meanings that can be identified and enumerated in fixed fields of reference. He thinks that the language games human beings play, the actual usage we make of words, is the only place to which we can turn when we want to give an account of language. He also thinks that usage is often stable, rigorous, and cohesive, because how else can a meaningful game be played?

In *Philosophical Investigations,* a book in which Wittgenstein asks questions and tests out possible descriptions in order to destroy any idea of a fixed realm of reference, I read #204 as a moment when he takes a stand and makes a commitment to the universal fact that what mankind does is play games:[1]

> As things are I can, for example, invent a game that is never played by anyone.—But would the following be possible too: mankind has never played any games; once, however, someone invented a game—which no one ever played?

The games are, of course, language games. One can invent a language that is never spoken by anyone. But ours is not a world in which the only language game ever to have existed was never played. To put it the other way around, in our world mankind inevitably plays language games (although not necessarily everyone all the time). Wittgenstein's rhetorical question is a *reductio ad absurdum,* and his point is a double one: people always play language games, and language games are always played by people. They exist only in their being played, not in the abstract. Language exists in usage, not as a formal structure.

The question then becomes one of rules, because Wittgenstein claims that every game from chess to ring-a-ring-a-roses has rules. The players know at least some of the rules in advance; rules are by definition used on multiple occasions, and rules also have to be obeyed by multiple players.[2] There are also, as we saw in the previous chapter, different sorts of game. Eleventh-century Arabic scholarship contains games in which the rules are laid out and debated, such as those for dialectical debate performances or for grammar. It also contains games

1. Wittgenstein (2006, #204).

2. Wittgenstein (2006, ##197, 199, 202, 243).

where the rules are not laid out but rather are known iteratively by the players, as they play:[3]

> Doesn't the analogy between language and games throw light here? We can easily imagine people amusing themselves in a field by playing with a ball so as to start various existing games, but playing many without finishing them and in between throwing the ball aimlessly into the air, chasing one another with the ball and bombarding one another for a joke and so on. And now someone says: The whole time they are playing a ball-game and following definite rules at every throw.
>
> And is there not also the case where we play and—make up the rules as we go along? And there is even one where we alter them—as we go along.

In this book, those people are ar-Rāġib, Ibn Fūrak, Ibn Sīnā, and al-Ǧurǧānī; the field is eleventh-century Arabic scholarship, and the ball is *maʿnā*. I find that Wittgenstein's account of a language game is the best way to give an account of the usage of *maʿnā* in the works that I have read.

Wittgenstein writes that "when we do philosophy we are like savages, primitive people, who hear the expressions of civilized men, put a false interpretation on them, and then draw the queerest conclusions."[4] (Ar-Rāġib and his contemporaries would agree with the heedless division of humanity into civilized and savage; in addition to their patriarchy, eleventh-century Arabic scholars tend to exhibit unselfconscious racism.) At this point in *Philosophical Investigations,* Wittgenstein is complaining about the imprecise way philosophers use language. He explains his criticism with an example, in which philosophers are describing the way an inanimate object, a machine, has something that they call "possibility of movement." Wittgenstein objects to this description. He says that a piece of machinery such as an engine, when not switched on or in operation, has for us some picture or history of experience that is its future movement. This "empirical condition" of the various parts being ready to move and not being broken or misaligned is "like a shadow of the movement itself." But what bothers Wittgenstein is that philosophers cover all this up with the blanket term "possibility of movement." They replace Wittgenstein's own multifaceted explanation, which he thinks is perfectly clear, with a single neologism. We are therefore effective language users when we say (updating Wittgenstein's example), "This mobile phone works" even when it is switched off. Our words are simple, but their usage in this case communicates a particular shadow picture of a phone-and-context-specific act of working that hasn't actually empirically happened, may not happen, and is (as this sentence shows) not really amenable to paraphrase.

3. Wittgenstein (2006, #83).

4. Wittgenstein (2006, #194).

This is why Wittgenstein complains that civilized men use words like "works" and then philosophers come along like savages and misinterpret them with phrases like "possibility of movement." Ibn Fūrak, ar-Rāġib, Ibn Sīnā, and al-Ǧurǧānī are the civilized men here, and we are the savages. They used simple words like *maʿnā* to talk about universal things like language and human minds very effectively, and then we come along and risk confusing their work, and ourselves, with a whole host of technical terms (sense, nominatum, denotation, illocution, signifier, signified, etc.), or alternatively with an after-the-fact assertion of conflicting meanings. (*Maʿnā* means this there, but that here, and so on.) Robyn Creswell, talking about poetry rather than theory, recently warned against thinking of Arabic as "a strange and potentially deranged exotic, whose speech shows no ability to connect one thought to another."[5] Ibn Fūrak, ar-Rāġib, Ibn Sīnā, and al-Ǧurǧānī used *maʿnā* to connect their thoughts with an unremarked-upon ease.

Wittgenstein was talking about machines because in *Philosophical Investigations* he was gradually establishing the machine as a metaphor for how language works. What interested him about machines was how they are both predictable and inert at the same time. They are like a number series, in which the subsequent unwritten numbers are both there and not there; so where are they?[6] This is the same question he asks about sentences and what happens when we read. The thrust of his argument is to deny that there is anything at all fixed to which words refer. His proof is that however hard he works to comprehend and explain a stable place in which meaning could reside, language is like the future numbers in the series and the future operations of the machine: it remains inexplicable without resorting to falsification. His examples of falsification are cover-ups such as "it has the possibility of movement" for the machine or "he understands the principle of the series" for the numbers.[7] He thinks that these are meaningless statements, whereas "This phone works" or "one, two, three, four . . ." is effective language in action. I think that the Arabic theory I have read for this book is also effective language in action, and I think we have to recognize it as such before we translate it.

Wittgenstein uses the machine as a metaphor for language, not as a model. It is not that language is like a machine, but that thinking about how machines work helps us think about how language works. It helps us because machines tend to be understood as things that work, not things that stand still. Language is the same: "The confusions which occupy us arise when language is like an engine idling, not when it is doing work."[8] Wittgenstein's famous explanation of signification as fam-

5. Creswell (2016, 452).

6. Wittgenstein (2006, ##143–52, 185–93).

7. Wittgenstein (2006, ##152, 194).

8. Wittgenstein (2006, #132).

ily resemblances is a metaphor too, not a model. Wittgenstein does not, I believe, think that a word can refer to clusters of ideas and that those ideas have family resemblances to each other. Instead, when it comes to a word like "game," which can refer to anything from ring-a-ring-a-roses to chess, he can "think of no better [metaphorical] expression to characterize these similarities than 'family resemblances,'" because the members of human families exhibit overlapping characteristics, like games.[9] It is not that there are things to which words refer that actually do have family resemblances to each other, just as it is not the case that language is actually a machine with fixed and permanent components.

Maʿnā does not have different meanings that share family resemblances, nor is it a fixed and permanent component of some linguistic machine. It is the ball in an eleventh-century language game. We need to read it as such, and then translate. Here, Wittgenstein's own practice provides some useful precedent for my experimental translation of the word *maʿnā* as "mental content." *Maʿnā* is not exactly the same thing all the time, just as Wittgenstein does not claim that a "game" is always exactly the same thing; sometimes it is ring-a-ring-a-roses, and sometimes it is chess. *Maʿnā* also does not mean lots of different incompatible things, for a game of ring-a-ring-a-roses and a game of chess are both games, both the same thing (whereas the bank of a river and the bank in which one puts one's money are not the same thing at all). Another example is "read"; whether one is reading this book or reading the expression on someone's face, one is still reading. One could, as Wittgenstein suggests, talk about the relationships between ring-a-ring-a-roses and chess, or between Ibn Fūrak's theological *maʿnā* and al-Ǧurǧānī's literary-critical *maʿnā*, as family resemblances, but this would be just a suggestive metaphor, rooted in Wittgenstein's twentieth-century mental picture of how different family members he had seen resembled and differed from each other. It is far better to follow the strategy on which Wittgenstein settled and track how eleventh-century Arabic scholars used the word *maʿnā* in their language games. My only *a priori* commitment is to the game itself; that is, I read the Arabic as if it made sense to the scholars writing it.

With this commitment in mind, it is worth returning briefly to Abū Hilāl's explanation for the use of *maʿnā* for both prelinguistic cognition and for the qualities or attributes of things. Where Wittgenstein reached for the metaphor of family resemblances, Abū Hilāl reached for the concept of *tawassuʿ*, semantic extension. The reason for this difference in strategy is that Abū Hilāl was committed to a lexically based theory of meaning, a structural account of language based on references made to *maʿānī*, which would have been anathema to Wittgenstein. Here is that irony: when the Arabic scholars used *maʿnā* to make sense of language and the world, they usually did so by positing exactly the kind of fixed cognitive

9. Wittgenstein (2006, #67).

and linguistic objects of which Wittgenstein was contemptuous. So Abū Hilāl wrote that variation in use could sometimes be explained by a stretching, broadening, or extension of a word's semantic field of reference. But Wittgenstein rejected the idea that any such account of meaning could be correct; he rejected the existence of the structure that Abū Hilāl was trying to stretch. Wittgenstein famously wrote, "You say: the point isn't the word, but its meaning, and you think of the meaning as a thing of the same kind as the word, though also different from the word. Here the word, there the meaning. The money, and the cow that you can buy with it."[10] This is exactly what the Arabic theorists did. Abū Hilāl thought that vocal forms referred to mental contents in fixed patterns that allowed for some stretching. Wittgenstein thought such accounts were nonsense.

But I use Wittgenstein because he provides me with a strategy for translation, not because he believed in the same model of language reference as eleventh-century Arabic scholars. The value of the translation strategy that Wittgenstein provides is that it does not allow us to simply replicate the accounts of reference in the work of the Arabic lexicographers, and it also refuses to allow us to substitute our own corrected accounts of reference mechanisms in place of theirs. Instead we need to ask, over and over again, What did they use *maʿnā* to do? I think asking this question has produced some valuable results, and this makes me in the end more optimistic about translation than was Wittgenstein. He thought that even with mastery of a strange country's language, we still could not really understand the people: "If a lion could talk, we could not understand him."[11] My task in this book is to make Arabic lions talk.

CORE CONCEPTUAL VOCABULARY (KUHN)

Kuhn's work on translation and on the incommensurability of conceptual vocabularies often seems to me as if it was written specifically for the problem of translating eleventh-century Arabic theories. He wrote that "incommensurability [is] always local, restricted to small sets of interrelated terms, ordinarily terms which must be learned together."[12] This is exactly the problem we face with *lafẓ, maʿnā,* and *ḥaqīqah,* a small set of interrelated terms that need to be learned together and are not commensurable with any set of terms in English. The problem is not that the Arabic scholars were doing something completely incompatible with twenty-first-century literary criticism or philosophy of language. After all, they too were socialized human beings using language to think about words, ideas, and things.

10. Wittgenstein (2006, #120).

11. Wittgenstein (2006, #190).

12. Kuhn (2009, 180).

Kuhn helps us notice that problems arise "when these terms or some other small clusters enter the text" and have an influence on our understanding of the text disproportionate to their small size and apparent simplicity. The problem is that they appear a great deal: "The most populous part of the lexicon . . . contains concepts learned in contrast sets and carrying normic expectations";[13] we meet *lafẓ, maʿnā,* and *ḥaqīqah* all the time when we read eleventh-century Arabic, and yet when we try to transpose them directly into English they seem to start to mean everything, anything, and nothing (as more than one colleague has remarked).

Kuhn knew what this incommensurability felt like. He famously related his experience as a graduate student struggling with Aristotle's physics and thinking it impossible that someone thought to be so intelligent could write such nonsense. Kuhn realized he needed to change "my way of reading, altering some of the concepts—the meanings of the words—that I, coming from a later age, had brought with me to the text."[14] As Alexander Bird puts it: "The appearance of absurdity was generated by the impossibility of properly translating Aristotelian ideas into a language inherited from Newton."[15] This is precisely the problem we face with the gap between our own vocabulary and that of eleventh-century Arabic.

The problem matches Kuhn's diagnosis: "Statements are not accessible by means of a translation that uses the current lexicon, not even if the list of words it contains is expanded by the addition of selected terms."[16] We cannot therefore simply solve the translation problem by transliterating key Arabic words and typing them into our European analyses. That would amount to nothing more than an expansion, by a few select terms, of our lexicon. It is for this reason that I propose a thought experiment rather than a translation mechanism. We should always try to think of *maʿnā* as mental content, and this thought process is what matters. The reason I have invariably translated *maʿnā* as "mental content" rather than relying on transliteration is that I want to make sure this thought experiment happens. *Maʿnā,* the romanized and italicized Arabic word, will not by itself ensure that readers think of *maʿnā* as some content that is in the mind. But the jarring neologism of "mental content" may help force the issue. The reason why I want to force the issue is that, following Wittgenstein, I think that if eleventh-century Arabic usage invariably uses *maʿnā* without qualification or explanation, then to capture that usage we need to replicate the word's unchanging omnipresence. The reason I want to use "mental content" rather than the romanized *maʿnā* is that, following Kuhn, this word is an item of core conceptual vocabulary that affects the

13. Kuhn (2000, 239).

14. Kuhn (2009, 179), (2000, 58–62).

15. Bird (2014, 157).

16. Kuhn (2000, 59).

entire thought system that uses it: we cannot simply slot it into our own English conceptual vocabulary as a foreign loanword. We need to experiment with letting this Arabic word change the way we think about language, mind, and reality. It is a burdensome process; translation has a chance of succeeding, Kuhn thinks, only when it ceases to be needed: at the end of a long process of language learning the reader becomes bilingual in the two conceptual vocabularies. (I consider elsewhere how al-Ǧurǧānī's bilingualism helped shape his translation theory.)[17] But even then the translation is limited to the language learners' conversations with themselves, for when new bilinguals speak to others they "must always remember within which community discourse is occurring. The use of one taxonomy to make statements to someone who uses the other places communication at risk."[18]

Kuhn's work helps us take Wittgenstein's insights about language in general and apply them to the specific problem of translating theories. For this is not a book about ordinary language in eleventh-century Arabic but rather a book about the scholarly theory of ar-Rāġib, Ibn Fūrak, Ibn Sīnā, and al-Ǧurǧānī. *Maʿnā* (mental content) is a piece of core conceptual vocabulary, and it is part of a small contrast pair with *lafẓ* (vocal form). *Ḥaqīqah* (accurate, getting it right) is a term that can be grasped only when *maʿnā* is understood. Compare this with Kuhn's account of "liquid," which requires mastery of "solid" and "gas" in order to be learned, or "force," which "must be learned with terms like 'mass' and 'weight.'" Indeed, "one cannot learn 'force' without recourse to Hooke's law and either Newton's three laws of motion or else his first and third laws together with the law of gravity."[19] Kuhn is here explaining that words like "liquid" and "force," which seem so obvious and ordinary to us, are in fact parts of sets of interrelated terms that need to be grasped as sets in use. Grasping them also requires knowledge of the historical theories that contributed to their meaning in our lexicon. We cannot understand "force" as it is used in Anglophone science today without Newton, and we cannot understand *maʿnā* as it was used in eleventh-century literary theory without Sībawayh and others.

Kuhn goes on to show that polysemy is not a successful workaround. It may seem as if we could capture the use of *maʿnā* across the broad range of disciplines reviewed in the previous pages by positing multiple terms: *maʿnā*$_1$ for grammar, *maʿnā*$_2$ for literary criticism, and *maʿnā*$_3$ for theology, for example. But *maʿnā* is (like the example Kuhn was using, "liquid") what Anglophone philosophers of language call "a kind term": words that classify or taxonomize the world into classes/kinds, so that one can say "that particular thing is a *maʿnā*" or "that

17. Forthcoming in the *Journal of Abbasid Studies.*

18. Kuhn (2000, 93).

19. Kuhn (2000, 230–31).

particular thing is a liquid."[20] (Cf. a recent article by Rodrigo Adem on the effects of another kind term across genres of scholarship: the word for explicit textual evidence, *naṣṣ*.)[21] Because *maʿnā* is a kind term, different uses of *maʿnā* will tend to overlap: one may have an instance of grammatical *maʿnā* that was also theological. In addition to the problem of overlap, kind terms are also often what Kuhn calls "normic"; they create expectations about the future. These are expectations for what a particular term will be used to refer to, and these expectations need to be compatible within a speech community.

Translation needs to align the expectations about what a term will be used to do. And this process of alignment is further complicated by the fact that in European languages we already have our own different core conceptual vocabulary, which we use when dealing with the same subjects. We can say that something connected to language or thought is "a meaning" or "a referent," or following Ferdinand de Saussure, "a sign," and when we use these kind terms we create sets of expectations wholly unconnected to the expectations created by Arabic kind terms functioning in their own contrast sets. This means that, as Kuhn said, we "describe the world differently and make different generalizations about it."[22] We see "epistemology" and "ontology" where they saw *maʿnā*. We live in different worlds: "If the terms to be imported are kind terms that overlap kind terms already in place, no importation is possible, at least no importation which allows both terms to retain their meaning, their projectability, their status as kind terms."[23]

Kuhn's work on the process of epistemological and scientific change is just that; it is not an account of a changing ontology but an account of changes in human beings' descriptions of what is out there in the world. It is an appropriate frame for my experiment in this book because the gap between Arabic eleventh-century conceptualizations of language and twenty-first-century Anglophone or European conceptualizations of language is, in the same way, an epistemological and not an ontological gap. The fact that language exists as a means of communication between human beings out in the world remains as true today as it was south of the Caspian Sea a millennium ago. And the human desire to understand how language works remains just as strong.

Kuhn also reminds us of what is at stake in the process of description, particularly when it comes to those central, small, interrelated sets of kind terms that create expectations. The centrality of kind terms comes from the fact that they are used to carve reality at the joints; when we use them, we are making the claim that our

20. Kuhn (2000, 232).

21. Adem (2017).

22. Kuhn (2000, 233).

23. Ibid.

language divides up the world accurately. This metaphor of carving nature is an old one, dating back at least to Plato's *Phaedrus,* where Socrates explained a pair of methodological principles: first the bringing together of scattered particulars; and second a cutting through of shapes and forms at the joints.[24] Kuhn sees this epistemological claim as itself helping to create the world being described.[25] *Maʿnā,* this piece of conceptual vocabulary for which we do not have an equivalent in European languages, is therefore in itself an act of carving. It was part of the lexicon, the core conceptual vocabulary, of the Arabic scholars who used it and "what this part of their lexicons supplies to community members is a set of learned expectations about the similarities and differences between the objects and situations that populate their world."[26] *Maʿnā* was a kind term that enabled the scholars who used it to say that something was a *maʿnā* of something else and thereby carve reality at the joints. We do not carve at the same joints; we stand over the same carcass with the knife but disagree about where to make the cut.

Kuhn also provides us with some helpful clarity about the degrees of disagreement within conceptual vocabularies and scientific communities. As the preceding chapter on precedents has shown, it is not the case that every Arabic scholar who used the word *maʿnā* did so to point at exactly the same object all the time. Wittgenstein has given us an explanation of how their language games could still function despite this, just as we are able in English to use the words "game" and "read" in a variety of different ways. Kuhn then gives us what could easily be a map of premodern Arabic use of the word *maʿnā:* kind terms create expectations, but in a single community a kind term does not need to always create exactly the same expectations. The work *maʿnā* does may differ from theology to literary criticism: scholars from different disciplines "may know different things about [*maʿānī*] . . . , but they will both pick out the same things, and they can learn more about those things from each other."[27] All Arabic scholars were using *maʿnā* within the same structure: "The lexicons of the various members of a speech community may vary in the expectations they induce, but they must all have the same *structure.* If they do not, then mutual incomprehension and an ultimate breakdown of communication will result."[28] The test of whether the language game worked is whether scholars from two disciplines ever had "incompatible expectations," with the result that one of them chose to "apply the term to a reference to which the other categorically denies that it applie[d]."[29]

24. Pl. *Phdr.* 265e: *to palin kat' eidē dunasthai diatemnein kat' arthra hēi pephuken.*

25. Kuhn (2000, 205–7).

26. Kuhn (2000, 239).

27. Kuhn (2000, 231). The interpolation is mine.

28. Kuhn (2000, 239).

29. Kuhn (2000, 231).

I have never seen this happen with *maʿnā* in an Arabic text from any disciplines of premodern scholarship, and it is my contention that if it had happened, then these lexically minded scholars would have noticed and discussed the problem. Communication did not break down over *maʿnā;* on the contrary the use of *maʿnā* redoubled and multiplied along with the continued explosion of text across the subsequent millennium. The language game continued to be played. *Maʿnā* was a core part of a shared lexical structure for eleventh-century Arabic scholars; it had a history of shared precedent stretching back to Sībawayh, and it had a future in the madrasa. The fact of language usage, the existence of the scholarly language game, kept its meaning stable and productive. Everyone knew what *maʿnā* was; everyone used it to carve their reality. We are the only people who don't know; outside the language game and outside the speech community, we need translation.

Maʿnā was often used in theoretical statements about what language is and how language works. It is what we may call a scientific, or even an abstract term. This makes it arguably harder to translate than simple descriptive language used for physical objects. Kuhn compared the process of translating such scientific terms to the process of translating literature, but this was a reach by a historian of science that casually and incorrectly allowed literature to represent difficulty, turbidity, and ambiguity. (Creswell, as noted above, recently defended Arabic literature on this very question.)[30] Willard Van Orman Quine's ideas about translation are more useful than Kuhn's here. Like Wittgenstein, Quine did not believe in a sphere of fixed meanings. He thought that the only way meanings could actually be shared between different people would be if those different people shared a single set of nerve endings.[31] Human beings do not share nerve endings, and so the only way they can know what other humans mean is by looking at what they do. This makes the truth of translation, and truth itself in any language, a matter of the "observable *reactions* of speakers to language and the world . . . patterns of [observed] assent and dissent."[32] This is easier with simple sentences about physical objects, and harder with abstract theoretical claims: "Observation sentences peel nicely; their meanings, stimulus meanings, emerge absolute and free of all residual verbal taint. Theoretical sentences such as 'Neutrinos lack mass,' or the law of entropy, or the constancy of the speed of light, are at the other extreme."[33]

How then can we translate Arabic theory? We lack what Kuhn calls a third neutral language of observation to stand between eleventh-century Arabic and

30. Creswell (2016), Kuhn (2000, 62, 164).

31. Quine (2004, 96).

32. Donald Davidson (2006, 74).

33. Quine (2004, 111).

twenty-first-century European languages.[34] His primary answer to this problem is that while translation recoils in the face of incommensurability, learning a second language is possible.[35] People who have learned the second language may then, although they struggle with it, work to provide a translation manual that includes "discursive paragraphs explaining how native speakers view the world, what sorts of ontological categories they deploy."[36] This book hopes to be just such a manual. But even with all the space the format provides me to work through the different usages of words such as *maʿnā*, problems remain. Quine imagines a linguist trying to work out and translate an unknown "jungle" language (my note above about unselfconscious racism in the eleventh-century applies equally well here) and finding that "he is not, in his finitude, free to assign English sentences to the infinitude of jungle ones in just any way whatever that will fit his supporting evidence; he has to assign them in some way that is manageably systematic. . . . He will put a premium on structural parallels: on correspondence between the parts of the native sentence, as he segments it, and the parts of the English translation."[37] Quine here is talking about the inevitability of one's own syntax affecting the way one deals with a new language, but the constraints he identifies are just as important for foreign theoretical concepts, and doubly so for theoretical language about language itself. Lydia Liu has identified the same problem: a "European Inquirer, who is undoubtably aware of the pitfalls of translations, nonetheless insists on having a Japanese equivalent of the European concept of language."[38] An Anglophone reader of this book who does not know Arabic is, in effect, in the position of Quine's linguist, if not necessarily Liu's European Inquirer. Your own segmentation of "meaning" and its usages is going to affect the way you engage with *maʿnā* when you see it in action.

MAʿNĀ$_1$, *MAʿNĀ*$_2$, *MAʿNĀ*$_3$, *MAʿNĀ*$_4$

This section deals with secondary scholarship; a non-Arabist may wish to skip ahead to Saussure. I am not proposing a sweeping correction of previous scholarship with my reading of *maʿnā* as mental content. Rather what I would like to do with this experiment is refocus our attention on the exact point at which problems of interpretation occur: the meeting point of language, mind, and reality, the confluence of epistemology and ontology. *Maʿnā* often appears when eleventh-century Arabic conceptual vocabulary is being used to talk about ideas,

34. Kuhn (2000, 162).

35. Kuhn (2000, 93, 163).

36. Kuhn (2000, 166).

37. Quine (2004, 109–10).

38. Liu (1995, 5).

qualities, or meanings located at this confluence. I am not the first person to notice this. Josef van Ess, writing about the statement of Ibn Kullāb that speech was "a *maʿnā* subsisting in the soul," notes that it is sometimes not easy to decide whether *maʿnā* is to be understood as an entity or a meaning. (Like Aristotle, Arabic used "soul" where we often use "mind" today in English.)[39] He also raises the question of whether *maʿnā* could have been used as a *passe-partout* when an author did not necessarily want to be precise.[40] Heinrichs, writing about early theological use of the related terms *ḥaqīqah* and *maǧāz*, says that "it is not always clear whether the pair . . . are used ontologically or linguistically. . . . Both strategies make sense and both are used."[41] Heinrichs is right that both strategies make sense. My take is that this is because they are, from the perspective of the original authors, one and the same strategy. In answer to van Ess's observation, authors did not necessarily need to be precise; their audiences knew what a *maʿnā* was and knew where their conceptual vocabulary located it. It is only we European and Anglophone audiences a millennium later who struggle to name that place as either language, or mind, or reality, as either epistemology or ontology.

There were no problems with use of the word *maʿnā* in the ninth through the eleventh century and beyond. The scholars whose Arabic books we read were untroubled by any threat of semantic breadth; they simply used the word to make their arguments. It is when we come to translate those arguments into English that problems arise. The translation strategy I propose locates the ambiguity in our European and Anglophone conceptual vocabulary and experiments with a reading of the Arabic that assumes it was unambiguous. In doing this I follow the late Richard Frank (d. 2009) of the Catholic University of America. In his Presidential Address to the 206th meeting of the American Oriental Society in 1996, he related experiences with Islamic theology very similar to those reported by Kuhn. Faced with difficulties interpreting theological discussions similar to those we have encountered in the previous chapter, he asked a colleague for help and was told, "This stuff wasn't really meant to make sense." But Frank refused to admit defeat in this way; he recognized that the sense the texts made was not immediately obvious "to the learned observer who views it from a distance and at an angle."[42]

Two Distinct Lexemes

For those readers who are familiar with the European-language scholarship on Classical Arabic, the question of *maʿnā* is indelibly connected to the name Frank.

39. Ivry (2012), Shields (2016).

40. هو معنىً قائم بالنفس. Al-Ašʿarī (1929–33, 425.10), van Ess (1991–95, 3:76, 4:186).

41. Heinrichs (2016, 256).

42. Frank (1996, 2).

A scholar of Islamic theology, he noticed that the word *maʿnā* appeared to play a number of different roles across Arabic scholarly disciplines, roles that were in some cases of critical importance to the disciplines' foundational debates. He is also the scholar who came closest to the approach I take to the word *ḥaqīqah;* he recognized that it was a word used for accurate cognitive judgments and the connected acts of linguistic description ("true meanings") in both theology and Aristotelian philosophy.[43] He wrote that the work of Islamic theologians from the ninth century through the twelfth was for the most part an internally consistent body of theory in which "the modern reader can find no key or clue to their vocabulary and conception outside the texts themselves and those other Muslim writings that belong to and form an integral part of their original context."[44]

However, Frank thought that *maʿnā* could occur "as two distinct lexemes" in a single sentence. It is at this point that I would like to propose an alternative translation strategy and depart from the scholarly consensus that we should contend with the word *maʿnā* by delineating and then naming its variant usages: assigning multiple meanings to a single word in order to make that word function in an Anglophone or European conceptual vocabulary. I do not believe that the multiple-meanings strategy necessarily results in incorrect interpretations; on the contrary I have benefited from its products (as the references in this book show). But what I think that strategy misses is the sense *maʿnā* made to those who used it in the eleventh century. Translation strategies that divide *maʿnā* into a series of previously unmarked alternatives give epistemological primacy to the target language. *Maʿnā* becomes multiple different words in English, whereas it was a single unmarked word in Arabic. What my experiment seeks to do is recapture the agency of the original sources and restore an epistemological supremacy that their authors assumed would remain unchallenged. No one in the Arabic eleventh century imagined that their assumptions would one day come into conflict, or conversation, with Saussure.

The understanding of how language works that I have developed with the help of Wittgenstein and Kuhn has confirmed my initial intuition about the use of *maʿnā:* that if an author used it twice in the same sentence without further qualification, then its meaning cannot have changed midsentence; it is unlikely to be, as Frank says, two distinct lexemes. This is not to say that distinct unmarked lexemes can never occur in any language. In English, for example, we can say that a bear can, in Alaska, bear very cold temperatures, and that upon seeing such a bear in

43. "The true and strict sense of a term and that which we really and truly mean and signify when we use the term in its strict sense and the being which is referred to when the term is so used": Frank (1982, 275), (1999, 184, 230).

44. Frank (1978, 5).

the headlights, a driver decided to bear left, which meant their car left the road. It is rather to say I believe that this is not how *maʿnā* worked in eleventh-century Arabic. I find the combination of Wittgenstein and Kuhn to be persuasive whatever the language: the theoretical explanation of this English sentence about the bear can rest on its syntax and context rather than on a structure of reference in which "bear" is set up as a word with more than one fixed meaning. Furthermore, the words "bear" and "left" are not functioning as core conceptual vocabulary in that English sentence: if they were, then we would not be able to sustain their roles as multiple unmarked lexemes.

What I would like to do is bring the uses of *maʿnā* back together, so that when it comes to translation we do not have to go as far as Frank did in his reading of a sentence as containing unmarked "distinct lexemes." Frank translated the sentence in question as: "the meaning of 'X is an accident' is that X is a something that exists in an atom" (accident is the Aristotelian word for a nonessential quality or attribute). The sentence in Arabic had used *maʿnā* twice: "The *maʿnā* of 'X is an accident' is that X is a *maʿnā* that exists in an atom."[45] Inserting "mental content" for *maʿnā* does not produce idiomatic English, but I think it is a productive thought experiment and a functional if clumsy translation: "The mental content of 'X is an accident' is that X is a mental content that exists in an atom." My translation forces us to ask what these mental contents were for the theologians: How could they be both meanings and atomic qualities?

Four General Headings

My disagreement with Frank is therefore over translation strategy and to a lesser extent over the specific use made of certain core items of conceptual vocabulary. There is no methodological disagreement involved, for as Frank said that 1996 Presidential Address (in which he cited Wittgenstein): "The aim is . . . to participate in a way of seeing things—to see how . . . things really do—or at least can, or might—appear that way and be thought about, talked about that way."[46] What I am proposing is an experimental reading and translation strategy that may help achieve the goals Frank laid out in the late 1990s. In an earlier and influential article, recognizing that theology was using a conceptual vocabulary taken from grammar, Frank noted that "the Ašʿarites . . . are fundamentally bound to the linguistic theory of the grammarians"[47] and identified "four general headings" under which the variant meanings of *maʿnā* could be grouped. They are: (1) the intent of

45. ومعنى قولِنا إنه عارضٌ أنه معنىً قائمٌ بالجوهر. In my quotation I have used "X" in place of Frank's original "it." Frank (1999, 182–83 n. 46).

46. Frank (1996, 9).

47. Frank (1982, 259), (1999, 230).

the speaker; (2) the referent of a noun or verb, which could be a real or an imagined thing; (3) what Frank calls a "semiotic equivalent" recoverable by paraphrase, which in the field of grammar may be the function of a conjunction; and (4) a "conceptual significate" grasped by a plurality of individuals, which could be an abstract proposition or concept.[48]

Let us take, as an example of these categories in action, az-Zağǧāǧī discussing the *maṣdar* (quasi-verbal event noun) according to the ninth-century Basran school of grammatical thought. The Basrans described the relationship of *maṣdar* to verb as analogous to the relationship of silver to silver jewelry: "Don't you see that silver is the root of everything that is made from it? For it is the existence of the *maʿnā* in the thing. If a tankard, jug, ring, bangle, anklet, or anything else is made from silver, then the *maʿnā* of silver exists in everything made from silver, but the *maʿānī* of the things made does not exist in silver on its own. It is the same with the *maʿnā* of the verbal noun, which is present in all the verbs derived from it, while the *maʿnā* of each single verb is not present in the *maṣdar*."[49] Frank translates *maʿnā* in this passage as "meaning," which is difficult to reconcile with the argument.[50] Can silver, in English, really have a meaning that is found in a silver ring? And could that meaning be the same meaning that maps across from the quasi-verbal event (the *maṣdar*) to the verb? The word "meaning" in our English conceptual vocabulary seems to be causing problems here. It is my contention that "mental content" causes fewer problems. Frank saw grammarians using *maʿnā* in what looked to him like different ways. But all these usages were unmarked in the original. The texts just used the single unremarked-upon word *maʿnā*. The dissonance appears only in the translation process.

Intrinsic Causal Determinants

In theology, Frank chose the translation "intrinsic causal determinant" for *maʿnā* in the work of Muʿammar and then later developed a translation of *maʿnā* as "entitative attribute" across Ašʿarī *kalām*. He was followed in the latter choice by Alnoor Dhanani and others.[51] My criticism of this translation strategy is simply that it moves *maʿnā* away from its usage in the Arabic texts and toward a different position in an Anglophone conceptual vocabulary. In this new position, there is a

48. Frank (1981, 314–18).

49. ألا ترى أنّ الفِضّة أصلٌ لجميعِ ما يُصاغ منها فهي موجودةُ المعنى فيه فإنْ صُنِعتْ كُوزاً أو إبريقاً أو خاتماً أو قُلْباً أو خخالاً وغيرَ ذلك فمعناها موجودةٌ في جميعِ ما يُصاغ منها وليس معاني ما يُصاغ منها موجودةً فيها مفردةً فكذلك معنى المصدر موجودٌ في جميع الأفعالَ المشتقّة منه وليس معنى فِعْلٍ واحدٍ منها موجودٌ في المصدر نفسه. Az-Zağǧāǧī (1959, 59.16–60.1).

50. Frank (1981, 283).

51. Dhanani (1994); Frank (1967, 253), (1999).

clear distinction assumed between epistemology and ontology, one that was not present in the original Arabic. Indeed, *maʿnā* was used most often in Arabic at exactly those points where the fundamental structures of what we now call epistemology and ontology were under discussion. This means that back-projecting our distinctions into their discussions risks anachronism.

Let us look first at what happens with "intrinsic causal determinant." We are back with Muʿammar's theory and al-Ḫayyāṭ's commentary from the previous chapter. Al-Ḫayyāṭ explained Muʿammar's position like this: "What led Muʿammar into the position attributed to him was his commitment to motion, at a point at which all the indications that something (whether motion or another similar accident) has happened are simply the motion itself. For Muʿammar wanted to enclose all the indications that something has happened within the thing itself. He did this because of his concern for the unity of God and his determination to see that unity prevail."[52] Al-Ḫayyāṭ was saying that Muʿammar developed his theory to maintain divine unity. But the theory in question was, as we have seen, an account of an infinite chain of causality, and any theory of infinite causal chains would seem to work against divine unity. If God's actions are caused by causes, which are caused by causes, which are caused by causes, and so on *ad infinitum,* then there would be multiple causal divinities. And it is here, at this critical point, that Frank's translation of *maʿnā* as intrinsic causal determinant may cause some problems: it paints Muʿammar as multiplying causes to infinity *because of* a commitment to divine unity. However, if we understand *maʿnā* in Muʿammar's theory as the same *maʿnā* we find in literary theory, grammar, or philosophy, then our interpretation changes and becomes consistent with al-Ḫayyāṭ's reading. Muʿammar developed a theory of *maʿānī* because this item of core conceptual vocabulary enabled him to explain accidents of motion and color while at the same time maintaining the unity of the thing in which he was explaining motion or color. Then, when the big test of applying a theory of accidents to God came along, there was no problem of multiplicity or polytheism. God had *maʿānī,* and at the same time God had divine unity. My argument is not that Frank got it wrong; *maʿānī* do indeed work for Muʿammar as causal determinants that are intrinsic. But I think that to fulfill Frank's promise that Islamic theology did and does make sense, we need to focus on the use theologians like Muʿammar made of *maʿnā* to explain the interaction of qualities with unity. This was a central topic of theology, and Muʿammar's claim was that qualities were caused by qualities. But why not say that using the Arabic word for qualities, *ṣifāt?* I think Muʿammar used *maʿnā,* a common word for the contents in our minds that can be expressed in speech, because he thought

52. والذي أَدخله في القول فيما حُكيتْ عنه تثبيتُهُ الحركةَ إذ كان مدارَ دلائلِ الحدث عليها وعلى أمثالها من الأعراض فأراد حِياطةَ دلائل الحدث عند نفسه لعنايته بالتوحيد ونُصرته له. Al-Ḫayyāṭ (1957, 46.24–47.2).

the multiplication of mental content was unproblematic, regardless of whether the target was a moving object or God.

Entities and Entitative Attributes

Frank later moved toward the translation "entitative attribute," in part after reading the work of Gimaret and others who translated *maʿnā* as *entité*.[53] Gimaret had said that "à tout qualificatif *(ḥukm, waṣf)* corresponde une entité (*maʿnā)* qui en est la cause, la raison d'*être* (*ʿilla*)" and that the *maʿānī* explain the differences between bodies by their presence as incorporeal existents that are the causes of differences and changes.[54] This is I think quite right, and the additional step my translation experiment helps us take is to ask, "To whom do the *maʿānī* explain?" My answer is that, of course, the *maʿānī* explain the world to us. It is our human qualifications and judgments that lead to our mental contents, which are therefore our explanations to ourselves of why things look or behave the way they do. Analytical philosophers today might call the *maʿānī* our language of thought (LOT). It is worth noting here that, just as we saw literary-critical disagreements about whether eloquence should be located in vocal form or mental content, so we find theological disagreements about whether speech is vocal form (the Muʿtazilī position) or *maʿnā* (the Ašʿarī position).

It was God's speech that was at stake in the theological polemics with which Gimaret was dealing. If God's speech is vocal form, then it is a created accident, whereas if it is mental content then it is eternal and divine. (The debate is reviewed by Peters.)[55] As a consequence, Gimaret struggles with an appropriate translation for *maʿnā*, deciding to distinguish a technical meaning of *maʿnā* as "entity" from its ordinary and more linguistic sense, "signification." I think that what causes Gimaret to do this is the French conceptual vocabulary in which he is writing, in which *signification* is a concept very different from *entité*.[56] But Arabic recognized no such difference; there was just *maʿnā*.

Frank makes the same distinction, in his case between *maʿnā* with the sense of reference and *maʿnā* with the sense of entitative attribute. But, much like Abū Hilāl, he explains the latter via the former: "The basic sense or connotation of '*maʿnā*' here—most conspicuously in the phrase '*maʿnan zāʾidun ʿalā al-ḏāt*'—is that of referent or, if you will, of a 'something' understood as the referent of one

53. Frank (1999, 213 n. 111).

54. "To every qualification corresponds an entity that is the cause, the purpose": Gimaret (1990, 26, 79).

55. Peters (1976, 308–12).

56. Gimaret (1990, 201–2).

of the terms, whether explicit or implicit, of the proposition in question."[57] I think that Frank is correct here, but I also think that the Anglophone conceptual vocabulary in which he is thinking produces, against the run of play in the language game from which it is being extracted, some confusion. There is also a degree of ambiguity with the word "entitative," a word by no means in everyday use in English. John Duns Scotus (d. 1308) used the phrase "entitative" to distinguish material existence (or haecceity) from abstract, logical existence in the mind.[58] This seems to be at direct odds with the Arabic *maʿnā;* the examples we have seen are paradigmatically logical and abstract categories such as accidents and qualities. "Entitative" has also, ironically, been used in modern psychology for the exact opposite purpose: "entitative" in Donald Campbell's work on social groups refers to the moment when we perceive a group of individuals as a group, when we give them an extra, cognitive, mental existence as group members.[59] This seems closer to the Arabic *maʿnā*, but the connection to speech that Abū Hilāl was so keen to preserve has been entirely lost. If we take "entitative" to mean simply "having existence," so that Frank's "entitative attribute" means "an attribute that exists," then the problem may be that "exists" pushes the user of English in the direction of extramental physical existence. This is especially risky if this "existence" is being opposed, as it is by both Frank and Gimaret, to a process of signification or reference connected to language. Frank was well aware of the uncertainty that he and Gimaret shared.[60] None of these problems existed in Arabic. All appear in translation.

I would like to end this section with an example taken from Dhanani's study of atomism. In it, Ibn Mattawayh (fl. early eleventh century) seems to speak to exactly this cluster of problems. Dhanani considers how we know accidents, and he quotes Ibn Mattawayh: "Accidents of location which we know immediately are known in a general and undifferentiated manner."[61] Now the Arabic that Dhanani provides includes the word *maʿnā*. My translation might read: "and we necessarily know this mental content as a collection. [I.e., "in a general manner."]" My translation serves to highlight the role *maʿnā* is playing and to make us ask, What is this mental content of which Ibn Mattawayh writes? The quotation comes from the beginning of a chapter on "existence." Ibn Mattawayh explained that "existence" can have different names depending on what it is doing, so that existence can be called "motion," or "rest," or "being-next-to," or at the start of some processes

57. معنىً زائدٌ على الذات. Frank (1999, 214).

58. Williams (2003, 119–20).

59. Campbell (1958, 16–17).

60. Frank (2000, 28–29 n. 62).

61. نَعْلَمُ هذا المعنى ضرورةً على الجملة. Dhanani (1994, 52).

simply "existence."[62] Ibn Mattawayh was therefore saying here that the mental content behind "existence" is this range of options, and we know all of them as a collective automatically, because we know what is happening when, for example, we stand up or sit down.[63] Schmidtke's edition of an anonymous twelfth-century commentary on the same work confirms this reading. The commentator said that Ibn Mattawayh used this chapter to "clarify the mental content of 'existence.'"[64] If we have thus confirmed that Ibn Mattawayh was talking about *maʿnā*, and that his usage had *maʿnā* as the stuff of cognition, the category in which any conception of an idea such as "existence" must be included, then let us return to Dhanani's translation. He uses the English phrase "are known" to stand in for the Arabic *maʿnā*. I seek not to criticize Dhanani's excellent work on atomism but rather to note the importance of a conceptual category central to the Arabic understanding and analysis of cognition: *maʿnā*. I do not think we should let it slip by. For it implies that epistemology blurs into ontology, that the content of things is the content of our understandings of them, and that our understandings have an ontological status equivalent to the ontological status of "motion" in a body. So equivalent a status, in fact, that the same word, *maʿnā*, is used without differentiation for both. This is the issue I will seek to address with Ibn Fūrak in chapter 5.

Divergent Concepts

Let us take a break from theology. Kanazi wrote, in his 1989 study of Abū Hilāl, that *maʿnā* was used by this lexicographer and literary critic "with reference to divergent concepts." Kanazi goes on to express concern: "Since it is essential to Abū Hilāl's theory, it should have been defined and systematically employed in an equivalent sense; yet . . . it remains undefined, being used to indicate a variety of heterogeneous notions."[65] This does not seem to match the care and rigor with which we saw Abū Hilāl explain his understanding of the difference between *maʿnā* and *ḥaqīqah*. Kanazi read and referenced that same passage but thought that it did not align with Abū Hilāl's literary criticism, where *maʿnā* was used for:

62. القولُ في الأكوان الكونُ هو ما يجيب كونَ الجوهر كائناً في جهةٍ والأسامي تختلف عليها وإنْ كان الكلُّ من هذا النوع فمتى حَصَلَ عَقيبَ ضِدِّه فهو حركةٌ وإذا بقي به الجوهرُ كائناً في جهةٍ أَزْيَدَ من وقتٍ واحدٍ أو وُجِد عَقيبَ مِثله فهو سكونٌ ومتى كان مُبتدأً لم يتقدّمه غيرُه فهو كونٌ فقط وهو الموجودُ في الجوهر حالَ حدوثِهِ فإنْ حَصَلَ بِقُرب هذا الجوهر جوهرٌ آخرُ سُمّي ما فيهما مجاورةً ومتى كان على بُعدٍ منه سُمّي ما فيهما مفارقةً ومباعدةً. Ibn Mattawayh (1975, 432), (2009, 1:237).

63. وقد نَعْلم هذا المعنى ضرورةً على الجملة وإنْ كان ممّا لا يُدْرَكُ وهو ما نَتصرّف فيه من قِيامٍ وقُعودٍ وغيرهما. Ibn Mattawayh (1975, 432), (2009, 1:237).

64. وجملةُ الكلام فيما أَوْرَدَهُ رحِمَه اللهُ في هذا الفصل أنْ يتبيّن معنى الكون. Ibn Mattawayh (2006, 136, fol. 68b l. 26).

65. Kanazi (1989, 83).

"a) an idea, thought or concept which is unformulated in the mind, or formulated when one expresses it in words; b) a theme; c) the meaning of a word, phrase or other constructions; and d) the quality or character of a certain object." (Joseph Sadan also has a very useful list.)[66] Kanazi then remarks in a footnote that "since, in some cases, one hesitates which of these numerous translations to adopt, I shall give the term in parenthesis, except in those rare cases where its interpretation is not open to question."[67] The quality of Kanazi's scholarship is not in question; like Frank, Kanazi identified his confusion and discussed it. But I do not think Abū Hilāl's use of *maʿnā* was confusing to Abū Hilāl, and I think that it is our job as philologists to try to recapture that clarity. We need to recognize that because literary criticism in Classical Arabic had a different conceptual vocabulary, it consequently had a different conceptual framework.

A Grid of Principles and Contexts

Recent scholarship on *maʿnā* has focused on the most famous of Arabic literary critics, and the subject of my chapter 7 in this book, al-Ǧurǧānī. In 2014, Nejmeddine Khalfallah published a study of al-Ǧurǧānī's semantic theory that focused on mental content: "le fruit de l'opération cognitive."[68] This was an important recognition that al-Ǧurǧānī's account of cognition and metaphor had a stable conceptual vocabulary and a logical order, "une grille de principes et de notions qui expliquent les conditions dans lesquelles émerge et fonctionne le sens."[69] My concern with this grid is that by placing *maʿnā* in different sections according to what Khalfallah sees as its different functions, we risk losing sight of the very aesthetic unity that I think al-Ǧurǧānī's theory was designed to capture. Al-Ǧurǧānī knew that if theory could achieve terminological eloquence it would stand the test of time, and concision was an important part of this eloquence. Ibn Sīnā had agreed: "If in the immediately apparent understanding of a vocal form there is something that will allow for concision, then choosing another route is a kind of weakness."[70] Al-Ǧurǧānī thought that the famed opening lines of Sībawayh's *Kitāb* achieved the terminological eloquence he was looking for: some parts of the fundamental books of scholarship have an inimitable elegance of vocal form and syntax, and indeed this is precisely what makes them fundamental. Sībawayh's universally

66. Sadan (1991, 61f).

67. Kanazi (1989, 84).

68. "The fruit of the cognitive operation": Khalfallah (2014, 351).

69. "A grid of principles and concepts that explain the conditions under which sense emerges and functions": Khalfallah (2014, 16).

70. وإذا وُجِد في ظاهرِ المفهوم مِن لفظٍ ما هو يقع به استغناءٌ واقتصارٌ كان المَصيرُ عنه إلى غيره ضرباً من العجز. Ibn Sīnā (1952c, 41.6–7).

memorized definition of the verb was an example of this.[71] Could al-Ǧurǧānī really have contemplated a theory in which there were four different unmarked kinds of *maʿnā* ("sens propres des mots," "sens grammaticaux," "sens psychologique," and "thème 'littéraire'")?[72] Is Khalfallah correct to read al-Ǧurǧānī with the conceptual vocabulary of French linguistic thought? Is he right to separate his accurate and philologically sensitive readings of *maʿnā* into four separate categories?

Lafẓ$_{1-3}$ *and maʿnā*$_{1-3}$

In 2016 Lara Harb published a fundamental study of al-Ǧurǧānī's work on "form, content, and the inimitability of the Qurʾān." I have benefited a great deal from this article, and from Harb's 2013 dissertation on wonder,[73] but I would like to propose a different translation strategy for *lafẓ* and *maʿnā*. Harb splits the former into *lafẓ*$_1$, *lafẓ*$_2$, and *lafẓ*$_3$, and the latter into *maʿnā*$_1$, *maʿnā*$_2$, and *maʿnā*$_3$. Let us first take *lafẓ*, which I argued above can be translated as "vocal form." Harb cites Abu Deeb and Heinrichs to make a division into "sound," "word combination," and "word choice,"[74] and it is indeed unarguable that al-Ǧurǧānī uses *lafẓ* to talk about things that we might call sound, word combination, or word choice in English or German. But what we are all working on here is al-Ǧurǧānī's theory, the language game he played, and in that language game there was only *lafẓ*. If we translate *lafẓ* with different versions of itself, then just as Kuhn has shown we risk obscuring the dynamics of al-Ǧurǧānī's own use of the word. Most important, we skew what Kuhn called the normic expectations generated by a kind term. In other words, when we split *lafẓ* into *lafẓ*$_1$, *lafẓ*$_2$, and *lafẓ*$_3$, we thereby create an entirely new set of expectations linked to each of these variants and the force of al-Ǧurǧānī's statement that something "is a *lafẓ*" is lost. The same thing happens with the tripartite division of *maʿnā*. Harb reads *maʿnā* as *maʿnā*$_1$ (the signified, paired with *lafẓ*$_1$ as the signifier), *maʿnā*$_2$ (the content, paired with *lafẓ*$_3$ as the combination of words or form), and *maʿnā*$_3$ (the image of meaning, *ṣūrat al-maʿnā,* which is composed of *lafẓ*$_3$ and *maʿnā*$_2$).[75] My concern here is twofold: first of all, that the terminological efficiency we know al-Ǧurǧānī was striving for is lost. Second, that the

71. والكتب المبتَدَءةُ الموجودةُ في العلوم المستخرجة فإنّا نَجِد أربابَها قد سَبقوا في فصولٍ منها إلى ضَرْبٍ من اللفظ والنظم أعْيا مَن بعدَهم أنْ يطلبوا مثلَه أو يجيء بشبيهٍ له فجعلوا لا يزيدون على أنْ يَحفظوا تلك الفصولَ على وجوهها . . . وذلك ما كان مِثلُ قولِ سيبويه في أوّل الكتاب وأمّا الفِعلُ فأمثلةٌ أُخِذتْ من لفظِ أحداثِ الأسماء. Al-Ǧurǧānī (1992a, 604.12–605.2), Sībawayh (1966, 1:12.4–5).

72. "The word's own meaning," the "grammatical sense," the "psychological sense," and the "literary motif": Khalfallah (2014, 27).

73. Harb (2013), (2015).

74. Abu Deeb (1979, 50), Harb (2015, 304), Heinrichs (1969, 70).

75. Harb (2015, 305–6).

influential changes that al-Ǧurǧānī made to the old pairing of *lafẓ* and *maʿnā*, and the new theoretical terms he proposed, lose their prominence. Harb's $ma\text{ʿ}n\bar{a}_3$ is not a variant or dissonant usage of *maʿnā* but, as she makes clear, a wholly different concept: *ṣūrat al-maʿnā*, which (as Harb brilliantly explains in her article and dissertation) is a new sphere of analysis created by al-Ǧurǧānī to allow him to explain his theories of aesthetic syntax. The argument I want to make here is not that Harb misunderstands al-Ǧurǧānī, for I have benefited from her work just as I have benefited from the work of Frank. What I want to do is propose a revision of their translation strategies, so as to dispense with a practice of dividing up words that I think causes more problems than it solves.

The process we see under way in the scholarship of Harb, Frank, and Khalfallah is that identified by Quine in the discussions above: the translator will inevitably "put a premium on structural parallels" and will segment the Arabic source in a manner that corresponds to the segmentation of the English, French, or German target vocabulary. (See also Mohamed Ait El Ferrane.)[76] The problem is that this takes the theoretical work of an eleventh-century scholar and explains it by a correspondence to the contemporary that can only be anachronistic; al-Ǧurǧānī did not speak twenty-first-century European languages. In translation, one theory becomes another. This is an acceptable procedure for the translation of literature, where one is dealing "with larger units than the word: the shape and syntax of sentences, the tone of voice, the weight of a phrase" (Creswell again).[77] But it is not so appropriate for theory, where the expectations created by the core conceptual vocabulary are so critical. This is even truer when the theory in question is itself a theory about language and cognition, when we are dealing with language about language.

Meaning

In English, the word "meaning" does a great deal of work. As we have already seen, it is often used to translate *maʿnā*. But "meaning" does not do the same work in English that *maʿnā* did in Classical Arabic. In his survey of Abbasid literary criticism, Abu Deeb recognized this fundamental difference. Arab critics had "a concept of meaning as an independent, complete, solid entity which it is possible to isolate, describe and express in differing ways of precision, concision and eloquence." This is exactly right, and the name for that "independent, complete, solid entity" was *maʿnā*. Abu Deeb goes on to say that "meaning" as he knew it in European and Anglophone scholarship, "meaning as a vague, undefinable,

76. El Ferrane (1990, 106f), Quine (2004, 109–10).

77. Creswell (2016, 449).

evolving presence in the text, inseparable from the language used to embody it, was hardly ever conceived of by Arab critics."[78]

THE DISTRACTION OF THE SIGN (SAUSSURE)

It is not just "meaning." In the sections above we have encountered other critical aspects of our twenty-first-century conceptual vocabulary that shape the domestication of Classical Arabic theory in English and other European languages. Some of the most prominent come from Saussure. The Swiss historical linguist is a primary point of reference for Anglophone and European discussions about what language is and how language works. Toril Moi has recently made a number of fundamental observations about Saussure's place in our intellectual world, the first of which is that his account of linguistics (published posthumously in 1916) was transformed across the second half of the twentieth century not just into a general philosophy of language but into one that had an outsize impact on literary criticism: "In the humanities today, the *doxa* concerning language and meaning remains Saussurean or, rather, post-Saussurean."[79] The subtle epistemological dominance of Saussure's model of language in European thought explains why he is a point of reference for Arabists, or at least a point of reference when we try to translate.

I have often tried to describe eleventh-century Arabic ideas about language to non-Arabist colleagues interested in language by asking them to imagine a world where everyone already knows and often uses the technical terms "signifier" and "signified." In English, these two words represent Saussure's *signifiant* and *signifié*, and refer to the theory of meaning and reference he developed in Switzerland, France, and Germany in the twentieth century. But knowledge of this intellectual history tends to be restricted to academics and linguists, and the words "signifier" and "signified" are not found in ordinary language, nor used widely or uniformly across twentieth- and twenty-first-century scientific and literary disciplines. The words that are found in ordinary language tend to be "word" and "idea," and the range of terminology available to describe processes of reference and meaning across literature, science, and philosophy is almost infinitely wide, from Jacques Derrida's trace to the notion of a theoretical term in the philosophy of science.[80] However, in this specific cluster of eleventh-century Arabic conceptual vocabulary, the ordinary language was the same as the technical terminology, and that technical terminology was shared across literary criticism, linguistics, politics, theology, and more. *Lafẓ*, *maʿnā*, and *ḥaqīqah*—vocal form, mental content, and

78. Abu Deeb (1990, 354).

79. Moi (2017, 15).

80. Andreas (2017), Lawlor (2016).

the accurate account—were both technical terms containing theoretical assumptions analogous to "signifier" and "signified," and at the same time parts of ordinary language analogous to "word" and "idea." When I introduce Saussure into the conversation, it is to show how far removed he is from Arabic.

Harb's contrasting approach uses Saussure to parse out separate referents for the word *maʿnā*. She writes that "if we were to borrow terminology from modern semiotics," then when al-Ǧurǧānī discusses the *lafẓ* and *maʿnā* of a single word he would be referring to the signifier and signified, respectively. She then captures al-Ǧurǧānī's rejection of the long-running literary-critical argument between adherents of *lafẓ* and adherents of *maʿnā* as a move away from *lafẓ* as signifier (*lafẓ*$_1$) to *lafẓ* as sign (*lafẓ*$_2$): "The proper meaning of *lafẓ* . . . is therefore not the 'signifier', which is limited to the 'sound-image' of a word, but the 'sign', which incorporates the meaning of the word."[81] The problem that Harb, Khalfallah, and I all face when we invoke Saussure as part of an explanation of al-Ǧurǧānī is this sign. It is Saussure's signature concept, and it is nowhere to be found in Arabic. Just like the word "meaning" in English, there is so much conceptual weight behind Saussurean vocabulary in English and French that the contours of eleventh-century Arabic theory are flattened when we mention Saussure. As Kuhn and Quine both said, audiences have no option but to domesticate a foreign vocabulary into their own in order to make sense of it.

Moi has shown how much of structuralism, poststructuralism, and even the more recent turn to materialism has stemmed from readings and misreadings of Saussure's idea of the sign.[82] The sign is a theoretical linguistic concept that has no basis in either ordinary human language or extramental reality. And here lies the epistemological risk inherent in translation strategies that use Saussure: they replicate Saussure's limits and project them onto the eleventh century. For example, Saussure's *la langue* served to remove consideration of usage from European language theory (*la langue* being the formal and artificial system he contrasted to untheorizable speech, *le langage,* and its individual human execution, *la parole*).[83] And the semiotics of Émile Benveniste and Paul Ricoeur did nothing to recover pragmatics after Saussure. But back in the eleventh century, whenever al-Ǧurǧānī talked about how language worked with *lafẓ* and *maʿnā,* he was giving the agency to human speakers who selected, under the restriction of precedent, vocal forms to communicate their mental contents. When he used on rare occasion the Arabic word for "sign" (*simah*), he was simply explaining the function of vocal form and its dependence on mental content: vocal forms indicate mental content, as do

81. Harb (2015, 305).

82. Moi (2017, 15–17).

83. Moi (2017, 115).

signs.[84] The epistemological or ontological category that we need to talk about is *ma'nā;* we need to ask what exactly the *ma'ānī* were and where they were located. Introducing Saussure's sign distracts us from this task. We do not need semiotics; rather we need intent and the lexicon.

When we ask what exactly these *ma'ānī* were and where they were located, we are asking how a kind term in eleventh-century Arabic conceptual vocabulary was used; we are not necessarily questioning the reality that this vocabulary sought to describe. In this translation process, we come to appreciate the utility of Wittgenstein's reminder that when we are talking about language, we need to look at usage. It is a mistake to elide our assumptions about some necessary structure to language that exists, something that is out there, in objective reality, that has a name in Arabic and a name in English or French. Such elisions generate the translation problems encountered above. There is an elided commitment to the actual existence of Saussure's sign behind any translation move that seeks to explain al-Ǧurǧānī using Saussure. Wittgenstein reminds us that there is not necessarily anything there, and if there is nothing there to refer to, no idea of the cow floating behind the cow, no objective reality of a permanent structure for language and meaning, *no sign,* then we cannot explain al-Ǧurǧānī by splitting his categories up into different categories in order to connect them to Saussure's categories. Instead we should follow al-Ǧurǧānī's usage of his own categories and think with the help of Kuhn how they enabled him to construct his account of linguistic structure.

HOMONYMY OR POLYSEMY?

The same dynamic, in which a translation strategy for Arabic contains elided commitments to certain European theories, can be seen with the question of homonymy and polysemy. Should we describe what is happening in Arabic with these two terms? We could say that *ma'nā* exhibits polysemy (in which the meanings are related) but it does not exhibit homonymy (in which the meanings are unrelated). The problem is that this requires us to be confident about the existence of meanings and about our ability to map their relatedness, which is exactly the path Wittgenstein warned against. Consider the linguist John Lyons: "The distinction between homonymy and polysemy . . . is very difficult to establish on general grounds, and may indeed rest upon ultimately untenable assumptions about the discreteness of the senses of lexemes."[85] When thinking about the meaning of the

84. هل كانت الألفاظُ إلا مِن أجل المعاني وهل هي إلا خَدَمٌ لها ومُصرَّفةٌ على حُكمها أو ليستْ هي سِمَةٌ لها. Al-Ǧurǧānī (1992a, 417.13–14).
وإذا قلنا في العِلم باللغة مِن مُبتدإِ الأمر أنه كان إلهاماً فإنّ الإلهام لا يرجع إلى معاني اللغات ولكنْ إلى كون ألفاظ اللغات سِمَاتٍ لتلك المعاني وكونِها مُرادةً بها. Al-Ǧurǧānī (1992a, 540.13–541.1). Cf. Ghersetti (2011, 100).

85. Lyons (1977, 2:544).

verb "play" in sentences like "she plays chess better than she plays the flute" or "he played scrum-half in the afternoon and Hamlet in the evening," Lyons concludes that however useful the categories of pure homonymy and pure polysemy can be as explanatory framing, "it may well be that the whole notion of discrete linguistic senses is ill-founded; and, if it is, there is no hope of defining lexemes on this basis."[86] This is linguistics with English as its target and subject matter. But distinctions that are questionable in English should not be used to frame and determine translations from Arabic. It is not the case that homonymy and polysemy are facts that exist regardless of context; they are theories of how language works that were developed in European and Anglophone linguistics. They are valuable, but they are a distraction from the task of translating eleventh-century Arabic, which had its own conceptual vocabulary and its own account of linguistic senses. The only fact on which we can ultimately rely is, as Wittgenstein said, the fact that Arabic scholars used the word *maʿnā* to do things, just as we still use words to do things today.

The Arabic conversation about homonymy, or polysemy, had in fact started with Sībawayh in the fourth section of *al-Kitāb*. After dealing with the parts of speech (noun, verb, and particle), desinential inflections, and predication, he described the different ways in which vocal forms can refer to mental contents. The Arabs whose language he was analyzing used (1) different vocal forms for different mental contents, and (2) different vocal forms for the same mental content (such as "to leave" and "to depart"), and (3) the same vocal form for different mental contents.[87] For this last category, Sībawayh's commentators tended to give the classic example of *ʿayn* (which can mean in Arabic "eye," "well/spring," and more),[88] while Sībawayh himself had stated that (3) was like the verb "found" in "I found him to be excited" and "I found my lost sheep."[89] If we focus on the difference between the examples given by Sībawayh and his commentators, we see that Sībawayh went with what we might call "polysemy," whereas his commentators went with what we might call "homonymy." Just as Lyons documents disagreements about whether a certain English usage is homonymy ("bank of a river" versus "money in the bank") or polysemy ("play rugby" versus "play the clarinet"), so we might see dissonance between the examples given by Sībawayh and by his commentators.

However, such an identification of dissonance would be entirely dependent on our prior commitment to the existence of a real difference between homonymy

86. Lyons (1977, 2:554, 569).

87. اعْلم أنّ مِن كلامهم اختلافَ اللفظين لاختلاف المعنيين واختلاف اللفظين والمعنى واحدٌ واتّفاقَ اللفظين واختلاف المعنيين. Sībawayh (1966, 1:24.8–9).

88. As-Sīrāfī (2008, 1:177.17–18).

89. واتّفاقُ اللفظين والمعنى مختلفٌ قولُك وجَدتُ عليه مِن المَوْجِدة ووجدتُ إذا أردتَ وِجدانَ الضالّة. Sībawayh (1966, 1:24.12–13).

and polysemy, two categories that are facts of twentieth-century linguistics but not necessarily facts of language as such. As Lyons said, the difference between the two categories rests on a belief in discrete linguistic senses that may be ill founded (and would certainly not meet with approval from Wittgenstein). This is exactly the process that Quine was talking about when he said that translators inevitably favor structural parallels. The extra problem that we are dealing with here is that the structural parallels are themselves accounts of linguistic structure, and that linguistic structure creates the framework for the existence of the categories under consideration themselves. The circularity can be damaging. We think in Saussure's terms, or in terms of a difference between homonymy and polysemy. We interrogate our beliefs about Saussure or the distinction between homonymy and polysemy when we do post-Saussurean or twentieth-century linguistics, but when we come to translate, the uncertainty inherent in these theories is flattened away, and their vocabulary starts to shape our reading of Arabic.

FOLK THEORY OR TECHNICAL TERMINOLOGY?

Roland Greene wrote at the beginning of his book-length study of five words that "words that maintain a disciplinary purchase but are also used in everyday life tend to be complex semantic events."[90] This is certainly true of *maʿnā*. We have already met *maʿnā* as a technical translation solution, a partisan position, and then in commonplace statements such as that "there is no *maʿnā* to someone's statement that . . ."[91] or "you have no *maʿnā* at the court of the caliph," which imply that *maʿnā* was an almost colloquial way of saying "meaning" or even "point." We are dealing with both what philosophers today call "folk theory" and what they call "philosophy." Folk theory is when nonphilosophers use commonplace words in regular patterns in everyday life based on rough shared assumptions; so, for example, the popular use of "word" and "idea" in English amounts to a folk theory of meaning, in which words refer to ideas. Philosophy, like science, is understood by its practitioners as more carefully defined. This more careful process of definition could be thought to give some of the words used more purchase, just as Kuhn thought that kind terms and core conceptual vocabulary could help create the worlds they described.[92] At the same time, however, we should be wary of privileging scientific discourse about language over the actual ordinary use of language. When the subject matter of concern is language itself, the ordinary language used becomes the data set for the scientific inquiry. If the Arabic scientific

90. Greene (2013, 6).

91. Ibn Fūrak (1987, 209.20).

92. Kuhn (2009, 182).

inquiry in which we are interested took place with a conceptual vocabulary that was also part of ordinary language at the time, the risks of confusion and circularity are substantial.

Frank made salient observations in this regard, but his strategy was to draw distinctions between theoretical terminology and ordinary language. (Peters did the same.)[93] This strategy held the same risks for the coherence of the original texts as did his strategy of dividing up *maʿnā* into separate words. He struggled to maintain the separation or to provide reasons why one word should be read formally whereas another has a technical meaning "intimately related" to "common use."[94] The problem with introducing a distinction between formal and ordinary language that is not present in the texts themselves is that it opens the door for other anachronistic concerns to follow. The problem that sneaks in here is the modern sensitivity to the difference between words and things (which we will meet again in chapter 5). When discussing the words *ḥaqīqah* and *ḥadd* ("accurate account" and "formal definition"), Frank wrote that both pointed to *maʿnā* and described how a *maʿnā* is indicated. He went on: "The meaning of these terms differs from that of their more common usage. In their usual occurrence . . . they are . . . commonly employed to talk about words and expressions." *Ḥaqīqah* "signifies the strict or lexically most proper meaning of a word, '*ḥadd*' its definition, and '*maʿnā*' its meaning." This makes sense, although the language here does not seem to be particularly ordinary. He then says, "In the formal use with which we are presently concerned, however, they refer not to words or intentions but to the objective reality of beings as such."[95] This is the moment where, in this important 1999 article, Frank's own conceptual vocabulary takes control. The sources themselves make no distinction between formal and ordinary language, nor do they have a concern with the difference between language and the "objective reality of beings as such." They do not appear to care about the same things that Frank cares about. This observation will lead us, in chapter 5, in some interesting directions. But first, the lexicon.

93. Peters (1976, 156 n. 234, 157).

94. Frank (1999, 172, 175).

95. Frank (1999, 178).

4

The Lexicon

When God spoke to the human race, his words indicated mental contents. Humans then tried, with the help of theologians and exegetes, to understand exactly what those mental contents were. When poets spoke to the human race, they did so with images and metaphors that made mental contents interact with each other, creating chain reactions of human cognition. Between God and the poets, these same reactions and connections between mental contents were the subject matter of logic, where they were manipulated by the Aristotelian syllogism. All the while, in a process that underpinned the language of God, the poets, and the logicians, the lexicographers wrote and curated dictionaries that mapped the connections between vocal forms (*alfāẓ*) and mental contents (*maʿānī*).

In this chapter, we will engage the lexical work and theory of ar-Rāġib and some of his contemporaries. Ar-Rāġib primarily worked in the linguistic disciplines of hermeneutics, lexicography, and poetics. In all of these places, the relationships of vocal forms to mental content were his primary concern. In the lexicon, which as we will see was much more than just a dictionary, there was nothing but the interaction between vocal form and mental content. The lexicon recorded and managed the connections between the two. Reading the lexicon also puts us in a position to understand two specific ways that vocal form and mental content connected with each other: pragmatics and nonliteral language. It is only by spending time with the lexicon, and the lexicographers who curated it, that we can understand what was at stake in discussing the intentions behind speech acts, and how those speech acts were understood to either follow some lexical precedent and be accurate (*ḥaqīqah*) or deviate from precedent and go beyond the lexicon (*maǧāz*).

The problem with hermeneutics is that it is always looking for a foundation. When one thinks about what things mean, where does one go to check one's conclusions? How can one prove, in an argument, that this interpretation is correct and that one is wrong? The answer in eleventh-century Arabic is the lexicon. It consisted of vocal forms that were connected to mental contents. Meaning was therefore always verifiable; one had only to return to the lexicon to establish what each vocal form indicated. The lexicon would always provide an account of an original connection between vocal form and mental content, a connection that was then the foundation for any subsequent hermeneutical work.

Then lexicon provides us with an account of its own constituent parts: vocal form and mental content. Ar-Rāġib defined *lafẓ* thus: "The 'vocal form' in speech is figuratively derived from the act of ejecting something from one's mouth or flour being discharged from a millstone."[1] He defined *maʿnā* thus: "The 'mental content' is what speech intends to communicate and that with which it is concerned."[2] As for speech (*al-kalām*), it was this pairing working in tandem: "The word 'speech' covers both the vocal forms when syntactically organized and the mental contents that lie beneath them."[3] Here we have the three components that make up the lexicon and that constitute the entirety of human speech: vocal forms, mental contents, and connections made between them. (Abū Sulaymān Ḥamd al-Ḫaṭṭābī, a contemporary of ar-Rāġib's, d. ca. 996, put the same trio into rhymed prose: *lafẓun ḥāmilun wa-maʿnā bi-hī qāʾimun wa-ribāṭun lahumā nāẓimun.*)[4] In the definitions ar-Rāġib provides for *lafẓ* and *maʿnā* we see two fundamental kinds of lexical statements. The first connects a vocal form to a mental content with a single statement: "mental content is what . . ." The second explains how a vocal form has come to mean something through a process of lexical development, in this case borrowing a vocal form originally connected to the acts of ejecting spittle from a mouth or flour from a millstone, and creation of a new use for that same vocal form to mean the ejecting of speech from the lips. Ar-Rāġib was prepared to argue for lexical connections from use and to give his own figurative explanations for those connections. He personified mental content and wrote that it was "the divulging of what the vocal form had encompassed."[5] He reported a popular etymology of

1. اللفظ بالكلام مستعارٌ من لفظ الشيء من الفم ولفظ الرحى الدقيق. Ar-Rāġib (1992, 743).

2. المعنى هو المقصود إليه من الكلام المهتمُّ به. ar-Rāġib (1988a, 178). I read المُهْتَمّ following three of the four manuscripts; only Chester Beatty has المبهم. ar-Rāġib (1280, fol. 12a.9), (1554, fol. 36b.29), (1680, fol. 61a.6), (n.d.[2], fol. 50b.2). *Pace* Key (2012, 111).

3. فالكلامُ يقع على الألفاظ المنظومة وعلى المعاني التي تحتها مجموعةً. Ar-Rāġib (1992, 722).

4. لفظٌ حاملٌ ومعنى به قائمٌ ورباطٌ لهما ناظم. "A vocal form that carries, a mental content that subsists in the vocal form, and a ligature that strings the two of them together": al-Ḫaṭṭābī (1959, 27.5–6).

5. والمعنى إظهارُ ما تضمَّنه اللفظ. Ar-Rāġib (1992, 351).

another word for speech (*nuṭq*) that related it to a belt or girdle (*niṭāq*) because "a vocal form is like a belt that surrounds and encompasses the mental content."[6] The role of the lexicographer is to regulate the connections between vocal form and mental content, provide their genealogies, manage their changing uses, and explain them to readers.

Arabic lexicography understood any connection between mental content and vocal form, between cognition and the physical existence of voice or writing, as a moment of "placing" (*waḍʿ*). This is the act of name giving or reference setting that is sometimes called "imposition" in Anglophone philosophy of language or was called "baptism" in European scholasticism: "Baptism, stripped of its religious connotations and understood as a pure naming ceremony, provides an excellent metaphor for the process by which, in the causal theory of reference, words are attached to things or sorts of things." (John Marenbon on the twelfth-century European philosopher Abelard.)[7] In Arabic, the source of the metaphor was more prosaic: the vocal forms had simply been "placed" or "put down" in the lexicon. I translate *waḍʿ* as "lexical placing," another uneasy neologism coined to reflect its epistemological independence from English. In the texts under consideration, therefore, vocal forms are lexically placed to communicate mental contents. Everyone writing about language in Arabic agreed that this was the operative process. There were disagreements, as we will see, about the exact history of this lexical placement and the degree of divine involvement, but all agreed that this was the structure within which language was created and existed.

The Arabic word for "lexicon" was *al-luġah,* often translated as "language" (and usually in modern Arabic used to mean just that). For eleventh-century Arabic a translation of *al-luġah* as "language" doesn't quite work. "Language" in English has to include the use human beings make of it. But the Arabic lexicon is the part of language that does not move during a conversation: humans refer to it for explanation and are limited by it when it comes to choice of expression; it is where one goes to determine meaning. When a scholar like ar-Rāġib or Ibn Fūrak says *al-luġah,* they mean this lexicon, they do not mean language. The centrality of this lexicon to eleventh-century Arabic theory cannot be overstated. It was foundational for grammar, legal theory, poetics, and all human and divine communication. Not everybody wanted to be restricted by it, and many of its curators were busy adapting it to circumstance, but everyone had to engage with it.

Where was this lexicon? It seems scarcely credible that it could be an actual book, but by the eleventh century that is exactly what scholars like ar-Rāġib and Ibn Fūrak thought the lexicon was. Their predecessors in Arabic scholarship had

6. وقيل حقيقةُ النُطق اللفظُ الذي هو كالنِطاق للمعنى في ضَمِّه وحَصْره. Ar-Rāġib (1992, 812).

7. Marenbon (2013, 156).

been producing Arabic-to-Arabic dictionaries since the eighth century and would continue to do so for another millennium at least. (See Ramzi Baalbaki and Tamás Iványi.)[8] These dictionaries were published books, available on the open market and written on the widely available medium of paper since the ninth century. They were all multivolume and comprehensive surveys of the entire language, and they were accompanied in the market by the separate genre of popular word lists on specific subjects like plants or particular animals (for an example, Larsen).[9] In an intellectual culture where memorization was praised as a scholarly faculty, this meant that authority was inevitably vested in the lexicographers who read the dictionaries to which they had access and then wrote their own, improved, extended versions. Ar-Rāġib was one such lexicographer, and although he did not claim that his dictionary was comprehensive beyond the vocabulary of the Quran, he could not resist including many words not found in revelation (like *maʿnā,* for example). In eleventh-century Arabic theory, hermeneutics had a physical foundation in the books on scholars' shelves.

PRINCIPLES (*AL-UṢŪL*)

Scholars in the eleventh century could look to the books on their shelves to find out what words meant, and therefore to understand what people and God intended. But their activity was more than just passive recourse; it was an active drive to produce more of the lexical reference that they were using, and thereby improve the stock of lexicography. (This is the sort of pun of which the lexicographers are fond: eleventh-century Arabic dictionary-writing both increased the number of available dictionaries in stock and raised the status, the stock, of the dictionary-writing endeavor.) It is important to remember how active this lexical drive to create meaning was, because the lexicon can appear static, and the rhetoric around its historical status stressed the conservative approach that lexicographers took to its modification. But when Arabic scholars were looking for meaning, they were creating meaning. There is no way to look at ar-Rāġib's Quranic glossary, or the dictionary of his contemporary Ibn Fāris (whom we met defining *maʿnā* in chapter 2.) other than as attempts to create meaning for the intellectual community. The primary way to do this was through statements about the origins of words and their morphological construction. The Arabic word here was *aṣl,* a root or root principle. Let us take the example of the word "lexicon" itself in Ibn Fāris's dictionary. We look it up under its morphological components, and we learn that the three core components (Arabic words are composed of ordered sets

8. Baalbaki (2014), Iványi (2015).

9. Ibn H̱ālawayh (2017).

of consonants; see Petr Zemánek)[10] of the word *luġah* are *l-ġ-w* and they have "two sound principles, the first of which indicates a thing that should not be counted, and the second indicates being addicted to a thing."[11]

Ibn Fāris goes on to explain, using the Quran and poetry (two of the paradigmatic lexical sources, the other being lexicographical fieldwork with nomadic native speakers), that the first of the two principles for *l-ġ-w* is "should not be counted" and that it plays out in usage as a failure to count members of a group of camels, or God not counting certain people as believers, or the error in perception when one sees someone approaching and initially gets their name wrong. The second principle, "being addicted to," is the source of the word *al-luġah,* and Ibn Fāris suggests an etymological process of derivation by which those who possess the Arabic lexicon are addicted to it, and it is thereby called "a quantity to which one is addicted."[12] A tone of conservative consistency must, by definition, run through all dictionaries, and Ibn Fāris's is no exception. But these principles were being built at the same time as they were being recorded in the eleventh century, and if we look to Ibn Fāris's contemporary the great grammarian and language theorist Ibn Ǧinnī, we read a very different lexical account of the same word for "lexicon." Ibn Ǧinnī's definition of the lexicon is: "The sounds with which all peoples express their aims . . . morphologically derived from the verb *laġā,* which means 'to speak.'"[13] Ibn Ǧinnī disagrees entirely with Ibn Fāris about the meaning of the verb from which they are agreed the word is morphologically derived. The substantial gap between "talking" and "addiction" should give the lie to any claim that eleventh-century lexicography was derivative rather than creative. At the same time, the tantalizing prospect of a semantic connection between "talking" and "addiction" should reinforce our understanding of Arabic lexicography as creative art. (It is worth noting in an aside that this art would reach fruition in 1855 when Aḥmad Fāris aš-Šidyāq published his novel dictionary *Kitāb as-Sāq ʿalā as-Sāq fī mā huwa al-Fāriyāq,* a book that joked about, criticized, praised, recaptured, and rewrote anew the Arabic lexicon.)[14]

A second answer to the question, "Where is the lexicon?" is that it is, of course, with God. He created the original lexicon (*aṣl al-luġah*), just as he created

10. Zemánek (2015).

11. اللامُ والغَين والحرف المعتلّ أصلان صحيحان أحدُهما يدلّ على الشيء لا يُعتدّ به والآخر على اللَهَج بالشيء. Ibn Fāris (1946–52, 5:255).

12. والثاني قولُهم لَغِيَ بالأمر إذا لَهِجَ به ويقال إنّ اشتقاق اللغة منه أي يلهَج صاحبُها بها. Ibn Fāris (1946–52, 5:356). Cf. Wright (1898, 1:175).

13. فإنها أصواتٌ يُعبّر بها كلُّ قوم عن أغراضهم .. فإنها فُعْلَةٌ من لَغَوْتَ أي تكلّمتَ. Ibn Ǧinnī (1952–56, 1:33.1–4).

14. Aš-Šidyāq (2013).

everything else. The Quran told ar-Rāġib, Ibn Fūrak, Ibn Fāris, Ibn Ǧinnī, and their predecessors and contemporaries that God taught all the names to Adam (Quran 2:31, al-Baqarah). There was an extended conversation among both lexicographers and theologians as to what form this teaching took. Did God teach the names (nouns) but not the verbs? Did he teach Adam certain names while language as such had actually been developed through convention, by humanity on its own? Did he teach Adam the *maʿānī*, as we saw al-Ǧāḥiẓ argue in chapter 2? I have edited and translated ar-Rāġib's position on this debate elsewhere[15] and will report only the conclusion to his discussion here: "God taught Adam all the names by teaching him the rules and principles to cover individual specifics and implementations. It is after all known that teaching the universals is a greater wonder and something closer to the divine than simply teaching a boy one letter after another."[16] Ar-Rāġib was at a critical epistemological moment here. With the existence of multiple human languages being an empirical fact, and with both the truth of the Quranic revelation and the monotheistic purity of the creator being articles of faith, ar-Rāġib had to provide an answer to the same question that vexed Plato in the *Cratylus:* Where does language come from? And at this critical moment ar-Rāġib made a rhetorical appeal to an epistemology of principles not instances, universals not particulars, and rules from which one could reason rather than examples that one had to repeat. This power of this appeal rested on an assumption that his readers were familiar with the vocabulary of both philhellenic logic and legal theory. Even though he was a lexicographer, ar-Rāġib thought that the principles behind a dictionary were more amazing than its entries.

Principles were simply more important. They underpinned all eleventh-century thought. (For the history of this methodological approach, see Endress.)[17] "Real accurate knowledge is knowledge of the principles that encompass applications and of the universal mental contents that comprise particulars. Examples of these mental contents include knowledge of the substance of the human being or of the horse." We are back to mental contents as the stuff of cognition here, and this mental content is what universal concepts are made of; *maʿnā* is the cognition of what we cannot see or touch ("horseness," for example). In the mind there are also "rules by which accurate accounts of things are known," which function as principles of multiplication in mathematics, dimension and quantity in geometry, and as principles of law, theology, and grammar. "Knowledge of particulars without knowledge

15. Key (2012, 123f).

16. فتعليمُ الله الأسماءَ كلّها إعلامُه القوانينَ والأصولَ المشتمِلة على الجزئيات والفروع وقد عُلم أنّ تعليم الكُلّيّات أعْظمُ في العجوبة وأشْبَهُ بالأمور الإلهية مِن تعليمنا الصبيَّ الحرفَ بعد الحرف. Key (2012, 297), ar-Rāġib (n.d., fol. 36b.15–17).

17. Endress (2002, 244f).

of their principles is not knowledge."[18] It therefore had to be the case that God taught Adam the principles of language, rather than going through every individual word one-by-one. This reinforces my observation that the lexicon was a human creation, and specifically a creation for which the lexicographers understood themselves as responsible. What, exactly, were they building? They were building knowledge of the world that was accessed through language: "One knows a name only when one knows the thing named, and when one attains this knowledge in one's consciousness. The information there can be substance, accident, quantity, quality, relation, and other accidents, according to all of which the name of the thing can differ. A human being has to know these mental contents both cumulatively and separately in order to know names."[19] This is ar-Rāġib's answer to the question of what language is and how it works: lexicon and cognition take center stage.

When the lexicon and cognition take center stage, lexicographers find themselves right at the heart of the relationship between God and humanity. Let us take an example from Ibn Fūrak. At the start of the twentieth chapter of his book, on the subject of "capability," Ibn Fūrak wrote that humans can be described with lexical accuracy as having capability (albeit according to the doctrine of acquisition, on which see further below.) He then said that God's "ability" cannot be called "capability," because there is no precedent for this description in divine revelation. However, he continued, if one looks at the question from the perspective of mental content, then ability is the same mental content as capability, "and the lexicographers do not distinguish between these two mental contents, just as they do not distinguish between ability and potentiality, or between knowledge and cognition, or between movement and transfer."[20] Unlike Abū Hilāl, Ibn Fūrak believed that multiple vocal forms in language can refer to the same mental content. What is interesting about this discussion is that two opposing hermeneutical dynamics are in play at the same time.

18. والصحيحُ أن العِلم في الحقيقة يتعلّق بمعرفة الأصول المشتملة على الفروع والمعاني الكُلّية المُنْطَوِية على الأجزاء كمعرفة جوهرِ الإنسان والفَرَس والقوانين التي تُعرف بها حقيقةُ الشيء كأصول الضرْب في الحساب وأحوال الأبعاد والمقادير والهندسة والأصول المَبنيّة عليها المسائلُ الكثيرة في الفقه والكلام والنحو فأما معرفةُ الجزئية مُتعرّيةً عن الأصول فليس بعلم. Key (2012, 296–97), ar-Rāġib (n.d., fol. 36b.10–14).

19. فثَبتَ أن معرفة الاسم لا يُحصل إلا بمعرفة المسمّى في نفسه وحصولِ معرفته في الضمير ثم المعلومات قد تكون جواهرَ وأعراضاً من كَميّة وكيفية وإضافة وسائرَ ذلك من الأعراض ويُجعل للشيء الواحد اساميَ بحسب هذه النظرات فلا بد أنْ يكون الإنسانُ عارفاً بهذه المعاني مُجتمِعةً ومفترقةً حتى يكون عارفاً بالاسماء التي يُجعل لها بحسبها. Key (2012, 297–98), ar-Rāġib (n.d., fol. 37a.3–6).

20. وكان يقول إنّ الله تعالى لا تُسمَّى قُدرتُه استطاعةً لأجل أنّ التوقيف لم يرِد بذلك فأما مِن طريق المعنى فالذي له من القدرة هو بمعنى الاستطاعة وأهلُ اللغة لا يُفرّقون بين معنَيَيهما كما لايُفرّقون بين القُدرة والقوية وبين العلم والمعرفة وبين الحركة والنقل. Ibn Fūrak (1987, 108.2–5).

On the one hand, there is the claim that evidence of God's word choice, found in language that comes from God, is the way to decide what God meant. We cannot guess what God meant, and so we have to follow his precedent as found in the lexicon he provided. However, there is another reading in play here, which Ibn Fūrak calls "the mental-content route." If we go down the mental-content route, then we say that when we find "ability" in revelation, it has the same mental content as "capability," and we therefore do not have to follow divine precedent. What mental content does here is enable Ibn Fūrak to posit a hermeneutical space for which there is no divine evidence and in which he can exercise his own judgment as to what God's words mean. The lexicographers are equally important in both these dynamics; whether lexical accuracy relies on divine precedent or human reasoning, the lexicon is still the place that connects specific vocal forms to mental contents, thereby enabling us to understand what God meant.

Ar-Rāġib shared Ibn Fūrak's respect for divine precedent, stating on more than one occasion that it was the only proper way to determine the correct words to describe God,[21] but he did not collapse multiple vocal forms into the same mental content with the frequency of Ibn Fūrak. He was therefore closer to Abū Hilāl, whose project was intended to demonstrate the complete absence of synonymy in Arabic and included analyses of how those vocal forms adduced by Ibn Fūrak (ability and potentiality, knowledge and cognition) did in fact refer to different mental contents in each case.[22] On the pairing of ability and potentiality, ar-Rāġib was particularly scathing, reporting how a senior scholar refused to even say the word "potentiality" while exclaiming: "This expression is used by philosophers so instead I say 'ability'!" Ar-Rāġib was unimpressed with this attitude to the lexicon: "It was as if he didn't know the difference between the two words in common usage, never mind among specialists!"[23] Clearly, the lexicographers do not in any sense represent a single authoritative source. Ibn Fūrak used them to argue that multiple vocal forms had the same mental content, and ar-Rāġib and Abū Hilāl used them to argue that multiple vocal forms had different mental contents. The lexicon was equally important in each case. In effect, "the lexicographers" was shorthand for a prolonged and iterative lexical argument about meaning, in which eleventh-century scholars could pick and choose as they saw fit.

21. ذكر أهلُ الأَثَر أنّ الله عزّ وجلّ لا يصح أنْ يُوصف إلا بما ورد السمعُ به . . . لا نَصِف اللهَ تعالى ولا نَصِف الأمورَ الإلهية إلا بما ورد به السمعُ. Key (2012, 77–80), ar-Rāġib (1988a, 79.13–14, 173.13–14).

22. الفرقُ بين العلم والقُدرة . . . الفرق بين القادر والقاوي. Abū Hilāl (2006, 93–94, 122).

23. وكأنه لم يعلم ما بينهما من الفرق في تعارف أعوام الناس فضلاً عن خواصهم. ar-Rāġib (2005b, 214).

INTENT

A theory of language that only has two components, vocal form and mental content, must account for the connections between them. Ar-Rāġib, his contemporaries, and his predecessors did this with intent. The idea that the intent of a speech act governed its meaning gained traction in European and Anglophone scholarship only in the twentieth century with the work of Paul Grice and J. L. Austin (and of course Wittgenstein). This gave subsequent theorists a set of new resources that they called "pragmatics." Kepa Korta and John Perry open their *Stanford Encyclopedia of Philosophy* entry on pragmatics with a quote from Voltaire: "When a diplomat says yes, he means perhaps; when he says perhaps, he means no.)[24] In the Arabic eleventh century, this was a well-established methodology. As we just saw with ar-Rāġib, one could intend either Zayd the person or Zayd the name while using the unchanged vocal form "Zayd." The connection between mental content and vocal forms was made by speakers' intent: people wanted to say things.[25] The theorizing of intent primarily took place in the discipline of legal theory, where in order to decide what speakers meant, the scholars had to account systematically for the intentions behind speech acts. This held for both God, whose commands in the Quran needed to be understood so that they could be followed, and for human beings themselves, whose contractual undertakings with each other needed to be codified so that they could be legislated. The secondary scholarship on legal theory is substantially more developed than in any other field of Classical Arabic language theory. Notable works are Mohammed M. Yunis Ali's synchronic analysis in *Medieval Islamic Pragmatics*, Robert Gleave's work on literalism, Joseph Lowry's study of the foundational monograph by the ninth-century aš-Šāfiʿī, Behnam Sadeghi's investigation of the frameworks in which laws were made, and David Vishanoff's diachronic survey of the jurisprudential responses to the question of what God meant.[26] This is how al-Ǧuwaynī (Imām al-Ḥaramyn, d. 1085: fl. in Nishapur and the teacher of al-Ġazālī) explained the relationship between law

24. Korta and Perry (2015).

25. أنّ المعنى إرادةُ كونِ القول على ما هو موضوعٌ له في أصل اللغة أو مجازها فهو في القول خاصّةٌ إلا أنْ يُستعار لغيره على ما ذكرنا قبل ولإرادةُ تكون في القول والفِعل. Abū Hilāl (2006, 143.20–21). And selections from passages already encountered:

. . . أنْ يكون زيدٌ في الحقيقة مراداً مع وجوده فدلّ . . . Abū Hilāl (2006, 45.18–19),

. . . ليس لدخولك إلى فلان معنى والمرادُ أنه ليس له فائدة تُقصَد ذكرَها بالقول . . . Abū Hilāl (2006, 45.21–22),

. . . لأنّ المعنى هو قصدُ القلب بالكلام إلى المراد . . . al-Qāḍī ʿAbd al-Ǧabbār (1965–74, 5:253.4–5),

. . . إلى كون ألفاظ اللغات سِمَاتٍ لتلك المعاني وكونِها مُرادةً بها . . . al-Ǧurǧānī (1992a, 540.14–541.1).

26. Ali (2000), Gleave (2012), Lowry (2007), Sadeghi (2013, esp. 24, 37–38), Vishanoff (2011).

and language: "Most of the work in legal theory deals with vocal forms and mental contents. Mental contents are dealt with as part of legal analogy. A concern with vocal forms is indispensable, for the divine revelation is in Arabic. . . . Legal theorists have a particular focus on those aspects of language that are not dealt with by lexicographers and grammarians. Legal theorists focus on bringing out the divine law, and they work on commands, prohibitions, statements of general versus particular applicability, and questions of exceptions from rules."[27]

The lexicon provided a framework for the divination of intent. How could one know what language users meant when they used a vocal form if not by reference to precedent and a history of usage in the speech community that was recorded by the lexicographers? The same is of course true of the quotation from Voltaire: only a history of usage can allow us to make sense of the idea that a diplomat might say "yes" and mean "perhaps." And yet that lexical precedent would almost never provide a single unimpeachable answer. In Arabic, there was always room to posit another meaning, perhaps a rarer meaning, which, as long as some lexical evidence was presented, could be made to stand up in argument with one's peers. The reason for this flexibility was the assumption that intent was how language functioned. The intent of a speaker was always an integral part of the model of signification, its third term or copula. For ar-Rāġib, the definition of mental content itself *was* intent: "Mental content is what speech intends to communicate and that with which it is concerned . . . contained as intent beneath the vocal form."[28] With a vocal form, a speaker intended a mental content, while the lexicon both restricted and registered their choice.

NAME, NAMED, AND NAMING *(ISM, MUSAMMĀ, TASMIYAH)*

There was a fraught exegetical and theological debate about the status of name, named, and naming that had started in the eighth century.[29] Ibn Fūrak reports that a group of theologians with whom al-Aš'arī had disagreed held that "the name is the thing named."[30] It was a statement that seems either counterintuitive or wildly

27. اعلمْ أنّ مُعظم الكلام في الأصول يتعلق بالألفاظ والمعاني أما المعاني فستأتي في كتاب القياس إنْ شاء الله تعالى وأما الألفاظ فلا بُد مِن الاعتناء بها فإنّ الشريعة عربيةٌ . . . وٱعتنوا في فنّهم بما أغْفلَه أئمةُ العربية واشتدَّ اعتناؤُهم بذكرِ ما اجتمع فيه إغفالُ أئمةِ اللسان وظهورُ مَقصد الشرع وهذا كالكلام على الأوامر والنواهي والعُموم والخُصوص وقضايا الاستثناء. Al-Ǧuwaynī (1979, 1:169.3–5, 10–12). Cf. translation in Miller forthcoming in the Journal of Abbasid Studies, and Cf. Vishanoff (2011, 116–20).

28. المعنى هو المقصود إليه من الكلام المُهْتَمُّ به . . . وقيل هو المُحتوَى تحت اللفظ مِن المقصود إليه. Ar-Rāġib (1988a, 178.2–4). See note 2 above.

29. Cf. al-Aš'arī (1929–33, 529.14–17).

30. مَن ذَهَبَ مِن أصحاب الصِفات إلى أنّ الاسم هو المسمى. Ibn Fūrak (1987, 39.1–2).

simplistic. It was an example of how problematic it was to do either hermeneutics or language theory without a stable conceptual vocabulary for reference and signification. Such a conceptual vocabulary was, of course, always available in the combination of vocal form and mental content. But in this particular debate, we are at a point in the early history of the archive when that structural assumption, which I have been arguing was everywhere, was not yet omnipresent. We are dealing with a theological debate that in the eleventh century must have seemed conceptually anachronistic. This is the context for Ibn Fūrak's reference, in a book full of careful delineations of reference and meaning, to an apparently simplistic theory in which "the name is the thing named." Let us now go back and reconstruct the debate with interpretative charity and brevity. (It has been dealt with in detail in the secondary literature.)[31]

The issue at hand is the relationship between linguistic acts of description of God, God's own revealed descriptions of himself and their ontological status, and the nature of God's divine self. In one of the earliest extant exegeses of the Quran, Abū ʿUbaydah (d. ca. 825) wrote that "in 'the name of God' is actually just 'in God' because the name of the thing is the thing in reality." Abū ʿUbaydah then referred to a poet from the time of the Quranic revelation (Labīd, d. 661) who used the referential function of language as an image: "The name of peace is upon them."[32] Abū ʿUbaydah's point was that Arabic speakers' primary and natural use of language was to refer to things, not to refer to words. When the poet said, "The name of peace is upon them," he did not mean that some linguistic act was floating above the people in question; he meant that they were actually in reality at peace. If a ninth-century exegete needed to make this apparently obvious point about how language works, we can infer that questions were being asked along the lines of, "What is the status of the 'name' in the Quranic phrase 'in the name of God' [the *basmalah*]? Is it separate from God himself? Is this something like the Christian Trinity?"

One initial theological response was to stress that language was completely separate from existence and that the fact that God has names means not that names exist alongside him but rather that human beings use names to describe his eternal divinity. This was the position of the Muʿtazilah, that the human use of a name (*tasmiyah*) can be distinguished from the thing named, that this use is the name, and that there is no other thing involved.[33] We read ʿAbd al-Ǧabbār in the eleventh century affecting shock at the naivety of the earlier statements and suggesting that the claim "the name is the thing named" stemmed from a

31. Brodersen (2014, 583–92), Frank (1982, 272–74), Gimaret (1990, 345–56), Massignon (1982, 3:172–76), Peters (1976, 377), van Ess (1991–95, 4:201–2, 628).

32. بسم الله إنما هو بالله لأنّ اسم الشيء هو الشيءُ بعينه قال لبيدٌ إِلَى ٱلحَوْلِ ثُمَّ ٱسْمُ ٱلسَّلامِ عَلَيْكُما. Abū ʿUbaydah (1954, 1:16).

33. وأنّ التسمية هي الاسم. Al-Ašʿarī (1929–33, 529.14), Frank (1978, 18).

desire to avoid the existence of a created Quran on earth, which containing God's name as it did would imply that God himself was created. "This is obviously false, because God is not literally *in* the Quran!" exclaimed ʿAbd al-Ğabbār; what is in the Quran is our linguistic statement of his name.[34] The problem with reading this debate is that neither side, fighting as they are polemical battles over right belief, is prepared to give the other side its due. All we can do is read the violent shifts in perspective between lines of analysis assuming the statement "God has a name" refers to two separate physical things and lines of analysis assuming "God has a name" to be tautology because the word "God" is itself a name. Shifting back away from ʿAbd al-Ğabbār to the original worry about the ontological status of names, we can read Abū Saʿīd ad-Dārimī (d. 894) writing with an apparently equal degree of shock and incomprehension that the problem with the Muʿtazilī position was that it implied God was a nameless person, unknown, with no idea who he was, until he created humans, they started talking about him in their language, and then they lent him a human name.[35] Outrageous! In the late tenth century, al-Bāqillānī agreed with ad-Dārimī and returned to the line of poetry that Abū ʿUbaydah had cited (noting that "lexicographers are the foundation stone!") to ask how the name (*ism*) could be the act of naming (*tasmiyah*) when the lexicographers had already said the poet didn't intend that a speech-act-of-naming-peace be upon those people, but rather that they just be at peace![36] I think that the shifts in perspective here in this debate are so extreme because it is language and its relationship to reality that is at stake. The analysis leaps from the world to the sounds and marks of linguistic activity without any intermediary, and this is what made it so unstable a conversation for both the Classical Arabic scholars taking part in it and for the twentieth-century scholars trying to read it. The missing intermediary is the mind. If a conceptual vocabulary is available that can clarify the relationship between things, ideas, and words, then the argument about how exactly they relate can take place more easily. It is exactly that role that we see *maʿnā* playing in other debates. The names-versus-named debate was an early and rare moment of fundamental confusion, and it throws into sharp relief the absence of such confusion in games that used the word *maʿnā*. It is also more than possible that scholars such as ad-Dārimī and al-Bāqillānī were not so much

34. وهذا ظاهرُ السقوط لأنّ القرآن ليس فيه الله في الحقيقة وإنما فيه قولُنا اللهُ الذي هو منظومٌ من حروف. Al-Qāḍī ʿAbd al-Ğabbār (1965–74, 7:164.12–13).

35. يَعنِي أنّ الله كان مَجهولاً كَشخْصٍ مجهولٍ لا يُهتدى لاسمه ولا يُدرى ما هو حتى خَلق الخلقَ فابتدعوا له أسماءً مِن مَخلوقِ كلامِهم فأعارُوها إيّاه مِن غير أنْ يُعرف له اسمٌ قَبل الخلق. Ad-Dārimī (2007, 280.20–23).

36. أَهْلَ اللغة الذين هم العُمدةُ . . . فكيف يكون الاسمُ هو التسمية التي هي قولُ المُسَمِّي وهُم قد جَعلوا الاسمُ نفسَ المسمَّى وإنْ كان شخصاً أو عَرَضاً هو الاسمُ . . . . Al-Bāqillānī (1957, 227.17–228.4).

confused as deliberately misinterpreting their theological opponents; not quite the "this stuff wasn't really meant to make sense" of Frank's interlocutor but certainly evidence of a lack of interpretative charity that may also have been present in the debate's earlier centuries.[37]

Indeed, what happened in subsequent generations was that the debate about the name and the named became a byword for the sort of theological confusion that scholars sought to avoid. In twelfth-century Baghdad, Ibn al-Ǧawzī (d. 1200) was a preacher, intellectual, and director of five madrasas. In his heresiographical polemic *The Deceit of Satan,* he attacked theology in the same way as we saw ar-Rāġib do over a century earlier and (while attributing the sentiment to the great ninth-century jurist Muḥammad b. Idrīs aš-Šāfiʿī, d. 820) wrote that "if you hear someone saying that the name is the named, or is not the named, then bear witness that he is a theologian and has no religion."[38] An alternative voice from the twelfth century, the even more famous al-Ġazālī, did not share Ibn al-Ǧawzī's rejection of theology and therefore had to take the opposite approach to the complex of problems around the name and the named. Al-Ġazālī's monograph, probably written around the year 1100, is an explanation of the mental contents of God's names.[39] The first chapter starts with the mental content of the name, the named, and the naming. The way to uncover the accurate accounts of this matter, wrote al-Ġazālī, is to distinguish the mental content of each vocal form and to recognize that things exist in three ways: as physical entities in the world, as language on the tongue, and as knowledge in the mind. He also wrote that one needed to deal with the mental content of the copula itself (what was meant by "is" in "the name *is* the named).[40] This is exactly the epistemological menu required to make sense of the matter at hand, and it was these ingredients that were absent in the earlier theological debates. Al-Ġazālī's intellectual debts to ar-Rāġib, and to Ibn Sīnā, have been established elsewhere,[41] and it should suffice to note here that the recognition of the importance of the copula comes from the Aristotelian tradition via Ibn Sīnā, and the foregrounding of mental content as an epistemological tool for both divine reality and human language comes from the eleventh-century language theory

37. See chapter 3 note 42.

38. قال وإذا سمِعْتَ الرجلَ يقول الاسمُ هو المسمَّى أو غيرُ المسمَّى فاشهَدْ أنه مِن أهل الكلام ولا دينَ له. Ibn al-Ǧawzī (1983, 81.2–3), van Ess (1966, 319).

39. Al-Ġazālī (1986, xv).

40. الفصلُ الأوّل في بيانِ معنى الاسم والمسمَّى والتسمية . . . ولا سبيلَ إلى كشْف الحقّ فيه إلا ببيان معنى كلّ واحدٍ من هذه الألفاظ الثلاثة مفرداً ثم بيان معنى قولِنا هو هو ومعنى هو غيرُه فهذا منهج الكشف للحقائق . . . إنّ للأشياء وجوداً في الأعيان ووجوداً في اللسان ووجوداً في الأذهان. Al-Ġazālī (1986, 17.2, 17.13–16, 18.8–9).

41. Janssens (2003), Madelung (1974).

exemplified by Ibn Fūrak and ar-Rāġib. I do not wish to argue that the conceptual vocabulary of mental content caused al-Ġazālī to make better analytical assessments of questions like the name and the named, but rather that *maʿnā,* mental content, was part of a conceptual vocabulary that enabled him to do so. The degree to which it enabled scholars to theorize can be seen from the pained arguments that took place in its absence.

Ar-Rāġib decided to take part in that conversation at the traditional trigger point of the first verse of the Quran and the *basmalah* invocation ("In the name of God, the merciful, the beneficent") that both was used before ritual recitation and is found in the Quranic text itself. Ibn Fūrak, on the other hand, decided to address the conversation as a foundation for his complete analysis of the divine attributes, and he split the difference between the two arguing sides reviewed above.[42] He disagreed with the statement that the name was the named, and he also disagreed with the statement that the name was just the use of the name. Ibn Fūrak wanted to preserve the separation of God from his divine attributes while at the same time maintaining a sphere in which those same attributes could exist unconnected to human language. The problem with the Muʿtazilī position was that (as ad-Dārimī had shown) it implied God was dependent on humanity; if human language was all that mattered (and the Muʿtazilah tended to assume language was a human convention),[43] then God's divine knowledge or ability became dependent on human beings' ability to name him as knowing or able. Ibn Fūrak's formulation was that "every use of the name is a name, but every name is not a use of the name."[44] This meant that God had divine attributes that could be named by humans but that these attributes also existed without reference to humans.

Ar-Rāġib dealt with the *basmalah* at the start of the Quran and quoted Abū ʿUbaydah and the line of poetry from Labīd approvingly. He equated the use of the name with the name itself, saying that "name" in this supplicative formulation was in effect functioning as a *maṣdar* (quasi-verbal event noun) and so "the name" and "the use of the name" were the same (not an inevitable lexical statement; cf. Abū Hilāl).[45] With regard to the theological argument about God's divine attributes, ar-Rāġib split the difference using a technique different from Ibn Fūrak's. He wrote that the two opposing sides were both right "from different perspectives." It was simply a matter of intent. One could say, "I saw Zayd" and thereby refer to the

42. اعْلَمْ أنّا قدّمْنا لك ذِكر هذا الفصل لنَبْنِيَ عليه ما بعدَه مِن ذِكر مذاهبه في معنى أسماء الله تعالى وصِفاته. Ibn Fūrak (1987, 38.15–16).

43. Peters (1976, 387).

44. لأنّ التسمية عنده اسمٌ للمسمّى وما عداها أيضا اسمٌ . . . مذهبُه أنّ كلّ تسميةٍ اسمٌ وليس كلّ اسمٍ تسمية. Ibn Fūrak (1987, 38.21–22, 39.4–5).

45. واسمٌ هاهنا مَوضوعٌ موضعَ المصدر أي التسمية. Abū Hilāl (2006, 40.3–41.3), ar-Rāġib (1984, 110.7).

actual named person Zayd, or one could say, "I called my son 'Zayd'" and thereby refer to the name itself in language. This leads to the existence of homonymous phrases such as "Zayd is beautiful," which can refer to either the name or to the person, depending on intent. Ar-Rāġib noted that there are a great many errors made with such statements.[46]

ACCURACY AND BEYOND (*ḤAQĪQAH* AND *MAǦĀZ*)

Connections between vocal forms and mental contents were recorded as precedent in the lexicon and that lexicon was then used and managed. Scholars such as ar-Rāġib made sense of the vastness of the lexicon by theorizing the existence of certain principles that structured it, and they made sense of actual language use by focusing on the intent behind specific speech acts. But the most important value applied to the lexicon was accuracy (*ḥaqīqah*), the conception of which was closely tied to the lexicon itself. It was accompanied by its twin and opposite, the process of going beyond the lexicon (*maǧāz*), which had its own epistemological and aesthetic value. *Ḥaqīqah* was always used to describe a process that was accurate, correct, real, and true. To provide the *ḥaqīqah* of something was to provide an accurate account of it, and this was a value that not everyone could necessarily access. When God showed Adam to the angels, they were unable to access the accurate accounts of the names. "We know only what you taught us" say the angels to God (Quran 2:32), but Adam, God's newly embodied language-capable creation, knew the names, their accurate accounts, and the principles with which to manage them.[47] He was the first lexicographer. Names in language were the way that things made their way into the heads of humans and angels alike, and when the accuracy of the resultant mental contents was at stake, ar-Rāġib used the word *ḥaqīqah*. If things that were coming into people's heads were speech acts or written words, then *ḥaqīqah* was used for a specific kind of accuracy that relied entirely on the lexicon.

This reliance took the form of a specific act of lexical placement that made a connection between a vocal form and a mental content, a connection deemed to be accurate by the lexicographers, who recorded it in the lexicon. There was consequently always a claim of consensus inherent in the use of *ḥaqīqah* as a value; the assumption was that if something was *ḥaqīqah* then everyone would agree

46. وما ذُكِر من الخلاف في أنّ الاسم هو المسمَّى أو غيرُه فقولانِ قالوهما بنظرين مختلفين وكِلاهما صحيحٌ بنَظَرٍ ونَظَر. Ar-Rāġib (1984, 110–11, 111.2–3).

47. وجُلُّ ذلك معدومٌ [من آيا صوفيا وفي جار الله معلوم وهو تصحيف] في المَلَك لعدْمِها كثافةُ الجسم المركَّب من الأمشاج واستغنايها [كذا] عن ذلك فبيّن اللهُ تعليمَه آدمَ هذه المعاني والأسامي وعَرْضَهم على الملايكة [كذا] وأنباءَ آدمَ بحقائقها . . . Ar-Rāġib (n.d., fol. 27a.14–15), (n.d.[3]). See note 16 above.

on it were they to have full access to the facts. This is why the *ḥaqīqah* connections in the lexicon were called *aṣl al-luġah;* the lexicon comprised only of accurate lexical placements was called "original" (*aṣl*) because it was a paradigm and a starting point. Ibn Fūrak wrote that there were certain fundamental truths that were necessarily known by all living things sufficiently endowed with senses and reason, and that if disagreement were to be permitted in these cases it would lead to mutual ignorance of the *ḥaqāʾiq;* mutual ignorance in the face of available accurate accounts was a contradiction in terms that proved the impossibility of disagreement about *ḥaqīqah.*[48] Any use of the word *ḥaqīqah* can therefore be read as a scholar making a claim for an accurate account of world or lexicon with which no one would disagree.

Ḥaqīqah was about truth and accuracy, but at the same time it was about a certain kind of linguistic truth and accuracy that consisted solely of lexical placing and precedent. Eleventh-century scholars used both kinds of accuracy to read texts produced either by God or by the poets and to play with the relationship between language and truth. The lexicographers noticed the gap between lexical truth and real truth. Ar-Rāġib explained *ḥaqīqah* as a word used to describe actual existence, deserved purview, true belief, sincere action, and speech that is neither lax nor exaggerated.[49] In all these cases *ḥaqīqah* was used for an accurate account of some truth that exists in the mind or in the world. Ar-Rāġib then went on to identify a language-facing usage of *ḥaqīqah* that was the specific terminology of the jurists and theologians,[50] one that he himself would later use in his own poetics: vocal forms used according to their original lexical placement.[51]

Abū Hilāl, on the other hand, maintained that *ḥaqīqah* was primarily a description of lexically accurate language and then secondarily, by the process of semantic extension we met above with *maʿna,* a description of accuracy with regard to ideas and things.[52] He also made some very meticulous observations about the potential use of a language-based account of accuracy to describe nonlinguistic things

48. وأما في الضروريات التي تقع ابتداءً فلا يصح فيها أيضا إلا المشاركةُ بين الأحياء وذوي الحوّاس والعُقلاء مع زوال الآفات وإنّ إجازةَ خلافِ ذلك تُؤدي إلى تناكُر الحقائق وإبطال الطُرق إلى إثباتها. Ibn Fūrak (1987, 16.22–17.2).

49. والحقيقةُ تُستعمَل تارةً في الشيء الذي له ثباتٌ ووجودٌ . . . وتارةً تُستعمَل في الاعتقاد . . . وتارةً في العمل وفي القول . . . لقوله حقيقةٌ إذا لم يكن مُترخِّصاً ومُتزيِّداً Ar-Rāġib (1992, 247/2.8–16).

50. وأما في تعارُف الفقهاء والمتكلمين فهي اللفظُ المستعمَل فيما وُضِع له في أصل اللغة. Ar-Rāġib (1992).

51. فالحقيقةُ اللفظُ المستعمَلُ فيما وُضِعَ له في أصل اللغة. Ar-Rāġib (ca. 14th C., fol. 4a.8–9).

52. والحقيقةُ أيضاً مِن قَبيل القول على ما ذكرنا وليستْ الذاتُ كذلك .. وتُوسَّعُ في الحقيقة ما لم تُوسَّعْ في المعنى فقيل لا شيءَ إلا وله حقيقةٌ ولا يقال لا شيءَ إلا وله معنىً ويقولون حقيقةُ الحركة كذا ولا يقولون معنى الحركة كذا. Abū Hilāl (2006, 45.22–24).

in the mind or in the world. First of all, he identified the truth-neutrality of the lexicon itself: "*Ḥaqīqah* is a speech act that is used according to its lexical place in the original lexicon, regardless of its good or bad qualities, whereas truth [*ḥaqq*] is what is used according to its place as judged by wisdom; it can therefore be only good." The process of verification (*taḥqīq*, which we briefly encountered above),[53] applies to both kinds of truth; accuracy with regard to "something being placed according to its place in either the lexicon or with regard to wisdom."[54] The foundation for ethics was wisdom, the ability to judge whether a thing was bad or good. The foundation for meaning, on the other hand, was lexical placement according to the stipulation of the lexicon. But accuracy was paramount in both cases.

Abū Hilāl thought that language was separate from reality. He wrote that *ḥaqīqah* was a quality of speech acts, but that essence (*ḏāt*) was not.[55] The proof that *ḥaqīqah* was a linguistic quality was that it necessitated the existence of *maǧāz*. The existence of accurate lexical connections necessitated the existence of other lexical connections that were not accurate in the same way. If one can use a vocal form according to its placement in the original lexicon, one can also use the same vocal form to go beyond that original placement, say something new, and generate a revised lexicon. This is the foundational concept of *maǧāz*, language that goes beyond the lexicon. Neither God nor the poets could speak without it. And *maǧāz* was, according to both Abū Hilāl and ar-Rāġib,[56] primarily linguistic. If *maǧāz* and *ḥaqīqah* were dependent on each other, and if *maǧāz* was linguistic, then Abū Hilāl argued that *ḥaqīqah* had to be linguistic too. This meant that things that were considered *ḥaqīqah*, things that were accurately accounted for as essences, could also be called *maǧāz*.[57] What did Abū Hilāl mean by that? It almost comes across as a throw-away remark in a passage where he is trying to explain that "logical definition" (*al-ḥadd*) and "accurate account" (*al-ḥaqīqah*) are not synonymous. But I think it is in fact a very meticulous observation about the boundary between language and the world.

53. See chapter 1 note 75.

54. الفرقُ بين الحقيقة والحقّ أن الحقيقة ما وُضِعَ مِن القول مَوضِعَه في أصل اللغة حَسَناً كان أو قبيحاً والحقُّ ما وُضِعَ مَوضِعَه مِن الحِكمة فلا يكون إلا حَسَناً وإنما شَمَلَهما اسمُ التحقيق لاشتراكهما في وَضْع الشيء منهما مَوضِعَه من اللغة والحكمة. Abū Hilāl (2006, 45.5–8).

55. والحقيقةُ أيضاً من قَبيل القول على ما ذكرنا وليست الذات كذلك. Abū Hilāl (2006, 45.3).

56. المجازُ اللفظُ المُستعمَل في غيرِ ما وُضِع له في أصل اللغة . . . والمجازُ من الكلام ما تَجاوَز مَوضِعَه الذي وُضِعَ له والحقيقةُ ما لم يتَجاوَز ذلك. Ar-Rāġib (1992, 211/2.25—212/1.2), (ca. 14th C., fol. 4a.9).

57. والحقيقةُ ما وُضِع من القول مَوضِعَه في أصل اللغة والشاهدُ أنها مقتضيَةُ المجاز وليس المجازُ إلا قولاً فلا يَجوز أنْ يكون ما يُناقِضه إلا قولاً ومِثلُ ذلك الصِدقُ لمّا كان قولاً كان ناقِضُه وهو الكِذبُ قولاً ثم يُسمَّى ما يُعبَّر عنه بالحقيقة وهو الذاتُ حقيقةً مجازاً. Abū Hilāl (2006, 44.6–9).

If we try and use a common example of language that goes beyond the lexicon, one that ar-Rāġib used in his poetics, the situation becomes clearer.[58] If you call an actual donkey "a donkey," then you are using the vocal form "donkey" with lexical accuracy, according to its precedent in the original lexicon. But if you call a stupid human being "donkey" you are going beyond the lexicon and using the vocal form "donkey" in a new way. This is how *ḥaqīqah* and *mağāz* are used as categories for language. But because *ḥaqīqah* can also be used to describe an accurate account of something in the world or the mind (either via semantic extension as per Abū Hilāl or as its primary usage as per ar-Rāġib), then the vocal form "donkey" when used to identify a stupid person is still pointing at some accurate conception of a donkey. What Abū Hilāl seems to have noticed here is that going beyond the lexicon requires keeping the original accurate lexical placement in play. This is exactly the insight that al-Ğurğānī would, as we will see, develop into a comprehensive theory of literary meaning. And the scale of *mağāz*, the extent to which language was able to go beyond the lexicon, cannot be underestimated. These scholars were relentless in their resort to the lexicon at the same time as they accepted a picture of ordinary language, technical and scientific language, divine language, and literary language in which usage went beyond the lexicon at all times and in every direction.

God and the poets both went beyond the lexicon. The Quran self-identified as an unparalleled literary event. Neither poetry nor make-believe, it was inimitable. And the scholarly response was to enumerate, taxonomize, and explain how this was so. Abū ʿUbaydah, the same highly regarded lexicographer whom we met above on the question of the name and the named, gave his exegesis the title *Mağāz al-Qurʾān* (*Going Beyond in the Quran*). The question of *mağāz* in Classical Arabic has received serious scholarly attention from Heinrichs and John Wansborough,[59] although work remains to be done. Heinrichs is the most persuasive, and he identifies *mağāz* in Abū ʿUbaydah as "a deep structure which materializes into two different surface structures equivalent to each other. [The two structures on the surface are the Quranic text and its *mağāz* paraphrase as provided by Abū ʿUbaydah.]"[60] This fits with how I have been trying to explain the accurate lexical account and usage that goes beyond it as two different epistemological accounts of language. Either language accords with the lexicon, or someone has made it deviate. What is interesting about Abū ʿUbaydah's work is that he is the one doing the deviation. God expressed content in an Arabic language that was immediately accessible to its original audience, the seventh-century Arabic speak-

58. كقولك حِمارٌ للبليد. Ar-Rāġib (ca. 14th C., fol. 4b.1).

59. Heinrichs (1984, esp. 137), (1991/92), (2016); Wansborough (1970).

60. Heinrichs (1984, 126).

ers of what is now Saudi Arabia. But for the audience of Abū ʿUbaydah, the grandson of a Persian Jew from Azerbaijan living in the new garrison city of Basra in Iraq,[61] the rare words, syntax, and brevity of the Quranic text needed explanation. So he wrote an exegesis that took each example of abbreviation, elision, or suppression of syntactical elements and made it deviate into a new, more accessible set of vocal forms.[62] For example, his opening example was the Quranic phrase "and their leaders came out; go and be patient" (Quran 38:6, Ṣād), which he explained as "and their leaders came out recommending to each other, or calling to each other, that they go and be patient."[63] This longer, clearer, version is Abu ʿUbaydah's *mağāz,* his deviation (or "going beyond") in vocal form while maintaining God's mental content.

Going beyond the lexicon is therefore not necessarily less accurate; we are not dealing with a situation in which there is truth (good!) and deviation (bad!). Instead we are dealing, as Heinrichs said, with different surface structures. These different surface structures had stable names that existed as a pair: *ḥaqīqah* and *mağāz* were defined, understood, and used together.[64] When they were used as a pair, it is clear to the reader that the two accounts of language structure that they described were interrelated. As we saw, Abū Hilāl used the fact of their interrelation to explain the meaning of *ḥaqīqah.* The question is whether this interrelationship still applied when the two terms were used separately. When Abū ʿUbaydah, Ibn Fūrak, or ar-Rāġib used *mağāz* or *ḥaqīqah,* did they do so with the assumption that all language was either one or the other? If so, what would be the *mağāz* version of a *ḥaqīqah* account of the extramental world? Can the translations "going beyond the lexicon" and "accurate account" be maintained? The reading I would like to advance is parallel to my reading of *maʿnā.* Just as I think *maʿnā* is best understood as "mental content," the stuff of cognition that can always potentially be expressed in vocal form, so I think that it is productive to read *ḥaqīqah* and *mağāz* as stable and mutually interdependent terms even in each other's absence. Although Abū ʿUbaydah never uses the word *ḥaqīqah* in his exegesis, it would not have been unrealistic for him to associate the Quranic text that he was deviating from with accuracy and correctness. *Mağāz* is therefore what moves away from

61. Weipert (2007).

62. فلمْ يحتجّ السلفُ .. أنْ يسألوا عن معانيه لأنهم كانوا عربَ الألْسُن .. وفي القرآن مِثل ما في كلام العرب من وُجوه الإعراب ومن الغريب والمعاني . . . ومِن مجازِ ما حُذِف وفيه مُضمَر. Abū ʿUbaydah (1954, 1:8.3–5, 6–7, 14).

63. ومِن المحتمل مِن مجازِ ما اختصَر وفيه مُضمرٌ قال وانطلَقَ الملأُ مِنهم أنْ امْشوا واصْبروا فهذا مختصَرٌ فيه ضميرٌ مجازُه وانطلق الملأُ منهم ثمّ اختصَر إلى فِعلهم وأضمَر فيه وتواصَوا أنْ امْشوا وتنادَوا أنْ امْشوا أو نحوَ ذلك. Abū ʿUbaydah (1954, 1:8.8–11).

64. Heinrichs (2016, 256).

some original and lexically validated literal, albeit without necessarily losing truth along the way. In a separate work, doing exegesis on poetry rather than revelation, Abū ʿUbaydah used the term *ḥaqīqah* to talk about a world of actual events that were reported in language. The poetry under consideration was from the famous Umayyad poet al-Farazdaq (d. ca. 728) and the line read:[65]

Do they offer vain threats?
Their impotent snakes have been seen.
It is a deadly serpent that bites and kills them.

Abū ʿUbaydah's lexicographical gloss for the verb "to make vain threats" was "mutual boasting without accuracy." The boast was inaccurate because it did not conform to a real world in which threats are made good upon. The threats were not real, and the poet had chosen to use a word that reflected a lack of accurate connection between speech and the world: al-Farazdaq's targets weren't "boasting"; they were "faking it."

For ar-Rāġib, the category of "going beyond the lexicon" is what happens when there is any deviation at all from the original lexical connection between vocal form and mental content. This could be anything from a complex metaphor to a dialect variation in pronunciation. The line above from al-Farazdaq, in which threats are impotent snakes, is quite clearly a departure from the lexicon, because vocal forms such as "snake" are not being used solely to describe animals in nature. A change of vowel pronunciation in certain dialects, however (such as moving from "love" to "luv" in English), is also going beyond the lexicon and moving away from the original act of placement.[66] This last example of vowel change should give readers a clue that what we have here with *maǧāz* is not a rejection of the lexicon or a call for its replacement with a realm of inexactitude. Instead, language that went beyond the original lexicon had now become part of a current one; this was one of the primary ways in which the lexicographers managed language change and development. They managed by enforcing restraint; in the lexicon the weight of precedent was heavy. All languages need rules based on the past, but at the same time languages need to adjust to changing circumstances and develop. This change could come from God, who altered the meaning of the word "prayer" when he stipulated the required prayers in his revelations, or from humans. In the eleventh century ar-Rāġib was well aware, as Abū ʿUbaydah had been in the ninth, that he was

65. أَيُفايِشُونَ وَقَدْ رَأَوْا حُفَّاثَهُمْ | قَدْ عَضَّهُ فَقَضَى عَلَيْهِ الأَشْجَعُ || قولُه أَيُفايِشُونَ قال المُفايَشَةُ المُفاخَرَةُ بلا حقيقةٍ. Abū ʿUbaydah (1998, 2:291.11–12).

66. الكلامُ ضرْبانِ حقيقةٌ ومجازٌ فالحقيقةُ اللفظُ المستعمَلُ في ما وُضِع له في أصل اللغة . . . [الحقيقةُ] اللفظُ المستعمَلُ في ما وُضِع له في أصل اللغة من غيرِ نَقْلٍ ولا زِيادةٍ ولا نُقصانٍ والمجازُ على عكسٍ من ذلك . . . فالمجازُ في المفردات .. نحوَ أَنْظُوْر في أَنْظُر. Ar-Rāġib (1984, 56.6–10), (ca. 14th C., fol. 4a.7–9).

no longer living in the speech community of the nomadic Bedouin, from whose pre-Islamic history of lexical precedent the first dictionaries had been collected. Ar-Rāġib remarked on this process of language evolution at multiple points in his Quranic glossary, using the word for "metaphor" (*isti'ārah,* a metaphor in which content is borrowed from a source). His dictionary sought to read God as having taken phrases from a nomadic lifestyle and turned them into language for a new community. The word *rawāḥ* ("afternoon passage") was borrowed from the rest (*rāḥah*) humans would take, or allow their camels to take, in the middle of the day.[67] The "abundant" (*midrāran*) rain had its lexical root in "milk" (*darr, dirrah*), and was one of the metaphors that borrowed the names and qualities of camels.[68] The verb "to pasture" came from the name of a thornless tree (*sarḥ*) that one fed to one's camel, and then every act of sending the camel to pasture came to have the same name. The verb "to release" in the Quran was borrowed from this pasturing of the camel, in just the same way as the word for "divorce" was borrowed from the setting-free of the camel.[69]

There is no question that what we are reading here is a theory of, and a taxonomical accounting for, language change that ascribes the changes to metaphorical usage. This was not unique to ar-Rāġib; over a century earlier al-Ǧāḥiẓ had used several of the same examples to explain that "if goaded, language will grow branches, and if its root principle is fixed, its arts will multiply and its pathways will broaden."[70] The process of language change had not stopped with the Quran in the seventh century, for the process of coining technical terminology required new word meanings that the lexicographers then had to record and curate: vocal forms "that specialists in any given discipline transfer from the initial conventional mental content to a different mental content of which only they are cognizant, so the vocal form in question remains shared between two mental contents. Vocal forms from divine revelation such as 'prayer' and 'tax' are examples of this process, as are the vocal forms which the jurists, theologians, and grammarians use."[71] All these new connections are, of course, departures from the lexicon. They are *maǧāz.*

67. وٱستُعيرَ الرواحُ للوقْت الذي يُراه الإنسانُ فيه مِن نِفس النهارِ ومنه قيل أَرَحْنا إبِلَنا. Quran 34:12 (Sabā'). Ar-Rāġib (1992, 371/1.4–6).

68. مِدْراراً وأَصْلُه مِن دَرّ والدِرّة أيْ اللبْن ويُستعار للمطر استعارةَ أسماء البَعير وأوْصافه. Quran 6:6 (al-An'ām), 11:52 (Hūd), 71:11 (Nūḥ). Ar-Rāġib (1992, 310/1.15–17).

69. السَرْحُ شَجَرٌ له ثمرٌ . . . وسَرَّحْتُ الإبلَ أصلُه أنْ تُرْعِيَهُ السرحَ ثم جُعِل لكلّ إرسالٍ في الرعْي . . . وقوله وَسَرِّحُوهُنَّ سَراحاً جَميلاً مستعارٌ من تسريحِ الأبل . . Quran 33:49 (al-Aḥzāb). Ar-Rāġib (1992, 406/1.21–/2.1–2,7–10).

70. والكلامُ إذا حُرِّكَ تَشعَّبَ وإذا ثُبِتَ أصلُه كَثُرتْ فنونُه واتَّسَعَتْ طُرُقُه. Al-Ǧāḥiẓ (1965a, 3:341.19–20), Miller (2016b, 64f, 75). The translation is mine.

71. هو الذي يَنقله أهلُ صناعةٍ ما عن المعنى المصطلَح عليه أوّلاً إلى معنىً آخرَ قد تفرّدوا بمعرفته فيَبقى

Departure from the lexicon is therefore not a route away from the truth or from accuracy. It could hardly be so when scholars actively used such departures to create new, more accurate and specialized technical terminology for their discipline of choice. What does this imply for the original accurate lexical connections? The most important implication is that the original lexical connection may not always be the best connection to make. This is true for hermeneutics and it is true for poetics. The accounts of literary innovation and eloquence that we will deal with in chapter 7, on al-Ǧurǧānī (I have dealt with ar-Rāġib's poetics elsewhere),[72] all rest on the breakdown of the accurate lexical connection between vocal form and mental content, and its replacement with a series of increasingly complex moves within mental contents themselves. When it came to hermeneutics the rewards were similar: "Some people pursue and demand accurate accounts in those verses where God uses analogy. They think that if the mental content in question doesn't have an accurate account then it is a lie."[73] Ar-Rāġib disagreed, because analogy could go beyond the lexicon and was central to all communication, including God's communication. It was also inherently valuable: "The analogy is the noblest vocal form because of the beauty of its comparison and syntax, and its brevity. The analogy is also the noblest mental content because it indicates both primary intent and subsequent connected intent, so it is a complete indication, not a partial one. It is oblique rather than straightforward, and there is a subtlety in oblique communication; it is the noblest level that speakers can attain."[74] When God compared paradise to a garden with rivers beneath it he was not using language according to the original lexicon, but he was using language effectively.

The combination of an accurate account of the world according to lexical precedent with the ability of speakers to go beyond that original lexicon gave language the potential to communicate more than the world and gave scholars like ar-Rāġib the ability to do poetics, hermeneutics, and philosophy at the same time. Mental content was at the heart of all three. An account of the world that was accurate was necessarily cognitive, and therefore was made up of mental content. An accurate reading of the language of others needed to identify their intent, which was their mental content, and then move it into one's own mind using the lexicon

---

من بعد مشترَكاً بين المَعْنِيَين وعلى ذلك الألفاظُ الشريعةُ نحو الصلاة والزكاة والألفاظُ التي يَستعملها الفقهاءُ والمتكلمون والنحويون. Ar-Rāġib (1984, 33.5–7).

72. Key (2012, 121f, 172f).

73. وبعضُ الناس تحرَّوا في آياتٍ ذكرها اللهُ تعالى على سبيل المَثَل تطلُّبَ الحقائق ورأَوا أنّ ذلك المعنى إذا لم يكن له وجودٌ على الحقيقة كان كِذباً. Ar-Rāġib (1984, 58.4–5).

74. فإنْ قيل فما الفائدةُ في العدول إلى المثل قيل المثلُ أشرفُ لفظاً لِما فيه من الصيغة في حُسن التشبيه والنظم واختصارِ اللفظ وأشرفُ معنىً لدلالته عل المقصود إليه وعلى غيره مما يُشاركه فدلالتُه دلالةٌ كلّيةٌ لا جزئيةٌ وتعريضٌ لا تصريحٌ وفي التعريض تلطّفٌ وهو أشرفُ منزلةٍ للمخاطبين. Ar-Rāġib (1988a, 183).

as a reference point. Poetics was about deliberately destabilizing that lexical reference point and equally about managing the degree of stability that remained. In all three spheres the taxonomical and theoretical activity of the scholars was indispensable. Someone had to write the accounts of mental content. Ar-Rāġib spent countless pages doing so. But the lexicographers were not the conservative recorders of Orientalist stereotype. As we have seen with Abū Hilāl and ar-Rāġib, they were prepared to follow their conceptual vocabulary and its linguistic origins into the thickets of the relationship between language, mind, and reality.

5

Theology

In this chapter, our scholars are talking about God. This is not the first time we have encountered him. God and the theological problems associated with his description have already appeared in chapter 4 on the lexicon, and they will appear again in chapters 6 and 7 on Aristotelian logic and poetics. Theological concerns, like concerns with language, cut across the genres and disciplines of eleventh-century scholarship. Everyone was playing the same game, in which the ball was *maʿnā* and the bat was *ḥaqīqah*. This is the chapter in which my translation of *maʿnā* as "mental content" comes under the most pressure.

FRAMING THEOLOGY

Islamic Theology (ʿilm al-kalām)

This chapter probes the sensitive boundary between words and things through a reading of theological debates at the nexus of language, mind, and reality. For Ibn Fūrak, *maʿnā* was a central theological concept at the core of an epistemology that linked humans to the divine. The word *maʿnā* appeared on both the human and the divine level, but it was an epistemological not an ontological framework that was being shared. Theology placed God and his creation in a single epistemological framework, where they were described by humans with the same conceptual vocabulary but remained incommensurable. This incommensurability is worth stressing at the outset.

A non-Arabist colleague recently asked me whether the theories I read in these Arabic texts were themselves coming out of a belief system, whether God and religion were driving eleventh-century Arabic accounts of meaning. After all, when one reads the accounts of how language signifies ideas or things in Samuel Coleridge, Walter Benjamin, or Paul De Man (to pick famous names on the question of language almost at random), the sign that is everywhere is a religious symbol.[1] The sign is Christ, a symbol of the eternal, opposed (for Coleridge) to the mechanical abstractions of allegory. But none of this helps answer the question of how the God of Islamic theology shared an epistemological framework with his creation, let alone how reference or allegory functioned in Arabic. A religious genealogy comparable to the Christian heritage of the sign is totally absent from the eleventh-century Arabic accounts of meaning. For the scholars under consideration in this book, the subject matter was unquestionably God, whereas the conceptual transmission history came from the disciplines of Arabic grammar and lexicography. Religion did not just lie in the background of Ibn Fūrak's epistemology; God was his epistemological goal. The knowledge was human, and the subject matter humans cared about knowing was divine.

The Arabic name of this discipline was *ʿilm al-kalām,* which up to this point I have simply been translating as "theology." But a literal translation would be "the science/discipline/knowledge of speech." How can theology, the study of God and his creation, have been given a disciplinary label related to speech? *ʿIlm al-kalām* did not contain, after all, any of the components we may expect a "science of speech" to contain in English. As we have seen, grammar, pragmatics, and lexical precedent were all studied elsewhere. The answer is that theologians like Ibn Fūrak knew that their discipline, which had grown up in the eighth and ninth centuries (Alexander Treiger),[2] was a discipline in which humans tried to talk accurately about both God and the world. What we have in *ʿilm a-kalām* is speech (people talking) about a variety of topics, structured according to foundational principles and subsequent statements. The speech had to be rational, and if it was not, Ibn Fūrak thought it would end up meaningless: "speech with no mental content behind it."[3] According to al-Ašʿarī, the variety of *ʿilm al-kalām* topics included "motion and rest, body and accident, colors and ways of being, the atom and the leap [the latter a contested argument against the indivisibility of atoms],[4] and finally the attributes of

1. Benjamin (1996), Coleridge (1816, 36–37), de Man (1983, 189).

2. Treiger (2016).

3. وكان [الأشعريُّ] يَبنِي الكلامَ في ذلك . . . وكان كثيراً ما يَبنِي كلامَه في . . . وعلى هذا الأصل يَبنِي الكلامَ في إطلاق القول بأنْ . . . وهذا كلامٌ لا يَحصل تحته معنى. Ibn Fūrak (1987, 101.7, 112.23, 162.8, 121.3).

4. Dhanani (1994, 160f).

the Creator."[5] Ar-Rāġib's definition was: "Knowledge of rational indicators, accurate demonstrative proofs, division and definition, the difference between reason and supposition, etc."[6] What we have before us here is a discipline that includes parts of what would be studied today in the natural sciences, philosophy, religion, and even in some parts of literary theory. And the name of this discipline in its eleventh-century Arabic context was "Speech about . . ." My reluctant working translation for *ʿilm al-kalām* will remain "theology."

This discipline of theology fits into our four scholars' careers in different ways. Both Ibn Fūrak and ar-Rāġib wrote creedal works designed to tell their readers what to believe,[7] and both wrote hermeneutic works designed to help their readers understand divine revelation. (Ar-Rāġib dealt with the Quran; Ibn Fūrak with both Quran and Hadith.)[8] Ar-Rāġib produced both a traditional exegesis of the Quran and an alphabetically ordered glossary.[9] Ibn Fūrak wrote a traditionally structured exegesis, which was itself largely structured as a verse-by-verse glossary: "If they ask you the mental content of this word, tell them it is . . ."[10] Ibn Fūrak also wrote on legal theory,[11] which ar-Rāġib did not, and ar-Rāġib composed books of ethics and of literary compilation and poetics,[12] which Ibn Fūrak did not. Ar-Rāġib's intellectual territory overlaps with Ibn Fūrak on questions of the divine, but his Neoplatonic/Aristotelian-flavored ethics and poetics also overlap with the work of Ibn Sīnā and al-Ǧurǧānī (the central figures of the next two chapters). Ibn Sīnā was cognizant of theological discourse but did not see himself as a participant. Al-Ǧurǧānī was in dialogue with theologians and made sure his account of language aesthetics was part of the discussion on God's language. The profile of ʿAbd al-Ǧabbār, the Muʿtazilī theologian whose work has already appeared in our discussions of translation, and whom we will meet again in this chapter, is closest to that of Ibn Fūrak. ʿAbd al-Ǧabbār and Ibn Fūrak both wrote exegesis of Quran and Hadith, legal theory, and theology.[13] They and al-Ǧurǧānī were taking part in the same conversations, which usually took the form of bitter arguments between

5. الكلام في الحركة والسكون والجِسم والعرض والألوان والأكوان والجزء والطفرة وصفات الباري. Al-Ašʿarī (1953b, #2).

6. معرفةُ الأدلّة العقلية والبراهين الحقيقية والتقسيم والتحديد والفرْق بين المقعولات والمظنونات وغيرِ ذلك. Ar-Rāġib (1984, 95).

7. Ibn Fūrak (1987), (2003); ar-Rāġib (1988a).

8. Ibn Fūrak (2003).

9. ar-Rāġib (1984), (1992), (2001), (2003).

10. Ibn Fūrak (2009a), (2009b), (2009c).

11. Ibn Fūrak (1906), (1999).

12. ar-Rāġib (1986), (1988b), (2006), (2007).

13. Heemskerk (2000, 36–52), (2007).

the Mu ʿtazilī and Aš ʿarī schools of theology about both substance and methodology. Every single scholar with whom I engage used the same core conceptual resources of *lafẓ*, *ma ʿnā*, and *ḥaqīqah* to talk about language, mind, and reality.

Relativism? Words or Things

In a discipline with "speech" in its title, translations of *ma ʿnā* must trace out the points at which Ibn Fūrak's concern for language shades into a concern for thought, or alternatively into a concern for the extramental world. But how do we know when we are reading his epistemology (a theory of knowledge), and when we are reading his ontology (an account of what actually is)? Ibn Fūrak's epistemology looks toward God, and his ontology includes God. But how does he mark the boundaries between language, mind, and reality? My predecessors have noticed with varying details of pained awareness that a linguistic threat always lurks when reading these Classical Arabic texts. Could they really just be talking about words? Was it all semantics rather than science? Michel Allard raised that very possibility in 1965.

Writing about the reportage in al-Aš ʿarī's *Maqālāt al-Islāmīyīn* on al-Aš ʿarī's famous Mu ʿtazilī teacher al-Ǧubbā ʾī, Allard argued that for the Mu ʿtazilah the empirical truth of the divine was unknowable and that discussions of the divine attributes were therefore just "opérations particulières de l'esprit humain qui essaye en son langage d'exprimer la totalité du mystère divin." These divine attributes, the things that God has or does, were a central topic in Islamic theology. (See Frank and Gimaret.)[14] For Allard, the judgments made by scholars like al-Aš ʿarī and al-Ǧubbā ʾī about God were rational but they: "ne l'atteignent pas dans sa réalite, mais manifestant la cohérence d'un langage humain."[15] The texts that led Allard to this conclusion were clear statements by al-Aš ʿarī that the Mu ʿtazilah held divine attributes to be aspects of speech acts, linguistic statements rather than actual things with ontological status.[16] (I deal with this doctrine below.) In 1965, Allard did not have access to the work of ʿAbd al-Ǧabbār, but al-Aš ʿarī's tenth-century assessment of the Mu ʿtazilī School was correct, and in the eleventh century ʿAbd al-Ǧabbār did state that the divine attribute is a human act of description.[17] It must have seemed to Allard that if scholars talk either about

14. Frank (1978), Gimaret (1988).

15. "Particular operations of a human spirit that was trying in its language to explain the totality of the divine mystery . . . did not reach God's reality, but rather showed the coherence of human language": Allard (1965, 122).

16. قالتْ المعتزلةُ والخوارجُ الأسماءُ والصفات هي الأقوال وهي قولُنا الله عالمٌ الله قادرٌ وما أشَبَه ذلك. Al-Aš ʿarī (1929–33, 172).

17. لأنّ الصفة هي القولُ كما أنه الوصف. Al-Qāḍī ʿAbd al-Ǧabbār (1965–74, 7:117).

words or about things, then the Muʿtazilah had been talking about words. Both Richard Frank and Johannes Peters inhabited the same twentieth-century world in which this was a key philosophical distinction and were extremely concerned at the prospect of *kalām* becoming not a science of the real but a vortex of linguistic relativism. Frank: "This is a distortion of both metaphysics and theology, for whatever feelings one may have about linguistic philosophy, to attempt to reduce the systematic thought of a medieval author to linguistic problems is to alienate it completely from its own proper sense."[18] Peters: "Should we conclude from all this that the qualities are the result of a purely intellectual activity which gives names to things, or even worse: Should we conclude that the qualities are only names and words arbitrarily given? Not at all."[19] Rarely in the literature do scholars take such a tone, and the fact that both men do so here is indicative of high twentieth-century academic stakes.

In his later work Frank came to see an "evocative richness" in the same overlap between language and external reality that had previously been of such concern, and he identified this richness as "a very basic aspect of their thought." But his translation strategy remained the same: the identification of different senses for key expressions that were "formally distinct but . . . nevertheless inseparably linked the one to the other."[20] This book is an attempt to continue the task that Frank began and work through more of the relationship between language, mind, and reality in these texts. But in order to do so, I would like to propose a different translation strategy, one that is in line with the methodology I outlined in chapter 3. As Frank and Allard both noted, we cannot afford to lose in translation the precision and rigor that these eleventh-century theologians brought to their work. They rarely appealed to some sphere of inexplicability, whether divine or human, but on the contrary constantly struggled to do what we now tend to call "science," a systematic attempt to understand how the world works. Their world included not just human beings but also God, and not just study of things in the extramental world but the study of language, meaning, and cognitive processes as well. Perhaps most important, however, scholars such as Ibn Fūrak were often very precise about the boundary between language and mind. For example, in his discussion of the optimal procedure for engaging in the dialectical theological debates of the eleventh century, Ibn Fūrak wrote that one should be careful not to give too much weight to aesthetically pleasing expressions but rather should "display the *maʿānī* to one's soul in order to determine what is true and what is invalid without reference to

18. Frank (1968, 299).

19. Peters (1976, 152).

20. Frank (1999, 189).

linguistic expressions."[21] I see this as a statement about cognition that privileges the mind over language; Ibn Fūrak thought that *maʿnā* was a sphere in which humans could exercise their judgment without language necessarily being involved.

In the eleventh century there was no cultural clash between scholars who cared about things and scholars who fetishized words. Instead, there was a conceptual vocabulary with *maʿnā* at its core. My argument resides in the experiment of reading Classical Arabic theology as *maʿnā*-centric and trying to work out from the evidence provided by usage both what sort of thing *maʿnā* was for them and how we can understand what it meant. Ibn Fūrak is my test case, and I hope that conclusions drawn here may prove informative for work on other scholars. My colleagues have noted the importance of language for these authors and the problem caused by the term *maʿnā*. Frank was well aware of language's cultural centrality,[22] and A. I. Sabra wrote that "the whole subject of language usage as a recognized argument in establishing *Kalām* doctrines deserves an extensive treatment, for which there is no space here."[23] Peters's important glossary of ʿAbd al-Ǧabbār's terminology has an entry for *maʿnā,* in which Peters writes that "some authors have been intrigued by this obscure concept. . . . To give a correct and clear translation of the word *maʿnā* is very difficult."[24] This is the point at which language and reality seem to overlap, the place where Frank located an "evocative richness," and it is here that we need to play their language games. *Maʿnā* is our ball.

THEOLOGIES DIRECTED AT THE WORLD

Language in ʿAbd al-Ǧabbār

The world that eleventh-century theologians wanted to understand was dominated by the observable phenomenon of human language. Scholars needed to use language to describe God, and in the process they needed to ask what language was and how it worked. Just as they were interested in the forces that caused objects to move in the world, with God inextricable from their accounts, so too were they interested in how language worked, and God was inextricable from these accounts too. In the above discussion of the threat of relativism, we encountered ʿAbd al-Ǧabbār's Muʿtazilī claim that God's divine attributes were in fact just human descriptions of him. Determined to preserve the ontological and epistemological transcendence and unity of the divine, the Muʿtazilah held that divine attributes

21. والطريق إلى التلخيص مِن ذلك عَرْضُ معانيها على النفس ليَفصِل بين حقّها وباطلها من دون العبارات. Ibn Fūrak (1987, 320.18–19).

22. Montgomery (2006, 38–39).

23. Sabra (2006, 209). Cf. Sabra (2009).

24. Peters (1976, 156 n. 234, 157).

were not eternal ontological things but rather human acts of description.[25] ʿAbd al-Ǧabbār then needed to explain how human acts of description worked. His explanation took the form of a structure of reference centered on how we use nouns.

When ʿAbd al-Ǧabbār wrote that *maʿānī* should not be confused with attributes, he was restating an established Muʿtazilī doctrine: "Attributes are speech acts, just as descriptions are speech acts."[26] Perhaps the clearest reason to make such a separation was that there was no theological risk involved in the multiplication of speech acts, whereas there was a substantial risk of polytheism involved in a theology that allowed the actual qualities or cognitive conceptions of God to multiply *ad infinitum*. The Muʿtazilah agreed with the Ašāʿirah about the existence and nature of *maʿānī*, just as they agreed about the monotheistic nature of the divine. The use of the word *maʿnā* was shared conceptual vocabulary between the two rival theological schools. They disagreed, but they did so from common conceptual ground, using shared terminological assumptions to play their language games.

Ibn Fūrak and ʿAbd al-Ǧabbār also shared a belief in the epistemological power of the lexicon and its lexicographer curators. The lexicographers were ʿAbd al-Ǧabbār's first point of call when he came to defend his statement about *maʿānī* being separate from attributes; it was they who represented language precedent and provided (alongside the Quranic text of the revelation) an epistemological backstop for his theories about language usage.[27] The lexicon was for ʿAbd al-Ǧabbār a stable system in which every expression communicated a certain matter, and it was the default state for language: "Absent any obstacles, expressions must be used to refer to everything that they specify."[28] This may seem to be a very tight and restrictive view of what language can do. But ʿAbd al-Ǧabbār was in fact arguing for the ability of language to do more, and he was using the lexicographers as his alibi. He was engaged in dismissing his own caricature of his opponents' position on the legitimacy of human descriptions of God: according to him they denied that God's speech could be described, but he said that lexicography proved that humans could and should use words to describe whatever those words applied to. ʿAbd al-Ǧabbār also had another division of language usage that we have not yet

25. قالت المعتزلةُ والخوارج الأسماءُ والصفات هي الأقوالُ وهي قولُنا اللهُ عالمٌ اللهُ قادرٌ وما أشبه ذلك. Al-Ašʿarī (1929–33, 172). لأنّ الصفة هي القولُ كما أنه الوصف. Al-Qāḍī ʿAbd al-Ǧabbār (1965–74, 7:117).

26. وبيَّنَا أنّ تسمية المعاني بأنها صفاتٌ لا تَصح لأنّ الصفات هي القولُ كما أنه الوصف. Al-Qāḍī ʿAbd al-Ǧabbār (1965–74, 7:117.10–11). Cf. Peters (1976, 151 n. 213).

27. Al-Qāḍī ʿAbd al-Ǧabbār (1965–74, 7:117.12, 5:251.19, 5:255.7f).

28. لأنّ كلّ عبارةٍ أفادتْ في اللغة أمرًا ما فيجِب إجراؤها على كلّ ما اختُصّ بذلك إلا المانع. Al-Qāḍī ʿAbd al-Ǧabbār (1965–74, 7:118.3–4).

encountered. He gave an account of how language worked as labeling (*laqab*) and an account of how language worked without labeling.

ʿAbd al-Ğabbār was discussing whether or not it was legitimate to describe God as a thing. This was another established and characteristic debate in Islamic theology. (For a representative review, see Brodersen.)[29] ʿAbd al-Ğabbār believed that God was a thing, and he held this position because of his understanding of what language was and how language worked. He wrote that "our speech act 'thing' records everything that can truly be known and reported on." To put this another way, we use the word "thing" for everything that we know and can talk about, everything we can predicate of something else, everything about which we can say, 'that is a . . .'" For this reason, we use "thing" to name all kinds of different things with different descriptions in different classes. ʿAbd al-Ğabbār immediately contrasted this way of using language with an epistemologically separate category of language use, the label (*laqab*): "If ['thing'] were a label, then it would single out something specific to the exclusion of everything else, and if what was being communicated was a class or an attribute, then it would equally be necessary for 'thing' to single out that class or attribute to the exclusion of all others."[30]

ʿAbd al-Ğabbār then sharpened the distinction between these two kinds of language usage. Using words as labels "communicates," but words can also be used to report on what is known without necessarily communicating what is known.[31] This seems to be counterintuitive, but he has a specific understanding of what it means to communicate here, which he makes clear with some examples from ordinary language. According to ʿAbd al-Ğabbār, the speech acts "I saw a thing" and "I saw" are identical with respect to what they communicate.[32] The word "thing" does not therefore communicate anything accurately, although it does report something that can be truly known. This is an account of how language reference works, an account that makes a distinction between language-as-label, which communicates, and language that does not meet that standard. ʿAbd al-Ğabbār was sensitive to the criticism that it is inappropriate to use the latter, less rigorously referential, kind of language to describe God. He wrote that words that do not communicate may still be used to report on a particular thing: "a body," for example, is a speech act that

29. Brodersen (2014, 473–76).

30. لأن قولنا شيءٌ يقع على كلِّ ما يَصح أنْ يُعلم ويُخبر عنه ولذلك تُسمّى به الأشياءُ على اختلافها واختلافِ أوصافها وأجناسها ولو كان لقباً يَختصّ شيئاً معيَّناً لَوَجَبَ أنْ يُخَصّ به دون غيرِه ولو أفاد جِنساً أو صفةً لَوَجَبَ أنْ يُختصّ به دون غيره. Al-Qāḍī ʿAbd al-Ğabbār (1965–74, 5:249.7–10).

31. هذا الاسمُ وإنْ كان يَجري على كلِّ ما يَصح أنْ يُعلم ويُخبر عنه فإنه لا يُفيد ذلك فيه. Al-Qāḍī ʿAbd al-Ğabbār (1965–74, 5:250.4–5).

32. لأنّ قولِ القائل رأيْتُ شيئاً ورأيْتُ في الفائدة سواء. Al-Qāḍī ʿAbd al-Ğabbār (1965–74, 250.8–9).

applies only to substances but that does not formally communicate "substance."[33] In these cases, it is possible to consider the noncommunicating speech act to be, in effect, working as a label, and this makes it acceptable for "thing" to be used for God.[34]

But there are still two separate kinds of language. Just like twentieth-century analytical philosophers of language, ʿAbd al-Ğabbār wanted to give an account of language (or at least of nouns) that was strictly referential: "The label is what specifies the thing labeled and singles it out so it receives a determination that functions in the same way as a physical gesture of indication."[35] But unlike twentieth-century advocates of language as reference, ʿAbd al-Ğabbār understood some ordinary language to fall short of that standard, in this case the word "thing." One the one hand, there was language that functioned according to a strict account of reference, in which a word applied to what it specified (whether an instance or a class) and nothing else. On the other hand, there was language that was used in context, speech acts that might at times work in the same way as labels but that did not provide the same epistemological specificity. Theology was the driver of this discussion, because the question of how to describe God forced theorists like ʿAbd al-Ğabbār to confront the degree to which they understood language as referential. (One cannot physically point at God.) He was also using vocabulary from earlier Muʿtazilī discussions of whether "thing" could be used for what God had not yet created.[36] And his vocabulary itself came from theories of grammar and lexicography in which the "label" was one way to talk about the proper noun or name. By the eleventh century, these resources enabled ʿAbd al-Ğabbār both to parse the theological legitimacy of certain speech acts and to reach conclusions about how language itself functioned. The conclusion he ultimately reached was that strict accounts of reference were possible, but strict reference did not work for God.[37]

ʿAbd al-Ğabbār reached this conclusion with the help of two conceptual frameworks with which we are already familiar, the lexicon and accuracy. The difference between the categories of label and not-label is that a label can be changed without

33. لأنّ قولنا جِسمٌ لا يقع إلا على الجواهر وإنْ كان لا يُفيد ذلك فيه. Al-Qāḍī ʿAbd al-Ğabbār (1965–74, 5:250.6–7).

34. فمِن حيث [الشيءُ] يقع على كلِّ ما هذه حالُه صار كأنه مُفيدٌ فلذلك وَصَفْنا اللهَ جلّ وعزّ به ولا يَمتنِع أنْ يقال إنه في حُكمِ اللقب وإنْ لم يكن لَقَبٌ. Al-Qāḍī ʿAbd al-Ğabbār (1965–74, 5:250.11–١٣).

35. لأنّ اللقب هو ما عيَّن الملقَّب وخصّص لِيقع به التعريفُ الجاري مَجرى التخصيص بالإشارة. Al-Qāḍī ʿAbd al-Ğabbār (1965–74, 5:250.13–14).

36. Al-Ašʿarī (1929–33, 161.8–10, 522.15f), Frank (1982, 262–63, 277–78 n. 9). Cf. Frank (1984, 49).

37. أنّ اللقب المَحْض الذي يَختص الأعيانَ هو الذي لا يَجري عليه تعالى . . . Al-Qāḍī ʿAbd al-Ğabbār (1965–74, 5:203.14–15).

affecting the lexicon (what Frank calls "arbitrary denomination"),[38] whereas nouns that are not labels cannot be changed without affecting the lexicon. As Abū Hilāl put it, describing a black thing as white is lying, but labeling a black thing "white" is not.[39] Just as we saw the lexicon function for ar-Rāġib and Ibn Fūrak as a limit, so the lexicon works for ʿAbd al-Ǧabbār as a ground in which he can anchor word usage that cannot be justified by a strict account of reference. A label simply points at something, but other nouns rely on the lexicon, and therefore on precedent, to make sense.[40] The paradigm of accurate reference is therefore the label, close to what we may call a proper noun, and independent of the lexicon. The vast majority of language, however, relies on the lexicon. In the lexicon, nouns point to *maʿānī*, and with some painfully circular Arabic syntax that I will avoid by way of paraphrase, ʿAbd al-Ǧabbār explained how these *maʿānī* could still make sense in the absence of accurate reference: the only *maʿnā* that the speech act "thing" communicates is a bringing together of everything that can be known and reported on with this noun.[41] That is how the noun "thing" is placed in the lexicon.[42] It communicates a *maʿnā*, and it is therefore appropriate to use it to talk about God, because the *maʿnā* in question is such that God is one of the things that can be reported upon. But "thing" cannot be a label for God.

What we see in the work of ʿAbd al-Ǧabbār, exemplified in this brief review of his position on whether or not God can be called a "thing," is a broad conviction that when it comes to the vast chasm between God and humanity, language falls on the human side. The lexicon was developed by human beings and is used by human beings. Language was a human lexicon, determined by precedent rather than reason or revelation.[43] The use that human beings make of their language does not have an impact on God: "Negating his name does not negate him."[44] Ibn Fūrak agreed that this separation existed, writing that if someone were to protest

38. Frank (1982, 263).

39. فالقائلُ للأسودِ أبيضُ على الصفة كاذبٌ وعلى اللقب غيرُ كاذب. Abū Hilāl (2006, 41.17–18).

40. إنّ شيءٌ [كذا] وإنْ لم يُفِد في الحقيقة على ما نُبيّنه بعدُ فإنه مخالِفٌ للّقبِ المحضِ ولذلك لا يصح تبديلُه مع بقاءِ اللغة كما لا يصح ذلك في الأسماء المفيدةِ ولذلك لا يصح أنْ يَزال عن جِهته مع بقاءِ اللغة كالألقاب. Al-Qāḍī ʿAbd al-Ǧabbār (1965–74, 5:202.3–5).

41. يُبيَّن ذلك أنّ ما له ولأجله لم يُفِد قولُنا شيءٌ معنىً يَرجِع إلى المسمّى دونَه وهو أنّ جميعَ ما يصح تسميتُه هو ما يَستعمِل عليه هذا الاسم وهو كلُّ ما يصح أنْ يُعلم وأنْ يُخبر عنه. Al-Qāḍī ʿAbd al-Ǧabbār (1965–74, 5:202.6–8).

42. Al-Qāḍī ʿAbd al-Ǧabbār (1965–74, 5:203.8–9).

43. أنّ استعمالَ الأسماء والأوصاف يَحسُن مِن جهة اللغة . . . اللغةُ هي الأصلُ كما أنّ أصلَ . . . ما يُعلم مِن جهة السمْع فأدِلّةُ السمْع هي الأصلُ وما يُعلم بالعقل فهو الأصلُ فيه. Al-Qāḍī ʿAbd al-Ǧabbār (1965–74, 5:197.4–7).

44. فليس في نفيِ الاسم نفيُه. Al-Qāḍī ʿAbd al-Ǧabbār (1965–74, 5:251.6).

that God, in commanding the unbeliever to believe, was ordering something he knew to be impossible (a key Muʿtazilī ethical argument with which the Ašāʿirah disagreed), then the answer should be: "Impossibility here is only in the speech act. The one who says 'impossible' moves a speech act away from the norms of truth and correctness and into error and falsity. It is not the person commanded who is impossible."[45] Neither Ibn Fūrak nor ʿAbd al-Ǧabbār thought that a human speech act could of itself create reality or determine the nature of God. But ʿAbd al-Ǧabbār came to this position through a thoroughgoing separation of human language from the divine sphere.

Atoms, Bodies, and Accidents with Ibn Fūrak

Ibn Fūrak's extramental world was composed of atoms that were combined into bodies. The eleventh-century theological texts do not all describe themselves as primarily engaged in the pursuit of atoms, but they almost all deal with atoms as an important question of fact, and this has proved a useful and productive lens with which to fit Islamic theology into the history of a scientific field that traditionally starts with Democritus and could be seen to end with the Large Hadron Collider.[46] Just as the beginnings of pre-Socratic Greek philosophy had been concerned with "the physical constitution of the universe," so a concern for atoms, accidents, space, and void had started in Arabic in the eighth century.[47] Atomism has been one of the central ways in which Anglophone and European scholarship has approached Islamic theology. But what would our reading of eleventh-century Islamic theology look like if it focused on *maʿānī* rather than on atoms? Ibn Fūrak was certainly concerned with the physical world; his investment in things both created and divine is clear. What did he say about atoms and *maʿnā*, and what happens if we try to continue the experiment of always translating *maʿnā* as "mental content"?

Chapter 37 of the *Muǧarrad* deals with the atom. It is the smallest division of reality possible, the "indivisible part" one reaches when dividing the composite bodies that constitute the world.[48] Ibn Fūrak describes this chapter as particularly subtle and intricate theology, subtle and intricate speech about God and the world.[49] He writes that all bodies in the world are composed of indivisible atoms according to the *maʿnā* that "every atom cannot be halved or divided into thirds

45. إنّ المُحال إنما يكون في القول وهو القولُ الذي أحالَه قائلُه عن سُنَن الحقّ والصواب إلى وجهِ الخطأ والبطلان وليس المأمورُ به مُحالاً. Ibn Fūrak (1987, 116.4–7).

46. Dhanani (1994); Sabra (2006), (2009); Wolfson (1976, 466f).

47. Gutas (2004, 199).

48. اعلمْ أنه كان يقول إنّ أجسام العالَم متركِّبةٌ من أجزاء غيرِ متجزّئة. Ibn Fūrak (1987, 202.13).

49. فصلٌ آخر في باب إيضاح مذاهبه في اللطيف من الكلام والدقيق. Ibn Fūrak (1987, 202.10).

or quarters. It cannot be contemplated that an atom could be divided or partitioned in such a way as to produce further divisions, parts, or atoms."[50] Ibn Fūrak also reported that belief in infinitely divisible parts was false, equivalent to the religiously controversial belief that bodies were cosmologically arranged in some form of vertical hierarchy: "There is no difference between the statement that every atom can be halved and the halves halved again, and the statement that every body has a body above it and a body below it."[51] Here we see an Islamic theological commitment to monotheism that uses avoidance of Neoplatonism as a reason to commit to atomism. (Cf. Herbert Davidson on Abū Yūsuf b. Isḥāq al-Kindī, d. ca. 870, and John Philoponus, d. ca. 570.)[52] We also see a determination to direct theology toward the real world. It is the physical bodies of the world that are at stake here.

But human cognition is involved. In Ibn Fūrak's quotation, al-Aš ʿarī used the word *maʿnā* in much the same way as Abū ʿUbaydah had: to introduce a conceptual paraphrase ("according to the *maʿnā* that . . .") A few sentences later, Ibn Fūrak used *maʿnā* again, this time as a label for causal factors in the agglomeration and subdivision of bodies. He explained that just as there was an upper limit on the process of combining bodies, so there had to be a lower limit on to what extent those combinations could be unwound to result in individual atoms: "The fact that there is a limited number of *maʿānī* by which bodies come together or are separated proves that the atoms are in themselves indivisible from all aspects."[53] This is a similar usage of *maʿnā* to Muʿammar's cause; *maʿnā* here, in Ibn Fūrak, is a factor that brings together atoms to make a body. (Cf. Herbert Davidson.)[54] We may in English introduce a conceptual paraphrase with "according to the idea that . . . ," and we may say that there is "a limited number of factors involved" in the combination or subdivision of bodies. Where we use "idea" and "factor," Arabic used *maʿnā*.

Atoms had *maʿānī*. For example, the quality of being is a *maʿnā* held to subsist in the atom itself. Another *maʿnā* is combination, which is in the atom when it is

50. اعلمْ أنه كان يقول إن أجسام العالَم متركّبة من أجزاء غير متجزّئة على معنى أن كلّ جزءٍ منها لا يصح أنْ يكون له نِصف أو ثُلث أو رُبع ولا يُتوهّم أنْ يَنقسم أو يتبعّض حتى يصير أقساماً وأبعاضاً وأجزاء. Ibn Fūrak (1987, 202.13–15).

51. وإنه لا فرْقَ بين قول مَن قال إنه لا جزءَ إلا وله نِصف ولنصفه نِصف وبين قول مَن قال إنه لا جِسمَ إلا وفوقَه جسم وتحته جسم لا إلى نهاية. Ibn Fūrak (1987, 202.16–18). Herbert Davidson (1987, 106f, 115). Thanks to Rodrigo Adem for the reference.

52. Herbert Davidson (1969).

53. وكان يقول إن ما دلَّ على حَدَث الأجسام دلَّ على تناهيها وإنّ ما فيها من الاجتماع والانضمام الذي عنه التجزّؤ والافتراقُ محصورٌ فكذلك ما يَعتقِبه من ضدّه من أجزاء الافتراق محصورٌ وانحِصارُ المعاني التي بها تجتمع وتفترِق دليلٌ على أنّ الأجزاء متناهيةٌ في نفسها من جميع جهاتها. Ibn Fūrak (1987, 202.19–22).

54. Herbert Davidson (1987, 55).

combined with another atom.[55] It is the *ma'nā* of being that makes a certain body actually be in a place.[56] Furthermore, the being *ma'nā*, just like a color *ma'nā*, is inevitable and necessary for any substance.[57] (Substance is the material substrate, composed of atoms, from which bodies are formed.)[58] So atoms combine to make bodies, and *ma'ānī* are present on both levels: a single atom that exists in a place has the *ma'nā* being, and a body made up of combined atoms has the *ma'nā* being. One thing that is apparent here is that atoms, like God, are an ontological category that works as a *terminus ad quem*, a final epistemological point beyond which there is nothing. But the same is not true of *ma'ānī*, which can be added on to various levels of extramental things in the world just as they can qualify things in the mind.

The *ma'ānī* that atoms had were accidents, those Aristotelian nonessential qualities or properties of things (for example, "red" as a quality of a chair).[59] For Ibn Fūrak, these *ma'ānī* accidents included, in addition to color, qualities such as being, which was necessary for an atom to exist, or being gathered together, which happened when atoms joined together to form bodies and substances.[60] An accident was a *ma'nā* that "does not subsist in itself."[61] The phrase "subsist in itself" was used to distinguish between bodies and substances on the one hand and accidents on the other: accidents did not subsist in themselves, and they required a place in which they could inhere,[62] whereas what did subsist in itself was a category largely reserved for the divine. (See below and Gimaret.)[63] Bodies composed of substance could also exist without a place, because Ibn Fūrak's system allowed for

55. وكان يقول إنّ الجزء الواحد يَحتمِل جميعَ الأعراض المتعاقِبة عليها وإنّ الذي به يكون كائناً في المكان إذا كان مكانٌ وهو كونٌ فيه موجودٌ وبه قائمٌ في كلّ حالٍ سواءٌ كان منفرداً أو مجتمعاً وإنْ كان مجتمعاً مع غيره كان ذلك المعنى اجتماعاً له مع غيره. Ibn Fūrak (1987, 203.4–7).

56. المعنى الذي يختصّ الجسمَ فيكون لأجله في مكان دون مكان هو الذي يُسمّى كون. Ibn Fūrak (1987, 262.15).

57. وإنّ الجوهر لا يجوز أنْ يخلو من الكون كما لا يجوز أنْ يخلو من اللون. Ibn Fūrak (1987, 242.11).

58. ويقول إنّ أقلّ ما يقع عليه اسمُ الجسم جَوهرانِ مختلفان. Ibn Fūrak (1987, 206.15–16). Cf. Peters (1976, 121).

59. Arist. *Metaph.* 1026b35–1027a1.

60. وكان يقول إنّ الجزء الواحد يحتمل جميع الأعراض المتعاقبة عليه وإنّ الذي به يكون كائناً في المكان إذا كان مكان وهو كونٌ . . . وإنْ كان مجتمِعاً مع غيره كان ذلك المعنى اجتماعاً له مع غيره. Ibn Fūrak (1987, 203.4–7).

61. العرض . . . فأما ما اصطلح عليه المتكلمون فهو المعاني التي لا تقوم بأنفسها. Ibn Fūrak (1987, 333.5).

62. حادِثٌ يَقتضي محلّاً يقوم به وهو العرض لا يصح حدوثه قائماً بنفسه. Ibn Fūrak (1987, 276.5–6).

63. See note 96 below and Gimaret (1990, 37).

the possibility of existence prior to the creation of the world.[64] Bodies could not be thought of as combinations of accidents, however, because an accurate account of "accident" was that it did not subsist in itself, and this held true even if it was combined with other accidents. Bodies had accidents (a chair could be red) but accidents didn't have accidents of their own. (Red couldn't be yellow, and a combination of different accidental qualities couldn't, without at least an atom, have an accident of its own.)[65] Accidents were also different from bodies, because accidents could have opposites, but bodies could not. (Black is the opposite of white, but a man is not the opposite of a horse.)[66]

Ibn Fūrak's discourse about accidents helps us see what his *maʿānī* were. They were not bodies composed of atomic substance but rather qualities that were dependent on those bodies and atoms. They were also subject to some simple logical operations, such as having an opposite. But this was not the only usage Ibn Fūrak made of *maʿnā*. As we saw in "Two Distinct Lexemes" above in chapter 3, Ibn Fūrak used *maʿnā* to talk about the mental content occasioned by speech acts: "The *maʿnā* of [the speech act] 'X is an accident' is that X is a *maʿnā* that exists in an atom."[67] When he argued with other scholars' understanding of "body," he talked about "the *maʿnā* of the body."[68] This refers to the mental content in the mind of the theologian when defining the concept "body." In play are not two separate lexemes but rather one piece of core conceptual vocabulary in Arabic that maps the mind and its interaction with language in a way that English does not. Let us consider how Ibn Fūrak talked about the *maʿnā* of being gathered together: "If the atom is gathered together with another atom, then the *maʿnā* in question is the atom's 'gathering together' with the other atom."[69] The first part of this translation, before the comma, deals with extramental reality. The second part, after the comma, deals with mental existence. The *maʿnā* here is a piece of content that is located in the theologians' minds and enables them to think about, and then name, the behavior of the two atoms in question.

64. وإنْ كان حادثاً لا في مكانٍ فهو بحيث أنْ لو وُجِد مكانٌ كان فيه. Ibn Fūrak (1987, 211.18–19).

65. . . . واعلمْ أنه كان يذهب إلى احالةَ قول مَن قال إنّ الجسم مركّب من أعراض جُمِعَتْ وأبعاض أُلِّفَتْ بل كان يقول إنّ العرض الواحد والأعراض الكثيرة حُكمُها سواء مِن قِبَل أنّ ما له من الحدّ والحقيقة لا يختلف بالقِلّة والكُثرة . . . وحُكم العرض الواحد وشرطُه أنه يستحيل أنْ يكون قائماً بنفسه محتملاً للعرض . . . فأما ما اصطلح عليه المتكلمون فهو المعاني التي تقوم بأنفسها. Ibn Fūrak (1987, 211.8–13, 333.5).

66. لا عَرَضٌ مِن الأعراض إلا وله ضِدٌّ مِن مُوافِقٍ أو مخالفٍ ولا يصح وجودُ عَرَضٍ لا ضِدَّ له وكذلك لا يصح وجودُ جوهرٍ له ضِدٌّ ولا وجودُ ضِدٍ لجوهر. Ibn Fūrak (1987, 261.20–21).

67. See chapter 3 note 45 above.

68. وإنْ أجاب مجيبٌ بأنّ حقيقة معنى الجسم . . . مَن ذهب من المعتزلة إلى أنّ معنى الجسم . . . Ibn Fūrak (1987, 29.19–20, 210.16).

69. وإنْ كان مجتمِعاً مع غيره كان ذلك المعنى اجتماعاً له مع غيره . . . Ibn Fūrak (1987, 203.6–7).

Bodies, composed of atoms, moved with a *maʿnā* that was movement. The accurate account of movement was that it was a *maʿnā* that took a body from one place to another; there was nothing else in movement of which one could give an accurate account.[70] As such, this *maʿnā* of movement was visible to the eye, just as the other *maʿānī* of color, combination, and separation were also observable.[71] But this *maʿnā* was not caused by another: *maʿānī* couldn't stack up behind each other in a causal chain as Muʿammar had thought. As always, the question looming in the background was the divine attributes of God. Whereas Muʿammar had said that God's essential attribute of knowledge was there because of a chain of infinite causal *maʿānī*,[72] Ibn Fūrak denied that there could even be two links in such a chain: God's knowledge was a *maʿnā*, and it couldn't have its own *maʿnā* of knowing.[73] This is compatible with Ibn Fūrak's account of the justice of God's acts: the justice is in the specific instance of an act; justice does not depend on a separate *maʿnā*.[74] Ibn Fūrak did not want to allow the proliferation of *maʿānī* behind the divine unity or command of God, and unlike Muʿammar he did not think that use of the word *maʿnā* was a way out of this monotheistic bind.

Ibn Fūrak's *maʿānī* had causal roles only when it came to the extramental reality of objects moving. When it came to God, the *maʿānī* were limited and static: God's knowledge was a *maʿnā*, but it was not caused by anything else, *maʿnā* or otherwise. The *maʿnā* as cause was a human issue. For example, Ibn Fūrak wrote that the word *ʿillah* (a cause or reason, translated by Frank as "ground") could, "like the accidents and the rest of the *maʿānī* that subsist in substances," be called a *maʿnā*.[75] Just as an accident was a specific kind of *maʿnā*, so the *ʿillah* was a different specific kind of *maʿnā*, the kind that was a cause requiring humans to act according to a specific scholarly ruling. We know these particular causal judgments were the

70. سأل [سائلٌ] فقال هل للحركة حقيقة سواءها فأجاب [الأشعريُّ] بأنه ليستْ لها حقيقةٌ غيرها بل حقيقتُها نفسُها وهى أنه معنىً يتحرّك به المتحرِّكُ ويُفرغ مكاماً ويَشغَل مكاناً. Ibn Fūrak (1987, 333.6–8).

71. وكان يقول إنّ الألوان والحركات مَرئيّةٌ لَنا الآن وكذلك الاجتماع والافتراق. Ibn Fūrak (1987, 333.10–11).

72. وأما معمّرٌ فحكى عنه محمدٌ بن عيسى السيرافي النظامي أنه كان يقول إنّ البارئ عالِمٌ بعِلمٍ وإنّ عِلمُه كان عِلمَه له لمعنىً وكان المعنى لمعنىً لا إلى غاية. Al-Ašʿarī (1929–33, 488.3–5), van Ess (1991–95, 5: 267–68).

73. ويأبى أنْ يُوصف العِلم بأنه عالِمٌ أو تُوصف الحركة بأنها متحرّكةٌ لأن ذلك يؤدي إلى قيامِ معنىً بها فلا يَحتمِل المعنى معنىً. Ibn Fūrak (1987, 39.18–19).

74. إنّ أفعال الله تعالى عدْلٌ وحِكمةٌ وحقٌّ وحَسَنٌ لِأَعْيانها لا لمعنى. Ibn Fūrak (1987, 140.12–13).

75. أنّ العلّة هو المعنى الذي يَتعلق به الحُكمُ المُوجَبُ عنه وكان لا يأبى تسميةَ المعاني التي تَقُوم بالجواهر كالأعراضِ الحادثةِ القائمةِ بها عِلَلٌ. Ibn Fūrak (1987, 303.4–5, 310.7f). Cf. Frank (2004, 755).

result of worldly hermeneutics, because they could be wrong: apostates had their false reasoning (*iʿtilāl*).[76]

One thing that brings all *maʿānī* together is the fact that they could always be expressed in language. This led to a tension, inherent in the development of these theories of theological physics, between the role played by the lexicon on the one hand and by human reason on the other. Ibn Fūrak complained that al-Astarābāḏī, the rival scholar who had scooped his book on al-Ašʿarī, had mistakenly adduced a statement that there was nothing in an accident of which one could give an accurate account. Ibn Fūrak said this could not be true because al-Ašʿarī had understood the accident "according to the lexicon" as simply "that which presented itself." One could, therefore, give an accurate account of the category of accident, a lexically accurate account.[77] Elsewhere, the position that bodies in the state of coming to be were not moving was characterized by Ibn Fūrak as being: "according to the lexicon, not according to reason, because the lexicographers call the body 'moving' when it is in one place and then is moved to another. The body in the state of coming to be, however, has not been in a previous place." In both these cases the lexicon is the arbiter of correct descriptions of forces in extramental reality. Ibn Fūrak calls this theorizing "from the perspective of the lexicon." But he goes on to say that while the existence of a body in a state of coming to be is not called "movement," it is nevertheless: "in the *maʿnā* of what is called 'movement.'"[78] This is theorizing "from the perspective of rational minds," and it uses *maʿnā* as the arbitrating structure. But even here, the lexicon is an indispensable part of the process: Ibn Fūrak can make the argument that the *maʿnā* of the vocal form "coming to be" is the same *maʿnā* referred to by the vocal form "moving" only because of the existence of a lexicon in which *maʿānī* map onto vocal forms. The same tension can be found in the opening chapter of the *Muǧarrad* on knowledge: al-Ašʿarī is asked for the causal factor behind God's knowledge, and he answers that God's knowledge is knowledge not because of some equation or relation but rather because the word "knowledge" is derived in the lexicon from the word "knowing." God is unquestionably "knowing," so there is no need for

76. . . . ومِثالُ ذلك في اعتلال الملحد فيما يدّعيه مِن قِدَم العالَم. Ibn Fūrak (1987, 296.17f).

77. ثم حكى عنه بعد ذلك أنه كان يقول إنّ العرَض ليستْ لها حقيقةٌ فهذا أيضاً خطأ فاحش لأنّ العرَض عنده ما يعرض من طريق اللغة ولا يختصّ ما يقوم بنفسه ممّا لا يقوم فأما ما اصطلح عليه المتكلمون فهو المعاني التي تقوم بأنفسها. Ibn Fūrak (1987, 333.3–5).

78. وكان يقول إنه لا يصح أنْ يكون [الجسمُ] متحرّكاً في حالِ حُدوثه من طريقِ امتناعِ تسميته بذلك مِن جهة اللغة لا مِن جهة العقول وذلك أن أهلُ اللغة سمّوا الجسمَ متحرّكاً إذا كان في مكانٍ ثم انتقَل منه إلى غيره والجسمُ في حالِ حُدوثه لم يكن كان في مكان قبله وانتقل عنه إليه ولذلك لا يُسمَّى ما فيه من الكون حركةً ولكنه هو بمعنى ما يسمَّى حركةً. Ibn Fūrak (1987, 211.20–24).

further investigation into the causes of his knowledge.[79] Here the lexicon is the ultimate adjudicator; it is the morphological structure of the Arabic language that provides the reason for God's knowledge. *Maʿnā* is the arbitrating structure, and it functions only through the lexicon.

Ibn Fūrak asked whether "re-creation" was in the same *maʿnā* space as "re-created." Should these two separate stages of a single process be placed in the same category?[80] This was a matter of whether, in an occasionalist world, things maintained their identity during a process of change. A black object, described as such, did not continue being black but rather was constantly recreated as black with a series of imperceptible handovers.[81] Being black was an accidental quality, but the same principle applied to substances themselves; a substance could have the *maʿnā* of continuance, and that *maʿnā* could be constantly recreated to ensure its stability.[82] This was Ibn Fūrak's Ašʿarī occasionalism. It applied only to the created world: God could have a permanent *maʿnā* of continuance, as we will see below, but in the world he continually re-created the *maʿnā* of continuance in bodies.

The problem with this theory was that when combined with the doctrine of different descriptions occupying the same *maʿnā* space, it led to contradictions. For example, a body that was being initialized would, at the time of its initialization, also be already re-created, because "initialization" was in the same *maʿnā* space as "re-creation," and "re-creation" was coterminous with "re-created." This is a theory of extramental physical forces and qualities: substances in the world have colors, and bodies in the world continue to exist. The problem for Ibn Fūrak was how to construct a rationally consistent account of these physical forces and qualities. He dealt with the initialization/re-created contradiction by making a distinction between *maʿnā* on the one hand and language on the other. It was true that an existent thing in the process of initialization had the same *maʿnā* as an existent thing that had been re-created. But escape lay in the lexicon: "An existent thing in the process of initialization is not actually named 're-created' in the

79. فسأل نفسَه فقال إنْ قال قائلٌ فلِما كان العالِمُ عالِماً ألأجل أنّ العِلم علمٌ أم لأجل أنّ العِلم عِلمٌ وأنه مضافٌ إليه فأبطلهما وقال إنما كان العالِم عالِماً لِما اشتُقّ منه اسمُ العالِم . . . [بياض في الأصل (جيمارت)] . . . استقرار اللغة ولا يحتاج في استحقاق إلى ذلك ولم يكن ذلك لأجل إضافة العِلم إلى العالِم Ibn Fūrak (1987, 11.1–6).

80. والصحيح على مذهبه أنّ الإعادة هي نفس المُعاد وأنّ معنى قولِنا إعادةٌ ومُعادٌ يرجع إلى حدوثٍ بعد حدوثٍ تخلّلهما عدمٌ. Ibn Fūrak (1987, 242.21–22).

81. وإنّ استدامة الوصف للأسود بأنه أسود وما توهّم الناظرُ إليه أنه باقٍ فذلك لتجدُّدِ أمثاله وتعذُّرِ الفصل بين ما يُعدَم منه ويُحدَث لتجانُسهما وتشاكُلهما لا لأجل أنه بقي إلى الثاني. Ibn Fūrak (1987, 242.9–11).

82. وعلى هذا الأصل فلا يُنكر عنده بقاءُ جوهرٍ مع عدمِ سائرِ الجواهر بأنْ يجدَّد بقاءٌ له. Ibn Fūrak (1987, 242.11–12).

lexicon."[83] Human language made a distinction between "initialization" and "re-created," but when it came to the operative *maʿnā* they were the same. The gap is clear: human language on one side and the operations of occasionalist physics on the other. Ibn Fūrak used an account of language usage and precedent to escape a conceptual problem that was posed in terms of *maʿānī.*

Another test of Ibn Fūrak's understanding of the relationship between *maʿnā* and extramental things is his description of the interaction between *maʿnā* and something that does not exist. He wrote that al-Ašʿarī "refused to call a nonexistent thing a name that would necessitate *maʿānī* subsisting within it." It was, he thought, impossible for a *maʿnā* such as knowledge or movement to be in something that did not exist. Even though use of the name "moving" or "knowing" established only the *maʿnā* of knowledge or movement and did not actually establish "the essence of the knowing person or the moving thing," nevertheless the presence of a *maʿnā* of knowing or movement did require there to be something existing in which that knowledge or movement could be.[84] In this statement from Ibn Fūrak we can see a clear separation between language on the one hand and mind and reality on the other. Language has a close relationship with mind: the use of a certain word inevitably produces a *maʿnā*. But this *maʿnā* does not then by itself affirm the existence of something in which the *maʿnā* could subsist or to which it could apply. The only way the existence of a *maʿnā* necessitates the existence of anything is by the logical argument that one cannot have movement in something that does not exist. Ibn Fūrak's mind was a rational place in which the law of noncontradiction held: "Two contradictory *maʿānī* cannot occur in the same place."[85] It was not a mental world that denied hypothetical or unreal things—"something that does not exist can be mentioned or known"—but it was a world in which those nonexistent things had to behave in rationally predictable ways: "The nonexistent cannot be killed or hit." Ibn Fūrak knew that language did not control extramental reality—"mentioning something does not make it exist"—but his mental content was internally consistent: the mental content of "having been killed" did necessitate the mental content of an act of killing.[86]

83. فإذا قيل على هذا ففي حالِ ابتدائه يجب أن يكون مُعاداً لوجودِ نفسه فالجواب أنه بمعنى ذلك وإنْ لم يُسمَّ به من طريق اللغة فلأنّ المُعاد والمبتدأ بمعنى واحد. Ibn Fūrak (1987, 243.1–3).

84. وكان يأبى أيضاً أنْ يُسمّى المعدومَ بالأسماء التي تقتضي قِيامَ المعاني به كقولنا إنه متحرّكٌ أم عالِمٌ لأنّ ذلك وإنْ كان إثباتاً للعِلم والحركة لا لِذات العالِم والمتحرِّك فإنّ ذلك يَقتضي وجودَ العالِم والمتحرِّك لاستحالة قيامِ عِلمٍ وحركةٍ بِمَعدوم. Ibn Fūrak (1987, 255.15–17). Cf. al-Ašʿarī (1929–33, 523).

85. وأن المعتبر عنده في معنى التضاد استحالة اجتماع المعنيين في محل من جهات الحدوث فقط لا معنى آخر. Ibn Fūrak (1987, 111.7–8).

86. وكذلك يستحيل أنْ يُوصَف المعدومُ بما يقتضي وجودَ معنىً به ممّا يقتضي وجودَه كنحوِ وَصْفِنا للمَقتول بأنه مقتولٌ لأنّ ذلك وإنْ كان يقتضي قيامَ قتلٍ بالقاتِل فإنه لا يصح قتلٌ لمقتولٍ معدومٍ ويصحّ وجودُ

Frank Griffel suggests that a good starting point for thinking about *maʿnā* in English is "anything that exists and is not a body." (Cf. Herbert Davidson, who simply uses "thing.")[87] I would like to suggest that we can add a location to this translation: *maʿānī* exist in the mind. The fact that they exist is critical: *maʿānī* have an ontological status and salience, as evidenced by the fact that they adhere to laws of noncontradiction. But their existence is a mental existence. The ultimate test of these readings, and of the concomitant translation of *maʿnā* as "mental content," is God. But the God revealed by reading Ibn Fūrak's Islamic theology never entirely gets away from human epistemology. Theology remains the human struggle to get to God, and for Ibn Fūrak this is a struggle with *maʿnā*.

There is a long section in the *Muğarrad* that deals with the possibility and permissibility of humans actually seeing God, where Ibn Fūrak considered the question of whether seeing God would mean that one acquired, with regard to God, a *maʿnā*. His answer was an attempt to maintain the necessary separation between the divine and humanity, and to promise a superlative affect to humans who reached such a stage, but despite this Ibn Fūrak remained committed to his human epistemology: "The person who sees necessarily attains a knowledge of what they see." Even when confronted with God, humans would process the superlative impact of this encounter with *maʿnā*.[88] The mechanism of sensory perception was the same for both language and reality: "Everything that exists can be seen and heard; everything we see has a 'vision,' and everything we hear has an 'audition,' that is in both cases specific to it and followed by a *maʿnā*."[89] *Maʿnā* was the stuff of cognition with which humans processed everything: their mental content. But at the same time, in an occasionalist world of Ašʿarī theology, it was God who made each specific mental content follow each vision and audition into the human mind; God was the cause of perception.[90]

ذكرٍ لمذكورٍ معدومٍ والفرقُ بينهما أنّ وجود الذكر لا يقتضي وجودَ المذكور ووجودُ القتل يقتضي وجودَ المقتول فلذلك جاز أنْ يُذكَر المعدومُ ويُعْلَم ولمْ يجزْ أنْ يُقْتَل المعدومُ ويُضْرَب. Ibn Fūrak (1987, 255.18–22).

87. Herbert Davidson (1987, 427), Griffel (2017, 14).

88. وكذلك كان يقول في جوابِ مَن يسأله فيقول [أ] إذا رأَيتُمُوه تَستفِيدون فيه معنىً أو لا بأنّ الفوائد إنما تَحْدُث في الرائي لا في المرئيّ وهو أنه يَحصل للرائي ضرورةً عِلمٌ بما يَراه مع أنواعٍ من اللّذّات زائدةٍ على كل لَذّة. Ibn Fūrak (1987, 89.18–20).

89. وإنّ كلّ مَوجودٍ يَجوز أنْ يُرى ويُسمع وإنّ لِكلّ مَرْئيّ لَنا رُؤيةً وإنّ لِكلّ مَسموع لَنا سمْعاً يَخصّه وله معنىً يعاقبه. Ibn Fūrak (1987, 80.13–15).

90. وإنما يُحدِث اللهُ الإدراكَ على مجرى العادة عند حُدوثِ معانٍ ومقابَلةَ أشياء لا لأجل تلك المعاني ولا لأجل المقابَلة. Ibn Fūrak (1987, 88.19–20).

THE WORLD CONNECTED TO GOD

"God created things and instances and made them exist as substance and accident." With this pithy statement Ibn Fūrak displays the difference between things in general (*šay'*, plural *ašyā'*) and particular instances of things (*ʿayn*, plural *aʿyān;* for discussion of these distinctions beyond Ibn Fūrak see Frank).[91] The theological point here is that the world and its things are created and not eternal (as the atheists claimed),[92] but the clear epistemological and ontological implication is that God's creation extends throughout and beyond physical reality. For it was not just that God created substance and accident but rather that substance and accident were all that he created; there were no other types of created thing.[93]

God's maʿānī

God's divine attributes shaped much of Islamic theological discourse, and theories about them helped create the epistemological structures Ibn Fūrak used for his descriptions of extramental reality. God has divine attributes that are *maʿānī* and that, unlike accidents, subsist in themselves. Alongside knowledge, another example of a divine attribute is "continuance" (*baqā'*). This is a *maʿnā* that God has, and God is thereby "continuing"; that is, he keeps on being God.[94] God's continuance *maʿnā* does not subsist in something else, as an accident would.[95] In typically circular formulations: "The continuance of the Creator continues for itself because its self is continuance,"[96] and "The continuance of the Creator continues, and it has a continuance that is its self."[97] These are *maʿānī* that subsist in themselves and do so by themselves without any extra causal factors. What Ibn Fūrak was doing here was working to preserve the monotheistic integrity of the creator. God could not continue with a *maʿnā* of continuance in his self because that would, under the conditions of strict monotheism, necessitate God's actual self being continuance as well as being God. And God cannot be two things. The continuance *maʿnā* had to be kept separate from the self of God. It had to subsist in itself. God and continu-

91. Frank (1999, 171f).

92. وكان يقول إنّ الله تعالى أَحْدَثَ الأشياءَ المُحدَثَةَ أشياءَ وأعياناً وأَوْجَدَها جواهرَ وأعراضاً . . . مَن خالَف في هذا الباب لازِمَه قولُ أهلِ الدهر في قِدَمِ الأعيان مِن الجواهر والأعراض. Ibn Fūrak (1987, 253.18–19, 254.3–4).

93. اعْلم أنه كان يقول إنّ أقسام المحدَثات نوعانِ جواهرُ وأعراض. Ibn Fūrak (1987, 265.22; cf. 93.14–15, 94.11, 95.14, 98.23–25).

94. أنّ البقاء معنىً مِن المعاني لأجله يَبقى الباقي . . . Ibn Fūrak (1987, 237.17–18).

95. ويَمنع أنْ يَقوم بقاءُ الباقي بغيره. Ibn Fūrak (1987, 43.4–5).

96. وكان يقول إنّ بقاء البارئ تعالى باقٍ لِنفسه لأنّ نفسَه بقاء. Ibn Fūrak (1987, 237.19).

97. وإنّ بقاء الباري تعالى باقٍ وله بقاءٌ وهو نفسُه. Ibn Fūrak (1987, 43.3–4).

ance could not be in the same *ma'nā* space.[98] I do not think it is too problematic to read *ma'nā* here as "mental content." Ibn Fūrak is talking about the human cognitive processes that explain divine functions. Humans have to make mental content separations between those different aspects of the divine being; our mental contents have to be logically ordered, and they must in their logical order adhere to the logic of monotheism. Ibn Fūrak uses *ma'nā* to talk about human cognition: "Something that continues, continues only because it has a continuance that is its mental content and its formal definition and its accurate account."[99] These three predicates for "continuance," mental content, formal definition, and accurate account, are all human epistemological processes. Ibn Fūrak is telling us how we should think about God. But he did not think God, or his divine attributes, were figments of human imagination; these mental contents had a target that was outside the mind.

Just as important for Islamic theology was how we should think about the world. Ibn Fūrak rejected the idea (which he attributed to al-Ǧubbā'ī, the Mu'tazilī theologian from a century previous) that the only thing that we can accurately think of as continuing was God.[100] Ibn Fūrak had no time for a theological statement that would reserve accuracy for God alone and deny humans the ability to give accurate accounts of the world. This was not a disavowal of God's complete separation from the world as its creator but rather a commitment to keep using the conceptual vocabulary of Islamic theology to describe things, instances, substances, and accidents. It was a stable vocabulary that enabled Ibn Fūrak to understand and then explain how God and human fitted together in the world.

Acquisition (kasb)

In Ibn Fūrak's Aš'arī School of Islamic theology, one of the primary ways that God and humanity fitted together was the theory of the acquisition of acts. This was a theory that explained how human beings could act in a world entirely created and controlled by God, and it gave scholars an account of human action and motivation with which to negotiate the ethics of theodicy. (See Frank and Thiele.)[101] Human beings can exert force on the objects in the world and be accountable for their actions, but the actual movement of the object in question is in fact done

98. ومُحالٌ أنْ تكون نفسُ البارئ تعالى في معنى البقاء. Ibn Fūrak (1987, 237.18–19).

99. إنّ الباقي إنما كان باقياً لأنّ له بقاءٌ ويقول إنّ ذلك معناه وهو حدُّه وحقيقتُه. Ibn Fūrak (1987, 237.3–4).

100. وكذلك كان ينُكِر قولَ الجبّائي في ذهابِه إلى أنْ لا باقٍ في الحقيقة إلا الله تعالى ويقول إنّ ذلك يُوجِب أنْ يَخُصّه بأوصافه ولا يُجيز مشاركةَ غيرِه له فيه حتى يُحيل أنْ يُوصف بكلّ وصْفٍ وُصِف هو به إلا هو وذلك مُحال. Ibn Fūrak (1987, 240.9–11).

101. Frank (1983, 210–15), Thiele (2016b).

by God. Humans are only local agents, and God is the real agent of change.[102] Ibn Fūrak's account of this core doctrine used the word *maʿnā* a great deal.

Ibn Fūrak wrote that "ability is a *maʿnā* that happens and is an accident. It does not subsist in itself, but rather it subsists in the living substance."[103] Humans can be accurately described as having ability,[104] and God created it, just he created the actual smell of something at the same time as the *maʿnā* of smell occurred in the human in question. These *maʿānī* are in human beings, while the actual referents of the *maʿānī* are created concurrently by God in the extramental world.[105] Humans may appear to be agents, but this is an illusion created by the divine action happening at the same time as the human cognition. On this reading the category of *maʿnā* becomes utterly central to one of the most famous doctrines of Ibn Fūrak's Ašʿarī School of theology.

Ibn Fūrak thought that ability was a *maʿnā* in the living extramental substance of another human or animal. But the word he used for this accidental quality was the same word that he used for human mental contents, and for his own cognition of those accidental qualities, a cognition that he could express in speech. It is not possible to show that he considered these two types of *maʿnā* as separate categories. On the contrary, the text itself shows how they overlap. The sentence quoted above is bracketed by the statement that "ability" is in the same *maʿnā* as "capability," "potentiality," and more. Using our Anglophone conceptual vocabulary, it makes little sense to say that "ability," "capability," and "potentiality" are all one and the same factor in an extramental substance, unless one means that "ability," "capability," and "potentiality" are all words for the same thing. Our conceptual vocabulary tends to push us either into a cognitive process in which the words "ability," "capability," and "potentiality" are judged to have the same meaning or into an extramental reality where "ability" is a faculty that exists in another living being. But Ibn Fūrak's conceptual vocabulary runs the two options together in the same sentence. There is no evidence that he considered them as either separate or different.

But Ibn Fūrak was a theologian equipped and prepared to make distinctions between language, mind, and reality. If he wanted to stress that something was

102. ويقول إنّ كَسْب العبد فعلُ الله تعالى ومفعولُه. Ibn Fūrak (1987, 91.22f).

103. اعْلم أنه كان يذهب إلى أنّ الاستطاعة هي القُدرة وأنه معنىً حادثٌ عَرَضٌ لا يَقوم بنفسه قائمٌ بالجوهر الحيّ. Ibn Fūrak (1987, 107.19–20).

104. وكان يقول إنّ الإنسان مستطيعٌ باستطاعةٍ هي غيرُه وإنه يُوصَف بذلك على الحقيقة. Ibn Fūrak (1987, 107.22–108.1).

105. يُحدِث [اللهُ] لوناً وطعماً ورائحةً عِند حُدوثِ بعض المعاني مِن أحدنا لا أنه هو الذي أَحْدَثَه وإنْ كان قد حَدَثَ عِند حُدوثِ ما يقع منه. Ibn Fūrak (1987, 213.17–19). Cf. al-Bāqillānī in Thiele (2016b, 268 n. 72).

linguistic rather than extramental truth, he did so. If he wanted to stress that what he was talking about was a real thing out in the extramental physical world, he did so. But here, at a central theological, ethical, and philosophical moment, he built a theory of the acquisition of acts that made none of those sharp distinctions. On the contrary, he used a conceptual vocabulary of *maʿnā* that elided the distinction between epistemology and ontology as if it were irrelevant to his concerns.

The selfsame doctrine of acquisition that he put forward may have enabled him to do this. The barriers that divide language, mind, and reality were lowered by God, who created both the *maʿānī* in human minds that made sense of action in the world and the extramental *maʿānī* that constituted that action. God managed both human cognition and extramental physics; humans still thought about physics with their cognitive processes, and *maʿnā* was the stuff of both. It is the translation process that makes us take a stand on the location of the *maʿānī*, not the theological texts themselves. Ibn Fūrak thought that both mind and reality were created and God had exactly the same amount of control over each one. God's control came through an account of causation that was occasionalist. Everything was created at its instant, and God could choose the opposite of the expected outcome or the visible accident at any time. (The undeniable existence of patterns in the world did nothing to disprove this, for God could choose to break them with miracles).[106] Bodies continued to exist only because God kept on renewing their continuance.[107] The same was true of accidents.[108] *Maʿnā* was a fundamental epistemological category that allowed Ibn Fūrak to talk about God while maintaining his commitment to monotheism, to develop a theory of extramental qualities and accidents, and to fit language, cognition, and perception together.

God's Speech

Let us hold onto this reading of *maʿnā* as mental content and move on to three more *quaestiones* that are familiar to Arabists. The theological doctrines of God's speech, God's names, and speech in the soul all deal with the nexus of language, mind, and reality, and all three help us understand what eleventh-century scholars thought language was and how they thought it worked. Language was the primary conduit between humans and the divine. So what did God do when he wanted

106. وكان يقول إنّ الحوادث كلّها مخترَعٌ لله تعالى ابتداءً مِن غير سببٍ يُوجِبها ولا عِلّةٍ تُولّدها وإنه ما مِن عَرَضٍ فَعَلَه مع عَرَضٍ أو بعدَه عَرَضٌ أو قبْلَه إلا وكان جائزاً أنْ يَفعَلَه مع خلافه أو على خلافِ ذلك . . . ولكنه تعالى قد أَجْرَى العادةَ في إحداثِ ذلك . . . ونقْضُ العادةِ إنما يكون مُعجِزةً وكرامةً ودلالةً للصادقين وإبانةً مِن الكاذبين. Ibn Fūrak (1987, 131.7–9, 134.7–9).

107. وإنّ الجسم يَبقى دائماً بتجدُّد البقاء له حالاً فحالاً. Ibn Fūrak (1987, 238.18–19).

108. وهكذا قولُه في سائر الأعراض إنه لا يصح وجودُ شيءٍ منها أكثرَ مِن وقْت واحد . . . ويَستحيل في حالَين متّصِلَين. Ibn Fūrak (1987, 12.22–13.3).

to communicate vital information to his creation? He spoke. Ibn Fūrak said on more than one occasion that absent such divine speech we are not in a position to determine much of what we should do, or much of what we could know to be true. God spoke to make the *maʿānī* of his speech clear to his creation. These *maʿānī* were available to humanity, and according to the same principles of occasionalism laid out above, God controlled this access.[109] Ibn Fūrak did not put as much effort as many of his contemporaries into determining the literary processes through which God communicated, agreeing with the prevalent assumption that God did so in an inimitably perfect way but not going into any great detail about how that perfection was inimitable. (The question of inimitability received substantially more attention from ar-Rāġib and al-Ǧurǧānī.) For Ibn Fūrak, the Quran was a miracle because it was eloquent, well structured, grammatically correct, and contained information humans would not otherwise have known.[110] He was more interested in the ontological and epistemological status of the speech itself.

God's speech was not an accident. On the contrary: it had a rare status for Ibn Fūrak as a *maʿnā* that was actually in God's very essence, with all the eternality, combination, and overlap that that might entail.[111] In the long-running debate on whether this eternality was a problem for Islamic monotheism, Ibn Fūrak held that the Quran's eternal *maʿnā* was in God's self, and the instances of it in human writing or recitation, or indeed divine writing on the heavenly preserved tablet, were outside, created, and accurately accounted for as no longer eternal.[112]

Maʿānī were therefore facts about how reality actually is, cognitive judgments that human beings make about reality, human thoughts and ideas that may or may not have anything to do with the world outside, the referents of the speech that humans engage in with one another, or the divine message that God seeks to communicate to humanity. God could choose to put them in human minds, or in external things, or in both. (Compare the ninth-century statement reported by al-Ǧāḥiẓ, via Jeannie Miller: "God can do what he wishes with names, just as he can do what he wishes with *maʿānī*.")[113] A translation strategy that identifies

109. وإنه [كلامُ الله] مسموعٌ على الحقيقة لله تعالى ولِمَن أسمعه مفهومٌ لمن فهّمه وعرّفه معانيه من المؤمنين . . . يَستدرِك [موسى] بها معاني كلامه [تعالى] والمرادَ بخطابه . . . حتى يَعلم [المرءُ] ابتداءَ مرادِ الله تعالى بخطابه وبمعاني كلامه إيّاه. Ibn Fūrak (1987, 59.13–14, 21, 64.20–21).

110. Ibn Fūrak (1987, 62.20f).

111. أنه كان يقول إنّ كلام الله تعالى صِفَةٌ له قديمةٌ لم يزل قائماً بذاته. Ibn Fūrak (1987, 59.11–12). Cf. Farahat (2016, 594), Vishanoff (2011, 153f).

112. وأنّ تِلاوتهم وقِراءتهم مُحدَثةٌ والمتلوُّ والمقروءُ بها غيرُ مُحدَث . . . وكان يقول إنّ كلام الله تعالى مكتوبٌ على الحقيقة بكتابةٍ حديثةٍ في اللوح. Ibn Fūrak (1987, 60.8–9, 61.22).

113. وزَعَم أنّ اللهَ تعالى يَحكُم في الأسماء بما أَحَبَّ كما أنّ له أنْ يَحكُم في المعاني بما أحب. Al-Ǧāḥiẓ (1965a, 3:329.16–17), Miller (2016b, 64). The translation is mine.

maʿnā as a core subject matter of Islamic theology helps us understand how this discipline can sometimes look on the surface as if it is all about naming, while at the same time it is also clearly very much about things. *Maʿānī* are the link. Omnipresent across the practice of Islamic theology (itself a "science of speech"), when *maʿānī* are expressed in language by a theologian, they inevitably become the mental content of that theologian along the way. (Cf. Frank on this same topic.)[114] But it is our conceptual vocabulary in English that forces us to posit the requirement for a movement from extramental fact or divine attribute to mental content. In Ibn Fūrak's conceptual vocabulary there was no such movement; *maʿnā* did not become mental content after having been an extramental or divine entity. It was just *maʿnā*.

So much of Islamic theology was about naming. This is one way we can read it as a "science of speech" (*ʿilm al-kalām*); the process in which the theologians were engaged was a process of making sure their *maʿānī* were aligned with God's *maʿānī*. Whether they were talking about his divine attributes or the physical forces observable in his creation, eleventh-century theologians were concerned to ensure that their minds had correctly and accurately mapped his *maʿānī*. For the backstop to these processes was always divine, whether it was the divinely placed lexicon that determined an accurate account or the divine act of creation that put the *maʿnā* of movement into a rolling ball and the *maʿnā* referent of speech into the minds of humans engaged in conversations with each other. God aligned *maʿānī* across the divide between this world and the heavens; the Quran was the moment when he did this with the Arabic language.

God's Names

Ibn Fūrak's fifteenth chapter is titled "Further Discussion Clarifying al-Ašʿarī's Positions on the *Maʿānī* of God's Names and Attributes Appearing in the Quran, Sunnah, and Community Consensus."[115] The theological category at stake here is *maʿnā*, which determines and structures the divine names and attributes. *Maʿānī* are, in effect, a set of ontological and cognitive pigeonholes into which different linguistic descriptions or theological functions can be placed by the theologian. For example, God is described as eternal, and the *maʿnā* of this description is that God is prior in existence to everything else, for ever. This is then the same *maʿnā* as the description of God as without beginning.[116] The two linguistic descriptions

114. Frank (2000, 28–32).

115. فصلٌ آخَرُ في إبانة مذاهبه في معاني ما وَرَد مِن أسماء الربّ تعالى وصِفاته في الكتاب والسُنة واتّفاق الأمة. Ibn Fūrak (1987, 42.7–8).

116. فأما وصفُه بأنه قديمٌ فهو إجماع الأمة ومعناه أنه متقدِّم بوجوده على كلِ ما وُجِد بالحدوث بغير غاية ولا مُدّة وهو معنى الوصف له بأنه أزليّ. Ibn Fūrak (1987, 42.19–20).

go in the same *maʿnā* pigeonhole. Ibn Fūrak had a theological concept of a critical aspect of God's divine nature: God was older than everything else. This was a *maʿnā*. He then placed the linguistic descriptions of God as being eternal or without beginning in this *maʿnā*. It was a way of thinking that allowed the complexity of theological possibilities to align with human reason, human language, and revelation. These three arenas revolved around *maʿnā*, the core category in which Ibn Fūrak's theological resolutions took place. It was a flexible structure; these *maʿānī* could be subject to internal subdivision. For example, the Arabic word *qadīm* could apply either to God or to his creation. God used it in the Quran to describe the way the moon appeared after waning, "like a *qadīm* date-palm stalk." (In English, we would translate this as "old.")[117] The same word was a theologically permissible description of God himself. (In English, we translate this as "eternal.") We can therefore give an accurate account of a created thing as *qadīm* if our intent is simply to refer to something that was before something else. But the *qadīm* that never ends—that is, God—is different. The *maʿnā* pigeonhole labeled *qadīm* has two shelves: one for an eternal God and the other for created things that are old.[118] These options were available for all God's names: the divine *maʿnā* was not the same as the created *maʿnā*. (Cf. ar-Rāġib's position that the created *maʿnā* was part of the divine *maʿnā*.)[119] And the shelf for the eternal God could have more than one linguistic description placed therein; not just "eternal" and "without beginning" but also "first."[120] But this pigeonhole metaphor can take us only so far. Can we still think of *maʿnā* as mental content? Ibn Fūrak is not dealing with meanings here; or if he is, they are unlike "meanings" in English: the *maʿānī* are stable categories or concepts that have ontological salience and can be expressed in language. "Mental content" is a clumsy placeholder, but it does at least do the job of reminding us that although the target of his cognition is divine, and although God controls his cognition, at least some of this work is taking place in the mind of the theologian.

We can see this play out in a series of claims throughout the *Muǧarrad*, where Ibn Fūrak reports on al-Ašʿarī's determination to place multiple quite different vocal forms within the same mental content. At one point he equated the mental

117. كان يقول إنّ المحدَث يُصف بأنه قديمٌ على الحقيقة إذ أُريدَ به تقدُّمه على ما حدث بعده كقوله حَتَّى عَادَ كَٱلْعُرْجُونِ ٱلْقَدِيمِ وإنّ العرجون كان قديماً على الحقيقة على معنى أنه تقدّم العراجين التي حدثتْ بعده. Ibn Fūrak (1987, 27.21–28.1).

118. وكان يقول إنّ القديم الذي لم يزل موجوداً هو أحد وَصْفَيْ القِدَم ونَوعَيْ معناه. Ibn Fūrak (1987, 28.1–2).

119. أجمعوا على إطلاقِ أسماء الله تعالى ومنْعِ أمثالها في المعنى واللغة. Ibn Fūrak (1987, 42.4–5). فمعناه المَوجودُ في الناس من المعنى الموجود لله تعالى ar-Rāġib (1992, 347/2.9–10). Cf. ar-Rāġib (1984, 115), (1988a, 270).

120. فأما معنى وصْفِه بأنه الأوّلُ فهو معنى وصْفِهِ بأنه قديمٌ أزلي. Ibn Fūrak (1987, 43.17).

content of eighteen different words from seven separate sets of consonants.[121] This would have been anathema to Abū Hilāl, but al-Aš'arī was not mapping mental content to make a point about fine semantic differences in the lexicon; he was making an argument about how human cognition dealt with God and negotiated the linguistic precedent of revelation: "Although revelation forbids that God be called 'supporting' or 'able,' with regard to the mental content both are correct."[122] Al-Aš'arī wanted to limit the number of things that could qualify God; with *ma'ānī* structured in this way he could replace eighteen divine attributes with one.

On the level of syntax, Ibn Fūrak talked about how the morphologies of words such "he did" and "he is doing" can have different forms while being "in the mental content" of each other. These are the "mental contents of syntax" (*ma'ānī an-naḥw*) that we encountered in chapter 2, and will meet again in chapter 7 on poetics.[123] It was a model of reference in which vocal forms existed, and both grammarians and theologians worked to map them onto mental contents, each according to his own wishes. These were the same *ma'ānī* that functioned as epistemological and ontological pigeonholes. Words referred to them, and they explained and described extramental objects. God passed his down to humanity through revelation, although he had already created them in human minds.

Speech in the Soul (kalām nafsī)

The final theological topic at the nexus of humanity, God, language, mind, and reality is the famous (among Arabists!) distinction between speech in the soul and speech on the lips (*kalām nafsī* and *kalām lafẓī*). It was a distinction intended to separate God's divine speech from human speech, in effect a recognition that the *ma'nā* of speech could not quite be the same for the eternal and the temporal. The standard position shared by Aš'arī theologians such as Ibn Fūrak and al-Bāqillānī (in disagreement with the Mu'tazilah) was that an accurate account of all speech was that it was *ma'ānī* in the soul, and that verbal (or written) repetitions thereof were indications of that original mental-content fact.[124]

121. وكان يقول إنّ معنى قولِنا مُحدَثٌ وإحداثٌ وحُدوثٌ وحادِثٌ وحديثٌ وحَدَثٌ وفِعْلٌ ومَفعُولٌ وإيجادٌ ومُوجَدٌ وإبداعٌ ومُبدَعٌ واختراعٌ ومُخْتَرَعٌ وتَكوينٌ ومُكَوّنٌ وخَلْقٌ ومَخلوقٌ سواءٌ في المعنى. Ibn Fūrak (1987, 28.6–9).

122. وإنّ الله تعالى لا يقال له آئدٌ ولا مُستطيعٌ لِمنْعِ السمْع منه فأما المعنى صحيحٌ . . . وكان يقول إنّ معنى القادر والقَويّ والقُدرة والقُوّة سواءٌ . . . وكذلك كان لا يفرّق بين العلم والدِراية والفِقه والفَهم والفطنة والعقل والحسّ والمعرفة. Ibn Fūrak (1987, 44.12–15).

123. وما هو على صورةِ يَفْعَلُ قد يكون بمعنى فَعَلَ. Ibn Fūrak (1987, 65.24–66.1).

124. Al-Bāqillānī (1963, 101f), Ibn Fūrak (1987, 59.11, 192.4f), Ibn Mattawayh (2009, 196f), Vasalou (2009, 221), Vishanoff (2011, 153f).

The following statement from Ibn Fūrak allows us to fill out more of the picture with regard to what he thought this mental content looked like when it was not instantiated in words on the lips or page. An accurate account of mental content is that it "has no letters, no morphological form, and no syntax. The letters and sounds with which the indications arrive are expressions of the speech of the speaker, his commands, prohibitions, and predications. They operate in the same way as the indications connected to intimations and physical gestures of communication, all of which serve to indicate the mental contents that subsist in the self."[125]

This account of speech as mental content in the soul holds true for both God and humanity (al-Bāqillānī).[126] It leads to a situation in which God has the eternal divine attribute of speech, and that attribute is of course a *maʿnā*, one of the *maʿānī* that subsist in themselves. At the same time, God's speech communicates his *maʿānī* and humans receive them via language in their own created minds as *maʿānī*. We do not have a category in English that covers all these bases, but Arabic did. Vishanoff has perceptively observed, in the context of a discussion of divine imperatives in which the legal force of the command comes from the *maʿnā* rather than the vocal form (*ṣīġat al-amr*), "Because *maʿnā* is both attribute and meaning, the ontological gap between God's eternal attribute of speech and its created expression is also a hermeneutical gap between meaning and the verbal form that expresses it."[127] Ibn Fūrak (and al-Bāqillānī) had a core conceptual vocabulary that assumed *maʿnā* was both the divine truth that they sought in revelation as exegetes and the eternal divine truth that they posited as theologians. In English, we would call the latter "an attribute" and the former "a meaning." But eleventh-century Arabic used the same word.

We learn here that the *maʿānī* we have been in pursuit of since the first page of this book do not for Ibn Fūrak come in the shape of words. But do they come in the shape of language? Are *maʿānī* some language of thought that does not necessarily have sound, letters, or syntax but that does still order itself in the pragmatic categories of command, prohibition, and predication? Is this what is sometimes called "speech" (as noted by Frank)?[128] Ibn Fūrak does not provide us with the answers to all these questions. What he does give us is a systematic account of how

125. فليس بحروفٍ ولا له صورةٌ ونِظامٌ وإنما هذه الحروفُ والأصواتُ التي تقع به الدلالات عبارةٌ عن كلامِ المتكلمين وأمره ونهيه وخَبَره فسبيلُها سبيلُ الكِناية والدلالاتِ المتعلَّقةِ بها وبالإشارة التي تكون دلالاتٌ على المعاني القائمة في النفس. Ibn Fūrak (1987, 192.5–8).

126. Al-Bāqillānī (1998, 2:5), Farahat (2016, 594).

127. Vishanoff (2011, 180). Thanks to David Vishanoff for an encouraging conversation on this question during the conference "Intention and Signification: Philosophy of Language across Islamic Disciplines, 800–1200" at Albert Ludwig University, Freiburg, in June 2017.

128. Frank (2000, 29).

human cognition used *ma ʿānī* to deal with the world and with God. It will be only with Ibn Sīnā and al-Ǧurǧānī in subsequent chapters that we start to see *ma ʿnā* given cognitive patterns and rules that stand at a certain remove from the vocal forms of language itself.

HUMAN ACCURACY

Objective Truth

Arabic theory understood accuracy in a linguistic framework. In this framework, there were only two ways that the plane of vocal form could connect to the plane of mental content: an accurate type of connection recorded in the lexicon (*ḥaqīqah*) and an alternative type of connection that went beyond the lexicon (*maǧāz*). Here I want to ask how persistent this linguistic framework was in Ibn Fūrak's theology. Did his conception of accuracy always contain the shadow, or even the presence, of language?

Arabic scholars in the eleventh century and earlier looked for accurate accounts of both things and ideas. Ibn Fūrak himself described the task of investigating knowledge as work on the "accurate mental content of al-Ašʿarī."[129] Pursuit of "accurate accounts of things" (*ḥaqāʾiq al-ašyāʾ*) was one of the most common ways to describe the practice of philhellenic philosophy (as noted in chapter 2.) In both these cases, whether words, things, or ideas were at stake, *ḥaqīqah* stood for getting it right.

Ibn Fūrak was committed to an objective sphere of truth, and he used *ḥaqīqah* to describe the accuracy available there. In a discussion of how necessary knowledge (inescapable knowledge, as opposed to what is acquired) must perforce be shared among all sentient beings, he wrote that if this principle did not hold, and necessary knowledge was disparately available to different people despite their equal access to it, "that would lead to collective disavowal of the accurate accounts and invalidation of the routes toward establishing them."[130] The accurate accounts are real knowledge of how things are, knowledge of the sort that would be at stake were we to lose the equalizing principle that two rational and sentient beings, in the absence of obstacles, know the same thing in the same way. Ibn Fūrak clearly cared as much about the pit of epistemological relativism as Peters and Frank.

129. فبدأنا عند ذلك بالكلام في العلوم ومداركها واقسامها وذكرِ حقيقة معناه على اصلِه. Ibn Fūrak (1987, 9.13–14).

130. وأمّا في الضَّروريّات التي تقع ابتداءً فلا يصح فيها أيضاً إلا المشارِكةُ بين الأحياء وذَوِي الحوّاس والعقلاء مع زَوالِ الآفات وإنّ إجازةَ خلافِ ذلك تؤدّي إلى تناكُرِ الحقائق وإبطالِ الطرق إلى إثباتها. Ibn Fūrak (1987, 16.22–17.2).

At one of the early points where he criticizes the work of al-Astarābāḏī, this accurate discernment of reality is the epistemological point of contention. Al-Astarābāḏī was wrong, Ibn Fūrak said, to write that accurate discernment of the truth or falsity of things was possible only through the Quran, prophetic example, scholarly consensus, and rational indicators. The problem with this standard list was that it omitted things that were known via sensory data and historical reports.[131] Ibn Fūrak wanted to extend the sphere of objective truth to include both those categories, and so to cover both observation and history. But the name both he and al-Astarābādī gave to what can be accurately known to be true or false was *ḥaqīqah.*

Later on, in chapter 40, Ibn Fūrak discussed how one person can know something in two different ways at the same time but cannot have two separate and identical knowledges of the same thing at the same time. Al-Ašʿarī apparently deduced this from the fact that an atheist (*ad-dahrī,* on whom see Patricia Crone)[132] could know a body existed (true) while believing it to be eternal (false). If the belief was false, then it could not be knowledge, "because knowledge has to be of the accurate account of what is known."[133] At this point, the appellation "knowledge" is reserved for those times when one gets it right (because if one's knowledge is false, then it is perforce just a belief) and the test is accuracy; one is right only when one knows the accurate account.

Accurate Language about the World

Accurate language about the world is an epistemological standard of accuracy that is structured with concepts that came from linguistic accounts of reference. There is a clear parallel between *ḥaqīqah* (accuracy) and *maʿnā* (mental content) here; both terms emerged from accounts of how language works and were then used to describe how cognition functions. Their continued use in cognition retains a strong linguistic flavor.

Let us take Ibn Fūrak's report on what al-Ašʿarī thought about the mental content of truth: "The vocal form 'the truth' contributes to multiple mental contents according to different aspects of usage. Truth cannot be enumerated in a concise vocal form." Al-Ašʿarī then compared "truth" to an Arabic word that had meanings so separate that some might call it a homonym in English: *ʿadl,* the verbal form of which could be used to say both "he *deviated* from the truth" and "he *behaved justly.*" Al-Ašʿarī wrote that the accurate account of *ʿadl* was that, like "truth," it could refer to different types of mental content. The next problem was

131. إذْ كلُّ الأشياء لا تُعرف حقيقتُها في صِحتها وفسادها من الوجوه التي ذَكَرها مِن الكتاب والسنة والإجماع ودلائل العقول بل أكثرُها يُعرف بغير هذه الطريقة وإنما الكتابُ والسنة والإجماع ودليل العقل يُعرف به بعضُ الأشياء دُون بعضٍ وجملةُ ذلك ما عَدا ما يُعلم بالحسّ وخبر التواتر. Ibn Fūrak (1987, 21.17–20).

132. Crone (2009), (2012).

133. لأنّ العِلم يجب أنْ يكون على حقيقةِ ما المعلومُ عليه. Ibn Fūrak (1987, 221.21).

a matter of pragmatics, of meaning in context: the question "Is unbelief true or false?" could be legitimately answered in both the affirmative (because unbelief is created by God) and the negative (because the unbelief acquired by humans is forbidden by God).[134] All these theological problems (two lexical homonyms and a matter of pragmatics) are linguistic; this is theology as the policing of language usage against the epistemological reference point of the lexicon. But these are also cognitive problems about the mental content of truth and the possibility of giving an accurate account of it. Ibn Fūrak identified two complementary methodological approaches to questions like these. The first was to explain how a vocal form could have more than one accurate account of its multiple mental contents. This approach rested on an attitude to the lexicon that assumed different names within it could point at the same mental content and occupy the same cognitive pigeonhole.[135] The second approach was to posit a category of *absolute* truth or *absolute* justice, for which a single mental content could be established in accordance with revelatory precedent. The account for "truth" was then ontological rather than linguistic and lexically based: "The mental content of absolute truth is that it is what has been verified as being and truly exists. . . . It inevitably either is or it will be."[136]

In chapter 8 of the *Muğarrad* Ibn Fūrak focused on "the mental content of the accurate account and the mental content of going beyond the lexicon."[137] He started by confirming that the accuracy is about more than language: "Our use of 'accuracy' may extend beyond vocal forms and statements to what is neither."[138] Ibn Fūrak goes on to report that "the accurate account of a thing is the self of that thing when it is as it is described . . . , and its accurate account is also its mental content, from which its description is derived." The accurate accounts of "black," "moving," "long," "short," "knowing," "capable," and "speaking" are in each case a mental content, from which these descriptions ("black," "moving," "long," and so on) are derived.[139] This is a presentation of the accurate account, in which it can

134. لفظة الحقّ مشتركةُ المعاني مختلفةُ الوجوه ولا يمكن حَصْرُه في لفظٍ مختصَرٍ وكذلك قال في معنى العدْلِ وحدّه وحقيقته لأنّ ذلك مما تتنوّع معانيها وتختلف ألا ترى أنه يقال عَدَلَ فلانٌ عن الحق وعَدَلَ على فلانٍ فالعدْلُ عن الحق جَورٌ والعدْل عليه ترْكُ الجَور . . . جواباً عن سؤالهم إذ قالوا الكُفْر حقٌّ أو باطلٌ أنّ مِن أصحابنا مَن قال إنه حقٌّ مِن حيث الخلْق وباطلٌ مِن حيث اكتسابه الكافرُ مَنْهِياً عنه. Ibn Fūrak (1987, 25.2–5, 9–10).

135. . . . أنّ الأصل [في كلمة ما] توقيفٌ وما في معناه يسمّى باسمه لِمُساواته له في معناه. Ibn Fūrak (1987, 41.22–23).

136. فعلى هذا يمكن أنْ يقال في معنى الحق المطلَق إنه هو الذي تحقَّق كونُه وصحّ وجودُه . . . هو كائنٌ أو سيكون لا محالة. Ibn Fūrak (1987, 25.16–17, 21).

137. فصلٌ آخر في بيانِ مذهبه في معنى الحقيقة والمجاز. Ibn Fūrak (1987, 26.10).

138. إنّ استعمالنا الحقيقةَ قد يتعدَّى الألفاظَ والأقوالَ إلى ما عداها أيضاً. Ibn Fūrak (1987, 26.12–13).

139. وحقيقةُ الشيء عنده نفْسُ الشيء إذا كان فيما يُوصف به الشيءُ ويُرْجَع إلى نفسه وحقيقته معناه

be used for both words and things. It is complemented by Ibn Fūrak's collection of formal definitions in legal theory, *Kitāb al-Ḥudūd fī al-Uṣūl,* where he writes that "'accuracy' can be used according to two mental contents, the first of which is the description of a thing that is its formal definition, its clarification, and the mental content on account of which this thing deserves that description. The second is the accurate account of speech, which also goes back to description in that it is a speech act according to original lexical placement."[140] In both the *Muğarrad* and the *Ḥudūd* there are two spheres in which theologians or legal theorists use *ḥaqīqah,* the word for accuracy. One sphere is language: accurate speech accords with lexical precedent. The other sphere, mental content, has no necessary correlate in vocal form and is actually prior to linguistic expression: we derive descriptions of things from the mental contents that are accurate.

Ibn Fūrak used *ḥaqīqah* as an indicator of accuracy, whether he was talking about the cognitive mental contents that enabled humans to think about the world and from which descriptions were derived, or when discussing word usage vis-à-vis the lexicon. The three domains of reality, mind, and language are inextricably connected by mental content, which sits in all three levels. We think about the world with mental content, and we refer to mental content when we talk. We then evaluate all this mental content according to the standard of the accurate account, an epistemological tool that enables certain cognitive processes and certain connections between vocal form and mental content to be privileged.

Accurate Accounts of Literature and Physics

The Arabic accurate account was not just a point where words and things combined; it was also an epistemological judgment that applied to both science and literature. By "science," I mean the systematic investigations by eleventh-century Arabic theologians and philosophers into the structure and behavior of the physical and natural world, and by "literature" I mean the specific set of approaches to aesthetics and poetry found in this period. For Ibn Fūrak and his contemporaries these included the study of imagery and the question of what a metaphor is and how it works, both tested against a self-consciously aesthetic canon of poetry and prose. This is the paradigmatically literary territory into which Ibn Fūrak moves only ten lines or so into chapter 8. For Arabists, it is no surprise that a discussion of physics (what it is to be moving) shades so quickly into a literary discussion of how metaphors work.

الذي يُشتقّ الوصفُ منه إذا كان جاريًا مجراه كقولنا أسودُ ومتحرّكٌ وطويلٌ وقصيرٌ وعالِمٌ وقادِرٌ ومتكلّمٌ حقيقةُ الأوصاف هذه تُشتقّ منها التي معانيه مجراه يجري وما ذلك جميعِ. Ibn Fūrak (1987, 26.13–15).

140. الحقيقةُ تُستعمل على معنيَين أحدُهما وصْفُ الشيء الذي هو حدّه وبَيانُه والمعنى الذي استحقّ الشيءُ لأجله الوجهُ الثاني هو حقيقةُ الكلام وذلك راجِعٌ إلى وصْفه بأنه قولٌ مستعمَلٌ فيما وُضِع له في الأصل. Ibn Fūrak (1999, 145.2–6).

It is a familiar feature of the Classical Arabic intellectual landscape and the corollary of its obsession with language; if one cares about language to the extent that its structures infuse one's ontology, then one's care for language cannot but extend to the creation of language as literature and the criticism thereof. Just as the chapters of this book move from mental contents in theology to mental contents in poetry, so Ibn Fūrak himself makes the same move inside a single short chapter: from accurate accounts of color and movement in a body to accurate accounts of reference in a line of poetry. The framework of the accurate account is constant throughout this move, just as mental content is a permanent part of the conceptual landscape.

Ibn Fūrak tells us what speech that goes beyond lexical placement looked like to him: "Some statements and vocal forms are called *maǧāz* according to a mental content that holds them to have moved away from that for which they were lexically placed to that for which they were not."[141] This is the accurate account applied to words and to their usage vis-à-vis the lexicon. It matches the lexicography and poetics of ar-Rāġib that we encountered in the previous chapter, and we will see al-Ǧurǧānī develop it in chapter 7. In the mind of the person who considers a speech act there is a mental content that constitutes their decision as to whether the vocal forms of the speech in question still have their original connections to the mental contents they encompassed in the lexicon. Speech acts consist of vocal forms and mental contents, while other mental contents make determinations about those speech acts. This is why I am comfortable translating *maʿnā* as "mental content" and understanding it as the stuff of cognition; mental content is in speech and is thought about speech, both part of literature itself and the material of literary criticism. There is a potential here that will be exploited by al-Ǧurǧānī.

When eleventh-century scholars said that speech went beyond the lexicon, they were giving an account of language that focused on a historic lexical relationship; a particular vocal form was known in the lexicon of the community to refer to a particular mental content, and this was the accurate account (*ḥaqīqah*). As soon as that link was altered, the speech act went beyond the lexicon (*maǧāz*). Ibn Fūrak, in this book of his about theology, explained speech that goes beyond the lexicon with three examples. The first is from the Quran, when the narrative voice is decrying those who plotted against the new religious community rather than joining it: "rather it was the scheming of the night and the day."[142] Ibn Fūrak makes the point that the scheming didn't really belong to the night or the day but rather happened during those times. The mental content of the verse is not that either night or day is a schemer but rather that the scheming took place during night

141. وإنما يقال لبعضِ الأقوال والألفاظ إنها مجازٌ على معنى أنه قد تُجُوّز به عمّا وُضِع له إلى ما لَم يُوضَع له. Ibn Fūrak (1987, 27.1–2).

142. بَلْ مَكْرُ ٱلَّيْلِ وَٱلنَّهَارِ. Quran 34:33 (as-Sabāʾ).

or day.[143] The verse as it stands in the Quran is therefore speech that goes beyond the lexicon. Accurate speech would be if the relationship of vocal form to mental content remained unaltered, and the night and day really had schemed. Ibn Fūrak then wrote: "This is like the statement of the poet: 'As for the day, it is in shackles and chains.'" He explained that the mental content was that the shackling occurred during the day, not that the day was itself actually wearing metal restraints.[144] The final example sees him switch back to the Quran and Moses coming across "a wall that wanted to fall down." Ibn Fūrak pithily notes that according to an accurate account walls don't want to do anything.[145]

The accurate account was a test of literature. But it was also a test of eleventh-century physics; when Ibn Fūrak wanted to say that accidents do not occupy space he wrote: "Accidents do not accurately have a spatial aspect, because they do not touch each other, and one accident cannot be a border for another."[146] The accurate account here is an epistemological standard of correctness, not necessarily connected to any linguistic sphere. This is made clearer a few lines later when he wrote that in a discussion like this, our expression "spatial aspect" is not accurate, and neither are the vocal forms "half," "third," and "quarter." This is because "the accurate account of a speaker's statement 'I took half a penny' is that they took a thing and left its exact like. The expression of this action with 'half' is a process of semantic extension."[147] The actual extramental reality of which one can give an accurate account is made up of atoms. All substances that exist can exist individually and separately from the rest: "This is the mental content of our statement that 'the atom cannot be subdivided' and that 'a substance cannot be divided or halved in its essence.'"[148] Because the world is actually made of atoms, the only accounts

143. فالمعنى أنّ المكْرَ يقع فيهما. Ibn Fūrak (1987, 27.3), (2009b, 139).

144. وهذا كقول الشاعر أَمَّا ٱلنَّهارُ فَفِيْ قَيْدٍ وَسِلْسِلَةٍ والمعنى أنّ التقيّد يقع فيه لا أنه يكون تقيّداً له. Ibn Fūrak (1987, 27.3–5).

145. فَوَجَدَا فِيهَا جِدَاراً يُرِيدُ أَنْ يَنقَضَّ. Quran 18:77 (al-Kahf). ولا إرادةَ في الحقيقة للجدار. Ibn Fūrak (1987, 27.5–6).

146. ويقول إنّ الأعراض لا يصح أنْ تكون لها جِهةٌ على الحقيقة مِن حيث لم يصح أنْ يُماسّ بعضُها بعضاً وأنْ يكون بعضُها حدّاً لبعض. Ibn Fūrak (1987, 203.19–20).

147. بل حقيقةُ قولِ القائل أخذتُ نِصفَ درهمٍ أنه أَخَذ شيئاً وتَرَك مثلَه فعبّر عنه بالنِصف توسّعاً. Ibn Fūrak (1987, 203.24–25).

148. وكذلك كان يقول إنّ عِبارتنا التي استعملناها هاهنا لهذا المعنى بلفظِ الجزء توسعٌ مِن قِبَل أنها لا حقيقةَ للبعض والنصف والثلث بل حقيقةُ قولِ القائل أخذتُ نصفَ درهمٍ أنه أخذ شيئاً وترك مثلَه فعبّر عنه بالنصف توسعًا فعلى هذا إذا قيل الجزءُ والبعضُ والنصفُ والثلثُ والربعُ فذلك توسّعٌ على أصله وحقيقتُه ما ذكرنا أنّ كلّ واحدٍ من هذه الجواهر المَوجودة لا يُنكَر أنْ يُوجَد منفرداً عن سائر الأجزاء مفارقاً لها وهذا هو معنى قولِنا إنّ الجزء لا يتجزّأ وإنّ الجوهر لا يَنقسم في ذاته ولا يتنصّف. Ibn Fūrak (1987, 203.23–204.4).

that can be strictly accurate according to this account of physics are those that make statements about individual atoms and their behavior. Every other grouping beyond the single atom is semantic extension, a broadening beyond an original strict accuracy. Ibn Fūrak therefore used "accurate account" to identify the moments when language gave an accurate account of the world as it was in extramental atomic fact. Frank's translation of *ḥaqīqah* here is a valuable one: "analytically strict [and] ontologically designative."[149] The nature of the world was at stake here, and the scientific framework being used to make sense of it was fundamentally linguistic. Ibn Fūrak used a core conceptual vocabulary for a scientific project. Atoms were understood to the extent that they could be spoken about. The vocabulary needs translation, and the project of naming and subdividing reality is still taking place in the Large Hadron Collider.

KNOWLEDGE IS EVERYTHING

We have come to understand that *maʿānī* were the primary building blocks of Ibn Fūrak's theology. They provided an interface between language, mind, and reality; they were the raw material for human perception of the world and understanding of God, and they were the cognitive source of the ideas that humans expressed in language. *Maʿānī* helped structure theological and scientific epistemologies and were themselves the stuff of those cognitive processes. There is a circularity here: *maʿnā* is both how we know and what we know. (Cf. Frank on the Muʿtazilī Abū al-Huḏayl al-ʿAllāf, d. 842.)[150] Knowledge (*ʿilm*) was everything. Ibn Fūrak was aware of this, and the first chapter of the *Muǧarrad* he titled "Clarification of al-Ašʿarī's School of Thought with Regard to the *Maʿnā* of Knowledge and Its Formal Definition."[151]

Ibn Fūrak started his chapter on knowledge with what he said was the fundamental and central statement of al-Ašʿarī around which all his other definitions of *maʿānī* revolved, that "the *maʿnā* of knowledge and its accurate account is that with which the knower knows the known."[152] This is concise and circular to the point of obscurity. But the theological problem that al-Ašʿarī and Ibn Fūrak faced was very real: how humans could best think of the divine. It was problematic to think of God as having a self that was his knowledge, because it was incoherent from the human perspective; it did not conform to the universal and accurate

149. Frank (1984, 50). Cf. al-Qāḍī ʿAbd al-Ǧabbār (1965–74, 7:130.3–10).

150. Frank (1969, 465–66).

151. الفصل الأول في إبانة مذهبه في معنى العِلم وحدّه. Ibn Fūrak (1987, 10–11).

152. معنى العِلم وحقيقتُه ما به يَعلَم العالِمُ المعلوم. Ibn Fūrak (1987, 10.12).

account of knowledge with which humans worked.[153] Daniel Gimaret has explained this doctrine as avoidance of the confusion of substance and accident, with both God and knower being substance and knowledge an accident. This is more than plausible, but the conceptual vocabulary of substance and accident is absent from these passages in al-Aš‘arī and Ibn Fūrak.[154] When al-Aš‘arī had discussed the same doctrine, he talked not about substance and accident but about *ma‘nā* and how humans conceive of knowledge: it was impossible for God to be "in the same *ma‘nā* as his attributes. Don't you see that the route by which it is known that knowledge is knowledge is that the knower has knowledge?"[155] Al-Aš‘arī was saying that we comprehend the *ma‘nā* of knowledge, we know what knowledge is, only by thinking of someone knowing something and thereby having knowledge. Our very conception of knowledge is of someone having it, not that someone is it. This is why God cannot be knowledge, nor be knowing in his self; we must understand him as having knowledge. (Cf. Frank on Abū al-Huḏayl).[156]

The theological process here is a policing of human speech acts that reflect human cognitive processes made up of *ma‘ānī.* Al-Aš‘arī made this clear in response to a hypothetical suggestion that God could be neither a knower in himself nor a knower with a separate *ma‘nā*. His response was that there is no third option: the knowledge is either a separate *ma‘nā,* or it is in God himself; we cannot affirm the knowledge in any other way.[157] I think that although it is clumsy, the translation of *ma‘nā* as "mental content" is still viable here: these are theories and debates about how humans should think of God. The pressure on my translation comes from the way the word "mental" calls into question whose mind the content is in. There is no doubt that the theological process is taking place in the mind of the theologian, but there is equally no doubt that the target of that process, the *ma‘nā* with which God knows, is divine and therefore not in the mind of the theo-

153. وعلى ذلك عوّل في استدلاله على أنّ الله تعالى عالِمٌ بعِلمٍ مِن حيث أنه لو كان عالِم بنفسه كان نفسُه عِلمٌ لأنّ حقيقةَ معنى العِلم ما يَعلَم به العالِمُ المعلومَ فلو كانتْ نفسُ القديم سبحانه نفساً بها يَعلَم المعلوماتِ وَجَب أنْ تكون عِلماً وفي معناه. Ibn Fūrak (1987, 10.12–15). Cf. al-Aš‘arī (1953a, 30 n. 18), Gimaret (1990, 37).

154. Al-Aš‘arī (1953a, #25), Gimaret (1990, 275).

155. ويَستحيل أنْ يكون العِلمُ عالِماً أو العالِمُ عِلماً أو يكون اللهُ تعالى بمعنى الصفات ألا ترى أنّ الطريق الذي [به (مكارثي)] يُعلَم [به (غرابه)] أنّ العِلم عِلمٌ أنّ العالِم به علم. Al-Aš‘arī (1953a, #25), (1955, 30.7–9).

156. فلما استَحال أنْ يكون الباري تعالى عِلماً استحال أنْ يكون عالِماً بنفسه فإذا استحال ذلك صحَّ أنه عالِمٌ بعِلمٍ يستَحيل أنْ يكون هو نفسه. Al-Aš‘arī (1953a, #25), (1955, 30.10–12). See also al-Aš‘arī (1953a, #18), (1955, 26.16–27.5); Frank (1969, 466–67).

157. فإنْ قال قائلٌ ما أنكرتم أنْ يكون الباري سبحانه عالِماً لا بنفسه ولا بمعنى يَستحيل أنْ يكون هو نفسُه قيل له لو جاز هذا لَجاز أنْ يكون قولُنا عالِمٌ لم يرجِع به إلى نفسه ولا إلى معنى ولم يَثبُت به نفسُه ولا معنىً يَستحيل أنْ يكون هو نفسُه وإذا لم يجز هذا بَطَل ما قالوه. Al-Aš‘arī (1953a, #26), (1955, 30.13–31.2).

logian. This is the same problem that we faced with the use of *maʿnā* in physics: theologians like Ibn Fūrak used a conceptual vocabulary based around *maʿnā* that did not inherently mark the boundary between the human mind and the world outside. The tension is a reminder that we do not have a word in English that does the work *maʿnā* did in Arabic.

Knowledge was everything, and it was different from other human or divine actions. One can know a taste, but taste itself is not knowledge.[158] Ibn Fūrak's choice of this example reminds us once again that he is seeking to apply to God conclusions developed with reference to humanity. This is arguably the central tension of Islamic theology. The lists of *maʿānī* other than "knowledge" that he provided in this first paragraph of his chapter 1 are evidence of this assumption: "movement, ability, color, and taste," and then "speech, movement, color, and taste." Both lists combine *maʿānī* understood to be unquestionably both divine and human (for example, "speech") and *maʿānī* that are consistently understood as theologically incompatible with God ("color" and "taste"). Ibn Fūrak also tells us how al-Ašʿarī asked himself whether the knower knows because knowledge is knowledge or because such knowledge is *relative* to the knower (in the same way as movement is relative to the mover).[159] Ibn Fūrak reported that al-Ašʿarī considered both alternatives invalid and wrote that "the knower knows only on account of that from which the name 'knower' is derived for him."[160] Ibn Fūrak then commented that "this is an intimation that this is the *maʿnā* of 'knowledge': that from which it is necessary to derive the name 'knowing' for whomsoever engages in knowing."[161] Once again, a *maʿnā* with an ontological significance that extends to the divine is constructed with reference to the lexicon.

Ibn Fūrak also distinguished knowledge from belief. (The Arabic word is *iʿtiqād,* which could also be translated as "firmly combined" or "compactly formed"; see Frank.)[162] He wrote that the root principle from which belief is derived "is investigated without *maʿānī.*"[163] In this short passage, Ibn Fūrak was

158. ألا ترى أنّ . . . الطعْم لا يصح أنْ يكون شيءٌ مِن ذلك عِلمٌ لمّا لم يجزم أنْ يكون عالِماً به عالِماً. Ibn Fūrak (1987, 10.16–18).

159. فلِماذا كان العالِمُ عالِماً ألأجل أنّ العِلم عِلمٌ أمْ لأجل أنّ العِلم عِلمٌ وأنه مُضافٌ إليه. Ibn Fūrak (1987, 11.1–2). . . . الحركةُ التي أُضيفتْ إلى المتحرِّك. Ibn Fūrak (1987, 26.21–22).

160. إنما كان العالِمُ عالِماً لما له اشتُقّ منه اسمُ العالِم وهو العِلم. Ibn Fūrak (1987, 11.2–3).

161. وهذا إيماءٌ إلى أنّ ذلك معنى العِلم وهو الذي يجب أنْ يُشتَقّ لِمَن قام به منه اسم. Ibn Fūrak (1987, 11.5–6).

162. Frank (1989, 42f).

163. وكان يُنكِر أنْ يكون معنى العِلم اعتقادُ الشيء على ما هو به وقال إنّ وصْفَ عِلمنا بأنه اعتقادٌ مجازٌ لأنه أصل العَقْد والاعتقاد إنما يَتحقّق بغير المعاني وإذا استُعمل في ذلك فعلى التوسُّع ومِن مذهبه أيضاً أنه لا

responding to an old Mu'tazilī doctrine, attributed to al-Ğubbā'ī, that knowledge is the belief that something is as it is.[164] In the roughly contemporary defense of that doctrine by 'Abd al-Ğabbār, we can see that for the Mu'tazilah there was a distinction between a broad category of belief and a narrower subcategory of belief called "knowledge," in which the belief came with certainty.[165] This is close to the Aš'ārī position of Ibn Fūrak that we encountered above: belief can be false, but knowledge is accurate.[166] The Mu'tazilah were firm in their location of the divine attributes in human language and cognition; there is no problem reading 'Abd al-Ğabbār's *ma'nā* here as "mental content," a conceptual category that was part of the human process of reasoning through the possibilities for accurate description of God. But what are the *ma'ānī* that Ibn Fūrak thought were not involved in belief? One way to think about them is to use the pigeonhole metaphor suggested above for *ma'ānī* as categories. Ibn Fūrak uses *ma'nā* in his theology because it provides him with a stable concept that can be separated from language and applied to both mind and reality (whether that reality is worldly or divine). If the *ma'ānī* are stable mental contents that reflect the world, then they cannot be false; one can of course have a false cognition of them, a flawed or corrupted idea, but the *ma'nā* itself is, perhaps, by definition true. We already know that an accurate human account of a *ma'nā* was called *ḥaqīqah,* and here we have a remark by Ibn Fūrak that suggests while *ma'ānī* are the stuff of human cognition, they are not the stuff of human false belief or faulty supposition. This fits with my assumption in chapter 2 that the *ma'ānī* of theology, lexicography, and grammar are one single category used in different ways. When scholars say that the *ma'nā* of X is Y, they are claiming to report fact. Scholars of course disagreed on the facts, and everyone from lexicographers to theologians disagreed about *ma'ānī,* but everyone agreed that in doing so they were concerned with facts about language, the world, or God. They were concerned, like Ibn Fūrak, with knowledge, not belief.

يُفرّق بين العِلم والمعرفة وكذلك اليقين والفهم والفتنة والدراية والعقل والفقه كلّ ذلك عنده بمعنى العِلم . . .
وكان يمنع وصْفَ العِلم والجهل بأنهما اعتقادان على الحقيقة وإنْ أجاز أنْ يُطلَق عليهما ذلك توسّعاً ومجازاً.
Ibn Fūrak (1987, 11.7–11, 13.23–24).

164. Frank (1969, 465), al-Qāḍī 'Abd al-Ğabbār (1965–74, 12: 25.18).

165. اعلمْ أنّ العِلم هو المعنى الذي يقتضي سكون نفس العالِم إلى ما تناوله . . . والذي يقول شيوخُنا رحمهم اللهُ في العِلم أنه من جنس الاعتقاد فمتى تعلَّق بالشيء على ما هو به ووقع على وجهٍ يقتضي سكون النفس. . . . العِلم هو الاعتقاد الواقع على بعض الوجوه Al-Qāḍī 'Abd al-Ğabbār (1965–74, 12: 13.1, 25.17–18, 27.8–9).

166. See note 133 above.

EVERYTHING IS KNOWLEDGE

When *maʿnā* worked to establish the strict monotheism of the Islamic God, it did so by moving the action into the human mind. We have seen scholars in this chapter reminding us that the words "description" and "attribute" refer to linguistic acts of description. We have not seen them engage in similar reminders that *maʿnā* refers to human cognition, but perhaps the reason no scholar said that *maʿānī* were cognitive is that there was no one around to disagree, whereas some creeds did indeed deny that God's descriptions and attributes were human and linguistic. The closest we get to a noncognitive *maʿnā* is the theory of Muʿammar, and in the absence of extant texts we cannot be sure exactly where he would have positioned his causal *maʿānī* between the mental and extramental realms. All we can be sure of is that he was using a core conceptual vocabulary that he shared with contemporary Arabic accounts of how language worked. However, with Ibn Fūrak we can at least consider the prospect that his cognitive *maʿānī* were located in human minds and that the effort he expended to prevent God being associated with internal multiplicity was focused on human cognition of God rather than on the extramental constitution of the divine being.

When the action moves to the sphere of human cognition, it starts to make more sense that language would be heavily involved. Again, this enables us to explain how so much of Islamic theology was about naming: the names given to things mattered because they reflected mental contents, and the mental contents reflected the extramental reality of the world. These two vectors of reflection were then critically evaluated according to the standard of accuracy. Theologians asked whether the vocal forms of language did in fact accurately reflect mental contents, and they could turn to the lexicon to adjudicate and negotiate their conclusions. Theologians also asked whether their mental contents accurately reflected the extramental world that their senses observed, and they could turn to reason and logic to adjudicate their conclusions. Theology was science for Ibn Fūrak and his contemporaries; the stuff of their debates was human mental content, and they wanted to make that content as accurate as possible. Humans had mental contents that resulted from their interactions with the world and mental contents that resulted from their considerations of the divine. Both needed to be assessed according to lexical precedent, revelatory precedent, reason, and sensory data as appropriate.

Ibn Fūrak's Ašʿarī theory of the acquisition of acts, as discussed above,[167] was relevant to this picture of human mental content. When we consider that theory, it seems logical to conclude that God had exactly the same control over human mental contents as he did over every single other atom or thing in his creation.

167. See section above: "Acquisition".

If this is the case, then theology was less about human cognition and reason and more about what God did with human mental contents. This makes theories like acquisition seem quite different: God created the human and created the extramental objects with which the human interacted. God also created the movements of those extramental objects and then created the human mental content that was human cognition of the movement of the extramental objects. On this reading, mental content simply provided God with a means to manage human minds. It is tempting to suggest that conclusions such as these may have been on the minds of scholars such as Ibn Fūrak's pupil al-Qušayrī, who contributed to the development of mystical epistemologies in which *maʿānī* and *ḥaqāʾiq*, accurate accounts of mental contents, became increasingly tightly connected to the divine and increasingly distant from the physics and linguistics of Ibn Fūrak.

However, the observation that Ašʿarī occasionalism contributes to a system in which God's omnipresence makes the location of *maʿānī* irrelevant would not have made sense to Ibn Fūrak. His typology of God's creation (things, instances, substances, and accidents) did not include *maʿānī*,[168] which suggests that he did not see them as a separate ontological category; they were just part of his process of thinking about things, instances, substances, and accidents. The observation about occasionalism rather comes out of the process of translating Ibn Fūrak into twenty-first-century English, a process that itself requires one to take a position on the location of the *maʿānī* between language, mind, and reality. The conclusion that I draw here is that *maʿānī* were connected to language because they could always (and only) be expressed in language. This meant that accounts of *maʿānī* were rooted in the lexicon. But Ibn Fūrak did not see the *maʿānī* as dependent on the lexicon or on human language. They were a category he could separate from language, a set of conceptual pigeonholes into which theological and physical concepts could be slotted and from which connections could then be made to specific linguistic vocal forms in contexts. The translation "mental contents," with the caveat that it does not produce fluid or easily read English prose, works for *maʿānī* on this account. The problem comes with the decision, forced upon us by the translation process but not necessarily experienced by the authors of these texts, as to whether the *maʿānī* are in human minds, outside in the extramental world, divine, or, while remaining themselves, in all three.

This is a moment at which some comparative philosophy may be useful. Twentieth- and twenty-first-century scholars of ancient Greece have encountered a similar problem with accidents, those Aristotelian nonessential qualities we encountered earlier in this chapter, and with universals. Mohsen Javadi makes the following important observation: "All concepts, including universals, exist in the

168. See note 92 above.

mind as mental qualities, but not [as] instances of substance. . . . Universals . . . are always present in the mind as mental qualities, as is the case with other accidents."[169] In Ibn Fūrak's theology we are not dealing with universals, or at least we are not dealing with the Aristotelian tradition of universals (that continued in Arabic, as the next chapter will show). But we are dealing with accidents, which as Ibn Fūrak said are a subcategory of *maʿānī*.[170] Javadi locates his clarity about the location of universals and accidents in the work of, among others, Ibn Sīnā: "As far as I know, this problem was not discussed in the West, but we can find a rich and detailed discussion of it in Muslim philosophy, especially in the discussion of 'knowledge' or 'mental existence' [*al-wuǧūd aḏ-ḏihnī*]."[171] We will come to Ibn Sīnā in the next chapter, where Javadi's observation will be shown to be correct. Ibn Sīnā was working with the same conceptual vocabulary as Ibn Fūrak and ar-Rāġib; he exploited the potential of *maʿānī* to build theories of cognition in a way that his predecessors in the Arabic Aristotelian tradition had not.

I would like to end this chapter on Ibn Fūrak with some observations made by Richard Cross about Duns Scotus (the thirteenth-century Scot whom we met in chapter 2 when considering the translation of *maʿnā* as "entitative"): "It makes no difference at all to cognition whether or not the object of cognition is inherent in the mind. Just the same causal story is told in both cases, and in both cases we can think of the mind as somehow or other including its object—even if that object is external to it." The theory of causality is what is important, not the location of the object of cognition: "The same nature can be said to exist in reality and in the mind, and to this extent extramental particulars, or aspects of such external particulars are, in a qualified way, themselves somehow 'in the mind.'"[172] Cross's analysis of Scotus has led him to the same point where our reading of Ibn Fūrak, an Islamic theologian working three centuries earlier, led us. In both thirteenth-century Europe and eleventh-century Iran and Iraq, a theory of theological physics could function with what looks to us now like a complete collapse between mind and world.

I suggested above that the blur between epistemology and ontology in Ibn Fūrak could be connected, via the Ašʿarī theory of acquisition, to the work of scholars like al-Qušayrī who are usually called "Sufi" or "mystic." I then noted that this is a connection that makes sense only in hindsight, arises only as an option in the translation process, and would not have made sense to Ibn Fūrak himself. Nevertheless, it is worth considering. Cross engages in a similar process with

169. Javadi (2013, 70).

170. See note 61 above.

171. Transliteration modified from Javadi (2013, 70).

172. Cross (2009, 294 [72]).

Scotus, and asks whether Scotus's assumptions "weaken the account of the self, such that the self is no longer a self-contained whole but extends out into the environment too." This is very much a question couched in the terms of twenty-first-century philosophy, which is no bad thing. Cross continues: "Mental contents are 'in' the mind whether or not they inhere in the mind. To be in the mind, all such contents have to be are actual objects of occurrent cognition." This matches the conclusions drawn in this chapter about *ma'ānī:* movements in living extramental bodies and divine attributes are both objects of cognition and mental contents. The explanation Cross gives for his reading is also useful: "Inner and outer theatres have the same observer—the mind or intelligence—and this breakdown of the distinction between representation and represented hinges on the loosening of what it is to be 'in' the mind: not as such inherent, but simply part of a causal story originating with semantic contents and issuing in an occurrent cognition."[173]

I have no intention of connecting Scotus's theory of the self to Ibn Fūrak, nor of suggesting that Ibn Fūrak's ideas necessarily made their way from Baghdad to the Scottish borders (or more accurately, to Oxford and Cologne). What I would like to do is use Cross's reading of Scotus as an alibi for my reading of Ibn Fūrak and suggest it as a possible resolution to the problems of interpretation identified by Frank, Gimaret, and Allard. If the inner and outer theaters of mind and extramental reality do indeed have the same observer, and that observer is the human intelligence of the theologian, then it is moot whether *ma'ānī* are mental contents, extramental forces and qualities, or divine attributes. *Ma'ānī* were the stuff of human intelligence, whether it was directed at the operations of grammar and syntax, linguistic precedent in the lexicon, extramental physics, or the nature of the divine. They were explicable categories that provided Ibn Fūrak with epistemological stability, clarity, and terminological concision, three merits that are lost when his Arabic is translated into our English.

173. Cross (2009, 300 [78]).

6

Logic

Ibn Sīnā inherited Greek and Arabic Aristotelianism and turned it into a new synthesis with a new conceptual vocabulary. Translation lay at the heart of this process. In the eleventh century, Ibn Sīnā wrote in dialogue with both the philhellenic commentary tradition and the Arabic tradition of thought about language. Where the Baghdad School of Aristotelian philosophers had claimed that logic enabled them to dispense with Arabic grammar (see my article with Peter Adamson),[1] and al-Fārābī had tended to use calques of Greek words (Zimmermann argues persuasively that he did so deliberately),[2] Ibn Sīnā chose to write Arabic with all the challenges and rewards such a decision entailed. He was faced with Aristotle in Arabic and translation choices made by other scholars. The Arabic conceptual vocabulary he developed gave him the tools to rethink human cognition, logical process, and the role of God.

IBN SĪNĀ BETWEEN GREECE AND THE WEST

Greece in the Arabic Eleventh Century

Ibn Sīnā was an Aristotelian. He was certain that he was engaged in the same intellectual project as Aristotle, and he structured his most comprehensive philosophical work, *aš-Šifāʾ* (*The Cure*) as a summa of the *Organon.* Aristotle had died over a millennium before Ibn Sīnā wrote *aš-Šifāʾ*, and across those centuries

1. Key and Adamson (2015).

2. Zimmermann (1981, cxxix–cxxxvii).

Aristotle's logical works, and more, had been curated into a single set of treatises understood as a tool (*organon*) for intellectual activity. Ibn Sīnā followed this commentary tradition. *Aš-Šifāʾ* starts with Porphyry's (d. 305) introduction to logic the *Eisagoge*, and then Aristotle's *Categories, De Interpretatione, Prior Analytics, Posterior Analytics, Topics, Sophistical Refutations, Rhetoric,* and *Poetics.* In all these cases *aš-Šifāʾ* is not a line-by-line commentary but rather a book-by-book analysis and reworking of Aristotle, al-Fārābī, and Aristotle's Greek and Arabic commentators. Ibn Sīnā saw himself "as a conscious reformer of the Aristotelian tradition,"[3] and after *Poetics* he stopped following the inherited Aristotelian order. *Aš-Šifāʾ* continued with Aristotle's *Physics, On the Heavens, De Generatione et Corruptione, Chemistry* (*Meteorology*), *Meteorology, On the Soul, Botany,* and *Zoology.* Then came mathematics with Euclid's (fl. 300 B.C.) *Elements,* Ptolemy's (d. 168) *Almagest,* Nichomacus's (d. 120) *Introduction,* and Ptolemy's *Harmonics.* Finally, closing out *aš-Šifāʾ* was Ibn Sīnā's own *Ilāhīyāt,* which took the theological and epistemological promise of Aristotle's *Metaphysics* and completely reworked it into a new Islamic philosophical synthesis.[4]

The benefit of writing out these titles here is that it forces the reader to remember just how much Greek there was in the Arabic eleventh century. This may come as a surprise when we consider the ways in which ar-Rāġib and Ibn Fūrak, the subjects of the previous two chapters, worked to understand and describe the world and mankind. They both knew the Greek was there, but their Islamic theology had the confidence to, for example, disagree with Democritus about atoms. Ar-Rāġib was opposed to any non-Islamic account of God whatsoever, but at the same time his ethics often came straight from Aristotle and Neoplatonism. Ar-Rāġib's claim that the physical act of doing things was central to both ethics and the purification of the soul is self-evidently both Aristotelian and Neoplatonic. Ibn Sīnā's account of the same process was very similar indeed; and his "with reason and revelation" was also one of ar-Rāġib's favorite ethicoepistemological slogans.[5] What we have in the eleventh century is a combination of Islamic theology and Arabic philosophy in which there is complete overlap at some points and total divergence at others. (For a paradigmatic example of the process, see Everett Rowson.)[6] Sometimes these two disciplines used the same Greek texts, and sometimes their wholly different approaches to the divine, the world, and humanity used completely separate epistemological resources. When we read Ibn Sīnā with a focus on

3. Gutas (1988, 115).

4. For details of these contents: Gutas (1988, 103f, 270f).

5. عقلًا وشرْعًا. Gutas (1988, 71), Ibn Sīnā (1952b, 196.17), Key (2011, 301–2).

6. Rowson and al-ʿĀmirī (1988).

the core conceptual vocabulary of *maʿnā* and *ḥaqīqah,* it brings to the forefront those moments when he was part of the conversation about language along with ar-Rāġib and Ibn Fūrak.

The Arabic Eleventh Century and the West

From our standpoint today in the twenty-first-century Anglophone and European academy, the historical genealogies of conceptual vocabulary go in more than one direction. It is not just the case that the Arabic reception of Greek philosophy moved into Europe through Ibn Sīnā, Ibn Rušd (Averroes, d. 1198), and others, or that Ibn Sīnā himself used Arabic translations of the same Greek texts we read today. There were also Roman and Christian traditions of thought about language that were accessed by European scholasticism yet were unavailable to Ibn Sīnā, despite their origins in the Middle East and Mediterranean. The works of Cicero (d. 43 B.C.), Varro (d. 27 B.C.), and Horace (d. 8 B.C.) were not available in Arabic. But there is little to be gained from pursuing of an account of influence or the lack thereof. Eleventh-century Arabic scholars and their predecessors moved and talked in ways that are not captured in the extant manuscripts. Furthermore, human beings are capable of having similar ideas in different places and at different times without this having been the result of a documentable transmission process. This is particularly true in relation to descriptions of languages and minds. Augustine of Hippo's (d. 430) theories of signification and epistemology, which famously helped Wittgenstein start *Philosophical Investigations* fifteen hundred years later, are one such case: they were not translated into Arabic at all.[7] But as Laurent Cesalli and Nadja Germann show, Augustine had a four-part map of signification that bears comparison to those found in the Arabic eleventh century. There were spoken words (*verbum*), spoken words that signified (*dictio*), intelligible contents (*dicibile*), and extramental objects (*res*). And there was a significant further component for Augustine: the sign (*signum*) that occurs "whenever something that sounds presents the mind with something to be cognized. . . . A sign is something which is itself sensed and which indicates to the mind something beyond the sign itself."[8] We find ourselves right back with Saussure, and it is much easier to sketch a genealogy of influence from Augustine to Saussure than it is to connect either to Arabic. All that we should say about the relationship between Augustine and eleventh-century Arabic is that they were playing different games with some of the same equipment. Furthermore, both the absence of Augustine from eleventh-century Arabic and the presence of Augustine in

7. König (2013).

8. Cesalli and Germann (2008, 131–32).

fourteenth-century Europe are important reminders that what came after Ibn Sīnā in Latin was both more and less than Arabic.

Translation in Three Directions (Greek, Latin, and Persian)

Ibn Sīnā wrote in Arabic and Persian, and as he did so he cared about Greek. He was well aware of the schools and stages of translation from Greek into Arabic that had enabled him to access Aristotle's texts. Ibn Sīnā's work was subsequently translated into Latin by scholars who knew Greek and who, as we have just noted above, were also reading Latin that predated Ibn Sīnā. *Maʿnā,* the term with which I am concerned, is an Arabic word that sits in between Greek and Latin, fitting neatly into neither. What did people think it meant in Latin? In their magisterial *The Development of Logic,* which traces formal logic from ancient Greece to the English twentieth century, William and Martha Kneale discussed the twelfth- and thirteenth-century European controversies about the intellectual soul and the connections made between Aristotle's *De Anima* and his *De Interpretatione.* The Kneales wrote: "Thought, it was generally held, proceeds by means of *propositiones mentales* formed from natural signs in the soul, and here again Arabic influence was important in the detailed elaboration of the theory. In the Arabic of Ibn Sīnā . . . a form in the soul was identified with a *maʿnā,* i.e. a meaning or notion, and when Ibn Sīnā's works were translated into Latin, *maʿnā* was rendered in all contexts by *intentio,* which thus came to have in medieval epistemology the technical sense of 'natural sign in the soul.'"[9] What happened here was that scholars such as Albert the Great (d. 1280) and Thomas Aquinas (d. 1198), while engaged in a European project of making Aristotle (and Ibn Rušd) compatible with Christian doctrine, used Ibn Sīnā's Aristotelian synthesis, which itself had used the Arabic word *maʿnā.* The result was a piece of Latin conceptual vocabulary, *intentio,* that did Christian work in Europe as equipment for a different language game. From a twenty-first-century perspective, this translation history can cause serious problems for philosophers reading Ibn Sīnā, as Dimitri Gutas has noted in a short discussion of what he calls an "evocatively polysemic word": "The fact that this *maʿnā* was translated as *intentio* in medieval Latin, the starting point of many a misled scholar, does not mean *by itself* that the term means 'intention' in any sense."[10]

When Ibn Sīnā's *maʿnā* was translated forward in time and into the European Latin language game, it started to play a necessarily new and different role within that game's Latin conceptual vocabulary. What about when *maʿnā* was translated backwards? Or rather, what conceptual vocabulary in ancient Greek philosophy

9. Kneale and Kneale (1962, 229).

10. Gutas (2012, 430).

became *maʿnā* in eleventh-century Arabic? Ullmann has already shown us how many of Galen's Greek words became *maʿnā* in the ninth century, and the array of options in the Arabic translation of *De Interpretatione* is indicative of the work *maʿānī* continued to do, and of the persistent problem of reading that work today in English: *pragmata, pathēma,* and *legō d' hoti!* First, we have an ancient Greek word for "things" (*pragmata*), which Aristotle used to refer to real objects. In the first chapter of *De Interpretatione,* J. L. Ackrill translates it as "real things." (Wolfson lists other occurrences.)[11] Next, a word for "passive emotion or condition" (*pathēma*), which Ackrill translates as "affections or impressions."[12] (The immediate Arabic translation was *āṯār,* but *maʿānī* were soon involved, as we will see below.) Finally, a phrase (*legō d' hoti*) that Aristotle used to express his authorial intent: "Now let me explain what I mean" (Harold Cooke; the phrase is elided by Ackrill).[13] Jon McGinnis, in an article on Ibn Sīnā's scientific method that looks forward to twentieth-century Anglophone philosophy of language and back to Aristotle, translates *maʿnā* as "certain (positive) accounts" and "intrinsic essential account."[14] (Cf. Gerhard Endress: "*maʿnā* ('Betroffenheit,' 'Intention') = *prâgma* 'Bedeutung.'")[15] John Wansborough has also noted the connection between the Greek word for "motif" or "theme" (*topos*) and the *maʿānī* of Arabic poetry.[16] It is clear that *maʿnā* in Arabic occupied a space that did not exist in Greek (just as it does not exist in English). Different games are played with different equipment.

The fact that *maʿnā* was used for this range of Greek meanings is evidence that it had a broad function in Arabic, and that it was a preexisting category in the conceptual vocabularies of the translators of Aristotle and his commentators, just as it had been a preexisting category in the translators of Galen. The question then becomes whether it developed specific, separate, technical functions in the Arabic vocabularies of the philhellenic philosophers and should be read as such, or whether it would be better to follow the practice established in the first five chapters of this book and read for a single stable usage. I would like to attempt the latter course; I think *maʿnā* was an Arabic word used for all kinds of Greek words across Aristotle, Galen, and more. *Maʿnā* in Arabic Aristotelianism is best looked at as a functional piece of equipment in the eleventh-century Arabic language game, and not as a series of distinct and incompatible alternatives.

11. Arist. *Int.* 16a7–8. Aristotle (1963, 43), Wolfson (1976, 115 n. 12).

12. Arist. *Int.* 16a5. Aristotle (1948, 1:99.6, 10), (1963, 43).

13. Arist. *Int.* 16b7–8. Aristotle (1938b, 119), (1963, 44).

14. McGinnis (2008, 137, 138).

15. Endress (1986, 280), (1989, 133).

16. Wansborough (1967, 57).

The Arabic Aristotelianism of Ibn Sīna used *maʿnā* to claim universal purchase on philosophy, regardless of the language in which it was written. At the end of his discussion of the first book of Aristotle's *Categories,* Ibn Sīnā noted that he was reading an account of the interface between language and thought that had been written in a language different from his own: "The Greek language uses a different convention here."[17] Ibn Sīnā had been reviewing Aristotle's third type of naming, *parōnuma* ("paronymous" for Ackrill, "derivatively" for Cooke), for which he gives the examples of "grammar" connecting to "grammarian" and "heroism" connecting to "hero."[18] Ibn Sīnā explained that what connects such names is a certain connection to a particular mental content, which can exist in the latter (eloquence exists in the eloquent person) or be for some work the latter does (the blacksmith, *ḥaddād,* works with iron, *ḥadīd*).[19] The variation in examples is a function of a millennium of translation and commentary. (The translation by Ḥunayn b. Isḥāq [d. 873] or his son Isḥāq b. Ḥunayn [d. 911] used by Ibn Sīnā is extant and has eloquence and bravery as the two examples.)[20] Ibn Sīnā goes on to explain how Arabic morphological changes to the vocal form can introduce variation in the mental content in different ways. (So a sword can be "Indian," *hindī* with the Arabic *nisbah* ending *-ī,* or it can be "an Indian-made sword," *muhannad,* in the form of the Arabic passive participle). He says this is specific to the convention of each different language, and ends with the remark about Greek I quoted above.[21] The Arabic translation of this passage of Aristotle did not use *maʿnā,* but Ibn Sīnā did, as had his predecessor in the Baghdad School of Aristotelian commentary, the Christian scholar al-Ḥasan Ibn Suwār (d. 1020).[22] *Maʿnā* was a useful word for discussions of comparative grammar in logic.

Elsewhere, in his Arabic commentary on *De Interpretatione,* Ibn Sīnā noted that Arabic Aristotelianism had established the Arabic "word" (*kalimah*) rather than "verb" (*fiʿl*) as a translation for the Greek "verb" (*rhēma,* on the translation of which see Ackrill).[23] Ibn Sīnā wrote: "Not everything that is a *fiʿl* in Arabic is a

17. ولليونانيات في الأمرَين اصطلاحٌ آخر. Ibn Sīnā (1959b, 17.13–14). On Ibn Sīnā's knowledge of Greek: Vagelpohl (2010, 260).

18. Arist. *Cat.* 1a12–15. Aristotle (1938a, 13), (1963, 3); Ibn Sīnā (1959b, 16.18–17.14).

19. والمُشتقُّ له الاسمُ هو الذي لمّا كانتْ له نسبةٌ ما أيْ نسبةٌ كانت إلى معنىً من المعاني سواء كان المعنى موجوداً فيه كالفصاحة أو له كالمال أو موضوعاً لعملٍ من أعماله كالحديد. Ibn Sīnā (1959b, 16.18–20).

20. Aristotle (1948, 1:33–34), D'Ancona (2013, n. 55).

21. فُعِلَ به فِعْلٌ آخَرُ يُوجِبه اصطلاحُ لغةٍ دون لغة. Ibn Sīnā (1959b, 17.5,12–14).

22. قال الحسن بن سُوار يُحتاج في تمامِ المشتقّةِ اسماؤه إلى خمسة أشياء أنْ تكون لها شِركةٌ في الاسم وشِركةٌ في المعنى واختلافٌ في الاسم واختلافٌ في المعنى وأنْ يكون اسمُ أحدِهما مأخوذٌ من الذي منه اشتُقّ الاسم. Aristotle (1948, 1:85 n. 24), Georr (1948, 371 n. 24).

23. Aristotle (1963, 118–20).

kalimah. For in Arabic, *amšī* ["I am walking"] and *yamšī* ["he is walking"] are both called *fiʿl*, but neither is unequivocally a *kalimah*. That is because the *a-* in *amšī* indicates a specific separate matter ["I"], as does the *-t-* in *mašaytu* ("I walked"). The statements "I am walking" or "I walked" can therefore be true or false."[24] Ibn Sīnā noted that the Arabic verb, which includes the subject as a prefix, is in effect a predication consisting of two terms, which can therefore be true or false. What matters for us here is Ibn Sīnā's combined clarity both about specific languages and about universal matters of logic such as predication.

Maʿnā was also available for Ibn Sīnā to use in his Persian logic as an Arabic loanword. This is not the place for an in-depth examination of the role of *maʿnā* in Persian philosophy, but suffice it to say that both *lafẓ* and *maʿnā* moved into New Persian along with a great deal of Arabic scholarly terminology around this time. As we know, Ibn Sīnā wrote a complete abridged philosophy in Persian at the request of the ruler of Isfahan, "apparently by translating into Persian sections that he had written earlier in Arabic" around 1027.[25] Vocal form and mental content are to be found there, just as they were in his Arabic logic.[26]

MENTAL CONTENTS IN IBN SĪNĀ'S CONCEPTUAL VOCABULARY

Maʿnā was a logical concept for Ibn Sīnā, and it was also the cognitive result of sensory input. Mental content is an unproblematic translation in both cases. *Maʿānī* were things in our minds that we do not sense directly; *maʿānī* such as the fear or enmity that one associates with a predator, or the sweetness that one associates with a yellow-colored substance thought to be honey.[27] In a famous example, Ibn Sīnā said that sheep see the shape and color of a wolf first, and then subsequently perceive a *maʿnā* of antagonism in the wolf that completes its form and leads them to be afraid and flee.[28]

24. وليس كلُّ ما يُسمّى في اللغة العربية فِعْلاً هو كلمةٌ فإنّ قولهم أَمْشِي ويَمْشِي فِعْلٌ عندهم وليس كلمةً مطلقةً وذلك لأنّ الهمزة دلّتْ على موضوع خاصٍ وكذلك التاء فصارَ قولُك أمشي أو مشيتُ صِدقاً أو كذباً. Ibn Sīnā (1970b, 18.12–14). Re: Arist. Int. 16b6f.

25. The *Dānišnāme-ye ʿAlāʾī* (*Philosophy for ʿAlāʾ ad-Dawlah*). Gutas (1988, 118–19, 424–25).

26. Ibn Sīnā (1952a, 11).

27. ثم إنا قد نحكم في المحسوسات بمعانٍ لا نحسّها إما أنْ لا تكون في طبائعها محسوسة البتة [مثل العداوة] وإما أنْ تكون محسوسة لكنا لانحسها وقْتَ الحكم . . . مثلاً شيئاً أصفر فنحكم أنه عسل و حلو. Ibn Sīnā (1959a, 166.5–7, 12–13). Cf. Black (2010, 74–75).

28. والفرْقُ بينِ إدراك الصورة وإدراك المعنى أنّ الصورة هو الشيء الذي يُدرِكه الحِسُّ الباطنُ والحسُّ الظاهرُ معاً . . . مثل إدراك الشاة لصورةِ الذئب أعني لشكله وهيئته ولونه . . . وأما المعنى فهو . . . مثل إدراك الشاة للمعنى المضاد في الذئب أو للمعنى المُوجِب لخوفها إيّاه وهربها عنه. Ibn Sīnā (1959a, 43.5–12).

Late in the *Eisagoge*, when Ibn Sīnā was exploring Porphyry's statement that "species are more extensive than genera,"[29] he wrote: "The species exceeds the genus with *maʿnā*, for it contains the *maʿnā* of the genus and the *maʿnā* of the specific difference in addition." Whereas a genus is obviously more general than a species and therefore exceeds it ("animal" is more general than "human"), a species such as "human" nevertheless contains within it both the *maʿnā* of animalness (its genus) and the *maʿnā* of speech (its specific difference).[30] This is how the apparently counterintuitive statement that a species can exceed a genus is true: a species such as "human" includes within it both the *maʿnā* of the genus of which it is a part (animal) and the additional *maʿnā* (speech) that differentiates it within that genus. The word *maʿnā* is functioning just as it did in Ibn Fūrak's accounts of God, as a stable category that helped explain epistemological relationships without necessitating any fragmentation of the concepts under consideration.[31] This shared vocabulary between Islamic theology and Aristotelian logic helps frame Ibn Sīnā's remark, in his analysis of sensory input, that "it has been the custom to call what is sensed a 'form,' and what is estimated a '*maʿnā*.'"[32] *Maʿnā* was the Arabic word for the stuff of cognition: mental content. The fact that this translation of *maʿnā* causes fewer problems in Ibn Sīnā than it did in Ibn Fūrak tells us that our conceptual vocabulary today shares more with Arabic logic than it does with Islamic theology. It tells us nothing about the divisions and consensus that existed in the eleventh century; for that we will have read more of Ibn Sīnā.

Mathematical Origins

Greek texts first began to be translated into Arabic in the eighth century, and Gutas makes a persuasive case for an early focus on mathematical disciplines that enabled the "accounting, surveying, engineering, and time-keeping" of the caliphs who founded Baghdad and whose bureaucrats needed to know "arithmetic, geometry, trigonometry, and astronomy." Euclid's *Elements* (which would serve as a mathematics textbook until the nineteenth century in the West) was consequently translated at some point before 775.[33] Then, from around 830 to 870, the scholar

Cf. Black (2010, 75), López-Farjeat (2016, 63–66).

29. Porph. *Eisagoge* 14.10f. Translation from Porphyry (2003, 14).

30. فالجِنسُ يَفضُل بالعُموم . . . والنَوعُ يَفضُل بالمعنى إذ يتضمّن معنى الجنس ومعنى الفَصْل زائداً عليه فإنه كما أنّ الحيوان يتضمّن بالعموم الإنسانَ وما ليس بالإنسان مما هو خارجٌ عن الإنسانية كذلك الإنسانُ يتضمّن بالمعنى معنى الحيوانية ومعنىً خارجاً عن الحيوانية وهو النُطق. Ibn Sīnā (1952c, 99.9–13). Cf. Thom (2016, 150).

31. Cf. Porphyry (2003, 261).

32. وقد جرتْ العادةُ بأنْ يسمّى مدرَك الحسّ صورةٌ ومدرَك الوهْم معنىً. Ibn Sīnā (1959a, 167.4–5).

33. Gutas (2004, 197–98).

known as the first Islamic philosopher, al-Kindī, was in a position to exploit the epistemological and rational potential of mathematics to work across all available fields of intellectual inquiry. Peter Adamson sketches the arc of a career that began with "the metaphysical and cosmological concerns typical of late Greek, Neoplatonizing Aristotelians" and then evolved into being "a practicing scientist and mathematician engaged in empirical research . . . more willing to . . . engage in criticism of the ancients."[34] Methodologically, for al-Kindī mathematics was everything. Gutas highlights the extreme nature of his rhetoric: "If number is removed, so also are the objects numbered." Adamson shows how, for example, his advances in optics and pharmacology relied on mathematical analyses, and Endress argues for a genealogical connection between the process of geometrical proof and the development of the syllogism.[35]

The knowledge that came from the Greeks was therefore always potentially associated with a certain kind of knowledge, the paradigmatic form of which was mathematics. This means that when al-Kindī stated his goal of reasoning the accurate accounts of things and achieving certainty through syllogistic proof,[36] the method he was envisioning to achieve that goal was via the numerical processes that Euclid had laid out, which he was engaged in applying to everything from metaphysics to music. Over a century later, the same honorific terms were being used in the eleventh century to describe the sort of certain knowledge that scholars like ar-Rāġib and Ibn Fūrak thought could be gained from revelation, or reasoning, or both. As noted above, for both Ibn Sīnā and ar-Rāġib, philosophy in the broad sense was the combination of thought and action (*ʿIlm* and *ʿamal* for both Ibn Sīnā and ar-Rāġib.)[37] As soon as philosophy moved into thought and action, one specific cognitive arena—language—that could be ignored in pharmacology or optics became unavoidable. When the subject matter of an intellectual endeavor moves from things to humans, language comes in along with the people. Both ar-Rāġib and Ibn Fūrak could comfortably accept the intrusion of language, in large part by not considering it an intrusion at all. For them, with hermeneutics and the divine revealed text always on the table as a source of certainty, the episte-

34. Adamson (2007, 12).

35. أما عِلم العدَد فبيّنٌ أنه أوّلٌ لجميعها [العلوم التي يحتاج الفيلسوفُ إليها] فإنّ العدَد إنْ ارتفع ارتفعتْ المَعدودات. Adamson (2007, 161, 167), Endress (2002, 241–43), Gutas (2004, 202), al-Kindī (1950, 1:369.14–15, 370.6–8).

36. العقلُ جوهرٌ بسيطٌ مدرِكٌ للأشياء بحقائقها . . . العِلمُ وِجْدانُ الأشياء بحقائقها .. اليقينُ هو سكونُ الفهم مع ثباتِ القضية ببرهان. Al-Kindī (1950, 1:165.5, 169.1, 171.4).

37. وسَعادتُه بتكميلِ جوهره وذلك بتزكيته بالعِلم بالله والعَمَل لله. Gutas (1988, 71), Ibn Sīnā (1952b, 196.15). لا تُحصَل إلا بزوالِ رجاسة النفس . . . المعارف الحقيقية. Ar-Rāġib (1988a, 93.6, 8). Cf. ar-Rāġib (1988b, chap. 23).

mological status of language was unquestioned (and the lexicographers benefited commensurately). But for Ibn Sīnā, the situation was very different. He knew and used the mathematical tools first identified in Arabic by al-Kindī, and his logical project was designed to fully integrate them into a set of empirical processes through which reason could start at the known and then arrive at the unknown. The epistemological promise of mathematics could not be ignored, but neither could the problem of language, nor the relationship of both mind and language to the extramental world.

Three Existences (triplex status naturae)

Ibn Sīnā's famous "threefold distinction of quiddity (*triplex status naturae* in Latin Europe),"[38] was built on a clear distinction between the world and the mind, albeit with terminology slightly different from that found in Ibn Fūrak and ar-Rāġib. For Ibn Sīna, the external, extramental, world was one of matter (*māddah*) that really occurs (*qiwām*), and the mental world of cognition was one of conception (*taṣawwur*). Actual instances (*aʿyān*) could exist in either the extramental or the mental world. Ibn Sīnā's distinction between these two existences is clearest when he comes to discuss *māhiyah* (an established term by the eleventh century, derived from the Arabic word *mā* ["what,"] translated as "quiddity" or "what-it-is-ness;" in philhellenic philosophy it has roots in Aristotle).[39] Ibn Sīnā wrote that "the what-it-is-ness of things can be in either the actual instances of things, or it can be in the conception."[40] As Alexander Kalbarczyk has shown,[41] Ibn Sīnā had profitable access to Simplicius's (fl. sixth century) commentary on the *Categories,* in which Simplicius had distinguished between the mental way a subject is and the extramental way a thing is: "There is a great difference between 'as in a subject' and 'as in matter.'"[42] Ibn Sīnā took this and turned it into three new categories: what-it-is-ness can be considered in three ways: (1) as unrelated to existence in either actual things or in conception; (2) as in actual things with the accidents specific to that existence; (3) as in conception with the accidents specific to that existence.[43] The

38. Bäck (1987, 365).

39. Arist. *Metaph.* 1029b21–23. See Cohen (2016), Endress (2002, 236).

40. وماهيّات الأشياء قد تكون في أعيانِ الأشياء وقد تكون في التصوُّر. Ibn Sīnā (1952c, 15.1). Cf. Black (2010, 70–71).

41. Kalbarczyk (2012, 313).

42. Simpl. *In Cat.* 46.22–23. Michael Chase's translation with Kalbarczyk's "subject" for *hupokeimenōi* instead of Chase's "substrate." Kalbarczyk (2012, 316), Simplicius (2003, 61).

43. فيكون لها اعتباراتٌ ثلاثةٌ اعتبارُ الماهية بما هي تلك الماهيةُ غيرُ مضافةٍ إلى أحدِ الوجودَين وما يلحقها مِن حيث هي كذلك واعتبارٌ لها مِن حيث هي في الأعيان فيلحقها حينئذٍ أعراضٌ تخصّ وجودَ ذلك واعتبارٌ لها مِن حيث هي في التصوّر فيلحقها حينئذٍ أعراض تخص وجودها ذلك. Ibn Sīnā (1952c, 15.1–5).

sort of accidents that attach to conceived things in the mind are "what-it-is-ness" and "accident," "subject" and "predicate." But out in the extramental world there is no such thing as an accident or a subject; the syllogism is in the mind, not in the world.[44]

What we are dealing with in Ibn Sīnā is a theory based on the process of conception, a process understood to happen in the mind. The mind is the location of the subject matter of logic: "Logic looks at things as predicates and subjects, universals and particulars,"[45] exactly those things that Ibn Sīnā knew did not exist in the extramental world. The stuff that is the result of conception is mental content: "Conception is the representation of the mental content of something in the mind."[46] This is where we find *maʿnā* in Ibn Sīnā: as the cognitive result of the process of conceiving of a thing, wholly separate from the question of whether or not it exists in the world. When he talks about conception (*taṣawwur*), he talks about the conception of mental content (cf. al-Fārābī).[47] Therefore, when he came to discuss the conception of being itself, which he had identified as the subject matter of Aristotle's *Metaphysics* as well as of his own, Ibn Sīnā used mental content to talk about existence: "We say that the mental contents of the existent, the thing, and the necessary are impressed upon the soul first, and this impression is not established on the basis of anything better known."[48] Mental content is primary, the first step in the cognition of anything. The components that make up our definitions, our meaningful conceptions of mental or extramental things, are *maʿānī*.[49]

This doctrine gives us clarity on the question of *maʿnā*. The mental contents are the stuff of conception, and conception is what happens when things exist in the mind. While Ibn Sīnā's actual instances can be in the mind or in the world, his conceptions and *maʿānī* can be only in the mind. In the work Gutas calls "his manifesto of the philosophical praxis as he came to formulate it later in his

44. فإنه ليس في الموجودات الخارجة ذاتيّةً ولا عرضيّةً ولا كونَ الشيءِ مُبتدأً ولا كونه خَبَراً ولا مُقدِّمةً ولا قياساً. Ibn Sīnā (1952c, 15.7–8).

45. وكذلك صناعةُ المنطق فإنها ليستْ تَنظر في مفرداتِ هذه الأمور من حيث هي . . . بلْ من حيث هي محمولات ومَوضوعات وكليّات وجُزئيات. Ibn Sīnā (1952c, 22.7–8, 10–11).

46. تمثَّل معناه في الذِهن. Ibn Sīnā (1952c, 17.8). Cf. Hodges (2011), (2016, 9–12).

47. Rudolph (2017, 605).

48. فنقول إنّ الموجود والشيء والضروريّ ومعانيها ترتسِم في النفس ارتساماً أوّلياً ليس ذلك الارتسامُ مما يُحتاج إلى أنْ يُجلَب بأشياء أعْرَفَ منها. Ibn Sīnā (1970a, 29.5–6).

49. فترتسِم حينئذٍ في العقل المعاني الأولى للمتصوَّرات ثم يُركَّب منها الحدود. Gutas (2012, 406), Ibn Sīnā (1938, 65.21–66.1). Ahmed's translation: "Thus, the primary meanings are imprinted in the intellect for [the process of] conceptualization. Then definitions are compounded out of them." Ibn Sīnā (2010, 135.24–26).

life"[50] (*Manṭiq al-Mašriqīyīn*), Ibn Sīnā wrote that "the subject matter of logic is the mental contents as they are placed for the composition that will enable them to help us attain something in our minds that is not yet there. The subject matter of logic is not the mental contents *qua* things that exist in actual instances such as substances, quantities, or qualities."[51] Logic is therefore about mental contents in specific logical arrangements. It is not about those mental contents that are instances of the cognitive conception of substance or the quality of a substance. (Although the conclusions of a logical arrangement of mental content, the results of logic that were previously unknown, may be cognitive instances of substance or quality.)

Does this mean that the results of logic *only* apply in the mind? Twenty-first-century scholars of logic have indeed noticed that Ibn Sīnā's syllogistic is not necessarily always *de re* (about the thing in extramental reality). Paul Thom writes: "Ibn Sīnā's characterization of the subject of these [modal] propositions as standing for whatever it applies to, 'be it so qualified in a mental assumption or in external existence . . .' leaves open two ways to construe the propositions."[52] The text that Thom uses here, from Ibn Sīnā's *al-Išārāt wa-t-Tanbīhāt,* states that with regard to "the predicative affirmation, for example 'the human is an animal,' the mental content of this is that the thing we suppose in our minds to be a human, whether or not it exists in actual instances, we suppose to be an animal."[53] So all that logic does here is take mental content and predicate mental content of it, with no necessary connection to the world outside. What sort of connection to the world outside did Ibn Sīnā envisage? He was surely not interested in a subjectivist or relativist rejection of extramental reality. And sure enough, back in *aš-Šifāʾ*, Ibn Sīnā talked about how mental contents could be congruent with actual existent things.[54] But even if we can settle our nerves with regard to the mind and its relationship to the world, what hangs in the background here is language.

Marks on the Soul (al-āṯār allatī fī an-nafs)

For Ibn Sīnā, the basic stuff of the cognitive process was conceived mental concept with a nonnecessary relationship to the outside world. But that same mental content could occur as a result of the noise of human language. Both Aristotle

50. Gutas (1988, 34).

51. وموضوعُه المعاني مِن حيث هي موضوعةٌ للتأليف الذي تَصير به مُوصِلةً إلى تحصيلِ شيءٍ في أذهاننا ليس في أذهاننا لا مِن حيث هي أشياءُ موجودةٌ في الأعيان كجواهر أو كمّيّات أو كيفيّات أو غير ذلك. Ibn Sīnā (1982, 31.9–12).

52. Thom (2008), 366.

53. Ibn Sīnā and aṭ-Ṭūsī (1983–94, 1:271.8–10).

54. وذلك المعنى [الإنسان] مُطابِقٌ لِزَيدٍ وعمرو. Ibn Sīnā (1952c, 26.13).

and his translator into Arabic, Isḥāq b. Ḥunayn, started *De Interpretatione* by affirming the need to discuss the noun, verb, affirmation, negation, statement, and sentence.[55] Ibn Sīnā, on the other hand, started by restating that there are two kinds of existence. There are things outside in the world, and thanks to sensory faculties, humans are able to draw secondary fixed impressions of those extramental things in their souls. The resulting impressions are not dependent on the continued existences of the sensed objects in the world, and subsequent impressions may be purely cognitive events shorn of connection to any external sensible form. "For things have an existence in extramental instance and an existence in the soul where they constitute marks on the soul."[56]

This vocabulary of marks or impressions on the soul came from Aristotle, who in the second sentence of *De Interpretatione* had introduced an influential epistemology of language, mind, and world: "Spoken sounds are symbols of affections in the soul, and written marks symbols of spoken sounds." And then while not all humans share a single language, "what these are in the first place signs of—affections of the soul—are the same for all; and what these affections are likenesses of—actual things—are also the same."[57] Isḥāq's Arabic translation reads: "What comes out in sound indicates the marks that are in the soul and what is written indicates what comes out in sound. . . . The things that sound indicates first are the soul's marks, and they are exactly the same for all, and the things of which the soul's marks are likenesses are the *maʿānī,* and they are also one for all."[58] Two conceptual vocabularies about language are meeting in translation, and in this tenth-century Baghdad moment a couple of interesting things have happened. The Greek token and sign (*sumbolon* and *sēmeion,* two nouns) have both become the Arabic process of indication (*dāllun,* an active participle). Deborah Black has observed that this process of indication connects all three parts of the language-mind-reality triad whereas al-Fārābī had restricted "indication" to the connection between language and mind. (And he followed Aristotle by connecting mind to reality with "likenesses.")[59]

55. Arist. *Int.* 16a1–3. Aristotle (1948, 1:99).

56. إنّ الإنسان قد أُوتِيَ قوةً حِسّيّة ترتسِم فيها صُوَرُ الأمور الخارجية وتتعدّى عنها إلى النفس فترتسِم فيها ارتساماً ثانياً ثابِتاً وإنْ غابَ عن الحسّ ثم ربما ارتسم بعد ذلك في النفس أمورٌ على نحوِ ما أدّاه الحسّ . . . فللأمور وجودٌ في الأعيان ووجودٌ في النفس يُكوّن آثاراً في النفس. Ibn Sīnā (1970b, 1.8–2.3).

57. Arist. *Int.* 16a3–8. Translation: Aristotle (1963, 43).

58. فنقول إنّ ما يَخرُج بالصوت دالٌّ على الآثار التي في النفس وما يُكتب دالٌّ على ما يَخرج بالصوت وكما أنّ الكتاب ليس هو واحداً بعينه للجميع كذلك ليس ما يخرج بالصوت واحداً بعينه لهم إلا أنّ الأشياء التي ما يَخرج بالصوت دالٌّ عليها أوّلًا وهي آثارُ النفس واحدةٌ بعينها للجميع والأشياءُ التي آثارُ النفس أمثلةٌ لها وهي المعاني تُوجَد أيضاً واحدةً للجميع. Aristotle (1948, 1:99.6–11).

59. Black (2010, 69 n. 13). Cf. Ibn Sīna at note 46 above.

The second observation is that *maʿānī* have made an appearance as objects in concrete reality (*pragmata*). What exactly are the *pragmata?* Recent scholarship has read Aristotle as using the word *pragmata* for bearers of truth or falsehood, certain states of affairs that are the objects of our cognitive and semiotic processes.[60] Wolfson has noted that in late antiquity *pragmata* was the word used to describe each of the three parts of the Christian Trinity,[61] thereby taking us back to *maʿnā* in Ibn Fūrak, where it was a word used to negotiate both gap and overlap between human minds and the divine. When Aristotle gave examples in his *Metaphysics* for false objects, false *pragmata,* his examples were "the diagonal's being commensurable [always false, because not all diagonals are commensurable] or your being seated [sometimes false but sometimes true depending on whether you are in fact seated]."[62] It seems that for Aristotle the *pragmata* grounded cognition in a realm of actual fact, whether conceptual or extramental. Further discussion of Aristotle is, however, beyond my scope here. To return to Arabic, we could speculate that Isḥāq was thinking of Islamic theology, or the Christian Trinity, or even of a grounding for the relationship between mind and world when he translated *pragmata* as *maʿānī,* but it would be guesswork. What we can say is that this is the translation that Ibn Sīnā worked from.

When Ibn Sīnā read Aristotle in Isḥāq's translation, it presented him with a *maʿnā*-shaped problem. His Aristotle told him that there were *maʿānī,* and that humans had likenesses of them as marks in their souls. His Arabic conceptual vocabulary, on the other hand, pushed him in the direction of seeing *maʿānī* as the mental contents in human souls. His solution was elegant: "What comes out in sound indicates what is in the soul and is called a mark. What is in the soul indicates things that are called mental contents or intentions of the soul. Just as marks in the soul, by way of analogy to the vocal forms, are also mental contents."[63] Both Black and Heidrun Eichener have analyzed this solution to good effect, Black in the context of Ibn Sīnā and Ibn Rušd's theories of intentionality,[64] and Eichener in an excellent passage of analysis that compares the translations as I have done and notes correctly that what we are dealing with here is logic "zwischen Ontologie

60. Ademollo (2015, 52–53), Crivelli (2004, 3f, 46f). Cf. David Larsen's discussion of Charles Sanders Peirce's theory of signs: Larsen (2007, 141).

61. Wolfson (1956, 4). See also chapter 2 note 95.

62. Arist. *Metaph.* 1024b18–21. My bracketed insertions into the translation from Ademollo (2015, 52).

63. فما يَخرج بالصوت يدُلّ على ما في النفس وهي التي تُسمّى آثاراً والتي في النفس تدُلّ على الأمور وهي التي تسمّى معانيَ أي مقاصدَ للنفس كما أنّ الآثار أيضاً بالقياس إلى الألفاظ معانٍ. Ibn Sīnā (1970b, 2.15–3.2).

64. Black (2010, 68–70).

und Epistemologie."[65] Riccardo Strobino also notes that the same word for "marks" reappears, when Ibn Sīnā deals with Aristotle's *Posterior Analytics,* as: "The attributes (*āṯār*) that are sought by demonstration to hold of the subject."[66] I would like to take a slightly different but complementary approach to explaining *De Interpretatione* in Ibn Sīnā.

On Ibn Sīnā's reading, the connection between the sounds of language and the human soul is a process through which impressions or marks are made on human souls. The connection between human souls and the world outside is a matter of mental contents. Ibn Sīnā said that these mental contents that connect the mind to the world could also be called "intentions of the soul," and this fits with the pragmatic relationship established in the previous chapters between mental content and what we want to say, our intent, our expression of the content of our souls. (It also gives an alibi to the Latin translators and their *intentio,* albeit no translations of Ibn Sīnā on *De Interpretatione* are recorded as having been made.)[67] I will return to intent in what follows. The soul therefore contains intentions, and it contains mental contents that connect to the world outside (although, as we have seen, the connection to the world outside is not a necessary one). The remaining problem for Ibn Sīnā is that his account of cognition in the soul now has three components: intentions, mental contents, and marks. The compatibility of intentions and mental contents is not a problem in Arabic. But Aristotle's marks have to be integrated, and Ibn Sīnā does this characteristically with an analogy (or perhaps even a rough Barbara syllogism in which > stands for "connect to"):

marks in the soul > sound	A > B
sound (i.e., vocal forms) > mental contents in the soul	B > C
marks in the soul are mental contents in the soul	A = C

As he put it: "The marks in the soul are also, by way of analogy to the vocal forms, mental contents." The autochthonous Arabic pairing of "vocal form" and "mental content" had already been used by Isḥāq to translate Aristotle (as noted by Eichner).[68] But here that Arabic pairing is doing a little more than providing a parallel; it is the framework on the Arabic side that actually enables Ibn Sīnā to translate Aristotle's concepts into Arabic (in the second line of the syllogism above). The Arabic assumption about signification, when placed in the syllogistic structure of demonstrative logic, is able to do what Ibn Sīnā wanted and effectively move one conceptual vocabulary into another.

65. "Between ontology and epistemology": Eichner (2010, 211–16, esp. 212).

66. Strobino (2016, 192, 206).

67. Bertolacci (2011, 48). Cf. Black (2010, 68).

68. Eichner (2010, 236).

Was this Ibn Sīnā's own idea? It seems likely. We do not know for sure which commentaries on *De Interpretatione* were available to him. The famous Baghdadi bibliographer Ibn an-Nadīm (d. 990) tells us that copies of commentaries by Alexander of Aphrodisias (fl. 200), Galen (d. 200), Porphyry (d. 305), Iamblichus (d. 325), and Proclus (d. 485) were available in Arabic then,[69] but they are not available to us now in Greek, Arabic, or Latin. Other works from that millennium between Aristotle and Ibn Sīnā that are available contain what could have been valuable resources, notably Stephanus's (fl. 6th–7th century) discussion of the relationship between sounds and thoughts as an analogy,[70] and Boethius's (d. ca. 524) long analysis, which states that the three fundamental components of speech are things, thoughts, and spoken sounds, and asks why Aristotle didn't simply call the "affections in the soul" thoughts. (Boethius suggests an affective relationship between the thing and the mind that bears some resemblance to the way *maʿnā* worked for Ibn Fūrak,[71] but we are in the realm of anachronistic guesswork just by bringing up such a resemblance; for while Boethius relied heavily on Porphyry's commentary on *De Interpretatione*,[72] which may have been available to Ibn Sīnā, there was no direct transmission of the Latin work Boethius did into Arabic.)[73]

For the commentary tradition, and that includes Ibn Sīnā, the opening of *De Interpretatione* was a moment to settle this question of words, things, and thoughts. It provided those working through the *Organon* in the traditional order with clarity after the equally traditional confusion about the subject matter of *Categories*, where Aristotle's readers asked whether he was talking about categories of words or categories of things. This was a long debate, and this is not the place to review it. (See the brief discussion in Adamson and Key, a much more detailed review in Bäck, and the foundational article by Sabra.)[74] Suffice it to say that Ibn Sīnā took a terse approach to the debate: Aristotle had not been thinking independently when he wrote the *Categories;* he had simply been imitating his predecessors.[75] Ibn Sīnā did not use Aristotle's ten categories (substance, quantity, quality, relation, place, time, position, possession, action, being acted upon), but rather the five universals of Porphyry's *Eisagoge* (genus, species, differentia, property, accident), and as for the question raised in the commentary tradition as to whether logic was about the

69. Gutas (2010a).

70. Stephanus, *In Int.* 6.15–21. Stephanus of Alexandria (2000, 122–23).

71. Boethius, *In Int.* 20.10–25, 33.25–34.25. Boethius (2010, 25, 32–33).

72. Marenbon (2010, 30).

73. Gutas (2010b, 12–13).

74. Bäck (2008, 47f), Key and Adamson (2015, 90), Sabra (1980).

75. أنّ واضِعَ هذا الكتاب لم يضعَه على سبيلِ التعليم بل على سبيل الوضع والتقليد . . . Ibn Sīnā (1959b, 6.9–10).

words or ideas, Ibn Sīnā was crystal clear: the logician needs vocal forms only to talk to his fellow logicians; he does not need them to do logic. If it were possible, it would be enough to learn logic from pure mental content. But it is not possible; our cognitive process of arranging mental contents is almost an internal linguistic whispering to ourselves with the imagined vocal forms of those mental contents, which means that the logician has to be aware of the patterns of vocal forms in order to be cognizant of the effect these patterns may have on mental content.[76]

Ibn Sīnā knew that logic was a cognitive process done with *ma῾ānī,* mental contents. The Arabic conceptual vocabulary of vocal form and mental content allowed him to be perfectly clear about the difference between language and thought, and how language has a carefully circumscribed role to play in logic. It is not words, or signs, or symbols that make their way into our cognitive processes; it is vocal forms that come in along with the mental contents. These are the vocal forms that we have previously used, or that we plan to use, to talk about our mental contents to our fellow logicians. They hang around in our minds, and the fact that when they are used in language they necessarily have certain patterns means that they bring the echoes of those patterns into our heads, with the potential for confusion. (Wilfred Hodges has suggested a formal account of this process.)[77] It is here that logic, the science of mental contents, comes in. Ibn Sīnā wants us to follow him through the logical chapters of *aš-Šifāʾ*, avoid being confused by the vocal forms of language, and then be equipped to proceed logically from the mental content we have in our possession to new mental content that is currently unknown to us.

The Lexicon

Gutas writes that Ibn Sīnā lived his philosophy: "His desire to communicate it beyond what his personal circumstances required, as an intellectual in the public eye, is manifest in the various compositional styles and different registers of language that he used."[78] It should therefore come as no surprise that while Ibn Sīnā clearly privileges logic as *the* epistemological discipline and talks with unprecedented clarity about how this makes cognition central, he nevertheless deals at

76. وليس للمنطقيّ مِن حيث هو منطقيٌّ شُغْلٌ أوّلٌ بالألفاظ إلا من جهةِ المخاطَبة والمحاورة ولو أمكَن أنْ يُتعلّم المنطقُ بفكرةٍ ساذجةٍ إنما تُلحَظ فيها المعاني وَحْدَها لكانَ ذلك كافياً . . . لكن لمّا . . . مِن المتعذِر على الرويّة أنْ تُرتّب المعاني مِن غيرِ أنْ تَتخيّلَ معها ألفاظَها بل تكاد تكون الرويّة مُناجاةً مِن الإنسان ذِهْنَه بألفاظٍ مُتخيَّلةٍ لَزِمَ أنْ تكون للألفاظ أحوالٌ مختلفةٌ تَختلِف لأجلها أحوالُ ما يُطابقها في النفس من المعاني. Ibn Sīnā (1952c, 22.13–23.1). Cf. Ibn Sīnā and aṭ-Ṭūsī (1983–94, 1:181), Key and Adamson (2015, 90–91), Sabra (1980, 763), Street (2004, 540).

77. Hodges (2012, slides 19–24).

78. Gutas (2016).

length with the lexicon, accurate lexical accounts, and the processes by which meaning can change.

The linguistic discussions that we find in Ibn Sīnā's logic do not focus on the framing and syntactic ordering of words, which is what one might have expected when reading his statement that patterns of vocal forms should be considered for their impact on the patterns of mental content. Instead, reading Ibn Sīnā with a focus on *maʿānī* leads us to moments when he talks about words themselves in the singular, and how their lexical histories affect the conceptions drawn from them. Ibn Sīnā is in exactly the same place as ar-Rāġib when it comes to the lexicon. Their rhetoric is very different, as indeed are the disciplinary conversations in which they were engaged. Ibn Sīnā was an Aristotelian philosopher, and ar-Rāġib an interesting combination of Hadith Folk, rationalist theology, and mysticism—three identities that would all have been anathema to Ibn Sīnā. They do, of course, share a certain metaphysical discourse describing God as necessarily existent (see Key, and Wisnovsky),[79] and they also share an ethical heritage in Aristotelian and Neoplatonic thought about the good life. But what I am concerned with here is a connection, which Ibn Fūrak also shares, that cuts across these disciplinary identities and boundaries. It is a connection to the Arabic language. We have seen how for ar-Rāġib this meant a valorization of the lexicographers. What did it mean for Ibn Sīnā?

In his discussion of *De Interpretatione,* Ibn Sīnā engaged with the origin of language, the question posed by Plato's *Cratylus* (although of course "no dialogue of Plato is known to have been fully translated into Arabic").[80] This is the same engagement that we have already encountered with ar-Rāġib, but Ibn Sīnā took a quite different tone. Whether or not language comes to us from God or from convention, he wrote, it still has to come from someone; there has to be precedent. And the connections are arbitrary: whether divinely or humanly instituted ("Have it as you wish!" he exclaims on that one), it is possible that the lexical placement could have been different.[81] Convention and the acceptance of precedent by language users (here Ibn Sīnā is in agreement with ar-Rāġib) was necessary to maintain a language once it had been created.[82] For Ibn Sīnā, however, that precedent was not primarily maintained by the lexicographers, as was the case with ar-Rāġib. Instead, a vocal form indicated, because once a human imagination hears a name,

79. Key (2012, 51); ar-Rāġib (1988a, 48, 56–58), (1988b, 40), (1992, 854); Wisnovsky (2003, 196f), (2004b, 88–90).

80. Gutas (2010a, 811).

81. وسَواءً كان اللفظُ أمْراً مُلْهَماً ومُوحاً به عُلِّمَه به مِن عند الله تعالى مُعلِّم أوّلٌ . . . كيف شِئتَ لَكان يجوز أنْ يكون الأمرُ في الدلالة بها بخلافِ ما صار إليه لو وَضَعَه. Ibn Sīnā (1970b, 3.6,15).

82. فالدلالةُ بالألفاظ إنما استمرَّ بها التعارُفُ بسببِ تراضٍ مِن المخاطِبين غيرِ ضروريّ . . . فإنه بحسبِ المشارَكة اصطلاحيّ. Ibn Sīnā (1970b, 4.1, 3).

a mental content is impressed in that human's soul, which is then able to maintain the connection.[83] The maintenance of the lexicon is individual and universal, not sociopolitical as it was for ar-Rāġib. Ibn Sīnā does mention the lexicographers in this section, but their work is accidental to logic.[84]

The question of which vocal form referred to which mental content was important for Ibn Sīnā only when it came to the technical terminology of the disciplines with which he was concerned. For example, Ibn Sīnā was concerned that other logicians used the vocal form *muqawwim* ("constituting") as a synonym for *ḏātī* ("essential" or "per se"; see Strobino).[85] This interfered with his own account of logical terminology, in which *muqawwim* applied only to a subset of *ḏātī*. What is important for our purposes here is to notice the moment when Ibn Sīnā starts to argue on the basis of the lexicon and linguistic precedent: "They have come with a synonym diverted away from its primary usage, a synonym that fails to indicate the mental content to which 'essential' has been transferred."[86] Ibn Sīnā, just like the lexicographers, used a conceptual vocabulary in which vocal forms indicate mental contents according to precedent. And just like lexicographers such as ar-Rāġib, who were policing language usage in theology, Ibn Sīnā was aware that the lexicon was a moving target. The closing phrase of the sentence quoted above, "the mental content to which 'essential' has been transferred," is a recognition of that fact. A few pages earlier Ibn Sīnā had noted that his preferred account of the meaning of "essential" (the word he thought people should be using) was in fact itself a deviation. The vocal form's original lexical placement had been for possession, and it was the convention of the logicians, of which Ibn Sīnā approved, that had caused it to deviate to from "possession" to "essential."[87] Linguistic precedent was a lexically authorized dynamic process through which word meanings could change.

83. ومعنى دلالةِ اللفظ أنْ يكون إذا ارتسم في الخَيال مسموعُ اسمٍ ارتسم في النفس معنىً فتَعرِفُ النفسُ أنّ هذا المسموع لهذا المفهوم فكلّما أورَده الحسُّ على النفس ٱلْتَفَتَ إلى معناه. Ibn Sīnā (1970b, 4.8–10).

84. وأيضاً فإنّ النظر في أنه أيّ لفظٍ هو مَوضوعٌ دالاً على معنى كذا وأيُّ كتابةٍ هي موضوعةٌ دالةً على معنى كذا أو أثرٍ كذا فذلك لصناعة اللغويين والكُتّاب ولا يتكلّم فيها المنطقيّ إلا بالعرض. Ibn Sīnā (1970b, 5.13–14).

85. Strobino (2016).

86. أما قولُهم إنّ الذاتي هو الُمقوِّم فإنما يَتناول ما كان من الذاتية غيرَ دالٍّ على الماهية فإنّ المُقوّم مُقوّمٌ لغيره وقد علمتَ ما يَعرض من هذا اللهمّ إلا أنْ يَعنُو بالمُقوّم ما لا يُفهَم من ظاهرِ لفظه ولكنْ يَعْنُو به ما عَنَيْنا بالذاتي فيكون إنما أتوا باسمٍ مرادفٍ صُرِف عن استعمال الأوّل ولم يدلّ على المعنى الذي نُقِل إليه. Ibn Sīnā (1952c, 33.12–16).

87. لكنّ قولنا ذاتيٌّ وإنْ كان بحسب قانونِ اللغة يدلّ على هذا المعنى النِسْبِيّ فإنه بحسبِ اصطلاحٍ وَقَع بين المنطقيين يدلّ على معنىً آخَر. Ibn Sīnā (1952c, 31.15–17).

Ibn Sīnā was also concerned with misconceptions about the correct form by which a statement can indicate what-it-is-ness. (For example, one can't just combine the most general mental content with anything more specific and thereby say "a speaking substance" to indicate the what-it-is-ness of the human.)[88] Ibn Sīnā's statement to indicate what-it-is-ness had to "include the complete accurate lexical account," which meant that "a transfer of the vocal form in question from its place in the lexicon to a secondary placement is not needed." Ibn Sīnā said he would explain later how his preferred solution "maintains the original lexical placement."[89] He did not deny the possibility that the logicians he was disagreeing with on this issue were using words differently, but he was prepared to state that they were not using words "according to their original lexical placement, nor according to a transfer for which there is textual evidence from specialist usage."[90] When logicians used language to talk to each other, as they were inevitably required to do, they had to engage with lexical placement and precedent just like the lexicographers and theologians.

This process was understood as not unique to Arabic. Ibn Sīnā introduced his discussion of genus in the *Eisagoge* with the remark that in Greek, the technical term "genus" was the result of a process of lexical change. The vocal form, in its prior lexical placement, had simply indicated the mental content of a shared characteristic such as familial descent or geographical origin.[91] The Greek logicians had then, needing a vocal form for the mental content "a single intellected thing with a relationship to multiple instances that share in it," transferred a name from its prior lexical placement and given it the new logical description "what is said of many different species in answer to the question, 'What is it?'"[92] Porphyry used

88. لو كان كذلك لَكان إذا أخذنا أعمّ المعاني كالجوهر وقرنّا به أخصّ ما يدلّ على الشيء فقلنا مثلًا جوهرٌ ناطق. Ibn Sīnā (1952c, 39.15–17).

89. مِن أنّ الدالّ على الماهية يجب أنْ يكون مشتمِلاً على كمالِ الحقيقة فيكون حينئذٍ هذا التكلّف يؤدي إلى أنْ لا يحتاج إلى نقلِ هذه اللفظة عن الموضوع في اللغة إلى اصطلاحٍ ثانٍ فإنا سَنُوضِح مِن بعد أنّ استعمالَ هذه اللفظة على ما هي عليه يَحفظ الوضعَ الأوّل لها. Ibn Sīnā (1952c, 40.2–5).

90. إلا أنّ ذلك لا يكون بحسب الوضع الأوّل ولا بحسب نقلٍ منصوصٍ عليه من المستعملين لهذه الألفاظ في أوّلِ ما استعملوا. Ibn Sīnā (1952c, 41.3–5).

91. فنقول إنّ اللفظة التي كانت في لغة اليونانيين تدلّ على معنى الجنس كانت تدلّ عندهم بحسب الوضع الأوّل على غير ذلك ثم نُقِلتْ بالوضع الثاني إلى المعنى الذي يسمّى عند المنطقيين وكانوا أولائك يُسمّون المعنى الذي يشترِك فيه أشخاصٌ كثيرةٌ جنساً مثل وَلَديتهم كالعَلَوية أو بلديتهم كالمصرية. Ibn Sīnā (1952c, 47.3–6).

92. فلما كان المعنى الذي يُسمَّى الآن عند المنطقيين جنساً هو معقولٌ واحد له نسبةٌ إلى أشياء كثيرة تشترِك فيه ولم يكن له في الوضع الأوّل اسمٌ نُقِلَ له من اسمِ هذه الأمور المتشابهة له اسمٌ فسُمّي جنساً وهو الذي يتكلم فيه المنطقيون ويرسمونه بأنه المَقولُ على كثيرين مختلفين بالنوع في جوابِ ما هو. Ibn Sīnā (1952c, 47.15–19).

the Greek word *sēmainomenon* ("sense," "meaning," noted by Jonathan Barnes), and his translator into Arabic, Abū ʿUṯmān Saʿīd ad-Dimašqī (d. after 914), used *ğihah* ("aspect").[93] But Ibn Sīnā used the Arabic core conceptual vocabulary of lexical placement, mental content, and transfer. This must have been a conscious choice; the philhellenic Arabic vocabulary used by ad-Dimašqī was available, but Ibn Sīnā chose to use the same words as his contemporaries working in theology and lexicography. (Al-Fārābī's précis of this same passage had made no mention of mental contents or the lexicon.)[94] Ibn Sīnā clearly felt that the Arabic conceptual vocabulary he was using was compatible with his logical and Aristotelian project: vocal forms connected to mental contents by lexical placement and intent—this was a stable and useful conceptual vocabulary with which to rethink Aristotelian logic.

In his composite philosophical work *an-Nağāh* (*The Salvation*),[95] Ibn Sīnā provided a short overview of the term *ḏātī* ("essential" or "per se," as discussed above) in which the Arabic conceptual vocabulary of mental content was at the center of the logical process. He dismissed a series of options for understanding "essential" as insufficient, and he located the action in mental content. It was "not enough to say that the mental content of 'essential' is that it cannot be separated from the thing in question." It was rather the case that "the essential is what if its mental content is understood . . . and if the mental content of what it is essential to is understood . . . , then the essence of the thing described cannot be understood without a prior understanding of the essential mental content in question." One cannot therefore understand "human" without already having understood "animal"; the mental content of animal is essential to the mental content of human.[96] "Understanding mental contents" was what mattered, just as al-Ǧāḥiẓ had claimed in a very different kind of Aristotelian book (Miller)[97] almost two hundred years earlier.[98] What Ibn Sīnā has done here is use the conceptual space of *maʿnā* to structure logical processes. His Aristotelian logical project did require new conceptual vocabulary

93. Porph. *Eisagoge* 1.20, 2.5. Aristotle (1948, 1058–60), Porphyry (2003, 50f).

94. Al-Fārābī (1986b, 24.2–8).

95. Gutas (1988, 115–17).

96. الذاتيُّ هو الذي يُقوّم ماهيةَ ما يقال عليه ولا يكفي في تعريف الذاتي أنْ يقال إنّ معناه ما لا يفارق فكثيرٌ مما ليس بذاتي لا يفارق ولا يكفي أنْ يقال إنّ معناه ما لا يفارق في الوجود . . . بَلْ الذاتيُّ ما إذا فُهِم معناه وأُخطِر بالبال وفُهِم معنى ما هو ذاتيٌّ له وأُخطِر بالبال معه لم يمكن أنْ يُفهَم ذاتُ الموصوف إلا أنْ يكون قد فُهِم له ذلك المعنى أولاً كالإنسان والحيوان فإنّك إذا فَهِمتَ ما الحيوانُ وفَهِمتَ ما الإنسانُ فلا تَفهَم الإنسانَ إلا وقد فَهِمتَ أولاً أنه حيوانٌ. Ibn Sīnā (1938, 6.14–16, 7.3–7). Cf. translation in Strobino (2016, 252).

97. Miller (2013, 58–90).

98. See chapter 2 note 48.

above and beyond vocal form and mental content, but the only way to explain that new vocabulary was with, of course, vocal form and mental content. Just as Ibn Fūrak used mental content to structure the interaction between human language and divine reality with a series of conceptual pigeonholes, so Ibn Sīnā used mental content to explain how a conception of something can be logically essential: there is a mental content of "animal" without which there cannot be a logically functional mental content of "human."

If understanding mental content was therefore what mattered, how could one know, with the sort of certainty for which Ibn Sīnā was looking, what people actually meant when they made logical statements? How can one account for potential ambiguity? As we have seen, Ibn Sīnā did not choose to have recourse to a sociopolitically charged lexicographical class of scholars like ar-Rāġib or a theological doctrine and school like Ibn Fūrak. Ibn Sīnā had himself written a dictionary, and could have considered himself a lexicographer like ar-Rāġib, but his philhellenic, philosophical, and logical commitments appear to have prevented him from locating truth in the books his contemporaries were iteratively curating. Instead Ibn Sīnā, just like twentieth-century Anglophone philosophers of language, turned to an account of what people meant that relied on intent, on pragmatics.

Intent

Pragmatics as Ibn Fūrak and ar-Rāġib understood it would seem to have been anathema to Ibn Sīnā, whose empiricism and logic was on the face of it inherently opposed to the subjectivity produced by accounts of meaning that give control to the speaker. For Ibn Fūrak and ar-Rāġib, this was not necessarily a problem, for they had both an actively curated lexicon and a confessional account of right belief to give them the confidence that they could divine what speakers meant. David Vishanoff has shown in chapters 5 and 6 of his *Formation* how the potential of a model of "performative speech intuitively grasped" was progressively exploited by Sunni legal theorists to get a great deal of what they wanted from the divine text.[99] But with Ibn Sīnā we are dealing with Aristotelian philosophy.

We have already encountered Ibn Sīnā's aside, in his commentary on *De Interpretatione,* to the effect that the mental contents in the soul are also intentions. This word for "intentions," *maqāṣid,* was not present in the Arabic translation of Aristotle that Ibn Sīnā used, and we do not have access to other Arabic commentaries that might help us identify a precedent. All we do know is that, as Kwame Gyekye showed in a 1971 article,[100] the Latin tradition bundled up mental contents

99. Vishanoff (2011, 190f).

100. Gyekye (1971, 35–37). See also notes 9 and 67 above.

(*ma'ānī*), intelligibles (*ma'qūlāt*), and intent (*qaṣd*) under the word *intentio.* Gyekye also confirms that Ibn Sīnā's mental contents are conceptually identifiable with al-Fārābī's intelligibles (on which see Zimmermann).[101] But neither Greek nor Latin provides us with a chronologically appropriate explanation for Ibn Sīnā's eleventh-century statement that "they are called mental contents: i.e., intentions of the soul."[102] I think that an Arabic assumption about pragmatics must be the source of this remark, because as we have already seen, mental content was often glossed as intent and vice versa in the earliest Arabic scholarly disciplines. This makes sense, because in the simple and elegant theory of meaning encapsulated in the Arabic core conceptual vocabulary, human beings had mental contents, and they intended to refer to them when they spoke with vocal forms. There was no separate ontological or epistemological category that could be "intent-separate-from-mental-content." There were just mental contents, vocal forms, and a process of intent that enabled the latter to indicate the former.

Ibn Sīnā used this conceptual vocabulary. For example, when he laid out the difference between simple and compound vocal forms in his *Eisagoge*, he did so by determining whether or not a vocal form could be divided into smaller component vocal forms each of which indicated an "*intended* mental content."[103] He then went on to identify the problem with the subjectivity of pragmatics that was always raised in Islamic exegesis and law (the question "How do you know what they mean?"). Ibn Sīnā's discussion of this problem took place in dialogue with logically inclined grammarians. It was a debate that had started almost a century earlier with the grammarian az-Zağğāğī. He had written that "others" had supplemented the logicians' standard definition of the simple noun (sound indicating mental content without time, a definition also adopted by some grammarians) with the phrase "and its parts do not indicate any of its mental content."[104] Ibn Sīnā identified the same development, albeit with slightly different contours: the teaching of the ancients described the noun as that whose parts did not indicate anything, but then scholars "considered that insufficient and made the necessary supplementation to the effect that the noun was that whose parts did not indicate anything apart from the mental content of the

101. Zimmermann (1981, xxxiiif, xli).

102. تُسمّى معانيَ أيْ مقاصدَ للنفس. Ibn Sīnā (1970b, 3.2).

103. إنّ اللفظ إنما مُفردٌ وإما مركَّبٌ والمركَّب هو الذي قد يُوجد له جزءٌ يدلّ على معنىً هو جزءٌ من المعنى المقصود. Ibn Sīnā (1952c, 24.13–14).

104. وليس هذا من كلام المنطقيين وإنْ كان قد تعلّق به جماعةٌ من النحويين . . . وقال آخرون الاسمُ صَوتٌ مَوضوعٌ دالٌّ باتّفاقٍ على معنىً بلا زمانٍ ولا يدلّ جزؤُه على شيءٍ من معناه وهذا أيضاً من كلام القَوم [المنطقيين وبعض النحويين] وإنْ كان فيه هذه الزيادةُ اليسيرةُ وقد مَضَى القولُ فيه. Az-Zağğāğī (1959, 48.11–13, 49.6–8).

whole."[105] It seems clear that Ibn Sīnā and az-Zağğāğī are referring to the same conversation. However, Ibn Sīnā then went on to say that this supplementation was a mistake, and was really only an explanation rather than a step necessary to complete the description. Why?

This is where intent makes its appearance: "Because the vocal form does not indicate by itself at all. Were that to be the case, then each vocal form would have a right portion of mental content from which it could not deviate. But this is not the case. The vocal form indicates only with the intent of the one who speaks it." A more thoroughgoing statement of pragmatics (and a clearer refutation of reference as the basis for theories of language signification) can scarcely be imagined! In *Manṭiq al-Mašriqīyīn,* Ibn Sīnā used the example of the Arabic compound proper name (ʿAbd Šams, "Slave of the Sun," the name of a famous pre-Islamic ancestor of the prophet) to illustrate how intent could determine whether such a compound vocal form referred to just a specific person or to that person's worship of the sun.[106] Back in his *Eisagoge,* Ibn Sīnā went on to give the example of a person using a word like *ʿayn* to mean "water source" in one speech act and "coin" in another speech act. An English equivalent is "bank" (of a river) or "bank" (where one keeps one's money). Vocal forms have no mental content in and of themselves.[107] A speaker can even intend no reference whatsoever, in which case no reference is to be found (the vocal form *ʿayn* could be meaningless if all the speaker meant was " ").[108] This statement of pragmatics then allows Ibn Sīnā to close the discussion of the simple and compound noun: a composite vocal form may have the potential to indicate its composite parts or its whole, but the only factor that matters in actual usage is the intent of the speaker.[109]

Ibn Sīnā, who is here in this book about *maʿnā* to represent the discipline of Aristotelian logic, had a philosophy of language that permitted language users to intend everything, or nothing, by their speech acts. The gaping maw of linguistic relativism would appear to be opening up again, and in a most unexpected

105. والموجودُ في تعليمِ الأقْدَم مِن رسْمِ الألفاظ المفردة أنها هي التي لا تدلّ أجزاؤُها على شيءٍ واستنقَص فريقٌ مِن أهلِ النظر هذا الرسمَ وأوْجَب أنه يجب أنْ يُزاد فيه أنها التي لا تدلّ أجزاؤها على شيءٍ من معنى الكل. Ibn Sīnā (1952c, 25.9–12).

106. مِثلُ قولِنا عبدُ شمسٍ فإنه إذا أُريدَ أن يُدَلّ به على شخصٍ مُعيَّنٍ مِن حيث هو شخصٌ مُعيَّنٌ لا مِن حيث يُراد أنْ يقال فيه عبدُ الشمس. Ibn Sīnā (1982, 32.4–7).

107. وذلك أنّ اللفظ بنفسه لا يدلّ البتة ولو لا ذلك لَكان لِكلّ لفظ حقٌّ من المعنى لا يجاوزه بل إنما يدلّ بإرادة اللافِظ فكما أنّ اللافِظ يطلقه دالاً على معنىً كالعين على ينبوعِ الماء فيكون ذلك دلالته ثم يطلقه دالاً على معنى آخَر كالَعين على الدينار فيكون ذلك دلالته. Ibn Sīnā (1952c, 25.15–18).

108. وكذلك إذا أخلاه في إطلاقه عن الدلالة بقي غيرَ دالّ. Ibn Sīnā (1952c, 25.18–19).

109. فلا يكون جزؤه البتة دالاً على شيءٍ حين هو جزؤه بالفِعل اللهمَّ إلا بالقُوة حين نجد الإضافة المُشار إليها وهي مقارنة إرادة القائل دلالةً به. Ibn Sīnā (1952c, 26.5–6).

place. But this is not the case. The reason that Ibn Sīnā is devoting so much of his *Eisagoge* to pragmatics is that he needs to identify the issues that come with vocal forms in order to focus on what really matters: mental contents. Logic, as he has already told us, is about mental content and not about vocal form. It is a matter of thought, not a matter of language. Ibn Sīnā was the first to really exploit the potential of the preexisting Arabic pairing of vocal form and mental content to be clear about what logic was and the extent to which language mattered for its pursuit. The questions of linguistic ambiguity that scholars like ar-Rāġib and Ibn Fūrak exploited in confessional hermeneutics were accurate reflections of how communication between human beings actually functioned, and Ibn Sīnā was not concerned to deny that reality. He knew that people had to guess what people meant. He also knew that logicians had no option but to use those ambiguous frameworks to talk to each other about logic. But what he was trying to establish in his work was an account, written in a consistent technical terminology, of how thought could be logically productive.

IBN SĪNĀ'S MENTAL CONTENTS IN ACTION

We have seen in this chapter that Ibn Sīnā used an Arabic core conceptual vocabulary to explain the workings of logic and language with influential clarity. I will now proceed to work through four topics at the heart of the nexus of language, mind, and reality in his philosophy. Two of them would become important for Latin philosophy in Europe (*pros hen* and *prima et secunda positio*). The third, "Attributes" (*ṣifāt*), represents Ibn Sīnā's engagement with Islamic theology, and the fourth, "Logical Assent" (*taṣdīq*), was the fundamental and most basic move of his logic. In all these cases, Ibn Sīnā used *maʿnā* to do great deal of work.

Being Is Said in Many Ways and pros hen

Thought needs to be logically productive in disciplines other than just logic itself, and Ibn Sīnā was very clear that metaphysics was one such discipline. Metaphysics was separate from logic, but it was part of the philosophical project that Ibn Sīnā identified in the Aristotelian tradition and then sought to bring to a completion that he thought the tradition had been unable to achieve. This book is not the place for an overview of that project. (For that, see Gutas in brief and McGinnis at length.)[110] It was a rational philosophical project with a unified methodology, and this book is not the place to take on a description of the methodology either (The essays in Adamson are a good place to start.)[111] What I would like to do is

110. Gutas (1988, 359–86), McGinnis (2010).

111. Adamson (2013).

take Ibn Sīnā's insights about language and mental content and apply them to one of the most famous considerations of ambiguity: *pros hen.* The issue here is how, in light of the clear distinction he made between vocal form and mental content, between thinking about language and about thinking about thinking, Ibn Sīnā read Aristotle's statement that "being is said in many ways."

At the beginning of Book Four (Gamma) of his *Metaphysics,* Aristotle wrote that "there are many senses in which a thing may be said to 'be.' but all that 'is' is related to one central point, one definite kind of thing, and is not said to 'be' by a mere ambiguity."[112] There is some central principle (the Greek word is *archē*)[113] that connects the different ways the word "being" is used, just as there is some principle that connects "healthy" when it is said of different things that may preserve health ("a healthy exercise regime"), or produce health ("a healthy juice drink"), or mark health ("healthy blood results"), or be receptive of the quality of health ("the healthy child").[114] These usages all go "toward one" (*pros hen*) principle. The Greek commentary tradition, dealing with echoes of the Platonic Forms that could no longer be heard by the time philosophy moved into Arabic, had ultimately taken this passage to be part of an Aristotelian account of the different ways in which language could refer to reality (Proclus, d. 485, and then Porphyry; see Alexander Treiger and Richard Sorabji).[115] The only Arabic translation we have extant is by Ustāṯ,[116] undertaken in the ninth century for al-Kindī and preserved as the text on which Ibn Rušd based his commentary. When it came to other books of the *Metaphysics,* Ibn Sīnā had access to a later version by Isḥāq, but we cannot be sure he had read anyone other than Ustāṯ when he was dealing with "being is said in many ways."[117] Ustāṯ told Ibn Sīnā that Aristotle said existence was not a matter of linguistic homonymy but was rather a matter of different things being related to a single first.[118] The epistemological status of this first principle was not in doubt: "The accurate account of all things is the knowledge of the thing that comes first, to which all the other things relate, and because of which they are named."[119] Ustāṯ

112. Arist. *Metaph.* 1003a33. Translation from Sennet (2015).

113. Arist. *Metaph.* 1003b6.

114. Arist. *Metaph.* 1003b2–4.

115. Sorabji (2005, 74, 131, 234–35), Treiger (2012, 336–38).

116. "The otherwise unknown Ustath . . . Eustathius, in all likelihood of Byzantine origin": D'Ancona (2013, n. 31).

117. Bertolacci (2006, 5–7, 14).

118. فالهُوية تقال على أنواعٍ كثيرةٍ ولا تقال بنوعِ اشتراكِ الاسم بل تُنسَب إلى شيءٍ واحدٍ وطِباعٍ واحد . . . تلك الأنواعُ تُنسَب إلى أوّلٍ واحد. Ibn Rušd and Aristotle (1938–52, vol. 5:2, pp. 300.13–14, 301.5).

119. والعِلمُ الذي هو عِلمٌ بالحقيقة في جميعِ الأشياء هو عِلمُ الشيء المتقدَّم الذي به يتّصل سائرُ الأشياء وبسببه تُسمّى. Ibn Rušd and Aristotle (1938–52, vol. 5:2, p. 302.1–2). Arist. Metaph. 1003b16–17.

translated the Greek word *kurios* ("decisive, authoritative, most important, principal": Liddell and Scott) that Aristotle had used to describe this knowledge with the central quasi-linguistic honorific for accuracy with which we have become familiar: *ḥaqīqah.*

On the one hand, what we have here is an epistemological framework of principles and instances, central ideas and related connections, roots and branches, that has echoes in ar-Rāġib's and Ibn Fāris's valorizations of the root principle in lexicography and the origins of language. Real accurate knowledge is always of a central principle from which one can produce further knowledge. And whereas in the Greek tradition such a framework would tend to engage commentators in a discussion of whether such principles should be connected to Platonic Forms, in an Arabic intellectual environment the root principle of language use was paradigmatically lexicographical. So when it came to Aristotle's statement that the epistemological principle behind "being" and "healthy" was not a homonym, Ustāṯ translated this exclusion of Aristotelian homonymy (*ouch homōnumōs*) as an exclusion of any species of Arabic homonymy (*lā . . . naw*ʿ*i -štirāki l-ism*).[120] Aristotelian homonymy was an account of the relationships between things in the outside world, established in *Categories* with the example of how a man and a picture of a man are both "animal,"[121] whereas Arabic homonymy was linguistic and lexical, such as we find with "bank" and "bank" in English (or ʿ*ayn* and ʿ*ayn* in Arabic). Aristotle had been trying to explain how "being" was an appropriate subject matter for his *Metaphysics,* hence the need to exclude what he thought was an unscientific type of connection such as that exemplified by "animal" in "picture of an animal" and "man is an animal." (He made exactly the same exclusion when trying to establish "the good" as the subject matter of his *Nichomachean Ethics,* a connection recognized by the Greek tradition.)[122] But the homonymy that the pre-Avicennian Arabic Aristotelians wanted to exclude was the homonymy of the lexicographers. (A century later, Ibn Rušd would carefully exclude both the homonymy of ʿ*ayn* and the homonymy of "man" and "animal.")[123]

What did Ibn Sīnā do with this complex of alternatives? What conceptual vocabulary did he choose to establish? It should be noted at the outset that I have benefited from Alexander Treiger's discussion of these same passages in an article in which he argues persuasively for a transcendental motivation in Ibn Sīnā's account of existence.[124] In what follows I take a quite different approach from

120. Arist. *Metaph.* 1003a34. Ibn Rušd and Aristotle (1938–52, vol. 5:2, p. 300.13).

121. Arist. *Cat.* 1a1.

122. Arist. *Eth. Nic.* 1096b25.

123. Ibn Rušd and Aristotle (1938–52, vol. 5:2, p. 302.14–16).

124. Treiger (2012).

Treiger, but as with Eichner's work I hope the result is complementary. Rather than ultimately focusing on high, as Treiger does with the One and necessary of existence, I restrict myself to looking at the most basic components of Ibn Sīnā's conceptual vocabulary, the building blocks of cognition and the question of their relationship to language. This does not necessarily tell us much about philosophy, but it should tell us something about *maʿnā.*

In his discussions of Aristotle's *Metaphysics* and *Categories,* Ibn Sīnā used *maʿnā* to talk about the complex of alternatives presented by Aristotle's epistemological framework for words such as "being" and the commentaries thereupon. The first chapter of Aristotle's *Categories* gives three ways that things can be connected through their names (homonymous, synonymous, and paronymous, rendered in Arabic as *muttafiqah, mutawāṭiʾah,* and *muštaqqah,* respectively). Ibn Sīnā described how synonymy was when the "statement about the substance" is the same, so "animal" is predicated as a synonym of both "man" and "horse." A man is not more animal than a horse. He glossed "statement about the substance" as "the distinguishing vocal form that indicates the mental content of the substance." This gloss (introduced with *ay,* meaning "i.e.") marks his movement from one conceptual vocabulary to another, from the Greek-into-Arabic translation of Isḥāq to his own Arabic framework of vocal form and mental content.[125] He makes the same move on the next line: "if the formal definition is one from every aspect—i.e. one in mental content."[126] With the equation between the two conceptual vocabularies established, he then divided homonymy into three: "either [1] the mental content in the different things is one in itself despite being different in some other way; or [2] the mental content is not one, but there is a certain similarity between the two things; or [3] the mental content is not one, and there is no similarity between the two things."[127]

Ibn Sīnā's first example for [1] was Aristotle's *pros hen* "being." The mental content in itself is the same ("being" is a stable category), but the form it takes is different in different things, some of which may be prior to others (a substance is prior in existence to its accidents).[128] The Peripatetics and the Stoics were all

125. *logos tēs ousias* / قَول الجوهر / أيْ اللفظ المُفصِّلُ الدالُّ على معنى الذات فيها كلّها Arist. *Cat.* 1a. Aristotle (1948, 1:33), Ibn Sīnā (1959b, 9:9–10).

126. وحدُّه واحدٌ فيها مِن كلّ وجْهٍ أيْ يكون واحدٌ بالمعنى. Ibn Sīnā (1959b, 9.11).

127. إما أنْ يكون المعنى فيها واحداً في نفسه وإنْ اختلفَ من جهةٍ أخرى وإما أنْ لا يكون واحداً ولكن يكون بينَهما مُشابهةٌ ما وإما أنْ لا يكون واحداً ولا يكون أيضاً بينَهما مُشابهة. Ibn Sīnā (1959b, 10.4–7). Cf. alternative translation: Treiger (2012, 353).

128. فمِثلُ معنى الوجود فإنه واحدٌ في أشياء كثيرةٍ لكنه يختلِف فيها فإنه ليس موجوداً فيها على صورة واحدة من كلّ وجهٍ فإنه موجودٌ لبعضِها قبلُ ولبعضِها بعدُ فإنّ الوجود للجوهر قبلَ الوجود لسائرِ ما يتّبِعه. Ibn Sīnā (1959b, 10.8–11), Treiger (2012, 353).

philosophers, but the work of the former was "more philosophical" than that of the latter.[129] Mental content is a key component in this epistemology: it is the stable form that "being" takes in the mind. While being is spoken of in many ways, and while extramental things exist in different ways, "being" stays the same in itself as a mental content, as does "philosophy": both are stable pigeonholes. Ibn Sīnā then introduces a new category of "modulated existence," which divides Aristotle's *pros hen* ambiguity into two.[130] This division (also identified by Kalbarczyk in an earlier commentary by Ibn Sīnā on *Categories*) is persuasively explained by Treiger as being motivated by Ibn Sīnā's desire to reserve a category of "being" that would apply only to God and maintain his unity.[131]

For group [2], things that Aristotle had called homonymous but did not share a common account, and may be in completely unrelated things, Ibn Sīna held that they could still share a name if there was a mental-content resemblance. He used Aristotle's example of "animal" predicated of both a horse and a picture of a horse.[132] What it is that connects the picture of the horse with a horse? Ibn Sīnā's answer is enabled, I think, by Arabic accounts of poetics rather than by the Aristotelian tradition. He says that the name "animal" has two original lexical placements in this case, one prior and one subsequent, to which it has been transferred.[133] The process of transfer from an original lexical placement is, of course, something we are familiar with from chapter 4 above, on the lexicon. No such structures were available to Ibn Sīnā from commentators such as Simplicius,[134] whom we know Ibn Sīnā had read from what are almost verbatim quotations a couple of pages later.[135] Ibn Sīnā is in conversation with Arabic poetics here. He talked about the way the constellations of Canis Major and Canis Minor and a living animal are all called

129. ولا تقال الفلسفةُ على التي في المشّائيين والتي في الروّاقيين على التواطؤ المُطلَق. Ibn Sīnā (1959b, 11.1), Treiger (2012, 354).

130. فما كان المفهومُ من اللفظ فيه واحداً إذا جُرِّد ولم يكن واحداً من كلّ جهةٍ مُتشابهاً في الأشياء المتّحِدة في ذلك اللفظ فإنه يسُمّى اسماً مُشَكَّكاً. Ibn Sīnā (1959b, 11.3–4), Treiger (2012, 354).

131. Kalbarczyk (2012), Treiger (2012).

132. وأما الذي لا يكون فيه اتّفاقٌ في قَولِ الجوهر وشرْحِ الاسم لكنْ يكون اتّفاقاً في معنىً يتشابه به فمِثلُ قولنا الحيوانُ للفَرَس والحيوانُ للمُصوَّر. Ibn Sīnā (1959b, 11.8–9).

133. ويكون الاسمُ في أحدِ الأمرَين موضوعاً وضْعاً متقدّماً ويكون في الثاني موضوعاً ثانياً فإذا قِيسَ ذلك الاسمُ إلى الأمرَين جميعاً سُمّي بالاسم المتشابِه وإذا قِيسَ إلى الثاني منهما سُمّي بالاسم المَنقول. Ibn Sīnā (1959b, 12.2–4).

134. Simpl. *In Cat.* 21.1–33.20. Simplicius (2003, 35–47).

135. وقد يتّفِق أنْ يكون الاسمُ الواحد مَقولاً على شيئين بالاتّفاق وبالتواطؤ معاً. Ibn Sīnā (1959b, 14.15). "There are, however, some things that are homonymous and synonymous with regard to one and the same name": Simpl. In Cat. 35.15–20. Simplicius (2003, 49–50).

"dog," but while the connection in the latter case is lexically accurate, the connection in the former is "borrowed" (the technical term for the Arabic metaphor to which we will return in the next chapter).[136] Like Ibn Rušd, Ibn Sīnā also carefully delineated this kind of homonymy from the complete lexical homonymy of "bank" and "bank."[137] He then paused to talk about lexical homonymy and say that he had no time for the claim that such homonyms exist because of infinite things and a finite number of words to describe them, a claim that ar-Rāġib had explicitly maintained.[138] From Ibn Sīnā's logical perspective, the theory of reference assumed in ar-Rāġib's claim was nonsensical. What determined names for Ibn Sīnā was the intent of the namers,[139] not any purported lack of availability of words or limit on the number of possible combinations of letters.[140] And while naming was a process of lexical expansion through metaphorical deviations from the accurate lexical placement, an account with which we are familiar from ar-Rāġib, Ibn Sīnā gave no curation role to a community of lexicographers. Instead he was content with chance and the possibility that different people in different places, or the same person at different times, may just use different deviations.[141]

Ibn Sīnā had an account of language that was keyed into the same Arabic lexical conversation as ar-Rāġib's. The most salient difference between the two was the weight ar-Rāġib gave to the lexicographical community. Just like ar-Rāġib, Ibn Sīnā used the pairing of vocal form and mental content to deal with some of the most important problems in his philosophy. When Ibn Sīnā came to *Metaphysics*, the same discussion of how being can be said in many ways, which Aristotle had tried to resolve with a *pros hen* relationship to a central principle, was for him a matter of mental contents and reference: "We say that 'existence' and 'thing' and 'necessary' have their mental contents impressed on the soul first, an impression

136. وربما كان هذا الاشتباهُ اشتباهاً حقيقياً وربما كان اشتباهاً مجازياً بعيداً مِثلَ قولهم كلْبٌ للنجْم وللكلْب الحيوانيّ وذلك لأنه لا تَشابُهَ بينهما في أمرٍ حقيقيّ إلا في أمرٍ مستعار. Ibn Sīnā (1959b, 12.7–9).

137. فما كان سبيلُ نقلِ الاسم إليه هذا السبيلَ فلا ينبغي أنْ يُجعل في هذا القِسم [الاسم المشكك] بل هو من القِسم الثالث الذي لا اشتراكَ حقيقياً ولا تَشابهَ فيه مِثل قولنا عينٌ للبصر وعينٌ للدينار. Ibn Sīnā (1959b, 12.10–12).

138. والأصلُ في الألفاظ أنْ تكون مختلفةً بحسبِ اختلافِ المعاني لكنّ ذلك لم يكن في الإمكان إذ كانت المعاني بلا نهايةٍ والألفاظُ مع اختلافِ تراكيبها ذاتَ نهايةٍ وغيرُ المتناهي لا يَحوِيه المتناهي فلم يكن بُدٌّ مِن وقوعِ اشتراكٍ في الألفاظ. Ar-Rāġib (1984, 29.5–7).

139. مِن حيثُ يَقصدها المُسمُّون بالتسمية. Ibn Sīnā (1959b, 13.8)

140. Ibn Sīnā (1959b, 12.12–13.14).

141. كأنّ بعضهم اتّفقَ له أنْ أَوْقَع اسمَ العين على شيءٍ والآخرُ اتّفقَ له أنْ أَوْقَعه على غيره فيجوز إذاً أنْ يكون سببُ الاتفاق هو اختلافُ حالِ مُسمِّيين أو لاختلافِ حالِ مُسَمٍ واحدٍ في زمانيين صار فيهما كشخصَين. Ibn Sīnā (1959b, 14.3–5).

that is not in need of any better known things to bring it about."[142] These are the central concepts of Ibn Sīnā's *Metaphysics*, analyzed accurately in the secondary scholarship as "intentional objects," and "primary, indefinable concepts." (I am quoting Robert Wisnovsky's discussion of "thing" with regard to Ibn Sīnā's what-it-is-ness and existence.)[143] They are mental contents. They are also the central concepts of Ibn Sīnā's logic. What is a universal? A mental content is universal when actually predicated of many (such as "is human"), or when possibly predicated of many although they may not exist (such as "is a heptagonal house"), or when it can be conceived of as predicated of many although a reason or cause may intervene (such as "is the sun," because there is only one sun).[144]

Mental content is the stuff of cognition, and if you are an Aristotelian philosopher like Ibn Sīnā, the Arabic conceptual vocabulary of mental content and vocal form provides you with a stable framework to talk about the relationship of language to logic, the nature of being itself, and to actually do logic, as we will see in the remainder of this chapter. The question that will take us into chapter 7 on al-Ǧurǧānī is: What if your aim was not a complete science of everything and the unfulfilled promise of Aristotle's project? What if you really cared about words? What if the subject matter that concerned you most was poetry? What if the question that drove you was not "What is it?" but rather "Why does it sound so good?"

Attributes (ṣifāt)

The answers to that question, "Why does it sound so good?" will in al-Ǧurǧānī be in part theological: "Why does God's word sound so good?" Here in the chapter on Ibn Sīnā, Treiger has opened the door to a consideration of theological motivation for Ibn Sīnā's epistemological categories, although Ibn Sīnā's Necessarily Existent One was as different from al-Ǧurǧānī's God as Aristotle's Prime Mover was from Zeus. In this short discussion of Ibn Sīnā's position on attributes I do not want to make the claim that Ibn Sīnā was doing theology in the same way as Ibn Fūrak, ar-Rāġib, or indeed al-Ǧurǧānī did Islamic theology.[145] What Ibn Sīnā shows us is that in his eleventh-century context there was a long-established theological

142. فنقول إنّ الموجود والشيء والضروريّ معانيها ترتسِم في النفس ارتساماً أوّلياً ليس ذلك الارتسامُ مما يُحتاج إلى أن يُجلب بأشياء أعْرَفَ منها. Ibn Sīnā (1970a, 29.5–6). Cf. translation by Michael Marmura: Ibn Sīnā (2004, 22).

143. Wisnovsky (2003, 158–59). Cf. Marmura (1980, 341f).

144. فيقال كليٌّ للمعنى من جهةٍ أنه مَقولٌ بالفعل على كثيرين مثل الإنسان ويقال كليٌّ للمعنى إذا كان جائزاً أنْ يُحمَل على كثيرين وإنْ لم يشترط أنهم موجودون بالفعل مِثل البيت المُسَبَّع . . . ويقال كليٌّ للمعنى الذي لا مانعٌ مِن تصوّره أنْ يقال على كثيرين إنما يَمنع منه إنْ منع سببٌ ويدلّ عليه دليلٌ مِثل الشمسِ والأرض. Ibn Sīnā (1970a, 195.6–12); cf. (2004, 148).

145. Cf. Gutas (2005, 62f).

debate with a stable vocabulary for God's attributes, of which Ibn Sīnā must have been aware (however antithetical it may have been to his philhellenic philosophical project). It was an Arabic conceptual vocabulary with a weight of scholarly precedent behind it. Now Ibn Sīnā had already, as we have seen, used the existing Arabic conceptual vocabulary of poetics in order to talk about the relationships of vocal forms to mental contents. When he used the vocabulary of poetics, he endorsed the theories of mental content that it carried with it, including the theoretical accounts of metaphor based on transfer, borrowing, and resemblance. But when he used the vocabulary of Islamic theology in his discussion of attributes, he did not endorse the theological assumptions in play. What, then, was he doing?

One answer is that the Islamic theological vocabulary of divine attributes was the inevitable basis for any discussion, even in logic, of what an attribute was. Moreover, unlike al-Fārābī, Ibn Sīnā was committed to using available Arabic words and avoiding the construction of neologisms. Another answer is that this was a moment when Ibn Sīnā contested the intellectual dominance of Islamic theology by a passive-aggressive (or ironic) use of theology's own vocabulary to do something different and philhellenic. If we follow the ironic interpretation, then an implication could be drawn as to the likely readership of Ibn Sīnā's logical work. Why write an ironic engagement with theology into logic if the only readers are one's fellow Aristotelians? If this implication is correct, then Ibn Sīnā wanted his logic to be read by scholars like al-Ǧurǧānī (Islamic theology and Arabic poetics) as much as he wanted to be read by scholars such as al-Ḥasan Ibn Suwār (Christianity, philhellenic philosophy, medicine). He included Islamic theology, alongside medicine, ethics, and more in his review of the foundational subjects of scholarly disciplines. (The starting point of theology was either obedience to divine law or the divine status of that law.)[146] Scholarship has already demonstrated the connections between Islamic theology before Ibn Sīnā and Ibn Sīnā's own work (Wisnovsky on Ibn Sīnā's *Metaphysics*), in addition to the impact that Ibn Sīnā had on theological discussions of atomism in the twelfth and thirteenth centuries (Dhanani).[147] What I am doing here is suggesting two further connections: first, that Ibn Sīnā brought parts of Arabic poetics and theology into his logic, and second, that scholars after Ibn Sīnā such as al-Ǧurǧānī used Ibn Sīnā's logic to do poetics.

With this framing established, let us turn again to Ibn Sīnā's *Eisagoge*. He had been discussing the difference between what-it-is-ness and accident as it stood in the Aristotelianism of his eleventh century, some three hundred years after

146. وإما أنْ تشترِك في مَبدأ واحدٍ مثل اشتراك موضوعات عِلم الكلام فإنها تشترك في نِسبتها إلى مبدأ واحد إما طاعة الشريعة أو كونها إلهية. Ibn Sīnā (1956b, 157.12–14), via alternative translation: Strobino (2016, 212).

147. Dhanani (2015), Wisnovsky (2003, 227f).

discussions of Porphyry's *Eisagoge* had begun in Arabic with Ibn al-Muqaffaʿ (d. 756). Ibn Sīnā started by dealing with the two types of accident identified by Porphyry: separable accidents such as "sleep" (and redness when embarrassed for Ibn al-Muqaffaʿ) and inseparable accidents such as "black" when used of ravens.[148] He then used the framework of mental and extramental existence to identify a third sphere in which, for example, a triangle necessarily had to have three angles that added up to 180 degrees. This fact about triangles, "triangleness," was not dependent on either existence in the mind or existence in the world: it was the what-it-is-ness of the triangle. The constituents of this what-it-is-ness (the fact of the three angles adding up to 180°) did not have to always be actually thought of when triangles were thought of, but whenever the what-it-is-ness of a triangle was thought of, these constituents were necessarily there too.[149] "If this is the case," says Ibn Sīnā, "then the attributes that we call essential for reasoned mental contents must necessarily be reasoned of a thing in this way; the what-it-is-ness of a thing cannot be conceived in the mind without their prior conception."[150]

This doctrine of what-it-is-ness would be influential for the subsequent millennium of both Arabic and European-language philosophy. (See, for example, statements by Wisnovsky and Klima.)[151] But I am interested in the move Ibn Sīnā made at the end of this discussion to talk about essential attributes, almost as if such a discussion was the justification for his analysis of what-it-is-ness. I am not claiming that this is the case; attributes (*ṣifāt*) rarely appear as a category in Ibn Sīnā's *Eisagoge*. But they do appear here, and the lesson that a theologian such as Ibn Fūrak might take would be that God can be thought of without necessarily thinking of his essential attributes (such as "speech" and "knowledge" for Ibn Fūrak) but that when the essence of God is thought of, then both speech and knowledge are necessarily constituents of that essence. It is as if Ibn Sīnā, having read Islamic theology in his youth,[152] was motivated to show his readers that his philhellenic logic, despite its programmatic and disciplinary separation from such theology (and despite the distinction philhellenic philosophy made between what-it-is-ness

148. Porph. *Eisagoge* 12.25. Porphyry (2003, 12).

فمن الأعراض مفارقٌ وغيرُ مفارق فأما المفارق . . . حُمرةُ الخجِل. Ibn al-Muqaffaʿ (1978, 8.1–4).

149. Ibn Sīnā (1952c, 34.12–35.3). See also note 43 above

150. وإذا كان كذلك فالصِفةُ التي نُسمّيها ذاتيةً للمعاني المعقولة يجب ضرورةً أنْ تُعقَل للشيء على هذا الوجه إذ لا تُتصوَّر الماهيةُ في الذهن دون تقدُّمِ تصوّرها. Ibn Sīnā (1952c, 35.3–5).

151. "Avicenna's innovations are a turning point in the history of metaphysics": Wisnovsky (2003, 266). "The most important influence in this [medieval European] period from our point of view came from Avicenna's doctrine distinguishing the absolute consideration of a universal nature": Klima (2013).

152. Wisnovsky (2003, 17).

and essence),[153] could still solve theological problems. Future generations would exploit this potential.

The other major discussion of attributes in the logical sections of Ibn Sīnā's *aš-Šifā'* comes in his discussion of the "fourfold classification of 'things there are'" in *Categories*, where Aristotle makes a distinction between things either in, or said of, the subject of a logical proposition.[154] I have not found in Porphyry, Simplicius, or the Arabic school notes, any indication that may frame the five-part scheme for the interaction of essence and attribute with which Ibn Sīnā replaces Aristotle's four categories.[155] Ibn Sīnā wrote that the attributes of things either: (1) are a mental content that settles in the essence but is external and attaches as a necessary concomitant or accident ("man is white," "man is laughing," Aristotle's "in but not said of"); or (2) settle in the essence and are not external but actually a part of the essence ("man is an animal," Aristotle's "said of but not in"); or (3) settle in the essence but are there to establish the essence while not being part of it (the relationship of form to substance); or (4) settle in the essence and are not attached externally but actually a part of the essence ("the animal is a body"); or (5) settle in the essence and attach to the essence either necessarily or accidentally ("matter occupies space" or "matter is white").[156] The disconnect between Ibn Sīnā and Aristotle (and between Ibn Sīnā and the commentary tradition) is symptomatic of the way he addressed the complex of problems around *Categories* with no concern for hermeneutical precedent. It may be an amusing exercise to slot Ibn Fūrak's concern for God's attributes into this scheme, and it is faintly conceivable that Ibn Sīnā had such epistemological assistance for theologians in mind (perhaps Ibn Fūrak would put God's knowledge into [5] and God's mercy into [1]?). It is worth noting that the word *ma'nā* appears only once in the scheme, and it does so as a word for an accidental quality in (1), just the same usage with which we became familiar in Islamic theology. The conceptual vocabulary in this passage is not particularly

153. Lizzini (2016).

154. Arist. *Cat.* 1a20f. Aristotle (1963, 74 notes).

155. Simpl. *In Cat.* 44–51, Porph. *In Cat.* 88f, Georr (1948, 359–87).

156. فاعلمْ أنّ صِفات الأمور على أقسامٍ لأنه إما أنْ يكون الموصوفُ قد استَقر ذاتَه معنىً قائماً ثم إنّ الصفة التي يُوصف بها تلحَقه خارجةً عنه لُحُوقَ عارضٍ أو لازمٍ وإما أنْ يكون الموصوفُ أُخِذ بحيث قد استقر ذاتَه لكنّ الصفة التي يُوصف بها ليستْ تلحَقه لُحُوقَ أمرٍ خارجٍ بل هو جزءٌ من قِوامه وإما أنْ يكون أُخِذ بحيث لا يكون قد استقر ذاتَه بعدُ والصفةُ تلحَقه لتقرّرِ ذاتِه وليستْ جزءاً من ذاته وإما أنْ يكون أُخِذ بحيث لا يكون قد استقر ذاتَه بعدُ والصفةُ ليستْ تلحَقه من خارجٍ بل هو جزءٌ من وجوده وإما أنْ لا يكون قد استقر ذاتَه والصفةُ تلحَقه لا لِنفس ذاتِه بل لُحُوقَ لازمٍ لمّا يُقرره أو عارضٍ له أوّلٌ ومِثالُ الأوّل قولُك الإنسانُ أبيض أو ضحّاك ومثالُ الثاني قولُك الإنسانُ حيوانٌ . . . ومثالُ الثالث الهيولى والصورة . . . ومثال الرابع الجوهرُ للجسم المحمول على الحيوان . . . ومثال الخامس الهيولى إذا وُصفتْ بالبياض أو السواد أو التحيّز. Ibn Sīnā (1959b, 18.5–19.7).

typical of Ibn Sīnā, and indeed he noted that he was using "subject" here in a specific technical way.[157] It is tempting to think that he took Aristotle's logical subject and used it to show Islamic theologians the sort of philhellenic resources that were available to them. But this is guesswork.

Logical Assent (taṣdīq)

Let us now put the amusement of imagining theological uses for Avicennian logic to one side and turn to Avicennian logic itself. The question is: What did *maʿnā* do here? In this section I will be presenting a basic account of logical categories and the syllogism with a focus on the conceptual vocabulary of mental content. This is an argument about what logic looks like from the outside, an argument designed to set up chapter 7, on al-Ǧurǧānī, who I will argue looked at logic from the outside (as I do!) and used its conceptual vocabulary to good effect in poetics. (For more detailed analysis of Arabic logic *qua* logic, readers should turn to a recent florescence in that field and to the work of Tony Street, Asad Q. Ahmed, Khaled El-Rouayheb, and others.)[158]

We have already established that the initial cognitive step for Ibn Sīnā was the process of conception, in which a particular mental content is established in the mind. This mental content can have a name in language (for example, "human") that enables it to be spoken about. But as a single mental content, not predicated of anything else, it cannot be true or false, and the question of truth and falsity is the concern of logic. Ibn Sīnā is here thinking of mental contents as language-facing, and one example of conceived mental content that cannot be true or false is the imperative speech act "Do that!"[159] You cannot take someone's order, the expression of their mental content, of their intent, and determine whether it is true or false. All that has happened is that mental content has been expressed. "X" cannot be true or false when conceived on its own, but faced with the statement "X is Y," we must decide whether or not to assent to its truth. The logical process begins when your brain does something to the mental content that language has delivered to you: "If someone says to you, 'Each instance of the color white is an accident,' then you do not just attain the mental content of that statement; rather you judge

157. فيجِب أنْ تفهَم مِن الموضوع هاهنا هذا وإنْ كان قد يُستعمَل فى مواضعَ أُخرى استعمالاتٍ غيره. Ibn Sīnā (1959b, 20.2).

158. Ahmed (2008); El-Rouayheb (2010), (2012); Ibn Sīnā (2010); Street (2004), (2015).

159. وكما أنّ الشيء يُعلم من وجهَين أحدُهما أن يُتصوّر فقط حتى إذا كان له اسمٌ فنُطِق به تَمثَّل معناه في الذِهن وإنْ لم يكن هناك صدقٌ أو كذبٌ كما إذا قيل إنسانٌ أو قيل إفْعَلْ كذا فإنك إذا وقفتَ على معنىً ما تخاطب به من ذلك كنتَ تصوّرتَه. Ibn Sīnā (1952c, 17.7–10). Cf. with translations Sabra (1980, 759–60), Street (2015). And for *tamtaṯṯala*, note 59.

it to be true."[160] This judgment is called "assent" (*taṣdīq*), and it comes after the initial cognitive language-facing process of conception (*taṣawwur*). The discipline of logic moves from known to unknown through both conception and assent.[161]

In this section Ibn Sīnā is clear that the language-facing mental content of initial cognition can be both single and composite. So when you hear "Each instance of the color white is an accident," your conceived mental content is of the form of the composition of the statement as well as of its individual components. Your subsequent assent concerns the correspondence (or lack thereof) in the relationship between that mental content and the actual things: Is each instance of the color white really an accident?[162] There is here no implication that the actual things have to be in the world outside as opposed to in the mind. At the start of the next section, on the subject matter of logic, Ibn Sīnā spelled out this distinction in terms of single and composite mental contents. The mind cannot do assent with single mental contents; they are insufficient because (for example) assent to their existence or nonexistence would (if the single mental content was all that was available to the mind) require their own cognitive existence or nonexistence. This would be impossible, because the cause of something (in this case the assent) cannot be a cause when it is possibly not there.[163] What actually happens when you assent to the existence of something or to its nonexistence is that you add a related additional piece of mental content.[164]

This is the critical statement about mental content that provided al-Ǧurǧānī with a conceptual vocabulary for poetics: language gives you a mental content, and your reason connects that mental content to other mental contents. What is more, the simple mental contents that make up composite mental contents have all kinds of extra issues that they bring along with them. Ibn Sīnā's example is the house composed of wood, clay, and bricks, each of which has qualities of which the builder must be aware. (Is the wood hard and straight, or soft and bent?) But the logician is not like the builder. The logician is unconcerned with the individual mental contents *qua* mental contents, and equally unconcerned with the question

160. فيكون إذا قيل لك مَثلاً إنّ كلّ بياضٍ عَرَضٌ لم يَحصل لك من هذا معنى هذا القول فقط بل صدّقتَ أنه كذلك. Ibn Sīnā (1952c, 17.10–12).

161. فهاهنا شيءٌ من شأنه أن يُفيد العِلم بالمجهول تصوّرُه وشيءٌ من شأنه أنْ يفيد العِلم بالمجهول تصديقُه. Ibn Sīnā (1952c, 18.2–3).

162. والتصور في مثل هذا المعنى يفيدك أن يَحدث في الذهن صورةُ هذا التأليف وما يُؤلّف منه كالبياض والعرض والتصديقُ هو أن يَحصل في الذهن نِسبةُ هذه الصورة إلى الأشياء أنفسِها أنها مطابقةٌ لها. Ibn Sīnā (1952c, 17.14–17); cf. (1938, 60.13–17), (1982, 29–30).

163. وليس يجوز أنْ يكون شيءٌ [المعنى المفرد] عِلةً [عِلةَ التصديق] في حالتَي عدمه ووجوده. Ibn Sīnā (1952c, 31.6–7).

164. وإذا قرنتَ بالمعنى وجوداً أو عدماً فقد أضفتَ إليه معنىً آخر. Ibn Sīnā (1952c, 31.9–10).

of whether and how they exist either in the mind or outside in the world. The logician cares only about the mental contents insofar as they are predicates, subjects, universals, and particulars. Everything else, from extramental instances to linguistic references, is accidental to logic.[165] Just as we saw happen with Islamic theology in the preceding sections, when Ibn Sīnā demarcated the discipline of Aristotelian logic he also managed, along the way, to provide conceptual vocabularies for the other intellectual pursuits of the eleventh century. Scholars of poetics are like the builder: they care about the implications that mental contents bring with them. The Classical Arabic poetic metaphor works only when each mental content is looked at from every possible angle.

First and Second Position (prima et secunda positio)

The logical process is one in which reason interacts with mental content. Syllogisms and logical definitions are composed of "reasoned mental content in defined compositions."[166] The labels for the parts of defined compositions such as the syllogism, or the logical definition, are themselves mental contents, but they are in second position. They are the subject matter of logic: the subject, the predicate, the universal, the particular, and so on. Logic uses a particular set of mental contents that do not exist in the world outside (there are no extramental real-life predicates) to structure all other mental content. Ibn Sīnā's description of these two types of mental content in his *Metaphysics* would prove influential in Latin Europe: "The subject matter of logic is the secondary reasoned mental contents, which depend on the primary mental contents." The argument is the same as he made in the *Eisagoge* quoted above, but the two types of mental content identified there are now in his *Metaphysics* given the names "primary" and "secondary."[167] The Kneales call this passage "the origin of that discussion of first and second intentions which continued until the end of medieval logic."[168] Latin Europe's concern had its roots (Sorabji *pace* the Kneales) in the "Neoplatonic theory of the two-stage imposition

165. Ibn Sīnā (1952c, 21.18–22.12).

166. وكل واحدٍ من القياس والحدّ فإنه مَعمولٌ ومؤلفٌ من معانٍ معقولة بتأليف محدود. Ibn Sīnā (1938, 3.15–16). Cf. translation Sabra (1980, 761).

167. *Eisagoge:*

وكذلك صناعة المنطق فإنها ليستْ تَنظر في مفرداتِ هذه الأمور من حيث هي على أحدِ نحوَي الوجود الذي في الأعيان والذي في الأذهان ولا أيضاً في ماهيات الأشياء من حيث هي ماهيات

Metaphysics:

والعِلم المنطقيّ كما علمتَ فقد كان موضوعُه المعاني المعقولةَ الثانيةَ التي تستنِد إلى المعاني المعقولة الأولى ولها الوجودُ العقليُّ الذي لا يتعلّق بمادةٍ أصلاً أو يتعلّق بمادةٍ غير جُسمانية. Germann (2008, 19), Ibn Sīnā (1952c, 22.8–10), (1970a, 10.17–11.2), (2004, 7).

168. Ibn Sīnā (1508, 70b/1.46–51), Kneale and Kneale (1962, 230).

of names."[169] Ibn Sīnā would have picked up this vocabulary, most probably, from Simplicius. But Simplicius was talking about the difference between Aristotle's *Categories* and *De Interpretatione,* and specifically about the grammatical categories of "noun" and "verb" therein.[170]

The problem in Arabic was that here a discussion of grammatical categories would run into the existing conceptual vocabulary that enumerated the mental contents of grammar. Al-Fārābī, who had been at this point a century or so earlier (see Zimmermann's detailed analysis)[171] had chosen to largely eschew the vocabulary of mental contents (*maʿānī*) in favor of "intelligibles" (*maʿqūlāt,* although he did use *maʿnā* for the target of conception).[172] But Ibn Sīnā was either more confident that he could overcome the grammarians or, as is perhaps more likely, by the eleventh century the boundaries between grammar and logic were no longer as polemically defined. (See Adamson and Key on this debate.)[173] Ibn Sīnā was doing logic, so he divided mental contents into two. Mental contents in first position enabled the conception of things that could be put into syllogisms or definitions (such as "instance of the color white" and "accident"). Mental contents in second position enabled the naming and classification of the structures of composition that created the syllogisms and definitions themselves (such as "subject" and "predicate"). When Ibn Sīnā made use of a pair of inherited philhellenic terms for these two levels, he was using terms with a genealogy that stretched back into ancient Greek grammar and forward into Latin European accounts of signification, but he was talking only about Arabic logic.

ARISTOTELIAN PHILOSOPHY DONE WITH ARABIC CONCEPTUAL VOCABULARY

The mental contents that are the stuff of Ibn Sīnā's logic were necessarily located in the mind. They are mental contents achieved through conception, in first or second position, and subject to assent. Through the formal structures of logic, the most important of which was the syllogism, they can be ordered so as to provide access to new information (if all A is B, and all B is C, then all A is C, a syllogism with a perfect proof, in Europe subsequently given the Latin mnemonic *Barbara*). The discipline of logic ensures accurate reference in the case of both conception and assent. Ibn Sīnā wrote that logic enabled the mind to check whether its

169. Simplicius (2003, 109 n. 182).

170. Simpl. *In Cat.* 15.1–5 via Zimmermann (1981, xxxii).

171. Zimmermann (1981, xxxi–xxxiii, 5–6). Cf. Gyekye (1971, 35–36).

172. For example, al-Fārābī (1972, 7f). See Rudolph (2017, 605).

173. Key and Adamson (2015).

conception of something really did give an accurate account of a what-it-is-ness, and if not, what had gone wrong with the logical statements of conception. Logic also enabled the mind to know how and whether logical statements produced certain and accurate assent that could not be unwound, or how and whether they could produce assent with a defined degree of uncertainty.[174] The logical statements in question (the Arabic word, *qawl*, may be translated as "speech act" in a discipline other than Aristotelian logic) are defined compositions of mental contents, compositional structures that are defined by the roles their terms play in the second position. For example, "man is an animal" is composed of subject plus predicate, as well as a species plus a genus. "Man" and "animal" are conceived mental contents in first position, and "subject," "predicate," "species," and "genus" are mental contents playing logical roles in second position.

In the case of both conception and assent, Ibn Sīnā describes the result as *ḥaqīqah*. As we have seen, this is a judgment about accuracy. It is not necessarily a judgment about language. In the case of conception, Ibn Sīnā means that the substance of the thing is accurately known in the mind; the mental content is accurate with respect to the thing. There is no necessary connection to language, and there is no necessary connection to extramental existence in the world outside. This is an accurate account that connects a mental content to a thing, wherever it is. Accurate conception is therefore integral to accurate assent.

If accurate conception and accurate assent are the goal of logic, what happens in cognition that fails to achieve this standard? How does Ibn Sīnā contend with inaccurate conception or assent, logical processes that he cannot describe as *ḥaqīqah?* We can suggest an answer by looking at his discussion of how logic enables the identification of statements that appear to produce an impression on the soul like assent but that are actually imagination.[175] The example he gives is honey, and we can read it as an example of what happens when conception, and therefore assent, are not accurate (what *taṣawwur* and *taṣdīq* look like in the absence of *ḥaqīqah*). Honey looks like bile (yellow and viscous) and on that basis, one might accept the logical statement "Honey is bitter and causes vomiting." The impression on the soul would be that honey is bitter, and so one should avoid it. The logical statement would through its compositional form and mental content have produced a

174. فغايةُ عِلم المنطق أنْ يفيد الذهنَ معرفةَ الشيئين [التصور والتصديق] فقط وهو أنْ يَعرف الإنسانُ أنه كيف يجب أنْ يكون القولُ المُوقِعُ للتصوّر حتى يكون مُعرِّفاً حقيقةَ ذاتِ الشيء وكيف يكون حتى يكون دالاً عليه وإنْ لم يُتوصَّل به إلى حقيقةِ ذاته وكيف يكون فاسداً . . . وأيضاً أنْ يَعرف الإنسانُ أنه كيف يكون القولُ الموقِعُ للتصديق حتى يكون مُوقِعاً تصديقاً يقينيّاً بالحقيقة لا يصح انتقاضُه وكيف يكون حتى يكون موقِعاً تصديقاً يقارب اليقين. Ibn Sīnā (1952c, 18.10–16).

175. وكيف يكون القولُ حتى يُأثّر في النفس ما يُأثِّره التصديقُ والتكذيبُ من إقدامٍ وامتناع. Ibn Sīnā (1952c, 18.19–19.1).

result in the soul parallel to the process of assent. But it would be wrong; it would not be assent! It would be (as Ibn Sīnā explains elsewhere) a judgment based on estimation and not on reason.[176] The problem with the statement that honey causes vomiting is that the conceptions and subsequent assents are not accurate. An accurate process of conception would associate the name "honey" with the property of sweetness and therefore would be able to judge that any assent to honey being bitter or causing vomiting is not accurate either. As Ibn Sīnā has just told us, logic shows how statements can accurately produce conception as well as how they can accurately produce assent. Logic would enable us to see how our conception of honey is not accurate, and it would ensure that our mental contents are accurate accounts of the what-it-is-ness of the thing in question. It should be noted that the thing in question (in this case "honey" and the properties it has when accurately conceived) does not need to be in the extramental world. The whole logical process can happen in the mind. In his *Eisagoge* Ibn Sīnā is describing a logical tool that applies across science, a tool he would use when he came to ask in medicine and biology whether honey really was sweet out there in the world.

This account of how *ḥaqīqah* in Ibn Sīnā interacts with *maʿnā* shows how the discipline of logic maintained the basic role of both these components of eleventh-century Arabic conceptual vocabulary. My approach here could enable a slightly different reading of texts in which Ibn Sīnā talks about things being accurate accounts, a reading that does not necessarily push toward extramental realities in the world outside but rather reaffirms the centrality of the mind. For example, let us take a passage from Ibn Sīnā's *Metaphysics*, analyzed to good effect by Wisnovsky. Ibn Sīnā was making a distinction between "thingness" (*šayʾīyah*) and "existence" (*wuǧūd*) in order to discuss "the relation between efficient and final causes" and resolve the question of how the final cause could be both final (i.e., last) and a cause (i.e., first).[177] Ibn Sīnā's conclusion was that the final cause is last with regard to existence (i.e., all other causes are before it in the Aristotelian chain of causality) but first with regard to thingness (i.e., its thingness is that it is the reason for the existence of the other causes in the chain).[178] But he needed to say how thingness and existence were different. Here, Wisnovsky translates *ḥaqīqah* as "inner reality": "The difference between a thing and existence is just like the difference between some entity and its concomitant. . . . Consider, once again, the case of man: man has an inner reality, consisting of his definition and his quiddity, which is not conditioned upon [his] existence's being particular or general,

176. Ibn Sīnā (1956a, 2:177.12–14) via Pormann (2013, 104).

177. Wisnovsky (2003, 161–62).

178. Ibn Sīnā (1970a, 293), Wisnovsky (2003, 162).

concrete or in the soul, or potential or actual."[179] Ibn Sīnā thought that the definition and what-it-is-ness (quiddity) of the human being is his thingness, and this is separate from his existence, which may be particular, general, or potential.

What happens if we read *ḥaqīqah* as "accurate account" in this same passage? My translation is: "The difference between the thing and the existent . . . is like the difference between something and its concomitant . . . for the human has an accurate account that is his logical definition and his what-it-is-ness, not conditional on a particular or general existence in actual instances or anything potential or actual in the soul."[180] I think that Ibn Sīnā thought that the *ḥaqīqah* of a human being, the accurate account of a human being, and the epistemological process that enables us to contend with the human being was the combination of logical definition and what-it-is-ness. To provide an accurate account of the human being, one could provide a logical definition, and one could state the what-it-is-ness. Logical definition was a human epistemological process, while what-it-is-ness was an independent construct that could (according to the *triplex*) be either in the mind or in actual instances of things.[181] What-it-is-ness and definition were therefore both accurate connections between logical statements and things. My focus on *maʿnā* and *ḥaqīqah,* on mental content and the accurate account in Ibn Sīnā, has not here produced a substantively different reading of his actual philosophical argument about final causation. What I hope to have done is complement Wisnovsky's analysis of this question with a new focus on the very first steps of Ibn Sīnā's thought process and the most basic components of his conceptual vocabulary. *Ḥaqīqah* can be translated not as "inner reality" but rather as Ibn Sīnā's epistemological judgment: in both logical definitions and statements about what-it-is-ness we get an instance of epistemological accuracy, an accurate account of a thing.

In *Manṭiq al-Mašriqīyīn,* as he defined the different scholarly disciplines that deal in practical or theoretical knowledge, Ibn Sīnā remarked on the mind's ability to engage with incorrect hypotheticals. He was describing the relationship of theoretical disciplines to extramental matter and wrote that in a theoretical discipline, the matters under consideration were either inevitably constituted by extramental matter (such as humanity or size) or were potentially conceivable as separate from matter (such as number, rotation, or the creator). The word *maʿnā* appears when the human mind is considering the possibility that anything could be human: "It is not impossible for the mind, at the beginning of its theorizing, to have humanity

179. Ibn Sīnā (1970a, 292.2–5), Wisnovsky (2003, 161). Wisnovsky translates *māhiyah* as "essence."

180. وفرْقٌ بين الشيء والموجود وإنْ كان الشيءُ لا يكون إلا موجوداً كالفرق بين الأمر ولازمه . . . فإنّ للإنسان حقيقةٌ هي حدُّه وماهيتُه مِن غير شرطِ وجودٍ خاصٍ أو عامٍ في الأعيان أو في النفس بالقوة شيءٌ من ذلك أو بالفعل. Ibn Sīnā (1970a, 292.2–5).

181. Ibn Sīnā (1952c, 15.1–3). Cf. Wisnovsky (2003, 160 n. 40).

inhering in every substance, but that would be classed as a mental error. To be correct, the mind must necessarily turn away from permitting this and know that the *maʿnā* of 'humanity' inheres in a substance only if there is another *maʿnā* that provides a structure for it."[182] *Maʿnā* is the stuff of cognition, the mental content with which we make sense of fundamental metaphysical questions and contend with the relationship between abstract categories and the extramental world. Ibn Sīnā was talking about theoretical scholarly disciplines and a process that took place in the mind; there can be no question about the location of the *maʿānī* in this passage. The scale and rigor of his philosophical project has ensured clarity on this point, and the action that is taking place is the same action that took place in Ibn Fūrak's theology: *maʿānī* both inhere in extramental substances and are the way our minds make sense of those substances. We do not have a word in English that does this work, but Ibn Sīnā had a word in Arabic that could.

Just like Ibn Fūrak, Ibn Sīnā used his conceptual vocabulary to clarify the difference between mind and reality. In *an-Naǧāh* he explained "thingness," the neologism we have just encountered with the help of Wisnovsky: "It is clear that thingness is different from existence in actual instances. For *maʿnā* has an existence in actual instances, an existence in the soul, and a shared matter that is thingness."[183] Thingness is that moment when *maʿnā* in the soul and *maʿnā* in actual instances align. To some extent, this must be a human epistemological process, and so just as with Ibn Fūrak the translation of *maʿnā* as "mental content" is imperfect but functional. In the *Eisagoge* chapter on universals (part of the *Eisagoge*'s mini-discussion of *Categories*), Ibn Sīnā used "animal" as an example for this type of mental content: "The animal is, as itself, a mental content, whether existing in actual instances or conceived in the soul. As itself it is neither general nor particular."[184] This state of existing in either instances or in the soul is exactly what Ibn Sīnā called "thingness" in the *Metaphysics.* In this philosophy, any extramental fact or actual instance in the physical world will inevitably become mental content as soon as logic's dual process of conception and assent starts to work. The parallel to Ibn Fūrak's theology is clear: any extramental fact concerning God or the extramental physical world will inevitably become mental content as soon as theology's dialectical and linguistic process starts to work. Mental content is

182. وإنْ كانتْ بحيث لا يمتنع الذهنُ في أوّل نظره عن أنْ يُحلّها كلَّ مادة فيكون على سبيلٍ مِن غلط الذهن بل يحتاج الذهنُ ضرورةً في الصواب أنْ ينصرف عن هذا التجويز ويَعلم أنّ ذلك المعنى [الإنسانية] لا يَحلّ مادةً إلا إذا حصل معنىً زائدٌ يُهيئها له وهذا كالسواد والبياض. Ibn Sīnā (1982, 25.15–20).

183. ومِن البيِّن أنّ الشيئية غيرُ الوجود في الأعيان فإنّ المعنى له وجودٌ في الأعيان ووجودٌ في النفس وأمرٌ مشترِكٌ فذلك المشترِك هو الشيئية. Ibn Sīnā (1938, 212.4–6). Cf. Wisnovsky (2003, 163).

184. إنّ الحيوان في نفسه معنىً سواءً كان موجوداً في الأعيان أو مُتصوَّراً في النفس وليس في نفسه بعامٍّ ولا خاصّ. Ibn Sīnā (1970a, 65.11–12) via Black (1999, 52–53).

what happens as soon as humans are involved. This necessarily happens in both logic and theology. The difference between Ibn Fūrak's theology and Ibn Sīnā's philosophy was what happened after humans got involved. For Ibn Fūrak, as we saw, mental content remained stable and may have been assumed to be controlled by God. Ibn Sīnā's philosophy, however, used mental content as human cognition of actual instances in the world and ideas in the soul. Mental content was both the abstract conception of "thingness" that underpinned metaphysics and the logical categories of subject and predicate with which logic was constructed. The mental content "animal" could be conceived of both in an actual instance of an animal and as an abstract logical category.

Ibn Sīnā's five universals were mental contents that could be natural, reasoned, or logical.[185] Mental content could conceive of animals out there in the world; it could reason the "thingness" category of animal, and it could assign the animal a logical category such as genus. This third logical stage involved the addition of another piece of mental content to the animalness.[186] Ibn Sīnā's accounting for mental content in this passage matches both his analysis of conception and assent and his analysis of hypotheticals: as soon as you assent to something, you add a piece of mental content to a piece of mental content, and so as soon as you conceive of something as a logical category such as genus, you are adding a piece of mental content to a piece of mental content. "The *maʿnā* of 'humanity' inheres in a substance only if there is another *maʿnā* that provides a structure for it."[187] This process of accounting for the workings of thought in terms of combining pieces of mental content is, I will argue in the next chapter, central to al-Ǧurǧānī's advances in the analysis of metaphor. It is how Ibn Sīnā used Arabic conceptual vocabulary to write Aristotelian philosophy, and in doing so develop that conceptual vocabulary into a tool that would be used for both philosophy and poetics across the subsequent millennium.

But Ibn Sīnā's goal was not to prepare the ground for al-Ǧurǧānī's poetics. Instead he was preparing the ground for his own metaphysics. At the start of this section Ibn Sīnā suggested organizing the three categories according to multiplicity. The reasoned category came first ("animal" conceived as a single mental content); then there was the multiplicity of instances in the world (lots of actual

185. فصلٌ في الطبيعي والعقلي والمنطقي وما قَبْل الكثرة وفي الكثرة وبعد الكثرة من هذه المعاني الخمسة . . . . إنّ منها ما هو طبيعيّ ومنها ما هو منطقيّ ومنها ما هو عقليّ Ibn Sīnā (1952c, 65.4–5). Cf. Black (1999, 52–53).

186. بل الحيوانُ في نفسه شيءٌ يُتصوَّر في الذهن حيواناً وبحسبِ تَصوُّره حيواناً لا يكون إلا حيواناً فقط. فإنْ تُتصوَّر معه معنىً زائدٌ على أنه حيوانٌ يَعرِض للحيوانية فقد تُصُوِّر معه عامٌّ وخاصٌّ وغيرُ ذلك Ibn Sīnā (1952c, 65.16–19).

187. See note 182 above.

animals), and then there was logical categorization of that multiplicity (statements such as "the human is an animal").[188] Then Ibn Sīnā discussed the question of which came first. Did the reasoned mental content come before the instances, and then the multiplicity in the world, or did the real-world multiplicity precede the scientific and logical determination that what these empirical facts displayed was genus and species? What caused what? With causation we are in the sphere of metaphysics, and Ibn Sīnā's resolution here (confirmed by a statement in his *Metaphysics* itself)[189] was: "All the different things that exist are related to God and the angels in the same way as our human crafts are related to the soul of each craftsman. For what God and the angels know is accurate knowledge of what is known, and perception of natural matters that exist before multiplicity. Each one of these reasoned things is a single mental content, and existence in multiplicity is subsequently produced for them. In extramental multiplicity there is no single general thing but rather complete separation. The next step after the extramental multiplicity is that the mental contents are produced for a second time in our rational processes."[190]

The single conceived mental contents that are the foundation of Ibn Sīnā's epistemology are here shown to be, like Ibn Fūrak's mental contents, of divine origin. For Ibn Fūrak and ar-Rāġib they were permanently under God's arbitrary control whether located in the mind or the world. But for Ibn Sīnā, God starts a process with simple mental contents that are conceived by angels. These conceived mental contents are then given real-world multiplicity. Finally, we human scientists and logicians study the multiplicity and reason logical categories from within it. Islamic theology and Arabic Aristotelianism turn out to be very different, and at the same time to share in *maʿnā*.

188. وربما قيل إنّ منها ما هو قبل الكثرة ومنها ما هو في الكثرة ومنها ما هو بعد الكثرة . . . Ibn Sīnā (1952c, 65.5–6f). Cf. Black (1999, 52).

189. فالحيوانُ مأخوذاً بعَوارضه هو الشيءُ الطبيعيُّ والمأخوذُ بذاته هو الطبيعةُ التي يقال إنّ وجودها أَقْدَمُ مِن الوجود الطبيعيّ بقِدَم البسيط على المركّب وهو الذي يخصّ وجودُه بأنه الوجودُ الإلهيّ لأنّ سببَ وجوده بما هو حيوانٌ عِنايةُ الله تعالى. Ibn Sīnā (1970a, 304.17–305.2) via Black (1999, 52).

190. ولأنّ جميعَ الأمور الموجودة فإنّ نسبتها إلى الله والملائكة نسبةُ المصنوعات التي عندنا إلى النفس الصانعة فيكون ما هو في عِلم الله والملائكة من حقيقة المعلوم والمدرَك من الأمور الطبيعية موجوداً قبْلَ الكثرة وكلّ معقولٍ منها معنىً واحداً ثم يَحصل لهذه المعاني الوجودُ في الكثرة فيحصل في الكثرة ولا يتّحد فيها بوجهٍ من الوجوه إذ ليس في خارجِ الأعيان شيءٌ واحدٌ عامٌّ بل تفريقٌ فقط ثم تحصل مرةً أخرى بعد الحصول في الكثرة معقولةً عندنا. Ibn Sīnā (1952c, 69.10–16). Cf. Black (1999, 53).

7

Poetics

With al-Ǧurǧānī, we move to aesthetics. Like ar-Rāġib, Ibn Fūrak, and Ibn Sīnā, he used the words *maʿnā* and *ḥaqīqah* to explain how human minds work. But he was asking a different question: What is it that makes language beautiful? His answer depended on, developed, and deployed a theory of how language and the mind interact. This theory was constructed with the lexicon, grammar, and syntax, and all three were made up of *maʿānī*. Lexical accuracy pointed at *maʿānī*, grammar structured *maʿānī* in sentences, and syntax manipulated the *maʿānī* of those sentences. Lexicographers, theologians, and logicians all wanted to align *maʿānī* to truth, whether the truths of reason, of the world, or of God. But the poets al-Ǧurǧānī was interested in wanted to manipulate *maʿānī*—mental contents—in order to create affect and make audiences feel and understand beauty.

Al-Ǧurǧānī did not write hermeneutics. He was concerned with how poetry worked, not what it meant. His poetics did not touch on questions of genre, mimesis, or the biographies of poets. He was not concerned with matters related to audience or culture. Instead, he wrote what we may call a linguistic, stylistic, and formalist criticism, in which he used the Arabic conceptual vocabulary of mental content to explain the processes at work. This vocabulary, the same vocabulary that we have read in lexicography, theology, and logic, enabled him to provide a map of the mechanisms with which humans create meaning. He was devoted to providing a literary theory that would explain why one could put a finger on a great line of poetry and say, "This is it!"[1]

1. وذلك ما إذا أُنشِدْتَه وَضَعْتَ فيه اليدَ على شيءٍ فقلتَ هذا هذا. Al-Ǧurǧānī (1992a, 88.13–14).

According to al-Ǧurǧānī, the poetic mechanisms that create affect are fundamentally grammatical and syntactical. Poets put words together in patterns that impact the minds of the audience. These patterns consist of mental contents, and the mental contents change and develop across the time it takes the audience to move through and come to terms with a sentence. This is where al-Ǧurǧānī locates affect, in *maʿānī an-naḥw* ("the mental contents of grammar"), the interactions of which constitute *naẓm* ("syntax"). I return to the translation of both terms below. The lexicographers' model of stable reference is given a dynamic and creative energy. Vocal forms no longer simply refer to mental contents; they are rather threaded into patterns of vocal form that generate patterns of mental content. The idea of a one-to-one correspondence between a vocal form and a mental content, already under pressure from lexical homonymy in ar-Rāġib, theological reason in Ibn Fūrak, and lexical homonymy again in Ibn Sīnā, was no longer tenable. Al-Ǧurǧānī recognized that while the arrangements of mental content in our heads are catalyzed by and potentially recaptured in arrangements of vocal form, they have their own cognitive and logical dynamics. Poetry makes the architecture of mental content in our heads shift and change. The ties that had connected a mental content to a vocal form when it was spoken or written can break in the mind of the audience. This means that the accuracy (*ḥaqīqah*) established by the lexicographers with their iterative management of lexical precedent, an epistemological standard that underpinned both Ibn Fūrak's theology and Ibn Sīnā's logic, became in the work of al-Ǧurǧānī something quite different.

Al-Ǧurǧanī's poetics was concerned with affect on the level of the sentence or the clause. Individual words can have grammatical and syntactical functions (the mental contents of grammar), but only combinations of words constitute syntax or produce images. In sentences and clauses, accuracy is both a foundation for departures of single words from the lexicon (*maǧāz*) and something that can help create and sustain the poetic image itself. In the poetic image as al-Ǧurǧānī sees it, accuracy still works to anchor the imagination, but it now has no curatable root in the lexicon. The theological and logical concern with extramental reality is no longer relevant. Within the triad of language, mind, and reality, poetry is concerned only with language and mind. There is an epistemological shift: poetry takes the lexicon up with it into the image, changing it along the way but rarely giving those changes a permanence that could survive the descent. Those moments when the lexicographers' lexicon changes to accommodate a new mental content achieved by metaphor, when the lexicon expands to include what will become a dead metaphor, are usually the products of simpler, syntactically shorter metaphors based on transfer. In the example that al-Ǧurǧānī used over and over again, the single word "lion" can come to be another lexically sanctioned way of saying "brave man." But the images he was interested in were of another order altogether:

As if the lightning was a Quran
in its reader's hand
closing and opening.

This powerful image is taken from a poem written in praise of a politically successful caliph by his cousin, the literary critic and poet Ibn al-Muʿtazz (861–908), who would himself become caliph for a single day before being deposed and executed.[2] The poet is comparing the caliph to lightning that illuminates the sky. Al-Ǧurǧānī had already cited another line, from later in the poem, as part of a separate piece of criticism nearly a hundred pages earlier in the *Asrār*:[3]

Everything comes together for us
in a leader who kills parsimony
and gives life to largesse.

These two images are each constructed across the space of a single Arabic line, just like all the images in this thirty-line poem with its regularly metered pairs of eleven-syllable hemistichs rhyming *āḥā-āḥā*, B-*āḥā*, C-*āḥā*, D-*āḥā*, and so on (I have altered the lineation and abandoned the rhyme in my translation). Al-Ǧurǧānī did not write about meter or rhyme. Nor was he interested in the irony of the poet's death or in the commentary on power and religion in these images. That was the subject matter of *adab*.

What al-Ǧurǧānī cared about—and in this he typifies Classical Arabic literary criticism—was the mechanism by which the two images, each taken on its own, produced affect. Nothing could be more different than a Quran and lightning, but at the same time nothing could be more similar, he thought, than a reader opening and closing a Quran, and watching lightning flash on and off. This combination of intense similarity with intense difference produces affect, and to achieve it the poet focused on the shape that he wanted the audience to see expand and then immediately contract.[4] Al-Ǧurǧānī cared about the formal mechanisms that manipulate the cognitive processes of the audience. He wanted to give a formal account of each and every mechanism that did this. He used the other image, of

2. وَكَأَنَّ ٱلْبَرْقَ مُصْحَفُ قَارٍ | فَٱنْطِبَاقاً مَرَّةً وٱنْفِتَاحاً. Al-Ǧurǧānī (1954, 140.6), Ibn al-Muʿtazz (1961, 141.6), Lewin (2012).

3. جُمِعَ ٱلْحَقُّ لَنا في إمامٍ | قَتَلَ ٱلْبُخْلَ وأَحْيَى ٱلسَّماحا. Al-Ǧurǧānī (1954, 50.14), Ibn al-Muʿtazz (1961, 141.18).

4. لم يُنظَر [ابنُ المعتز] من جميعِ أوصافِ البَرق ومعانيه إلا إلى الهيئة التي تجدها العينُ له من انبساطٍ يَعقبه انقِباضٌ . . . فأصابَ ذلك فيما يَفعله القارئُ من الحركة الخاصّة في المصحف إذا جعل يَفتحه مرةً ويُطبقه أُخرى ولم يكن إعجابُ هذا التشبيه لك وإيناسُه إيّاك لأنّ الشيئَين مختلفانِ في الجِنس أشدَّ الاختلافِ فقط بل لأنْ حَصلَ بإزاءِ الاختلاف اتفاقٌ كأحْسَنِ ما يكون وأتمِّه فَبِمَجْموعِ الأمرَين شدّةُ ائتلافٍ في شدّةِ اختلافٍ. Al-Ǧurǧānī (1954, 140.8–14).

the leader killing parsimony, to demonstrate how a metaphor might be dependent on the objects of any transitive verbs involved. It is only the object of such a verb that leads us to classify the verb as "borrowed." The verb "kills" is a metaphor only because its object is parsimony; if enemies were being killed there would be no metaphor.[5] A logical grammar of predicative combination creates the image.

WHAT IS GOOD *MAʿNĀ?*

Poetics in Arabic asked the question, What makes for good *maʿnā?* The place to start looking for the answer is the two most important books of Arabic poetics: al-Ǧurǧānī's *Asrār al-Balāġah* and *Dalāʾil al-Iʿǧāz.* I do not think this judgment is hyperbole. (See the *Journal of Abbasid Studies* 5:1–2, a special issue devoted to al-Ǧurǧānī.) He knew that when people spoke they could do more than just refer to mental content; they could choose to create beauty. People made a choice when they spoke, a choice to make their words not just correct, but better crafted. Not just fact, but art. Not just grammar, but beauty. Al-Ǧurǧānī wanted to explain why some literature was better than other literature. He was always looking for that something extra that gave language an aesthetic edge. (The Arabic word he used for this something extra was *mazīyah,* a distinguishing virtue, terminology already in use with ʿAbd al-Ǧabbār.)[6] Unlike Ibn Fūrak's, ar-Rāġib's, and Ibn Sīnā's, al-Ǧurǧānī's theory was first and foremost aesthetic. His aesthetics then required that he develop an account of what language was and how language worked. *Maʿnā* was the heart of that account.

What was the literature of which he was a critic? In the Arabic eleventh century, al-Ǧurǧānī's concern was not quite what the word "literature" refers to today. But it was the same human and divine canon that we have already encountered, consisting of poetry, the Quran, and short selections of eloquent prose. Pre-Islamic Arabs had produced poetry that was still a reference point for al-Ǧurǧānī nearly five hundred years later. God had revealed a Quran that had not only changed the course of history but remained a literary event. The four Islamic centuries that preceded al-Ǧurǧānī had seen the canon of Arabic poetry massively expanded and developed, along with a host of innovations in subject matter and form. Increasingly, in the ninth, tenth and eleventh centuries, this development and expansion was accompanied by a lively critical discourse that argued about matters of style and the relative merits of parts of the canon. Unsurprisingly, given the degree of technical complexity with which we have become accustomed in

5. فَقَتَلَ وأحيَى إنّما صارَا مستعارَينِ بأنْ عُدِّيَا إلى البُخل والسماح ولو قال قتل الأعداءَ وأحيَى لم يكن قَتَلَ استعارةً بوجه ولم يكن أحيَى استعارةً على هذا الوجه. Al-Ǧurǧānī (1954, 51.1–3).

6. مَزِيّة. Al-Qāḍī ʿAbd al-Ǧabbār (1965–74, 16:199.10, 14).

the previous chapters, this critical practice was decisively theoretical. Perhaps the most famous poet, Abū Ṭayyib al-Mutanabbī (d. 965), reportedly said of the theorist Ibn Ǧinnī, "he knows more about my poetry than I do."[7] Classical Arabic literary criticism has been the subject of sustained scholarly attention. (See in particular the encyclopedia edited by Julie Scott Meisami and Paul Starkey, Abu Deeb's entry in *Abbasid Belles Lettres,* Wen-Chin Ouyang's monograph, and Ḫalafallāh's brief review.)[8] This was a criticism oriented toward the single line of poetry, and in the poetry itself enjambment was rare. Aesthetic judgment came at the end of the line. (The value placed on the structural unity of complete poems has been debated by van Gelder, Andras Hamori, and more recently Raymond Farrin.)[9] By the eleventh century this was the established critical practice, and it had a symbiotic relationship with the art itself: poets and critics were in the same places, taking part in the same conversations. This literature shared its patronage and performance spaces with its own criticism. Poetry and criticism shared a commitment to the image and to the line, as well as a deep involvement with the formal complexity of both. But poetry did more than just develop intricate single images in series: it spoke to power and to social reality about fate, money, beauty, love, and loss. These subjects and more were integral to the engagement with poetry that took place outside literary criticism in the prosimetrical genre of *adab:* books about how to live and what life meant, characterized by an iterative approach to truth and a multiplication of narratives.

Just as poetry's remit expanded beyond that of its formal criticism to the world of meaning interrogated in *adab,* literary criticism had a scope that extended beyond poetry to revelation. One of its most important critical and theoretical conversations was an argument about the relative aesthetic merits of the sacred Quran and profane poetry. Quranic language was fundamental to al-Ǧurǧānī's project; it was an example of how language could be beautiful. Virtually no one was prepared to say that poetry was better than the Quran, and the Quran clearly differentiated itself from poetry,[10] but there was an argument about whether or not one could theorize the Quran as a literary text in such a way as to demonstrate its superiority. (Geert Jan van Gelder has drawn my attention to the extreme example of Abū al-ʿĀtāhiyah [d. ca. 825], a canonical poet with "unorthodox religious beliefs" who was said to have claimed he had

7. ابنُ جِنّي أَعْرفُ بشعري منّي. Ibn Ǧinnī (2004, 1:469), al-Yamānī (1986, 200).

8. Abu Deeb (1990), *Encyclopedia of Arabic Literature* (1998), Ḫalafallāh (1944, 48f), Ouyang (1997).

9. Farrin (2011), Hamori (1974), van Gelder (1982). Cf. Sharlet (2015).

10. See statements at Quran 21:5 (al-Anbiyāʾ), 26:224 (aš-Šuʿarāʾ), 36:69 (Yā Sīn), 37:36 (aṣ-Ṣāffāt), 52:30 (aṭ-Ṭūr), and 69:41 (al-Ḥāqqah).

written a poem better than a Quranic *sūrah* [chapter].)[11] As ar-Rāġib and many others had done before him,[12] al-Ǧurǧānī leapt into this argument, committed to making his theories work in such a way as to explain both why poetry was good and why the Quranic text could not be replicated by humans. This would require two slightly different versions of the same argument and so generated both the *Asrār* and the *Dalāʾil.* This debate about Quranic inimitability framed and fueled al-Ǧurǧānī's literary-critical work but did not define or constitute it. The Quran was just one more reason why the question *How does literary language work?* needed to be answered.

"To make an aesthetic judgment is to stake one's authority on nothing but one's own experience: when we declare that something is beautiful we have nothing but our own judgment to go on. While we may spontaneously feel that others simply *must* see what we see, we can't ground the claim in anything more tangible than our own judgment. . . . This feels risky."[13] Toril Moi identifies a genealogy for this risk of aesthetic subjectivity that goes back to Kant. But she could just as easily have gone back to Classical Arabic, where critics worked to give accounts of poetry that strove to avoid a collapse into the subjectivity of personal experience. In a passage quoted in full by ar-Rāġib, the literary critic al-Qāḍī Abū al-Ḥasan ʿAlī al-Ǧurǧānī (d. 1002) explained great eloquence as what one cannot explain, for which one cannot give a reason.[14] An epistemological risk of this kind is different from the one we have encountered in previous chapters, when secondary scholarship (also in the long shadow of Kant) feared a collapse into linguistic relativism. Here, the risk for theory is that all one is left with is the plaintive question *Can you see what I see?*[15] Reading Ibn Fūrak and Ibn Sīnā has shown us that the epistemological risk of linguistic relativism was not necessarily a problem should one choose to share their conceptual vocabulary of mental content. But here, in a chapter on poetics, the differences between our European and Anglophone present and the Arabic eleventh century are less evident. The experience of the beauty of poetry and the question of taste in art put us and al-Ǧurǧānī (both ʿAbd al-Qāhir and Abū al-Ḥasan!) in the same place. They asked exactly the same question as Moi. There is, says ʿAbd al-Qāhir al-Ǧurǧānī, some poetry whose quality you know

11. Quran 78 (an-Nabāʾ). Abū Faraǧ al-Iṣfahānī (1964–74, 4:34.8–9), Creswell (2009).

12. Key (2010).

13. Moi (2017, 313). Cf. Kant (1987, ##32, 33, 145–49).

14. ثم لا تَعلم وإنْ قايستَ واعتبرتَ ونظرتَ وفكرتَ لهذه المزيّة سبباً ولِما خُصَّتْ مقتضياً . . . Al-Qāḍī al-Ǧurǧānī (1966, 412.7–8). Cf. ar-Rāġib (ca. 14th C., fol. 38b.4–5). See also chapter 1 note 15 above and al-Andalusī (1987, 192.3–4).

15. Cavell (2002, 93), Moi (2017, 326).

when you hear it, even if you don't know the poet: "It is as if you can put your hand on it and say, 'This is it!'"[16]

When he explained the cognitive and affective mechanisms at work in poetry, al-Ǧurǧānī was working in an established tradition of Arabic literary criticism that, unlike the philosophical tradition, was uninvolved with the Greek past. He did not use Aristotle's *Rhetoric* or *Poetics.* This was also an Arabic tradition unconnected to a European future. The Latinate rhetoric of commentaries on Cicero and Horace made no use of Arabic, and although Latin rhetoric shared with Arabic a connection to grammar, it did so in a very different way: Latin grammar and rhetoric was about language pedagogy (see the remarks of Hermannus Alemannus in Rita Copeland and Ineke Sluiter's translation),[17] whereas Arabic grammar and poetics was about theoretical accounts of cognition. It was therefore through Ibn Sīnā's Arabic logic that al-Ǧurǧānī would use the Greeks, at several degrees of remove and in translation.

Scholars working in Arabic were of course not ignorant of the ancient Greek and late-antique discussions of literature. Maria Mavroudi has shown that Homer's *Odyssey* and *Iliad* were translated into Syriac in the ninth century and that Ḥunayn, the translator of Aristotle whom we have already met, recited Homer in Baghdad.[18] Furthermore, philhellenic Arabic philosophers did write commentaries on Aristotle's *Poetics* and *Rhetoric,* but they either kept them separate from the autochthonous Arabic tradition (Ibn Sīnā) or in a very few cases outside the eleventh century attempted combining the two traditions (al-Fārābī in the tenth century and Ḥāzim al-Qarṭāǧannī, on whom see Heinrichs, in the thirteenth, while Ibn Rušd's twelfth-century synthesis would arguably have more impact in Latin than in Arabic).[19] Deborah Black has shown how a commitment to the *Organon* curriculum shaped philhellenic Arabic philosophy's dealings with Aristotle's *Poetics* and *Rhetoric;* Wolfhart Heinrichs and others have discussed Ibn Sīnā's and al-Fārābī's uses of the Aristotelian syllogism to discuss poetry, and Uwe Vagelpohl has analyzed the reception of the *Rhetoric* and *Poetics.*[20] M C. Lyons's edition has shown the limitations of the Arabic translation of the *Rhetoric,*[21] and Abu Deeb (cf. Ḫalafallāh)[22] devoted an entire chapter to successfully demonstrating how al-Ǧurǧānī's work did not connect with the *Poetics.*[23]

16. See note 1 above.

17. Copeland and Sluiter (2012, 739).

18. Mavroudi (2015, 324–25).

19. Aouad (2009), Aristotle (1953), Copeland and Sluiter (2012, 735), Heinrichs (1969).

20. Black (1990), Heinrichs (2008); Vagelpohl (2008), (2015).

21. Aristotle (1982), Wansborough (1984).

22. Ḫalafallāh (1944, 67f).

23. Abu Deeb (1979, 303–22). Cf. Larkin (1995, 146–50).

Ignorance was not the problem, but the disconnect survived. The Greek and Arabic aesthetic traditions had different epistemological structures and different cultural assumptions about the forms and genres of art itself. There was no prestige genre of formal dramatic tragedy in Classical Arabic. There was nothing equivalent to *adab* in ancient Greek. Al-Ǧurǧānī and his peers did not think that an answer could be found in theories of genre, culture, or mimesis to the question *How can we explain what poetry does to us?* Ṭaha Ḥusayn has suggested that the source of influence for Classical Arabic literary criticism was "Aristotle's general ideas and methodology" via Ibn Sīnā,[24] but here I would like to be more specific. I argue that al-Ǧurǧānī found resources in theories of cognition, and the place to look for an account of cognition in the eleventh century was Arabic logic. The machinery to ground an account of cognition in a set of assumptions about how language worked already existed in Arabic grammar and lexicography. This was al-Ǧurǧānī's poetics: a theory of literature that bypassed genre and culture to rely instead on grammar and then follow logic out into the imaginary.

Al-Ǧurǧānī's poetics was a project that shaped the subsequent millennium of work on Arabic literature, and it has not gone unnoticed in Arabist secondary scholarship. (For a brief review, see Harb and Key)[25] On the one hand, for scholars trained in Arabic-speaking institutions, al-Ǧurǧānī's work has proved important beyond all others for the production of conceptual vocabularies that combine eleventh-century Arabic theory with twentieth-century European theory. I am thinking in particular of Ahmed Moutaouakil, who wrote his highly functional synthesis of al-Ǧurǧānī and Saussure in French.[26] Another example, from the field of theology, is Naṣr Ḥāmid Abū Zayd's engagement with Ibn ʿArabī (d. 1240) and Western semiotics (Thomas Hildebrandt).[27] As for scholars trained in European and Anglophone institutions, they work in a frame created by the absence of connection between literary criticism in Greek, Arabic, and Latin. Abu Deeb is absolutely clear that his book is motivated by a profound sense of shock at the scale and depth of the connections between al-Ǧurǧānī's theory and twentieth-century Anglophone literary theory. (He was also following the connections that Ḫalafallāh had made with European theories of affect in 1944.)[28] Abu Deeb wrote to effect a connection, and to develop a new critical tool that combined al-Ǧurǧānī's theory with those of T. S. Eliot and others, precisely because the object of study was the

24. Quoted in Ḫalafallāh (1944, 20, 76f).

25. Harb and Key (forthcoming).

26. Moutaouakil (1982).

27. Abū Zayd (2005), Hildebrandt (2007, 501f).

28. Ḫalafallāh (1944, 42f).

same: poetry. Al-Ǧurǧānī "is aware of the various types of images, sensuous, non-sensuous, visual and non-visual, which have been studied in modern criticism."[29]

In *Al-Jurjānī's Theory of Poetic Imagery,* published at the same time as Edward Said's *Orientalism,* Abu Deeb wrote: "It is altogether unfortunate that European writers ignore the achievement of other cultures in many areas and thus find themselves 'discovering' principles . . . already discovered and developed to an amazing degree of sophistication in these other cultures." Furthermore, al-Ǧurǧānī's theory had to be used not just because it was first but because it still worked: "the first genuinely structuralist analysis of imagery I know of and its value goes far beyond the historical." Al-Ǧurǧānī's "achievement . . . precedes by nine centuries the work of Croce, Bradely, Wimsatt, Richards, and Beardsley, who are among the most outstanding critics of our era."[30] Writing from a department of comparative literature in 2017, what is so frightening about Abu Deeb's project is that he was right and that the project failed. Benedetto Croce (d. 1952), A. C. Bradely (d. 1935), William Kurtz Wimsatt (d. 1975), I. A. Richards (d. 1979), and Monroe Beardsley (d. 1985) may no longer quite be of my era (which began in 1979), but in any case al-Ǧurǧānī's name and the translations of the *Asrār* and *Dalāʾil* into German and French, respectively,[31] are not to be found alongside them in the syllabi and bibliographies of Anglophone literary criticism. Time has exposed the risk Abu Deeb took: his book links al-Ǧurǧānī so effectively with mid-twentieth-century Anglophone literary theory that in the early twenty-first century al-Ǧurǧānī appears doubly dated.

SELF-CONSCIOUSLY THEORETICAL ANSWERS IN MONOGRAPHS

Al-Ǧurǧānī's literary theory was written in a style consistent with its theoretical content. As he wrote the *Asrār* and *Dalāʾil,* he circled around the most important questions, returning to them over and over again, trying out new phraseology for the theoretical arguments he was trying to make and, in the later parts of the *Dalāʾil,* testing his new terminology on his audience. (His most oft-quoted theoretical statements tend to come from the final sections of each monograph.) This was how he thought that theory itself should work. There was not a single, fixed model that could enable the sort of taxonomy of rhetorical figures that scholars like ar-Rāġib found so attractive. Instead, there were principles and zones that anchored meaning and enabled its analysis. These principles and zones supported

29. Abu Deeb (1979, 13, 96).

30. Abu Deeb (1979, 32, 58, 81).

31. Al-Ǧurǧānī (1959a), (2006).

dynamics that could coexist or overlap and could be described in multiple ways with or without examples. It was a different way of doing literary criticism, discursive and formalist rather than taxonomical. Al-Ǧurǧānī's narrative voice circled and looped over a complex literary landscape populated by language users and marked by moments of special significance such as the Quran or a great metaphor.

Al-Ǧurǧānī's criticism was self-consciously theoretical. It was a poetics that claimed universal applicability across the languages spoken by its author. (See my separate article on al-Ǧurǧānī and translation theory.)[32] It was also a poetics that deliberately provided principles that were intended to be applied across the canon by other scholars. Its author therefore took great care with his terminology. Al-Ǧurǧānī knew that one's choice of terms is fundamental to the prospects for one's theory. He was very aware of the different stages of technical terminology and their relationship to ordinary language. Throughout his work we can see this commitment to the curation of terminology in the face of pressure from ordinary language. When making the argument that syntax was a matter of organizing mental content rather than vocal form, he made it clear that he was working against a folk theory of language that tended to associate the act of making syntactical connections with vocal forms rather than mental contents.[33] When making his argument about the correct understanding of metaphor, he was aware that he was working against a popular and problematic tendency to talk about metaphor as a simple transfer.[34] When making his argument about the way a specific arrangement of mental content could take on a form, he made it expressly clear that there was a preexisting scholarly consensus on the use of the word *ṣūrah* ("form," "image"; see below) and that he should not be constrained by that established terminology.[35]

Al-Ǧurǧānī's extant works are either grammar or literary criticism. His grammar works are structured conventionally, whether as long and detailed line-by-line commentaries with a short dedicatory or an explanatory preface[36] or as concise pedagogical tools.[37] But when it came to literary theory he wrote differently and

32. Key forthcoming in the *Journal of Abbasid Studies*.

33. ومما يُلّبس على الناظر في هذا الموضع ويُغلّطه أنه يَستبعد أنْ يقال هذا كلامٌ قد نُظِمتْ معانيه فالعُرفُ كأنه لم يَجري بذلك. Al-Ǧurǧānī (1992a, 53.3–4).

34. ومِن شأنِ ما غمضَ من المعاني ولطفَ أنْ يَصعب تصويرُه على الوجه الذي هو عليه لعامةِ الناس فيقع لذلك في العبارات التي يُعبِّر بها عنه ما يُوهِم الخطأ وإطلاقُهم في الاستعارة أنها نقلٌ للعبارة عمّا وُضِعتْ له من ذلك. Al-Ǧurǧānī (1992a, 435.1–4).

35. وليس العبارةُ عن ذلك بالصورة شيئاً نحن ابتدأناه فيُنكِره مُنكِرٌ بل هو مستعمَلٌ مشهورٌ في كلام العلماء. Al-Ǧurǧānī (1992a, 508.13–14).

36. Al-Ǧurǧānī (1982), (2007).

37. Al-Ǧurǧānī (196-), (1987), (1988), (1990).

was conscious of doing so. The *Asrār* and the *Dalāʾil* are two substantial monographs, most probably written in that order, of around 80,000 and 130,000 words, respectively. The *Dalāʾil* in Muḥammad Šākir's 1984 edition includes a separate epistle on Quranic inimitability.[38] Šākir's inclusion of this epistle is in accordance with his base manuscript, dated 1177 (Hüseyin Çelebi 913 at the İnebey Yazma Eser Kütüphanesi in Bursa, Turkey).[39] The inclusion of the twelve-thousand-word epistle after the end of the *Dalāʾil* makes sense to readers of the printed edition today just as it did to readers of the manuscript in the twelfth century: it is consistent with the structure of the work itself. Al-Ǧurǧānī's monograph ends formally on page 478 of Šākir's edition but is immediately followed by a series of attachments and short epistles found in Hüseyin Çelebi 913. (Šākir [1984], Rašīd Riḍā [1952], and Muḥammad aš-Šinqīṭī [1978] each placed the last of these, "Introduction to the *Dalāʾil*," at the beginning of his printed edition.)[40] Šākir's reasonable suggestion (following a note on the manuscript itself)[41] is that these extras were transcribed from separate notes in al-Ǧurǧānī's hand after his death, but whatever the case, we know from remarks within them that al-Ǧurǧānī saw them as part of a single literary-critical project. At the start of one such attachment, on page 525, the author directly addresses "the reader of our book" and writes that such a reader should by this stage be comfortable with his account of creative syntax, but nevertheless goes on, in order to "truly, honestly, make sure that the reader is not troubled by exhaustion,"[42] to write another ten pages of clarification. Scholars today can only dream of being afforded such space or the sort of reader whose fatigue is decreased by more reading!

What is the significance of this manuscript history, and of the fact that both the *Asrār* and the *Dalāʾil* roam so discursively that the latter can expand for more than a hundred pages after it ends without that affecting its structural integrity? Thankfully, al-Ǧurǧānī provides the answer himself. Half of his answer is explicit; half, implicit. The implicit half has been identified by Larkin, Šākir, and others: it is the scholarly context of an eleventh century in which al-Ǧurǧānī was engaged in argument, polemic, and theoretical debate with scholars in literary theory and theology. The later sections of the *Dalāʾil* are most often couched in terms that make it clear that the author was responding to specific criticisms of his basic ideas about syntax, Quranic inimitability, and the way that language works. Al-Ǧurǧānī

38. Al-Ǧurǧānī (1959b), (1992a, introd. *lām*. 1–2), (1992b).

39. Al-Ǧurǧānī (1172/77, fol. 180b).

40. Al-Ǧurǧānī (1172/77, fol. 181a–183b), (1952, 13–20), (1978, 2–8).

41. Al-Ǧurǧānī (1172/77, fol. 176b.1).

42. رَجَوْنا ... رَغْبةً صادقةً تَدفع عنك السأمَ وأريحيةً يَخفّ معها عليك تعْبَ الفكر وكدَّ النظر. Al-Ǧurǧānī (1992a, 525.12–526.1).

was constantly trying out new ways of describing and explaining his theories in order to persuade his audience that he was right.

Al-Ğurğānī was working with words in order to communicate ideas about words. Faced with this universal scholarly problem, he laid out a defense of theory and a critique of taxonomy. Instead of the innumerable subdivisions required to taxonomize a topic such as comparison (*tašbīh*) in poetry, he wrote that he aimed to provide an indication or a pointer, a gesture, the form of which would be sufficient to inform readers. He would also provide counterexamples, because things get clearer alongside their opposites.[43] Literary theory had often tended, before al-Ğurğānī, to function through the use of examples. Each separate rhetorical figure was therefore encapsulated and understood in terms of a representative line of poetry. But al-Ğurğānī aimed to establish the formal principles of poetics that validated these examples.

Let us take an example to see how he did this. As part of his long discussion of metaphor in the *Asrār*, he defined one subset of metaphor as being that in which the operative comparison is between forms, composed of mental content, that are reasoned out by the audience. (I will return to his idea of "form," *ṣūrah*, below.)[44] These were the best kind of metaphor, because the term of comparison was not accessed through its membership in a certain class, nor by some natural critical instinct of the audience, nor by some form already existing in an audience member's psyche.[45] Instead, "the pattern of this . . . principle of metaphor is that it takes a point of comparison between two reasoned things. The paradigmatic and most widely applicable example of this is a comparison that goes from [1] something's existence to its nonexistence or [2] from something's nonexistence to its existence. As for [1], the underlying mental content here is that when a thing loses those specific mental contents by which it comes to have measure and reference, its actual existence becomes a nonexistence."[46] This is a deliberately logical and abstract account (Ritter

43. ولا يمكن الانتصافُ منه [التشبيه المُفيد] إلا بفصولٍ جمّةٍ وقِسمةٍ بعدَ قسمة وأنا أرى أنْ أقتصِر الآن على إشارةٍ تُعرّف صورتُه على الجملة بقدرِ ما تراه وقد قابل خلافَه الذي هو غيرُ المفيد فيتمّ تصوّرُك للغرض والمراد فإنّ الأشياء تَزداد بياناً بالأضداد. Al-Ğurğānī (1954, 31.12–15).

44. See notes 75–77 below.

45. وهذا كما تَعلم شَبَهٌ لستَ تَحصل منه على جنسٍ ولا على طبيعة وغريزة ولا على هيئة وصورة تَدخل في الخِلقة وإنما هو صورة عقلية واعلمْ أنّ هذا الضرب هو المنزلة التي تبلغ عندها الاستعارةُ غايةَ شرفها. Al-Ğurğānī (1954, 60.14–17).

46. مثالُ الأصل الثالث وهو أخْذُ الشِبه من المعقول للمعقول أوّلُ ذلك وأعمُّه تشبيهُ الوجود من الشيء مرةً بالعَدَم والعدمِ مرةً بالوجود أما الأوّل فعلى معنى أنه لما قلَّ في المعاني التي بها يَظهر للشيء قدْرٌ ويصير له ذكرٌ صار وجودُه كلا وجود. Al-Ğurğānī (1954, 67.8–11).

calls it "complicated logical analysis"),[47] and there are two more pages of theory before al-Ǧurǧānī provides some lines of poetry, which include:[48]

I cannot stop leaning in
to embrace the memories of days past; they give me
something more fragile than nothingness.

The poet, Abū Naṣr ʿAbd al-ʿAzīz Ibn Nubātah (fl. ca. 950), is justifying his reminiscences of youth with a deliberate lack of conviction. These memories offer him comfort so gossamer-thin that a nonexistent thing in a state of nonexistence would be thicker.

Al-Ǧurǧānī's logical and abstract literary-critical framework enables us to see that on reading or hearing this line the audience has no choice but to reason through its counterintuitive and hypothetical impossibility in order to posit for a moment a new form not encountered before in nature or science. This reasoned form gives the line its meaning.[49] It is a form composed of mental contents: "something thinner than a nonexistent thing in a state of nonexistence." This is not an intervention in language that can be preserved in the lexicon; it is a moment of creation that produces affect through reason.

Al-Ǧurǧānī wanted to lay out a theoretical structure with a technical vocabulary that could inform critical engagement with poetry. His abstract explanation of the comparison that goes from nonexistence to existence reads: "It works according to the following mental content: the thing ceasing to exist had existed and was then lost and vanished. But when it leaves behind beautiful traces, they give life to its memory and make permanent its name among the people; it therefore becomes as if it existed."[50] This is self-evidently a theory designed to encompass the *aṭlāl,* that most famous of tropes in pre-Islamic poetry in which the poet mourns his beloved's departure at the remains of her encampment. At the very beginning of the *Asrār,* al-Ǧurǧānī had quoted the canonical example of this trope, the opening line of Imruʾ al-Qays' *Muʿallaqah:* "Stop! Let us weep . . ."[51] There he had asked rhetorically whether the line depended on its word order (of course it does!), and here he gives a literary-critical account based on rational conceptions of existence and nonexistence that enables him to identify

47. Al-Ǧurǧānī (1954, 16).

48. مَا زِلْتُ أَعْطِفُ أَيَّامي فَتَمْنَحُني | نَيْلاً أَدَقَّ مِن ٱلْمَعْدُومِ فِي ٱلْعَدَمِي. Al-Ǧurǧānī (1954, 69.14), aṯ-Ṯaʿālibī (1983, 455.11).

49. . . . وإنما هو صورة عقلية . . . Al-Ǧurǧānī (1954, 60.16).

50. وأما الثاني فعلى معنى أنّ الفاني كان موجوداً ثم فُقِد وعُدِم إلا أنه لمّا خلّف آثاراً جميلةً تُحيي ذكرَه وتُديم في الناس اسمَه صار ذلك كأنه لم يُعدم. Al-Ǧurǧānī (1954, 67.12–13).

51. قِفَا نَبْكِ مِنْ ذِكْرَى حَبِيبٍ وَمَنْزِلِ |. Al-Ǧurǧānī (1954, 3.13).

the dynamic architecture of mental content that produces its affect: a thing that does not exist is being reasoned into existence. Rhetorical figures are no longer taxonomized according to their exemplars, but rather they are organized and read according to rational and abstract theories about the forms that mental content can take.

This was a theory contained in a long monograph that needed to be read. This discussion of the reasoned metaphor stretches over more than twenty pages in Helmut Ritter's edition. Al-Ǧurǧānī knew what he was doing. In an age of chapters, subchapters, and increasing concern for pedagogical practicality, he was writing books that needed to be read from start to finish. In the *Dalāʾil* he said so, and this is where we find his explicit authorial statement of monograph structure: "The only way to know whether this is all correct is to allow my statement to be complete and to reach the end of what I have put together for you."[52] It is not a book that the author can summarize at the beginning; it is a process that will complete al-Ǧurǧānī's account of how language works and what makes it good: "I am not prepared to tell you, here at the beginning, what will happen at the end of this book, or to name for you the chapters that I intend to compose if God allows me. I do not want you to know what will happen before it does. Know instead that there are chapters that will follow each other, and that this is the first."[53] It is a radical statement, but one that matches al-Ǧurǧānī's work. It is an ethics of reading applied to an entire monograph.

It was complemented by an ethics of reading that worked on the level of syntax, centered on the process of building up mental-content connections across a sentence or a clause, where a poet could manipulate grammar and syntax in order to set the audience up for the maximum impact (Abu Deeb).[54] This was an ethics of reading in which the literature came in small evocative snatches of a few lines or less. Al-Ǧurǧānī thought *his* readers should work their way productively and iteratively through his long monographs, but although he had the theory to deal with the whole long Classical Arabic poem, he usually chose to work on a smaller scale. (Cf. van Gelder, Larkin, and Abu Deeb on analysis that does stretch through a poem.)[55] It is tempting to suggest that al-Ǧurǧānī worked this way because he thought theory of the complex sort that he was writing had a discursive struc-

52. واعلمْ أنه لا سبيلَ إلى أنْ تَعرف صحةَ هذه الجملة حتى يَبلغ القولُ غايتَه وينتهي إلى آخِره ما أردتُ جمعَه لك. Al-Ǧurǧānī (1992a, 38.4–5).

53. وليس يتأتّى لي أنْ أُعلّمك مِن أوّل الأمر في ذلك آخرَه وأنْ أُسمّي لك الفصولَ التي في نِيَّتي أنْ أُحرّرها بمشيئة الله عزّ وجلّ حتى تكون على عِلمٍ بها قبلَ مَوردها عليك فاعْملْ على أنّ هاهنا فصولاً يجيء بعضُها في إثرِ بعضٍ وهذا أوّلها. Al-Ǧurǧānī (1992a, 42.9–12).

54. Abu Deeb (1979, 255).

55. Abu Deeb (1979, 100–102), al-Ǧurǧānī (1954, 30.12f), Larkin (1995, 126), van Gelder (1982, 136).

ture that a reader could maintain across hundreds of pages but that *literature*—art, beauty, and poetry functioned in the listener's head at the moment of audition. Long poems might well have unities, but the aesthetic impact he was interested in came in a few seconds.

Let me now briefly sketch out the contents of the *Asrār* and *Dalāʾil.* My suggestion, *pace* Ritter and via Heinrichs,[56] is that although there is no clear evidence as to which book was written first, the *Dalāʾil* feels like a final, conclusive review, one that assumes the argument of the *Asrār* is already proved. Whatever the case, they are very different books when it comes to subject matter. Al-Ǧurǧānī wrote one book on metaphor (the *Asrār*) and one book on syntax (the *Dalāʾil*). *Ex nihilo,* the *Asrār* revolutionized Arabic poetics, and then the *Dalāʾil* engaged with debates in both theology and poetics. Both books primarily deal with the Quran and poetry (the *Asrār* with slightly more poetry, the *Dalāʾil* with slightly more Quran; see Khalfallah's tabulations),[57] and both state that their conclusions apply equally to prose. Al-Ǧurǧānī's opening argument in the *Asrār* was that everyone knew that great poetry was good, but no one had been able to effectively theorize why the canon was the canon. Literary theory, faced with vocal forms and mental content, had lazily attributed aesthetic quality to the vocal forms and forgotten that metaphors are only ever constructed in and understood by the mind with mental contents. This was why al-Ǧurǧānī had to reexamine the most basic concepts (Abu Deeb)[58] of Arabic language about language: vocal form and mental content. He had to say anew what language was in order to explain how it worked. Writing within the iterative structure he had set for himself, he also needed to say what language was over and over again. This is why, I think, scholars in both the madrasa and the twenty-first-century academy have sometimes identified inconsistencies in his position on vocal form and mental content. But as Lara Harb notes, these inconsistencies appear when excerpts from his work are "read out of context."[59] Taken as a whole, al-Ǧurǧānī's argument is clear: an exclusive binary of vocal form and mental content is insufficient for literary criticism, and when critics focus myopically on either category, they are mistaken.

In order to prove that a critical focus on vocal forms was a failure of literary criticism, al-Ǧurǧānī started the *Asrār* with an analysis of wordplay and paronomasia, poetic techniques that would appear on their face to be entirely about vocal forms rather than mental content. Al-Ǧurǧānī showed how wordplay was in fact entirely dependent on the cognitive responses of audiences, and then after a good

56. Al-Ǧurǧānī (1954, introd. 6), Heinrichs (1991/92, 276 n. 54).

57. Khalfallah (2014, 311–21).

58. Abu Deeb (1990, 380).

59. Harb (2013, 192–96), (2015, 304).

twenty pages he started the book proper with an exhaustive analysis of metaphor. This analysis of the loan metaphor is the core of his argument, bookended with a discussion of lexical accuracy and going beyond the lexicon. The *Dalāʾil* opens with a defense of grammar and a defense of poetry. Both are key to understanding the literary status of the Quran. Al-Ǧurǧānī then came back to the pairing of vocal form and mental content with a slightly different angle from that taken in the *Asrār,* because now he wanted to explain his theory of syntax. Creative and subtle syntax, the positioning of words in a sentence, negation and predication, connections and appositions all were ways in which vocal form reflected and catalyzed mental content.

His word for these techniques was *naẓm,* the same word used for stringing pearls on a thread. This was the subject matter of the *Dalāʾil:* "the way a sentence is constructed in light of the syntactical relationships between its words."[60] I use the word "syntax" in English. Al-Ǧurǧānī used the word *naẓm* and saw it as constituted by *maʿānī an-naḥw,* the mental contents of grammar.[61] It must be noted here that the discipline of grammar, *naḥw,* itself contained two subdisciplines: *naḥw* and *ṣarf,* which are usually translated as "syntax and morphology" (just as in English, the discipline of grammar contains syntax and morphology.) This puts some pressure on my translation of *naẓm* as "syntax," because "syntax" is also a subdiscipline of grammar. *Naḥw* was the science of how words connected to each other; *ṣarf* was the science of how individual words were formed, and *naḥw* was also the word for both these sciences taken together as a scholarly discipline. But *naẓm* was something bigger, a space in which there was the potential for beauty and affect, whereas in *naḥw* there was only right and wrong. In the *Asrār* and *Dalāʾil,* al-Ǧurǧānī was not interested in whether combinations of words were grammatically correct but rather in how a poet could manipulate their correct mental contents in a dynamic syntactical pattern. The English word "syntax" is not a perfect translation for this creative process, but it has the advantages of familiarity and concision, serving as well to locate the action exactly where al-Ǧurǧānī located it: in the formal combinations of words. As Baalbaki has observed, there is in Arabic a "self-explanatory" "kinship" between the study of grammar and eloquence (*naḥw* and *balāġah*): they are both concerned with syntax. But whereas grammarians tended to be concerned with the syntactical operation of case markers, scholars working on eloquence focused more on the impact created by syntactical variation.[62] It is this latter understanding of the importance of word choice

60. The quotation is a definition of *naẓm:* Harb (2015, 305).

61. وكلّه من معاني النحو كما ترى وهكذا السبيلُ أبداً في كلّ حُسْنٍ ومَزيةٍ رأيتَهما قد نُسِبا إلى النظم. Al-Ǧurǧānī (1992a, 86.18–20).

62. Baalbaki (1983, 8–9).

and combination that al-Ǧurǧānī sought to capture with his concept of *naẓm* and that I engage with under the heading "syntax."

POETICS FROM AXES TO ZONES (*AQṬĀB* AND *AQṬĀR*)

Al-Ǧurǧānī's eleventh-century theory was not a madrasa-ready pedagogical tool. It did not have a clear taxonomical structure, and it consciously required the reader to work through two long monographs on metaphor and syntax, developing along the way an understanding of how language worked and what made some of it beautiful. On this journey, the reader would meet the core dynamics of al-Ǧurǧānī's poetics over and over again. Comparison, analogy, and metaphor were "axes around which mental content revolved" and "zones that encompassed mental contents according to the perspective of each." They could not be encapsulated or enumerated in a taxonomy of representative examples.[63] They overlapped in dynamic ways that cannot be clearly mapped.

This is the problem for scholarship on al-Ǧurǧānī's poetics: his program for how theory should be written and read does not make the task of the secondary analyst easy. The work of Abu Deeb, Harb, Khalfallah, Larkin, and myself demonstrates that in the twentieth or twenty-first century one has no option when writing about the *Asrār* and *Dalāʾil* but to do exactly what Arabic scholars in the twelfth and thirteenth centuries did: develop one's own theoretical scheme and fit al-Ǧurǧānī into it. For the creators of the madrasa textbooks, those schemas tended to be primarily taxonomical. For more recent European and Anglophone academics, these schemas have tended to be thematic (subjective poetics, theological reasoning, wonder, signification, or translation theory). My own attempts in this chapter focus on the most fundamental building blocks of al-Ǧurǧānī's conceptual vocabulary, *maʿnā* and *ḥaqīqah,* and so look to Arabic grammar and philhellenic logic for poetic potential. I have tried to validate and explain al-Ǧurǧānī's own claim that syntax was the "pursuit of the mental contents of grammar" and that it was the heart of poetics.[64]

Let us orient ourselves a little further in al-Ǧurǧānī's poetics. Metaphor (*istiʿārah*) was one of the three axes of his theory and the primary subject of the *Asrār.* It always involved comparison (*tašbīh,* another axis), and it could include analogy (*tamṯīl,* a third axis). The basic meaning of the Arabic word for metaphor is "borrowing" and this refers to the rough idea that a characteristic

63. القولُ على التشبيه والتمثيل والاستعارة فإنّ هذه أصولٌ . . . وكأنها أقطابٌ تَدور عليها المعاني في متصرَّفاتها وأقطارٌ تُحيط بها من جهاتها ولا يقنع طالبُ التحقيق أنْ يقتصر فيها على أمثلة تُذكَر ونظائر تُعَدّ. Al-Ǧurǧānī (1954, 26.6,8–10).

64. تَوَخّي معاني النحو. For example, al-Ǧurǧānī (1992a, 84.12–13, 361.1–2).

is borrowed from the source and given to the target. (*Istiʿārah* can be translated more precisely as "loan metaphor.")[65] Al-Ğurğānī's book-length treatment of metaphor is substantially more complex, and this is not the place to review it. Abu Deeb has already done an excellent job. He defines al-Ğurğānī's *istiʿārah* for an Anglophone audience as "metaphor, but more exactly a type of metaphor based only on similarity or analogy."[66] Al-Ğurğānī himself defined metaphor in terms with which are already very familiar: "Metaphor, taken as a whole, is when a vocal form has an original lexical placement that is known and can be indicated by evidentiary precedent. Someone, whether poet or not, then uses that vocal form somewhere other than in that original lexical place. This person transfers the vocal form to a new place in a move that is not strictly necessary."[67] Metaphor comes from a free choice to use a word outside of precedent. And the result of metaphor is new mental content, a new poetic end or object, that would not exist were it not for the metaphor.[68] It is worth noting that in English poetics we tend to pair metaphor, by way of contrast, with metonymy. This is not the case in Arabic: metaphor (*istiʿārah*) is not part of a contrast pair with metonymy (*kināyah*), nor is Arabic metonymy understood in the same way as English metonymy (Harb).[69] Arabic metonymy is, however, given serious attention in the *Dalāʾil*,[70] where the standard example is "long of the sword strap" to describe a tall man. Al-Ğurğānī defines metonymy as "when the speaker intends to affirm a certain mental content but does not speak of that mental content using the vocal form placed for it in the lexicon. Rather, the speaker comes to another mental content that follows or succeeds the first mental content in the sphere of existence."[71] When you think of a long sword strap, you think of the tall man who must wear it.

The most famous subdivison of metaphor (*istiʿārah*) is make-believe (*taḫyīl*). Al-Ğurğānī's development of this concept has received substantial attention from

65. Heinrichs (1977).

66. Abu Deeb (1979, ix).

67. اعلمْ أنّ الاستعارة في الجملة أنْ يكون للفظٍ أصلٌ في الوضْع اللغويّ معروفٌ تَدلّ الشواهدُ على أنه اختُصّ به حِين وُضِع ثم يَستعمله الشاعرُ أو غير الشاعر في غير ذلك الأصل ويَنقله إليه نقلاً غير لازم. Al-Ğurğānī (1954, 29.1–3).

68. وأما المفيدُ فقد بانَ لك باستعارته فائدةٌ ومعنىً من المعاني وغرضٌ من الأغراض لو لا مَكانُ تلك الاستعارة لم يَحصل لك. Al-Ğurğānī (1954, 31.9–10).

69. Harb (2013, n. 643), (2015, n. 5).

70. Abu Deeb (1979, 164).

71. والمرادُ بالكِناية هاهنا أنْ يُريد المتكلّمُ إثباتَ معنىً من المعاني فلا يَذكره باللفظ الموضوع له في اللغة ولكن يجيء إلى معنىً هو تاليه ورِدْفُه في الوجود فيُومئ به إليه ويَجعله دليلاً عليه مِثالُ ذلك قولُهم هو طويلُ النِجاد يريدون طويلَ القامة. Al-Ğurğānī (1992a, 66.5–8).

scholars, most notably in the remarkable volume of essays and translations edited by Geert Jan van Gelder and Marlé Hammond.[72] Make-believe is about combinations of imagery, and in the process of combining images the poet completely destabilizes the usual relationships of predication and the usual connections between vocal forms and groups of mental content. Make-believe has to start in sensory reality but then escape it.[73] The audience needs to get on board with the process, but the aesthetic rewards are substantial.[74] New forms of combined and interacting mental content are produced: new poetic images. Al-Ǧurǧānī's technical phrase for these new images was *ṣūrat al-maʿnā,* a new terminological label for the form taken by a certain syntactical combination of mental contents, described by Harb as "the final image in which a meaning is articulated."[75]

There was a precedent for understanding a reasoned set of mental contents as a "form" (*ṣūrah*), and it is to be found in logic, where Ibn Sīnā used the phrase "form of composition" (*ṣūrat at-taʾlīf*) for the form that a logical statement takes in the mind,[76] and al-Fārābī had used *ṣūrah* for the form in which a logical statement combined subject, predicate, and copula.[77] Both thought that logical statements created fixed and functional patterns of reasoned mental contents. These patterns were in the mind, and they produced logical conclusions. Al-Ǧurǧānī then used *ṣūrah* for the final form taken by a set of mental contents in the minds of audience members when they had finished listening to (or reading) and thinking about a single image.

Logic also provided al-Ǧurǧānī with a tool to explain how make-believe comparisons differed from other comparison, and this tool was conversion (*ʿaks*). A simple comparison could be easily converted: "Zayd is a lion" can be converted into "a lion is Zayd" without changing the mental content. But a comparison between a person's manners and musk in which the point of comparison is their shared pleasantness cannot so easily be converted. One can say, "he has manners like musk," but one cannot say "this musk is like his manners" without entering the zone of make-believe.[78] It is only in the zone of make-believe that musk could be imagined to have manners. The musk changes from being an animal secretion with a sweet scent (in "he has manners like musk") to being a make-believe person

72. van Gelder and Hammond (2008).

73. كيف ولو لا سَبْقُ المعرفة مِن طريق الحس . . . Al-Ǧurǧānī (1954, 218.1).

74. Abu Deeb (1979, 157f), Harb (2013, 159f).

75. Abu Deeb (1979, 52f); Harb (2013, 196f), (2015, 306–7); Larkin (1995, 110f).

76. يُفيدك أنْ يَحدث في الذهن صورةُ هذا التأليف. See chapter 6 note 162.

77. Al-Fārābī (1986a, 90.8), Zimmermann (1981, comm. 22.18, 171.15).

78. فكما لا يصحّ أنْ يُعكَس فيُشبَّه . . . كذلك لا يصحّ أنْ تقول هذا مِسكٌ كخلقِ فلانٍ إلا على ما قدّمتُ مِن التخيل. Al-Ǧurǧānī (1954, 217.16–18).

who behaves sweetly (in "this musk is like his manners.") For al-Ǧurǧānī, it is the logical mechanism of conversion that helps us see this.

Al-Ǧurǧānī's poetics depended on these logical mechanisms because it was reason, not words, that created truth. It was impossible for a rational judgment to be dependent on a linguistic formulation, because the lexicon was only signs and marks that have no mental content until they are used to indicate something.[79] As Khalfallah has observed, "dans toutes les occurences où l'auteur parle du *ʿaql* ou de *maʿqūl,* il fait en réalité référence au sens que l'intellect perçoit à travers l'évocation du mot."[80] And the conceptual vocabulary for mapping these rational processes came from logic. It did not come from theology, where the only conceptual resources al-Ǧurǧānī would have had were remarks such as ʿAbd al-Ǧabbār's that "language that goes beyond the lexicon may be more eloquent because it is like reasoning with the lexicon; most likely, however, it is more eloquent because it makes additions to lexical precedent."[81] ʿAbd al-Ǧabbār did not recognize, as al-Ǧurǧānī did, the centrality of the cognitive process and of mental content therein (as noted by Larkin and, in an engaging brief survey from outside the Arabist field, Michiel Leezenberg).[82] This is one of the moments—of which there are many (see Larkin)[83]—in which it seems very much as if al-Ǧurǧānī was reacting to Muʿtazilī theories that, although they identified syntax as important, had failed to provide any account of how language users made connections between vocal form and mental content. "Makes additions to lexical precedent" was simply not a sufficient explanation for al-Ǧurǧānī. In ʿAbd al-Ǧabbār's epistemology we read of vocal forms that can sound nicer than others, and mental contents that can be more elevated than others. But he thought that there could be no aesthetic quality in mental content because an ugly-sounding word could indicate a pure and beautiful idea; beauty could therefore reside only in vocal form.[84] Al-Ǧurǧānī disagreed.

79. أنّ كلّ حُكم يجب في العقل وجوباً حتى لا يَجوز خلافُه فإضافتُه إلى دلالة اللغة وجَعْلُه مشروطاً فيها مُحالٌ لأنّ اللغة تَجري مجرى العَلامات والسِمات ولا معنى للعَلامة والسِمة حتى يَحتمل الشيءُ ما جُعِلتْ العَلامةُ دليلاً عليه وخلافه. Al-Ǧurǧānī (1954, 347.18–21, 348.6–7). وأنْ يقال ما ضَرَبَ زيدٌ وقد كان منه ضَرْبٌ يُوجِب على أصلهم إخلاء اللفظ من معناه الذي وُضِع لِيدلّ عليه وذلك ما لا يُشكّ في فساده. Al-Ǧurǧānī (1992a, 532.7–9).

80. "Whenever the author speaks of *ʿaql* or *maʿqūl,* he is actually referring to the sense in which the intellect looks into the evocation of the word": Khalfallah (2014, 34).

81. بلْ رُبما كان المجازُ أدْخَلَ في الفصاحة لأنه كالاستدلال في اللغة والغالب أنه يَزيد على المواضعة السابقة. Larkin (1995, 74), al-Qāḍī ʿAbd al-Ǧabbār (1965–74, 16:200.15–16).

82. Larkin (1995, 65–66), Leezenberg (2001, 47–48).

83. Larkin (1995, 55–56).

84. ولِذلك نجد المعبّرين عن المعنى الواحد يكون أحدُهما أَفْصَحَ مِن الآخر والمعنى مُتّفِقٌ وقد يكون أحدُ

SYNTAX TIME

Lexicography claimed to be static, and although the dictionaries themselves were constantly and iteratively being developed, the new lexical placements they documented claimed permanence. But in poetics, the movement of mental content was the core of the theory. Al-Ǧurǧānī's poetics was a theory of syntax, and it is in the very nature of syntax that the language user moves along the sentence as a series of discrete steps, with their cognitive processes changing along the way. This meant that the passage of time, and the interface of time with mental content, was one of al-Ǧurǧānī's central dynamics.

He wrote:[85] "If you want to define analogy, even though there is very little need to do so. If you want to be able to identify it without pausing, then consider what al-Buḥturī said:"[86]

> *Coming close to the hands of those who seek favor*
> *but remote. A liberality beyond every rival*
> *above everyone else in the game.*
> *Immoderately high like the moon*
> *his light the good fortune of companionship*
> *for a band of night travelers.*

This was written by al-Buḥturī (d. 987) in praise of his patron. Think, says al-Ǧurǧānī, "think of the state you are in, and the state of the mental content that is with you when you are in the first line ["Coming close to the hands of those who seek favor . . ."], heedless of the second line ["Immoderately high like the moon . . ."]. You have not contemplated how the second line will rescue the first line, nor how it will provide an analogy for the first line. The analogy will concern something that a person's eyes dictate to them, something to which a person's sight leads them. Then, when you have grasped the analogy and considered its two parts, compare the two states you have been in. You will see the distance you have traveled and how much more firmly the mental content you have is fixed after the second line. . . . You will then grant me the truth of my analysis."[87]

المعنيين أَحْسَنَ وأَعْرَفَ والمعبّرُ عنه في الفصاحة أَدْوَنَ فهو مما لا بدّ مِن اعتباره وإنْ كانت المزيةُ تَظهر بغيره على أنّ نَعلم أنّ المعاني لا يقع فيها تَزايُد. Al-Qāḍī ʿAbd al-Ǧabbār (1965–74, 16:199.15–18).

85. وإنْ أردتَ أنْ تعرف ذلك وإنْ كان تَقِلّ الحاجةُ فيه إلى التعريف ويُستغنَى في الوقوف عليه عن التوقيف فانظرْ إلى نحوِ قول البحتري. Al-Ǧurǧānī (1954, 102.18–19).

86. دَانٍ عَلَى أَيْدِيْ ٱلْعُفَاةِ وَشَاسِعٌ | عَنْ كُلِّ نِدٍّ فِي ٱلنَّدَى [فِي ٱلْعُلَا (الصيرفي)] وَضَرِيْبِ
كَٱلْبَدْرِ أَفْرَطَ فِي ٱلْعُلُوِّ وَضَوْءُهُ | لِلْعُصْبَةِ ٱلسَّارِيْنَ جِدُّ قَرِيْبِ
Al-Buḥturī (1963–, 248–49 lines 27–28), al-Ǧurǧānī (1954, 103.1–2).

87. وفكِّرْ في حالك وحالِ المعنى معك وأنتَ في البيت الأول لم تَنتبه إلى الثاني ولم تَتبدّر نصرتَه إياه وتمثيلَه له فيما يُملي على الإنسان عيناه ويؤدي إليه ناظراه ثم قِسهما على الحال وقد وقفتَ عليه وتأملتَ طرفَيه

In order to understand the power of analogy, al-Ǧurǧānī wants you to travel through syntax time and notice how different you feel after the journey. The first line in Arabic is, "Coming close to the hands of those who seek favor. . . . above everyone else in the game." On hearing this line (which the lineation of my translation has turned into three lines), you grasp that the patron is aloof and more generous than his peers, but that is all you grasp. Then you hear the second line: "Immoderately high like the moon . . . for a band of night travelers." This is an analogy, a *tamṯīl.* (The Arabic term literally means "the making of an example.") It is a sensory analogy; you imagine looking up at the moon in the sky, and suddenly the patron's aloof generosity has new dimensions: he shines, and the light he provides guides those beneath. By the end of the second line, at the end of the analogy, you have a great deal more to think about.

Time also controlled ambiguity. In the American twentieth century, John Ransom (d. 1974) famously wrote that ambiguity arises when two different readings are possible, or when there is a certain diffuseness in the reference.[88] Classical Arabic poetics, with a technique based around the movement of mental contents that was more mechanical than New Criticism, dealt with ambiguity through the relationship between vocal form and mental content. Ar-Rāġib had stated in his poetics that one could intend two different mental contents with a single vocal form. In Rabīʿah b. Maqrūm's (d. ca. 672) line:

Water, its supply tainted, deserted.
The wild beasts dig at its edges.

the vocal form "water" indicated both a liquid and a place.[89] Ar-Rāġib's lexicographical framework did not include a consideration of the syntax time that passed as the audience read or heard this poem, and he implied that the vocal form indicated two mental contents at the same time.

However, when al-Ǧurǧānī discussed a similar phenomenon in the *Dalāʾil,* he wrote that an indefinite noun, when found at the start of a phrase, could frame the audience's response by telling them that what followed would fall into a certain class of thing. So if one heard: "only evil makes a fanged animal snarl," one would be alerted upon hearing "evil" to the fact that speaker intended to talk about something, not yet precisely defined, that was not good.[90] The use of a definite article here

---

فإنك تَعلم بُعدَ ما بين حالتَيك وشِدة تفاوتهما في تمكُّن المعنى لدَيك . . . وتَحكُم لي بالصدق فيما قلت. Al-Ǧurǧānī (1954, 103.3–7).

88. Ransom (1979, 102, 111).

89. وَمَاءٍ آجِنِ ٱلْجَمَّاتِ قَفْرٍ | تَعَقَّمَ فِي جَوَانِبِهِ ٱلسِّبَاعُ. Ar-Rāġib (ca. 14th C., fol. 4a.4). Cf. translations: Key (2012, 115), Lane (1863–93, ʿ-q-m).

90. واعلمْ أنَّا لم نُرِدْ بما قلناه مِن أنه إنما حَسُنَ الابتداءُ بالنكرة في قولهم شَرٌّ أهرَّ ذا ناب لأنه أُريدَ به

would have produced different, albeit equally inauspicious, mental content: "only *the* evil . . ." But, wrote al-Ǧurǧānī, one could also use an indefinite noun in a situation where the intent was not to frame what followed as belonging to a certain class of things. If you say, "Did a man come, or two men?" then the mental content that you intend with "a man" is not the class of men. With "evil," the indefinite vocal form leads the audience to consider a class of evil things. But with "a man," the indefinite vocal form leads the audience to consider a single undefined man. As al-Ǧurǧānī put it: "The vocal form can indicate two matters, and then the intent can determine one of them and exclude the other. The excluded matter, because it is not part of the intent, becomes as if it is no longer part of the indication of the vocal form."[91]

Grammar provides options, and speakers choose between them. Syntax has rules. Although a vocal form can be potentially ambiguous, when the mind of the audience comes to the end of the sentence, there is no space for ambiguity or diffusion. The gap between the potential ambiguity and the eventual certainty is a gap in time. Time was what al-Ǧurǧānī's theory of creative syntax exploited. He disagreed with ar-Rāġib about the possibility of two mental contents being in play at the same time. Whereas ar-Rāġib used a model of static and paradigmatically lexical connections between vocal form and mental content, al-Ǧurǧānī's model of creative syntax enabled the poet to negotiate ambiguity as the sentence developed.

Arabic grammar had an established discourse about elision, the functions it performed, and the contexts in which it occurred. But al-Ǧurǧānī connected elision to poetic affect. He knew that this was a theoretical intervention, writing that a serious reader of his monograph would come to see that when "I emphasize and elevate elision to a position where it is almost magic and overwhelms the mind, the situation is in fact as I say it is."[92] It was an intervention that, as Baalbaki has shown, consciously expanded grammar into aesthetics.[93] One particular short section on elision in the *Dalā'il* starts with a deliberate irony of presentation. With a rhetorical flourish, al-Ǧurǧānī wrote that this section was only for those who were really interested in the minutiae of poetics and motivated to discover how reason works. Such people, his desired audience, "do not

---

الجنسُ أَنَّ معنى شرٌّ والشرُّ سواءٌ وإنما أَرَدْنا أَنَّ الغرض من الكلام أنْ نُبيّن أنَّ الذي أَهرَّ ذا الناب هو مِن جِنسِ الشرّ لا جنسِ الخير. Al-Ǧurǧānī (1992a, 143.9, 144.6–14). Cf. Sībawayh (1966, 1:329.9–10).

91. وعكسُ هذا أنك إذا قلتَ أَرجلٌ أتاك أم رجلانِ كان القصدُ مِنك إلى كونه واحداً دون كونه رجلاً فاعرفْ ذلك أصْلاً وهو أنه قد يكون في اللفظ دليلٌ على أمرَين ثم يقع القصدُ إلى أحدهما دون الآخر فيصير ذلك الآخر بأنْ لم يَدخل في القصد كأنه لم يَدخل في دلالة اللفظ. Al-Ǧurǧānī (1992a, 144.16–145.2).

92. أنّ الذي قلتُ في شأنِ الحذف وفي تفخيمِ أمره والتنويه بذكره وأنّ مَأخَذه مَأْخَذٌ يُشبه السحرَ ويُبهر الفكرَ كالذي قلت. Al-Ǧurǧānī (١٩٩٢a, ٧–١٧١,٥).

93. Baalbaki (1983, 16).

race to the first thing that occurs to their minds."[94] For theory requires a slower reading process. But the theory that he is talking about in this section is about the aesthetic impact of the first thing that occurs to one's mind! Al-Ǧurǧānī had an ethics of reading for theory and criticism that valorized slow, iterative process through long books, yet here that criticism is an ethics of reading sentences that values the speed with which images present themselves. (On that speed, see Harb and Abu Deeb.)[95] In this section, al-Ǧurǧānī took the following image from al-Buḥturī:[96]

> *How often you defend me from*
> *the burden of each new event*
> *intensity of days that cut*
> *to the bone.*

and focused on the phrase "cut to the bone." He wrote that in the elision of "flesh" ("cut [the flesh] to the bone," the phrase not having in Arabic quite the ubiquity it has now in English) there was a "wonderful and glorious something extra."[97]

The impact of elision came from the steps of reasoned imagination that the listener no longer had to take. If the poet had included the flesh and written, "intensity of days that cut the flesh to the bone," then the audience would have imagined, after hearing the word "flesh" and before hearing the words "cut to the bone," that the cutting of flesh in question was a matter of flesh wounds, or skinning, or some other way in which flesh can be cut. Then when they heard the words "to the bone," they would have realized what type of cutting was intended. But the power of elision in this case was to "free the listener from that imagination, to make the mental content occur at the first moment and to allow the listener to conceive in his soul from the very beginning that that cut went through the flesh and nothing stopped it until it reached the bone."[98] This was the best kind of conception for al-Ǧurǧānī, imagery that was in the soul and more eloquent than if it had been indicated by vocal form, and yet imagery that relied entirely on syntax creating meaning in time. His literary criticism took Ibn Sīnā's logical vocabulary of mental contents conceived in the soul and turned that vocabulary to the diagnosis of affect across the time it took to read a sentence.

94. لِمَنْ نَظَرَ نَظَرَ المُثبَّت . . . ولا يَعْدو الذي يَقع في أوّلِ الخاطر. Al-Ǧurǧānī (1992a, 171.1–5).

95. Abu Deeb (1979, 255), Harb (2013, 99f).

96. وَكَمْ ذُدْتَ عَنِّي مِنْ تَحامُلِ حادِثٍ | وَسَوْرَةِ أَيَّامٍ حَزَزْنَ إِلى ٱلْعَظْمِ. Al-Buḥturī (1963–), (2018, l. 43).

97. أنّ في مَجيئه به محذوفاً وإسقاطِه له مِن النُطق وتركِه في الضمير مَزيةً عجيبةً وفائدةً جليلة. Al-Ǧurǧānī (1992a, 171.14–15).

98. ليُبْرئَ السامعَ مِن هذا الوهم ويَجعله بحيث يقع المعنى منه في أُنُف الفهم ويتصوَّر في نفسه مِن أوّلِ الأمر أنّ الحظّ مَضى في اللحم حتى لم يَردَّه إلا العظم. Al-Ǧurǧānī (1992a, 172.6–8).

LEXICAL ACCURACY (*ḤAQĪQAH*)

Lexical accuracy was a fundamental aspect of language that the critic could identify regardless of whether the techniques in play were classed as comparison, analogy, metaphor, make-believe, or metonymy. Lexical accuracy was central to al-Ǧurǧānī's project. But how did he think of the lexicon? He certainly knew the lexicographers, remarking that when the authors of dictionaries (such as Abū al-ʿAbbās Ṯaʿlab, d. 904) gave their books titles such as *The Eloquent* (*al-Faṣīḥ*), the eloquence to which they were referring was only a matter of precedent and adherence to morphological and lexical rules.[99] Al-Ǧurǧānī thought that while the lexicon was the structural foundation for language use, it was not the source of aesthetic value or creativity; beauty came from syntax and from metaphor.[100]

Al-Ǧurǧānī moved away from previous theories of Arabic poetics grounded in the lexicon. They had assumed words could have more meaning when used in poetry, that when vocal forms were in poetic images they could suddenly start referring to more mental content than usual. This had tended to be the assumption behind the valorization of concision by ar-Rāġib and others.[101] Al-Ǧurǧānī, on the other hand, wrote at the end of the *Dalāʾil* that the collections of mental content entrusted to each vocal form never change beyond the lexical placement intended by the language giver. He too was discussing the aesthetic value of concision, but he wanted to clarify that eloquent concision that communicated "a lot of mental content with a little vocal form" did not change the actual lexical-placement connections between vocal forms and collections of mental content. In al-Ǧurǧānī's theory, via a purely cognitive process, the initial mental content that resulted from a vocal form could connect to other, subsequent, mental contents and create a poetic image without altering any original lexical connections.[102] What made al-Ǧurǧānī's theory different was that it turned a static, lexicographical model into a dynamic, syntactical one. Rather than words having more meaning when poets put them into images, the words kept their meanings, and it was the syntax that created new forms of meaning in the audience's mind. Rather than poetry break-

99. . . . ورأَوا أبا العباس ثَعْلَبَ قد سَمَّى كتابَه الفصيحَ مع أنه لم يَذكر فيه إلا اللغةَ والألفاظ المفردة ولم يَعلم أنّ المعانيَ في وصْف الألفاظ المفردة بالفصاحة أنها في اللغة أَثْبَتُ وفي استعمال الفصحاء أكثرُ أو أنها أَجرَى على مقاييس اللغة القَوانينِ التي وضَعَها. Al-Ǧurǧānī (1992a, 458.13–459.1). Partial translation: Khalfallah (2014, 36).

100. Al-Ǧurǧānī (1992a, 250.9–13).

101. Key (2012, 182f, 185), ar-Rāġib (ca. 14th C., fol. 5bf).

102. وهو أنّ العاقِل إذا نَظر عَلِمَ عِلْمَ ضرورةٍ أنه لا سبيلَ له إلى أنْ يُكثّر معانيَ الألفاظ أو يُقلّلها لأنّ المعاني المُودَعة في الألفاظ لا تَتغيّر على الجملة عمّا أَراده واضِعُ اللغة وإذا ثَبَتَ ذلك ظَهر منه أنه لا معنى لقولنا كَثْرةُ المعنى مع قِلّة اللفظ غيرَ أنّ المتكلم يَتوصّل بدلالة المعنى على المعنى إلى فوائد. Al-Ǧurǧānī (1992a, 464.2–6).

ing down lexical accuracy, poets instead used syntax to create images that combined lexical accuracy with imaginative predications.

Al-Ğurğānī held that critics could recognize beauty in literature only when they understood the mechanisms by which it moved in relation to language's lexical foundations. (Stefan Sperl would reach the same conclusion as al-Ğurğānī many centuries later, writing of "the creation of concord or discord between signifier and signified" as the defining characteristic of what he called the "mannerism" of the ninth-century poets such as Abū Tammām.)[103] The primary structure governing language in the lexicon was, as we have already seen, the distinction between lexical accuracy (*ḥaqīqah*) and language that went beyond the lexicon (*mağāz*). In order to explain how poetic imagery could be both unreal and lexically accurate, al-Ğurğānī made a distinction between lexical accuracy as it applied to single words and lexical accuracy as it applied to sentences or clauses. (See Heinrichs, who is keen to make a distinction between aesthetic and theological disciplines, a distinction that I am comfortable allowing to collapse.)[104] In sentences, lexical accuracy was a matter of predication: was A really B? (The single-lexeme verb was included with sentences because in Arabic it contained a pronoun and therefore an affirmation: "He did.")[105] When it came to single words, al-Ğurğānī had his own account of lexical placement. Every word used according to its original placement was lexically accurate if the connection between vocal form and mental content was direct and simple. In an aside that can have been intended only for his Muʿtazilī interlocutors, al-Ğurğānī added that you could, if you wanted, call that lexical placement "the process of lexical placement,"[106] which was the term used by ʿAbd al-Ğabbār, among others, to claim that language was constantly being created by human lexical placement rather than having been created all at one time by God.[107] In any case—and here he adopted the same tone as Ibn Sīnā—it doesn't matter whether one thinks that language was imposed in a divine act of placement or that it had developed iteratively according to shared convention from the earliest Arabic tribal dialects to the present day. In either case, the same definition of lexical accuracy applies.[108] It is a matter of how one uses words.

103. Sperl (1989, 180).

104. Heinrichs (1991/92, 278).

105. وأما فَعَلَ فلم تَنْقُله عن الموضِع الذي وضعَتْه اللغةُ لأنه كما مَضى موضوعٌ لإثباتِ الفِعل للشيء في زمانٍ ماضٍ. Al-Ğurğānī (1954, 378.20–379.1).

106. كلُّ كلمةٍ أُريدَ بها ما وقعتْ له في وضعِ واضعٍ وإنْ شِئتَ قلتَ في مُواضَعة وُقوعاً لا تَستند فيه إلى غيره فهي حقيقة. Al-Ğurğānī (1954, 324.8–10).

107. Peters (1976, 304–5, 386–87), al-Qāḍī ʿAbd al-Ğabbār (1965–74, 16:199).

108. وهذه عِبارةٌ تَنتظم الوضعَ الأوّلَ وما تَأخَّر عنه كلغةٍ تَحدُث في قبيلة مِن العرب أو في جميع العرب أو في جميع الناس مثلاً أو تُحدَث اليوم. Al-Ğurğānī (1954, 324.10–12).

Lexical accuracy was a quality that all words could have, right down to simple particles of comparison such as "like." If you say "Zayd is like a lion," then you are using "like" with lexical accuracy; comparison is a mental content like any other, and it is connected by precedent to the vocal form "like."[109] Conversely, if you use "the hand" for "the blessing" because humans have tended to use their hands to give blessings, then the word can be judged to be beyond the lexicon. (This is a reference to the exegetical discussion about God's hands in the Quran and anthropomorphism.)[110] But even here the original lexical placement is still in play: without some maintenance of reference to the human appendage the metaphorical usage makes no sense.[111]

Think, said al-Ǧurǧānī, about how you use the word "lion" to refer to the wild beast. "You will see how your statement fulfills all its own requirements. This is because your intent was that to which you know the word 'lion' connects according to lexical placement. You are also aware that this connection does not rely on anything other than the wild beast. You are not forced by some potential confusion or the memory of some concept to conceive of an additional principle that could lead you to the wild beast."[112] This is al-Ǧurǧānī's lexically accurate account, and its definition contains the seeds of his entire critical project. "Lexical accuracy" is the name for the connection between vocal form and mental content that you make when you are simply following the precedent of other language users. All language users, wherever they are, can be placers of the lexicon according to al-Ǧurǧānī; he says that this is why he deliberately kept the nouns in his definition of lexical accuracy indefinite ("a placement by a placer").[113] This direct connection between vocal form

109. لأن التشبيه معنى من المعاني وله حروف واسماء تدل عليه فإذا صرح بذكر ما هو موضوع للدلالة عليه كان الكلام حقيقة كالحكم في سائر المعاني فاعرفه. Al-Ǧurǧānī (1992a, 222.4–5).

110. Quran 3:26, 3:73 (Āl ʿImrān), 5:64 (al-Māʾidah), 23:88 (al-Muʾminūn), 36:83 (Yā Sīn), 48:10 (al-Fatḥ), 57:29 (al-Ḥadīd), 67:1 (al-Mulk). Cf. ar-Rāġib (1992, 889/2.6f).

111. وهو أنْ يقع نقْلُه على وجهٍ لا يَعْرَى معه من ملاحظةِ الأصل ومعنى الملاحظة أنّ الاسم يقع لِما تقول إنه مجازٌ فيه بسببٍ بينه وبين الذين تَجعله حقيقةً فيه نحو أنّ اليد تقع للنعمة وأصلُها الجارحة لأجل أنّ الاعتبارات اللغوية تتبع أحوالَ المخلوقين وعاداتِهم وما يَقتضيه ظاهرُ البِنْيَة وموضوع الجِبِلّة ومن شأن النعمة أنْ تَصدُر عن اليد ومنها تصل إلى المقصودِ بها وفي ذكر اليد إشارةٌ إلى مَصْدَرِ تلك النعمةِ الواصلةِ إلى المقصود بها والموهوبةِ هي منه. Al-Ǧurǧānī (1954, 365.6–12; cf. 325.19f).

112. فانظُرْ إلى قولك الأسدُ تُريد به السبعَ فإنك تَراه يؤدّي جميعَ شرائطه لأنك قد أردتَ به ما تَعلم أنه وَقَعَ له في وضْعِ واضعِ اللغة وكذلك تَعلم أنه غيرُ مستندٍ في هذا الوقوع إلى شيءٍ غير السبع أيْ لا يَحتاج أنْ يُتصوَّر له أصلٌ أَدّاه إلى السبع مِن أجلِ التِباسٍ بينهما ومُلاحَظة. Al-Ǧurǧānī (1954, 325.7–11).

113. وهذا الحُكمُ إذا كانتْ الكلمةُ حادثةً ولو وُضِعتْ اليومَ متى كان وضعُها كذلك وكذلك الأعلامُ وذلك أنّي قلتُ ما وَقَعتْ له في وضعِ واضعٍ أو مُواضعةٍ على التنكير ولم أقل في وضعِ الواضع الذي ابتدأ اللغةَ أو في المواضعة اللغوية. Al-Ǧurǧānī (1954, 325.11–14).

and mental content, enabled by precedent, can be recognized by the absence of any need to rely on any other cognitive component. As soon as some memory of the speech act's context, or some commitment to reading metaphorically, or some surface lack of clarity intervenes, the direct link is broken, and the audience starts trying to connect the lexically accurate mental content to some other mental content in order for the speech act to make sense. The resultant mental gymnastics, which can be very simple or tremendously complex, are what make language beautiful.

But the lexicon was always present, anchoring the aesthetically pleasing loops of mental content. The lexicon was, for al-Ǧurǧānī, the naming precedent of the speech community, constantly in development. It, was communal habit that governed the success or failure of metaphor, not divine precedent. So although the prophet Muḥammad had compared the believer to a date palm (for its firm roots, etc.), one cannot simply say "I saw a date palm" and have it mean that you saw a believer. Al-Ǧurǧānī borrows a phrase from Sībawayh here: this mistake would make you "a riddler who has abandoned the sort of speech that goes straight to people's hearts." (Sībawayh had been talking about declensions of case and elided verbs, whereas al-Ǧurǧānī was talking about metaphor, but the invective proved attractive.)[114]

How did al-Ǧurǧānī conceive of this lexicon's functioning? If there was no divine moment of original lexical placement, and no sociocultural curation by an elite class of lexicographers, what was the accurate mental content delineated by an act of lexical placement? In the *Asrār,* al-Ǧurǧānī provided an answer through an analogy to changes of costume. He was explaining how metaphors always had an underlying comparison, even in the absence of a particle such as "like" or "as," and this explanation relied on the concept of accuracy.[115] The single noun, he wrote, is a shape that indicates the class of a thing. It is like the clothing of kings, or of market folk. You can take off those clothes, remove every indication that a person belongs to the market or the monarchy, and then dress each in the clothes of the other, leaving the audience unable to perceive the change without external corroboration. If you do this, then you have borrowed the shape and clothes of market folk or kings, and done so "accurately."[116] If, however, you do not completely denude the person of every single mental content that indicates their status, and some indication remains that the person is in fact a king or from the market, then you have not accurately borrowed the clothes or the shape of the noun. The metaphor depends on the accuracy: all the clothes have to change in order for the audience to be forced to look outside the syntax; this is how metaphors work. There is also a

114. إنّ مَن رام مِثل هذا كان كما قال صاحبُ الكتاب مُلْغِزاً تاركاً لكلامِ الناس الذي يَسبُق إلى أَفئدَتهم. Al-Ǧurǧānī (1954, 227.4–5), Sībawayh (1966, 1:308.7).

115. Al-Ǧurǧānī (1954, 300.5–301.2).

116. كنتَ قد أَعَرْتَه هيئةَ الملك وَزِيّه على الحقيقة. Al-Ǧurǧānī (1954, 300.9–10).

difference between the way a noun behaves and the way a garment behaves: while the garment is a single thing that can have distinguishing properties, the shape of a noun actually determines a group of things together, and it is this group of mental contents that indicates the class of thing shaped by the noun.[117] Garments do not make metaphors; nouns make metaphors.

What al-Ǧurǧānī has done here is explain how his accurate lexical placement works. Nouns indicate groups of mental contents, and if a noun is used to refer to the whole group of mental contents, then it is being used accurately. The lexically accurate single noun was therefore a type of connection between vocal form and mental content in which a vocal form indicated all the mental contents that precedent had associated with that noun. What this means is that a noun can be used in a make-believe and metaphorical way but still be considered accurate because it is still indicating its full set of mental contents. If we could think of Ibn Fūrak's use of mental content as a set of pigeonholes into which rationally commensurate qualities and ideas could be slotted, we can think of al-Ǧurǧānī's mental contents as bundles of qualities and ideas that help constitute an essence (on which see more below) and that are attached to vocal forms by precedent. If the whole bundle is there in the audience's mind, then the word remains accurate, however unreal the image.

This maintenance of the accurate account in a metaphor is what often gives metaphors their strength. Al-Ǧurǧānī ends this passage with the following example: "If someone hears you say 'Zayd is a lion' and fails to imagine that you intend 'lion' accurately, then the name 'lion' will not adhere to Zayd, and you will not have borrowed it for Zayd in a sound and complete fashion."[118] Metaphors depend on the accurate account remaining in play, but al-Ǧurǧānī's accurate account is not like ar-Rāġib's fixed and curated dictionary connection. It is rather a value that attaches to the connection made in a speech act between the vocal form of a noun and a collection of mental contents. The full bundle of mental contents that is attached to the vocal form "lion" must remain in play when we compare Zayd to a lion because he is brave: if only the bravery is in play, then we are just using "lion" as a noun that means "brave," and the image is not a metaphor. The audience has to imagine that you mean "lion" accurately in order for the image to work.

Al-Ǧurǧānī's starting point had been that established by preceding generations of scholars: going beyond the lexicon (*maǧāz*) is what happens when someone

117. وإنما أَعْتبِر الهيئةَ وهي تَحصل بمجموع أشياء وذلك أنّ الهيئة هي التي يُشبِه حالُها حالَ الاسم لأنّ الهيئة تَخصّ جِنساً دُون جنسٍ كما أنّ الاسم كذلك والثوبُ على الإطلاق لا يَفعل ذلك إلا بخصائص تقترِن به وتُرعَى معه. Al-Ǧurǧānī (1954, 300.15–16).

118. فإذا كان السامعُ قولَك زيدٌ أسدٌ لا يَتوهّم أنك قصدتَ أسداً على الحقيقة لم يكن الاسمُ قد لَحِقَه ولم تكن قد أَعَرْتَه إيّاه إعارةً صحيحةً. Al-Ǧurǧānī (1954, 300.17–301.1).

uses a vocal form and intends mental content not its own.[119] And the choice to be lexically accurate or go beyond the lexicon was the speaker's; a factually or empirically incorrect statement could still be "accurate for the person who said it."[120] Al-Ǧurǧānī wrote that going beyond the lexicon was a broad category that encompassed metaphor, metonymy, and analogy,[121] and this had naturally led critics to associate it with aesthetic quality: "always more eloquent than lexical accuracy."[122] But the situation was not that simple. (See Heinrichs.)[123] "It has been our custom to say about the difference between lexical accuracy and going beyond the lexicon the following: lexical accuracy is when the vocal form keeps to its place in the lexicon, and going beyond is when it ceases to be in that place and is used somewhere other than its lexical placement."[124] But what happens is in fact the complete opposite. When we call a brave man a lion, we have not completely moved the vocal form "lion" away from its lexical meaning; what we have done is claim that the man is included in the mental content of "lion." The metaphor is in the predication, not in the word itself. The vocal form "lion" still means "lion," because it is clearly invalid to imagine that the speaker of the phrase "he is a lion" meant only and exactly "he is brave." There must be more to what the speaker meant than simply "he is brave."[125]

Al-Ǧurǧānī had abandoned the established consensus that lexical accuracy was a stable category of reference and that going beyond the lexicon was constituted by any and all deviations from that category. Instead, lexical accuracy was a zone or principle that anchored and caused affect. It was not a hermetically sealed category. When we say "the man is a lion," the lexically accurate mental content of that fearsome beast is still in play. (Cf. Heinrichs.)[126] What anchors the metaphor

119. ذكرتَ الكلمةَ وأنتَ لا تُريد معناها. Al-Ǧurǧānī (1992a, 293.4).

120. الذي] أَطْلَقَه بِجهله وعَماه . . . لا يُوصف بالمجاز ولكنْ يقال عِند قائله أنه حقيقة وهو كذب وباطل]. Al-Ǧurǧānī (1954, 356.1–3).

121. هذه المعاني التي هي الاستعارةُ والكِناية والتمثيل وسائر ضروب المجاز. Al-Ǧurǧānī (1992a, 393.6–7).

122. إنه أبلَغُ مِن الحقيقة . . . يكون أبداً أَبْلَغَ مِن الحقيقة. Al-Ǧurǧānī (1992a, 367.12, 427.3–4).

123. Heinrichs (2016, 252–57).

124. وذاك أنّ العادة قد جرتْ بأنْ يقال في الفرْق بين الحقيقة والمجاز إنّ الحقيقة أنْ يُقرَّ اللفظُ على أصله في اللغة والمجاز أنْ يُزال عن مَوضعه ويُستعمَل في غيرِ ما وُضِع له. Al-Ǧurǧānī (1992a, 366.13–15).

125. فإنّ الأمر بعدُ على خلافه وذاك أنا إذا حققنا لم نجِد لفظَ أسدٍ قد استُعمِلَ على القطْع والبتّ في غيرِ ما وُضِع له . . . فالتجوُّزُ في أنْ ادّعَيتَ للرجل أنه في معنى الأسد . . . وهذا إنْ أنتَ حصلتَ [فهو] تَجوُّزٌ مِنك في معنى اللفظ لا اللفظِ وإنما يكون اللفظُ مُزالاً بالحقيقة عن مَوضوعه ومنقولاً عمّا وُضِع له أنْ لو كنتَ تجِد عاقلاً يقول هو أسدٌ وهو لايُضمِر في نفسه تشبيهاً له بالأسد ولا يُريد إلا ما يريده إذا قال هو شُجاعٌ وذلك ما لا يُشكُّ في بطلانه. Al-Ǧurǧānī (1992a, 367.2–10).

126. Heinrichs (1991/92, 280).

is the bundle of accurate mental contents for "lion," which includes the strength and fearlessness of the animal.[127] This new way of looking at the categories of lexical accuracy and going beyond the lexicon meant that al-Ǧurǧānī could no longer sustain the taxonomical clarity that had led ar-Rāġib to say that any elision or abbreviation was a departure from the lexicon. Such extraneous alterations in the vocal forms had no significance for al-Ǧurǧānī; they did not involve the intent to communicate extra mental content. (See Heinrichs.)[128] What interested al-Ǧurǧānī was images. Images are sentences or clauses, predications or affirmations in which the poet claims that something is something else: he is a lion, or she is a gazelle. On the level of the sentence, there is no lexical accuracy, because the person in question is not actually a lion or a gazelle. But on the level of the individual word, there is lexical accuracy, because the poet intends the whole bundle of mental contents that precedent has connected to the vocal form "lion" or "gazelle" to be in play. Lexical accuracy therefore helps explain why images create more affect than factual statements: it is the combination of loss of accuracy on the sentence level with maintenance of accuracy on the word level that makes "he is a lion" more beautiful than "he is brave."

Al-Ǧurǧānī used the standard example of "he is a lion" to establish his theory of lexical accuracy, predication, and metaphor. But the goal of this theory was not to explain such commonplace statements. The target of his criticism was the most famous and complex images of Classical Arabic poetry. Let us take the toolbox we have assembled in the paragraphs above and turn to the make-believe metaphor and a subdivision thereof in which the poet pretends that neither metaphor nor any points of actual comparison are relevant any longer. The poem is now functioning in a wholly imaginary but still lexically accurate sphere. When Abū Tammām (d. 845) wrote in an elegy for a general that:[129]

He rose so high
that the ignorant thought
he had work to do
in the sky,

he was pretending to forget the underlying comparison of physical ascent with increased social status and was instead constructing a new comparison in the

127. أنه في معنى الأسد وأنه كأنه هو في قوة قلبه وشدة بطشه وفي أن الخوف لا يخامره والذعر لا يعارض له. Al-Ǧurǧānī (1992a, 367.5–6).

128. وذلك أن حقيقة الزيادة في الكلمة أن تعرّى من معناها وتذكر ولا فائدة لها سوى الصلة ويكون سقوطها وثبوتها سواء ومحال أن يكون ذلك مجاز لأن المجاز أن يراد بالكلمة غير ما وضِعت له في الأصل. Al-Ǧurǧānī (1954, 384.11–14), Heinrichs (1991/92, 278).

129. وَيَصْعَدُ حَتَّى يَظُنُّ ٱلْجَهُوْلُ | بِأَنَّ لَهُ حَاجَةً فِي ٱلسَّمَاءِ. Abū Tammām and at-Tabrīzī (1994, 2:200.58), al-Ǧurǧānī (1954, 279.6).

sphere of make-believe. Without the pretending-to-forget, the image has no impact.[130] This process revolved, for al-Ǧurǧānī, around the wonder experienced by the audience. (This wonder is also the starting point for Harb's analyses.)[131] What is interesting for our purposes here is the role that lexical accuracy played in his theory.

Al-Ǧurǧānī was dealing at this point in the *Dalāʾil* with a phrase from a poem by al-Farazdaq:[132]

> *My forefather is the more praiseworthy of the two heavy rains.*

The critic first identified the absence of an explicit comparison made between the bountiful behavior of the poet's forefather and the bountiful impact of the rain, as if "it was not even in the poet's mind that the phrase went beyond the lexicon."[133] The poet also appears to assume that the similarity of forefather and bounteous rain is well established and well known. Then, al-Ǧurǧānī notes that the specific grammatical structure of the phrase in Arabic forces the audience to imagine two rains together, one of which *is* the forefather. The Arabic syntax makes it very difficult for the audience to think of the forefather and the rain as two separate things. (A phrase such as "he is comparable to the rain" would allow this, and thereby create less wonder.) It is exactly because it is difficult to get out of the image and back to the real world of comparison that this kind of poetry has aesthetic value. What matters to al-Ǧurǧānī is that "departure from the lexicon is joined with lexical accuracy in the compact of the dual form of the noun."[134] Arabic nouns can have singular, dual, or plural forms. In this case, "two rains" is a single lexeme, *ġayṯāni*, in which al-Ǧurǧānī locates a lexically accurate rain, a rain that goes beyond the lexicon, and the poetic affect itself. Next, al-Ǧurǧānī turned to an image from al-Buḥturī that praised a patron's lion-hunting ability:

> You are the two hardest-fighting lions
> I have ever seen at war.

The patron becomes a lion in the image (beyond the lexicon) while the lion he is fighting remains a lion (lexically accurate).[135]

130. ومِثالُه استعارتُهم العُلوَّ لزيادة الرجل على غيره في الفضل والقَدْر والسلطان ثم وَضْعُهم الكلامَ وضْعَ مَن يَذكر عُلوّاً مِن طريق المكان ألا تَرى إلى قولِ أبي تمام ويصعد حتى يظن الجهول بأن له حاجة في السماء . . . لَما كان لهذا الكلام وَجْه فلو لا قَصْدُه أنْ يُنسى التشبيهَ ويَرفعه بجهده. Al-Ǧurǧānī (1954, 279.3–8). Cf. translation in van Gelder and Hammond (2008, 57).

131. ومَدارُ هذا النوع في الغالب على التعجُّب. Al-Ǧurǧānī (1954, 281.11), Harb (2013, 159f, 169f).

132. أَبِي أَحْمَدُ ٱلْغَيْثَيْنِ . . . Al-Farazdaq (1987, 329.12), al-Ǧurǧānī (1954, 293.13).

133. ومَن لا يخطر بباله أنه مجازٌ فيه ومتناوِلٌ له. Al-Ǧurǧānī (1954, 293.15–16).

134. أنْ يُضَمَّ المجازُ إلى الحقيقة في عَقْد التثنية. Al-Ǧurǧānī (1954, 295.11). Translation of this passage: van Gelder and Hammond (2008, 67–69).

135. فَلَمْ أَرَ ضِرْغَامَيْنِ أَصْدَقَ مِنْكُمَا | عِرَاكاً . . . لأنّ أحد الضرغامين حقيقةٌ والآخر مجاز. Al-Buḥturī

In these three examples (rising in the sky, the two rains, and the two lions) we can see the framework provided by grammatical structures in syntax for the cognitive process catalyzed by poetry; al-Ǧurǧānī located the power of the image of the two rains *in* the Arabic declension of a noun as dual. We can also see his understanding of lexical accuracy as a dynamic category: these are make-believe images far removed from reality; no one actually fought with any lions or became a downpour, and yet the epistemological category of lexical accuracy remains in play. It anchors al-Ǧurǧānī's analyses. A make-believe situation can itself be read as containing accurate accounts; the poet creates a new accuracy when he makes a man into a lion that actually fights another lion. This is not accuracy as Ibn Sīnā or Ibn Fūrak understood it. It is closest to the accuracy of ar-Rāġib, but whereas the lexicographer ar-Rāġib had such a static understanding of lexical connections that he had to categorize all poetic action (and dialect) as going beyond the lexicon, al-Ǧurǧānī's sense of lexical accuracy as dynamic allowed him to explain how images can be both true and false.

SYNTAX (*NAẒM*)

Syntax was the base structure of language in which the axes and zones of poetic technique played out. Syntax was also al-Ǧurǧānī's central resolution for the problem of how the Quran is inimitably eloquent. This diagnosis enabled him to complete the work of the *Asrār* and in the *Dalāʾil* extend his account of beauty in language to cover everything about words and how they relate to each other: all the quality he located in poetry and eloquent prose came from combinations of words. (See Antonella Ghersetti.)[136]

When God said in the Quran that "those who fear God are the scholars," his specific intent could not be recovered by a paraphrase that altered the syntax. "The scholars fear God" does not have the same mental content.[137] Our minds react differently to the two phrases, and our disparate reactions can be traced through the time it takes to hear or read the sentence. During this time, there is more happening in the syntax than simply word order and grammatical particles. Syntax *requires* the inclusion of metaphor, metonymy, and analogy to achieve its aesthetic goal.[138] But at the same time syntax, as a zone of analysis, remained "the pursuit

---

(1963-, 1:200 l. 43), al-Ǧurǧānī (1954, 295.13–14), van Gelder and Hammond (2008, 68).

136. Ghersetti (2011, 97f).

137. ولو أُخّر ذِكرُ اسمِ الله وقُدّم العلماءُ فقيل إنما يَخشَى العلماءُ اللهَ لَصار المعنى على ضِدّ ما هو عليه الآن ولَصار الغَرَضُ بيانَ المخشيّ مَن هو. Quran 35:28 (Fāṭir). Al-Ǧurǧānī (1992a, 338.3–339.6).

138. ذلك يَقتضي دُخول الاستعارة ونظائرها فيما هو مُعجزٌ وذلك لأنّ هذه المعاني التي هي الاستعارة والكِناية والتمثيل وسائر ضروب المجاز من بعدها مِن مقتضَيات النظم وعنه يُحدَث وبه يكون. Al-Ǧurǧānī

of the mental contents of grammar." Al-Ǧurǧānī's poetics in the *Asrār* and *Dalā'il* was a study of the aesthetic functions of those mental contents. (He dealt with their strictly grammatical functions elsewhere; see Versteegh.)[139]

In his section in the *Dalā'il* on predication, al-Ǧurǧānī dealt with the definite article ("the") and the different ways in which it can deliver the mental content of prior knowledge, completeness, or paradigmatic nature. This productive variation is called by al-Ǧurǧānī the "ineffable magic of clarity."[140] He did not use grammar as just a source of epistemological frameworks to explain metaphor and comparison; he invested grammatical categories with aesthetic value. He located beauty in the definite article. There was no more powerful instantiation of the definite article, al-Ǧurǧānī wrote, than the pronoun that in Arabic introduces the definite relative clause ("which/who"). It impacts on imagination. Al-Ǧurǧānī started off with two lines of poetry that at the time of the *Dalā'il* were around 450 and 300 years old, respectively. The first was from Ḥuǧǧayah b. al-Muḍarrab (fl. ca. seventh century):[141]

It is your brother who will answer your call when misfortune strikes;
if you are angry he will be angry,
angry with the sword.

The second was from Baššār b. Burd (d. 784):[142]

It is your brother who if you doubt him will say
'I must have given cause to doubt.'
If you then criticize him
he will accept it.

Al-Ǧurǧānī's analysis of these verses focused on the imaginary estimations in the audience's mind. Just as the definite article could make the listener imagine the paradigmatic instance of a class and then subsequently realize that the person being described was one such paradigm, so in these two quotations the relative pronoun "who" makes the listener estimate a person who could behave as the poets describe. Such a person then appears in the audience's mind without them actually knowing such a person. This is how the poet teaches the listener to

---

(1992a, 393.5–8).

139. Al-Ǧurǧānī (1982, 1:391), Versteegh (1992, 126).

140. مِن سِحْرِ البيان الذي تَقصُر العبارةُ عن تأديته حقّه. Al-Ǧurǧānī (1992a, 184.8).

141. أَخُوْكَ ٱلَّذِيْ إِنْ تَدْعُهُ لِمُلِمَّةٍ | يُجِبْكَ وَإِنْ تَغْضَبْ إِلَى ٱلسَّيْفِ يَغْضَبِ. Al-Ǧurǧānī (1992a, 184.16), al-Marzūqī and Abū Tammām (1991, 1177).

142. أَخُوْكَ ٱلَّذِيْ إِنْ رِبْتَهُ قَالَ إِنَّمَا | أَرَبْتُ وَإِنْ عَاتَبْتَهُ لَانَ جَانِبُهْ. Baššār b. Burd (1976, 1:326.1), al-Ǧurǧānī (1992a, 185.2).

connect this ideal imagined person with the brother they may actually know.[143] Poetry creates imagined images in the minds of the audience, and the epistemological structure that brought al-Ǧurǧānī to this conclusion was grammar. It was a structure he reified and with which he was constantly in dialogue. (See Baalbaki on this same topic of the relative pronoun.)[144]

Grammar provided al-Ǧurǧānī with epistemological structures and a conceptual vocabulary to describe the impact that language had, across syntax time, on the mind of a speaker. (This was itself an intervention in grammatical theory, as Ghersetti and Baalbaki have shown.)[145] It was al-Ǧurǧānī's answer to the question, Why do certain images affect us so much? The achievement of his literary-critical project was to explain how the simple, logical mechanics of grammar manipulate our mental contents in a process that develops across the time it takes a listener to hear and fully apprehend an image. In poetry, words affect us in series, and grammar is the only way to explain this effect.

Let us end this section with one of al-Ǧurǧānī's examples of superlative syntax in poetry. These three lines are from a poem by Ibrāhīm b. al-ʿAbbās aṣ-Ṣūlī (d. 861), praising his employer in the caliphal bureaucracy, vizier to three successive caliphs and patron of translations from Greek, Muḥammad b. ʿAbd al-Malik az-Zayyāt (d. 847).[146] These lines are all that has been preserved from the poem:[147]

Should an epoch fade, a master be disavowed,
enemies take power, and a protector be absent,
My home would be outside Ahwaz
on high ground.
But measures have passed, and matters have occurred.
And I hope after this,
Muhammad,
for the best that a brother and a vizier can expect.

143. فهذا ونحوها على أنك قَدَّرتَ إنساناً هذه صِفتُه وهذا شأنُه وأَحَلْتَ السامعَ على مَن يَعِنُّ في الوهم دون أنْ يكون قد عَرَفَ رجلاً بهذه الصفة فأَعلمتَه أنّ المستحِقَّ لاسمِ الإخوة هو ذلك الذي عرفه حتى كأنك قلتَ أخوكَ زيدٌ الذي عرفتَ أنك إنْ تدعه لِملمّة يُحبّك. Al-Ǧurǧānī (1992a, 185.3–6).

144. Baalbaki (1983, 11).

145. Baalbaki (1983), Ghersetti (2011, 102).

146. Gutas (1998, 130–31).

147. فَلَوْ إذْ نَبَا دَهْرٌ وَأُنْكِرَ صَاحِبٌ | وَسُلِّطَ أَعْدَاءٌ وَغَابَ نَصِيْرُ
تَكُوْنُ عَنِ ٱلأَهْوَازِ دَارِي بِنَجْوَةٍ | وَلٰكِنْ مَقَادِيْرٌ جَرَتْ وَأُمُوْرُ
وَإِنِّي لَأَرْجُوْ بَعْدَ هٰذا مُحَمَّداً | لِأَفْضَلِ مَا يُرْجَى أَخٌ وَوَزِيْرُ
Al-Ǧurǧānī (1992a, 86.7–11). Cf. with ms. variants aṣ-Ṣūlī (1937, 132).

Al-Ǧurǧānī located the beauty in four syntactic moves: (1) the poet's decision to place the temporal adverbial element "should (an epoch fade)" before the verb that governs it: "(my home) would be." (2) The decision to fully conjugate that verb, "be." (3) The decision to make "an epoch," "a master," "enemies," and "a protector" indefinite. (4) The use of the passive "a master be disavowed" instead of an active "I disavowed a master." Al-Ǧurǧānī wrote that these four moves created the beauty and that they were all "the mental content of grammar, as you can see."[148]

If we unpack these moves using his methodology, we see that starting with the adverbial element (1) creates dramatic tension throughout the first line, a sense of as-yet-unexplained high stakes that would be absent if the poet had written "my home would be outside Ahwaz on high ground should an epoch fade." Then (2), the rules of Arabic grammar would have permitted the poet to use an invariable perfect verb "to be" in the second line. Such an invariable verb would have placed the being of the house in the same tense and aspect as the fading, disavowing, taking power and being absent of the first line. As it is, however, the feminine imperfect verb chosen both tells the reader to expect a grammatically feminine subject (which turns out to be the house), and places the presence of the house in an imperfect tense, which denotes continuing action. It is as if we switch from an epic hypothetical ("should an epoch fade") to the reality of a domestic present ("my home would be"). The string of indefinite nouns at the beginning of the quotation (3) has the same effect that al-Ǧurǧānī discussed above with "an evil."[149] The audience is free to consider all kinds of epochs, masters, enemies, and protectors, right up until the appearance of the patron ("Muḥammad"). By the time we arrive at the end of the quotation (or perhaps earlier, if we had access to the whole poem), we know that the poet is talking about his relationship with his own employer and patron. But by using the passive voice ("to be disavowed") instead of making it clear that he would be doing the disavowing (4—which is al-Ǧurǧānī's reading), the poet maintains the universal and hypothetical voice of the first line. The passive voice keeps the direction of rejection imprecise: the master could be himself reviled by the caliph, or the master could be rejected by his own poet. Syntax works to deliver all these effects.

148. إنما كان مِن أجلِ تقديمه الظرفَ الذي هو إذ نبا على عامله الذي هو تكون وأنْ لم يقل فلو تكون عن الأهواز داري بنجوة إذ نبا دهْرٌ ثم أنْ قال تكون ولم يقل كان ثم أنْ نَكّر الدهرَ ولم يقل فلو إذ نبا الدهرُ ثم أنْ ساق هذا التنكيرَ في جميع ما أتى به من بعدُ ثم أنْ قال وأُنكِر صاحبٌ ولم يقل وأَنكرتُ صاحباً لا تَرى في البيتين الأوّلين شيئاً غيرَ الذي عَددتُه لك تَجعله حُسناً في النظم وكلّه من معاني النحو كما ترى. Al-Ǧurǧānī (1992a, 86.12–20).

149. See note 90 above.

LOGIC AND GRAMMAR

Al-Ǧurǧānī wrote at the beginning of the *Asrār* that it was impossible to imagine metaphor being a cognitive process unique to the Arabs. To think such a thing would be equivalent to believing that only Arabic could produce speech from two nouns put together, or a noun and a verb, or that only Arabic could maintain a variety of means of predication.[150] The fact of the matter was that universal rules existed, and one could produce a formal definition about a linguistic matter that would apply in any language. The example al-Ǧurǧānī gave later on in the *Asrār* for such a rule was "The predicate is what can be true or false," and then he went on to make the following passionate complaint: "There are many rules such as these, and this is just one of the issues that people forget and that confuses them to such an extent that they think that this discipline of knowledge has no rational laws and that its *quaestiones* resemble the lexicon in that they are conventional and can be imagined, transferred, or exchanged. Their error in this point has become atrocious, and this is not the place to speak about it further."[151] What al-Ǧurǧānī was saying is that grammar is a linguistic discipline but that it is logical, and its logic can be universal. He thought that seeing the predicate as a place for truth conditions was a grammatical way of thinking. Like Ibn Sīnā, al-Ǧurǧānī had no time for the idea that grammar was for the Arabs and logic for universally rational philhellenic philosophers. But unlike Ibn Sīnā, al-Ǧurǧānī's logic was a logic of grammar; it was logic as grammar, and grammar as logic.

This collapse of grammar into logic and vice versa appears problematic from our twenty-first-century perspective. It would also have been a problem for Ibn Sīnā, whose Aristotelian heritage gave him a disciplinary incentive to separate logic from other sciences. Ibn Sīnā would probably have agreed with Quine that "logic chases truth up the tree of grammar."[152] But for al-Ǧurǧānī, a grammarian writing language theory after Ibn Sīnā, there was no such problem. A very short detour into Quine may be useful here, because although he was writing in the post-Fregean twentieth century, Quine was clear, like Ibn Sīnā, that logic needed to chase grammar up the tree in order to succeed. Quine's statement that "logic

150. إلى طريقةٍ في المعقولات لا يَعرفها غيرُ العرب أولم يتّفق لِمَن سِواهم لأنّ ذلك بمنزلةٍ أنْ تقول أنّ تركيب الكلام من الاسمَين أو مِن الفِعْل والاسم يَختص بلغة العرب وذلك مما لا يُخفى فسادُه. Al-Ǧurǧānī (1954, 33.3–6); cf. Key forthcoming in the *Journal of Abbasid Studies.*

151. ألا تَرى أنّ حَدَّك الخبرِ بأنه ما احتمل الصدقَ والكذبَ مما لا يَخص لساناً دون لسان ونظائرُ ذلك كثيرةٌ وهو أحدُ ما غفل عنه الناسُ ودخل عليهم اللبسُ فيه حتى ظنّوا أنه ليس لهذا العِلم قوانينُ عقليةٌ وأنّ مسائله مُشْبِهَةٌ باللغة في كونها اصطلاحاً يُتوهَّم عليه النقلُ والتبديلُ لقد فَحُش غلطُهم فيه وليس هذا موضِعُ القول في ذلك. Al-Ǧurǧānī (1954, 325.2–6).

152. Quine (1986, 35).

explores the truth conditions of sentences in the light of how the sentences are grammatically constructed" could have come from Ibn Sīnā; "in the light of" was what Ibn Sīnā meant by the "patterns" of vocal forms that carried over into and affected mental contents.[153] But al-Ǧurǧānī went further than either Ibn Sīnā or Quine with his assumption that logic was grammar and grammar was logic.

The best way to parse the three scholars' attitudes is to focus on the extent to which each was concerned with the extramental world. The truth that Quine's logic (like Gottlob Frege's) cared about was a truth of things out there in the world. But the truth that al-Ǧurǧānī cared about was cognitive: it was a truth of mental content that could, in rules such as the one above about the predicate, be universal. This was also, I think, Ibn Sīnā's ultimate concern: his logic was about how the mind worked and about creating new knowledge, not about predicting how the world was. (Other parts of his philosophy did do that, of course.) Looking at it this way makes Ibn Sīnā and al-Ǧurǧānī appear similar, and different from Quine. Eleventh-century Arabic was committed to, and used *maʿnā* for, logical analyses of cognition. Ibn Sīnā and al-Ǧurǧānī shared an acceptance of the centrality of language to those logical analyses. Ibn Sīna thought that a central epistemological principle such as "predication has truth value" was logic. Al-Ǧurǧānī thought that the same principle was grammar. But they were the same thing.

THE GRAMMAR OF METAPHOR AND COMPARISON (*ISTIʿĀRAH* VS. *TAŠBĪH*)

Al-Ǧurǧānī, a grammarian by trade and repute, made grammar the fundamental explanatory realm of his theory. Syntax was grammar (Larkin).[154] And the central dynamic of grammar was the act of predication (Abu Deeb, Khalfallah).[155] In fact, all knowledge was grammatical predication, and that predication was either affirmation or negation.[156] (On "affirmation," see Harb.)[157] All lexically accurate language revolved around affirmation and negation: "Don't you see that predication is the first mental content of speech, the most fundamental, and that upon

153. See chapter 6 note 76.

154. إعلم أنّ ليس النظمُ إلا أنْ تَضع كلامَك الوضعَ الذي يَقتضيه عِلمُ النحو وتَعمل على قوانينه وأصوله. Al-Ǧurǧānī (1992a, 81.6–7). Cf. translation in Larkin (1995, 65–66).

155. Abu Deeb (1979, 29), Khalfallah (2014, 69f).

156. فاعلم أنّ معاني الكلام كلّها معانٍ لا تُتصوّر إلا فيما بين شيئين والأصلُ والأوّلُ هو الخبر . . . [و] لأنه يَنقسم إلى إثبات ونفي. Al-Ǧurǧānī (1992a, 541.5–8).

157. العِلم بالإثبات والنفي وسائر معاني الكلام في غرائز النفوس ولم تُوضَع أمثلةُ الأفعال لتُعلَمَ هذه المعاني في أنفسنا. Al-Ǧurǧānī (1992a, 561.2). Translation: Larkin (1995, 58). Harb (2013, 190f).

which all the other mental contents rely and around which they are organized?"[158] This meant that what happened in the human brain was, for al-Ǧurǧānī, grammar. Grammar did two things: it set up a series of mutually interacting mental contents in the mind, and it was the logical structure according to which the reason could predicate (A is B; x is y). Grammar was inevitably mental rather than extramental (How could grammar be outside the mind?), and it was also inevitably a language (and a natural language, at that). The language of thought was grammatical. One of the most important consequences of this epistemological structure was that al-Ǧurǧānī, influenced no doubt by the long-established Arabic grammatical tradition of positing semantic reconstructions to explain the case of nouns and verbs (so "dogs!" is in the accusative case because there is an implied imperative: "[Release the] dogs!"),[159] conceived of the language of thought as including mental contents not explicitly instantiated in vocal form. If one said, "good" in reply to the question "How is Zayd?" one would inevitably be predicating that "good" of another piece of mental content impressed alongside it in one's mind: "[Zayd is] good."[160] The scale of al-Ǧurǧānī's ambition for grammar feels very much like the scale of Ibn Sīnā's ambition for logic. Mental contents were what mattered, and they did not simply reflect vocal forms.

But the question that al-Ǧurǧānī was asking was: How do vocal forms and mental contents combine to create affect? He knew that the answer could not simply be grammar: there was no extra quality without craft.[161] But he was looking to grammar, and to the way that grammar must inevitably be a matter of syntax, to explain how affect was created. In the *Asrār,* he offered a way to look at the difference between the broad function of comparison and the specific construction of metaphor. He wanted to explain how there were two different processes behind "Zayd is a lion" (a comparison) and "I saw a lion" (a metaphor if one is describing Zayd).[162] He wrote that when you decide whether or not a noun is a metaphor, you are deciding whether or not it is a predicate. Al-Ǧurǧānī was not doing grammar here, he was using grammar as an epistemological resource. When he dealt with the actual grammar of predication in his long work on syntax, he explained

158. ألا ترى أنّ الخبر أوّلُ معاني الكلام وأَقْدَمُها والذي تَستند سائرُ المعاني إليه وتَترتّب عليه. Al-Ǧurǧānī (1954, 338.11–12).

159. وذلك إذا حُقِّق الأمرُ كان كلاماً بتقدير الفِعل المضمَر الذي هو . . . دليلٌ عليه وعلى قِيام معناه في النفس. Al-Ǧurǧānī (1992a, 8.2–4).

160. فانظرْ إذا قيل لك كيف زيدٌ فقلتَ صالحٌ هل يكون لقولك صالحٌ أثرٌ في نفسك مِن دون أنْ تُريد هو صالح. Al-Ǧurǧānī (1992a, 527.13–14).

161. لا فضيلةَ حتى تَرى في الأمر مَصنعاً. Al-Ǧurǧānī (1992a) 98.2–3). Cf. translation in Larkin (1995, 58).

162. Al-Ǧurǧānī (1954, 302.3–304.3).

why and how predicates and their attributes had certain case markings.[163] Here in the *Asrār,* a work on metaphor, he was using the relationships that grammar had established between subjects and predicates to lay out a logical account of how reference (the way that vocal forms indicated mental contents) worked in metaphor and in comparison. Ibn Sīnā, of course, had used Aristotelian logic to do the same job, but Arabic grammar had more traction for al-Ǧurǧānī. (It is, however, harder to write about in English, as the following passages will show!) Al-Ǧurǧānī identified his theory with grammar. He devoted the first two hundred pages of the *Dalāʾil* to grammar, and grammar was his epistemological sphere of choice throughout both the *Dalāʾil* and the *Asrār.* My use of Quine above was intended to frame these accounts of how the linguistic structures behind metaphor are logical, but logical through grammar. Al-Ǧurǧānī had a grammatical logic, one far removed from our own English conceptual vocabularies, but we know he intended it to be universal.

In the *Asrār,* al-Ǧurǧānī was making a distinction between metaphor and comparison based on predicates. Predicates either could be the objects of a verb (for example, "I am *a man*" or "I know *that man*") or they could be words functioning as predicates in what the Arabic grammarians called a "circumstantial construction," wherein something is added to the predicate (for example, "I brandished a sword *that was cutting through the enemy*).[164] Comparisons also have predication; if you say "Zayd is a lion," you make the source (lion) a predicate of the target (Zayd). When a noun is predicated of something, this happens in one of two ways: it is either an affirmation of a description derived from the predicated action (e.g., the departure in the statement "Zayd is departing") or it is an affirmation that something belongs to a class (e.g., "this is a man"). The comparison "Zayd is a lion" is of the latter type, but the class of "lion" is not accurately affirmed of Zayd; all that is being affirmed is a similarity to a class. This is the grammatical background for the theoretical statement that al-Ǧurǧānī wanted to make: in the case of "Zayd is a lion," we have brought the noun in order to create a comparison with it right now, and we fix it in this new place and make it part of the space of affirmation.[165] So al-Ǧurǧānī defines comparison as the grammatical process of pulling a noun into the space where predicates affirm. Comparisons are when vocal forms indicate

163. Al-Ǧurǧānī (1982, 1:255f).

164. وهو أنّ الحالة التي يختلف في الاسم إذا وَقع فيها أ يُسمّى استعارةً أم لا يُسمّى هي الحالةُ التي يكون الاسمُ فيها خبرَ مبتدإٍ أو مُنزّلاً منزلتَه أعني أنْ يكون خبرَ كان أو مفعولاً ثانياً لبابِ علِمتُ لأنّ هذه الأبواب كلّها أصلُها مبتدأ وخبر أو يكون حالاً لأنّ الحال عندهم زيادةٌ في الخبر فحكمها حكمُ الخبر. Al-Ǧurǧānī (1954, 302.4–8).

165. فقد اجتلبنا الاسمَ لِنُحْدِث به التشبيهَ الآنَ ونُقرّره ونُدخِله في حيّز الحصول والثبوت. Al-Ǧurǧānī (1954, 302.1–2).

bundles of mental contents, and one piece of mental content is affirmed as belonging to both vocal forms. The poet makes this affirmation, and the audience reasons it. The grammatical structure in which this takes place is predication.

In metaphors, the grammatical structure of predication is still present, but the metaphor itself does not either predicate or affirm. It simply assumes that predication has occurred somewhere offstage in the speaker's soul and proceeds on that basis. The critical relationship is still between vocal form and mental content. In the metaphor "a gazelle sang to us," the vocal form "gazelle," while actually engaged in predicating and affirming something else (that the gazelle *is singing*), tries to take hold of the intended target (a beautiful woman) and claim that she is a member of the class of gazelles, that class for which "gazelle" was first lexically placed.[166] The audience realizes that the predication "she is a gazelle" must have taken place offstage. Metaphor is different from comparison because of this different relationship to predication. In a metaphor, wrote al-Ǧurǧānī, "The noun is not brought to affirm mental content for something, nor are the words lexically placed for that reason. Both those things require a subject with a noun as its predicate."[167] But in al-Ǧurǧānī's metaphor, what is being affirmed can be the agent of a verb, or the object of a verb, or an annexing noun, or another subject. "In all these cases, you speak in order to affirm something other than the mental content of the noun in question."[168]

This is a critical moment for al-Ǧurǧānī, or at the very least a revealing moment for our analyses of him. What makes a metaphor different from a comparison is not some relationship with or deviation from the lexicon. (We have already seen how lexical accuracy is a quality that can persist in metaphor and provide it with impact.) Neither are metaphors different from comparisons because of some relationship or lack thereof to extramental reality and the real world outside language. What makes a metaphor different from a comparison is a variance in how vocal forms are used to indicate mental content. This is a variance that is mapped by grammatical structures. The combination of subject and predicate (x is y) is a decision to affirm the mental content of a noun, whether with lexical accuracy (Zayd is a man) or by going beyond the lexicon in a comparison (Zayd is a lion). Metaphor is different: it is what happens when you say "a lion approached me" or "I passed

166. وإذا كان كذلك بانَ أنّ الاسم في قولك زيدٌ أسدٌ مقصودٌ به إيقاعُ التشبيه في الحال وإيجابُه وأما في قولك غَنَّتْ لنا ظَبْيةٌ وسَلَلْتُ سيفاً على العُدوّ فوُضِع الاسمُ هكذا انتهازاً واقتضاباً على المقصود وادّعاءً أنه من الجنس الذي وُضِع له الاسمُ في أصل اللغة. Al-Ǧurǧānī (1954, 303.19–304.3).

167. فهي حالةٌ إذا وَقع الاسمُ فيها لم يكن الاسمُ مجتلِباً لإثباتِ معناه للشيء ولا الكلامُ موضوعاً لذلك لأنّ هذا حُكمٌ لا يكون إلا إذا كان الاسمُ في منزلةِ الخبر من المبتدأ. Al-Ǧurǧānī (1954, 303.5–7).

168. فأما إذا لم يكن كذلك وكان مبتدأً بنفسه أو فاعلاً أو مفعولاً أو مُضافاً إليه فأنتَ واضعُ كلامك لإثباتِ أمرٍ آخر غيرِ ما هو معنى الاسم. Al-Ǧurǧānī (1954, 303.7–9).

by a lion." In these cases what you are affirming is the approach or the passing by. You are not affirming the mental-content bundle of the lion, because the lion is the agent of the verb (in the first case) and the indirect object of the verb (in the second).[169] It is the same when you say "a gazelle sang to us" and intend a woman singing; you are not using the noun "gazelle" to affirm the very comparison that you intend. ("Gazelle" is not your predicate.) You do not even mention the target of the metaphor. (Cf. Abu Deeb.)[170] Your metaphorical language forces the audience to go back to the hidden state of your soul.[171]

ESSENCE

Essence is a slightly different technical concept in each of the scholarly disciplines dealt with in this book, but in all of them it is an epistemological claim made about an ontological reality. Furthermore, in both logic and grammar essence is a fundamental structuring principle that was always understood in terms of *maʿnā*. When we encountered Ibn Sīnā's work on essence and existence (and what-it-is-ness), we saw how it was enabled by the Arabic conceptual vocabulary of mental content. This also applies to al-Ǧurǧānī, for whom *maʿnā* was a way to talk about essences and accidents in poetry; how a horse, for example, was essentially a horse and accidentally brown. The connection between the vocal form "horse" and the mental content of horseness was a lexical and accurate connection. But it was also another key to the functioning of metaphor that al-Ǧurǧānī was trying to explain. Both Larkin and Khalfallah have identified al-Ǧurǧānī's ease and familiarity with logical relationships at a basic level (causality, argumentation, and division for Khalfallah; "logical parsing of figures" for Larkin).[172] What I would like to do here is ask how the conceptual vocabulary of mental content enabled al-Ǧurǧānī to conceive of essences themselves before considering how they helped him explain poetry.

Larkin put the basic dynamic well: for al-Ǧurǧānī nouns "call up the essence" of an entity.[173] But what vocabulary did al-Ǧurǧānī use? He said that speakers intend

169. فالكلامُ موضوعٌ لإثباتِ الإقبال [أو المجيء أو الرؤية] للأسد لا لإثباتِ معنى الأسد. Al-Ǧurǧānī (1954, 303. 12–13).

170. Abu Deeb (1979, 152).

171. ثم قلتَ غنّتْ لنا ظَبْيةٌ وهززتُ سيفاً صارماً على الأعداء وأنت تعني بالظبية امرأةً وبالسيف رجلاً لم يكن ذِكرُك للإسمَين [ظبيةٌ وسيفٌ] في كلامك هذا لإثباتِ الشَبَه المقصود الآنَ وكيف يُتصوّر أنْ تَقصِد إلى إثباتِ الشَبَه منهما بشيء وأنتَ لم تَذكر شيئاً يَنصرِف إثباتُ الشَبَه إليه وإنما تُثْبِت الشَبَهَ من طريق الرجوع إلى الحال والبَحْث عن خبيءٍ في نفس المتكلم. Al-Ǧurǧānī (1954, 303.15–18).

172. Khalfallah (2014) 238–43), Larkin (1995, 108).

173. Larkin (1995, 107).

mental contents. He then had an account of how those mental contents connect to nouns that was dependent on the lexicon. Bundles of mental content were connected to nouns, and some pieces of mental content in each bundle were more central to a noun than others. The function of the lexicon was to preserve via accurate connections the full set of reference to the whole bundle. Toward the end of the *Asrār*, al-Ǧurǧānī wrote: suppose that we claim in a metaphor that a man has lionness, to the extent that he deserves the name 'lion.' In this we do not go so far as to claim that he has the form and shape of a lion, nor the thick neck nor claws of a lion, nor the rest of the descriptions that are externally apparent to the eye. Although bravery is one of the most specific and firmest fixed descriptions of the lion, the lexicon still placed the name "lion" not with bravery alone but rather with a body, form, shape, teeth, claws, and all the other limbs. If the lexicon had placed the name "lion" for bravery alone, then it would be an attribute, not a name, and everything that is connected to bravery would deserve to be accurately included under "lion."[174] In such a case, even though our metaphor, "he is a lion," would not indicate any mental content not already contained under the name "lion" in its original lexical placement, we would still have stripped the name of some of that for which it was placed and made it indicate some of the mental contents that are internal to the lion and its nature, separate from those mental contents that are externally apparent. This change would mean that the name had moved from its original place in the lexicon.[175]

What this long paraphrase tells us is that al-Ǧurǧānī understood the lexicon to be made up of names that indicate sets of mental contents through precedent. He used the word "definition" (*ḥadd*) to refer to this group, but he did not mean the formal logical definition that we met in Ibn Sīnā. Instead, al-Ǧurǧānī's definitions were bundles, constellations, sets, or groupings of mental contents. These bundles are lexically accurate if and when they are complete. This accuracy is judged, as we saw above with the analogy of the king and his clothes, with regard to the impact it has on the audience, not the relationship it has to extramental reality. To call the use of a noun "lexically accurate" is to say that it must have been intended to refer to a person like Zayd or a class of thing like lion. The noun in both "Zayd knows" and "the lion knows" is lexically accurate.[176] Lexical accuracy is a commitment to

174. ولو كانت وَضَعَتْهُ [اللغةُ] لتلك الشجاعة التي تَعرفها وحدَها لكان صفةً لا اسماً ولَـكان كلُّ شيء يُفضي في شجاعته إلى ذلك الحدّ مستحِقّاً للاسم استحقاقاً حقيقياً لا على طريق التشبيه والتأويل. Al-Ǧurǧānī (1954, 381.7–9).

175. Al-Ǧurǧānī (1954, 381.1–14).

176. ومعلومٌ [في الحقيقة] أنّ ما هو كالمنفعة من الاسم أنْ يُوجِب ذكرُه القصدَ إلى الشيء في نفسه فإذا قلتَ زيدٌ عُلِمَ أنك أردتَ أنْ تُخبِر عن الشخص المعلوم وإذا قلتَ أسداً عُلِمَ أنك عَلّقتَ اللقاء بواحد من هذا الجنس. Al-Ǧurǧānī (1954, 301.9–12).

use a noun to indicate an actual person or a complete bundle of mental contents. Just as in Ibn Fūrak, accuracy is an epistemological value judgment, but here in al-Ǧurǧānī the intent behind a speech act is being judged, not the truth of a claim about divine ontology.

The reason al-Ǧurǧānī spent so much time explaining these underlying structures of language is that poets use them to create beauty. "It is their craft," he wrote, "if they want to increase or decrease the virtue of someone, or to praise or blame them, to attach some of the descriptions in which the persons shares but that are not the lexically accurate reason for the quality in question."[177] For example, al-Buḥturī wrote:[178]

The whiteness of the falcon is
upon consideration
more truly beautiful
than the black of the crow.

He was talking about the relative merits of old age (white hair) and youth (black hair). What al-Ǧurǧānī was interested in was the deliberate focus on descriptions that are not central to the bundle of mental contents to which they belong in the lexicon. (Whiteness is not central to old age in the way that bravery is central to lions.) Whiteness is also not the same as lionness. One can affirm and conceive of an attribute while also knowing that attributes don't have independent extramental existence: "You can't have the existence of blackness [and whiteness] or movement without a place, but blackness [and whiteness] and movement can be known as themselves. The fact of the matter is that the reliance, in existence, of something on something else does not prevent that thing from being known independently."[179] Ibn Fūrak would have agreed.[180]

177. ومِن ذلك صنيعُهم إذا أراد تفضيلَ شيء أو نقصَه ومدحَه أو ذامَّه فتعلَّقوا ببعضٍ ما يشاركه في أوصاف على الحقيقة . . . ليستْ هي سببَ الفضيلة. Al-Ǧurǧānī (1954, 246.12–14). Cf. translation in van Gelder and Hammond (2008, 33).

178. وَبَياضُ ٱلْبَازِيِّ أَصْدَقُ حُسْناً | إِنْ تَأَمَّلْتَ مِنْ سَوَادِ ٱلْغُرَابِ. Al-Buḥturī (1963–, 1:84 l. 10), al-Ǧurǧānī (1954, 247.1), van Gelder and Hammond (2008, 33).

179. إذا ضُمّ إلى اسمٍ إثباتُ الضرب لمسمّى ذلك الاسم فهو موضوعٌ ليدلّ على وقوعِ إثباتٍ منك ووجودِهِ في نفسك وليس في أنّ الإثبات لا يقع إلا متعلّقاً بشيئَين ما يَمنع أنْ يكونَ الإثباتُ معنىً مستقلّاً بنفسه معلوماً ومثلُه أنه لا يصحّ وجودُ صفةٍ مِن غير موصوفٍ ثم لا يَمنع ذلك أنْ تكون الصفةُ في نفسها معلومةً تفسيرُ ذلك أنه لا يصحّ وجودُ سوادٍ وحركةٍ في غير مَحَلٍّ ثم لم يَمنع ذلك أنْ يكونا معلومَين في أنفسهما وجملةُ الأمر أنّ حاجةَ الشيء في وجوده إلى شيءٍ آخر لا يَمنع أنْ يكون شيئاً مستقِلّاً بنفسه معلوماً. Al-Ǧurǧānī (1992a, 561.7–15).

180. See chapter 5 note 84 above.

Al-Ǧurǧānī's poetics relied on an account of basic categories of predication, essence, and attribute that came from theology and from logic (where they were in second position) and were constructed with mental content. Only when literary criticism shared logic's understanding of the difference between "lionness" and "whiteness" and used a vocabulary of logical predication could a literary critic start to describe what poetry did to manipulate those categories and mechanisms in order to affect both our minds and our emotions. Al-Ǧurǧānī did this work himself: across two monographs he both developed the core conceptual vocabulary he needed from theology and logic, and then used it to describe how poetry was beautiful. When the poet said "he is a lion" (rather than just "he is like a lion"), it was not just a claim of similarity, but a readjustment of the lexical relationship between vocal form and mental content. It was a claim that bravery, the quality being mapped across from source to target, was in fact the dominant quality of the lion *qua* lion; the essence of lionness was no longer the bundle of mental content established by precedent, but now it was bravery and all other qualities were secondary. With this claim established in the image, the bravery could then be mapped across to the person in question, and he could be called a lion without any doubt.[181]

Al-Ǧurǧānī had taken essence and attribute from theology and logic and used them to explain the whiteness of al-Buḥturī's falcon and the blackness of his crow in comparison to the bravery of a lion. He had taken static bundles of mental content curated by lexicography and shown how syntax could make them dynamic. He had taken logic's account of how mental contents interacted and shown what could happen when these interactions took place not with the fixed terms of a syllogism but with dynamic bundles of mental content and with make-believe accuracy.

181. Al-Ǧurǧānī (1954, 231.10–232.2).

8

Conclusion

Maʿnā is mental content. It was central to the conceptual vocabularies of lexicographers, theologians, logicians, and literary critics. It enabled them to build theories of meaning, cosmology, truth, and beauty at the nexus of language, mind, and reality. Reading the eleventh century through the lens of this concept helps us see how those theories worked.

Maʿnā helps us recognize that eleventh-century Arabic lexicography was fundamental to all other scholarly pursuits and that while it was iteratively conservative it was also epistemologically creative. The lexicographers managed a lexicon of precedent that anchored an accurate (*ḥaqīqah*) connection between a vocal form (*lafẓ*) and a mental content (*maʿnā*).

Maʿnā helps us grasp that Islamic theology in the eleventh century was lexical and linguistic and at the same time scientific, and targeted at both God and the extramental world. *Ḥaqīqah* was the theologians' goal: to accurately align their mental contents (and their vocal forms) with the truth of the divine creation.

Maʿnā helps us understand how Aristotelian logic became, in the eleventh-century Arabic of Ibn Sīnā, a comprehensive epistemology that policed with rigor and success the boundaries between language and mind. *Ḥaqīqah* was the accuracy that this system demanded for both its two primary cognitive steps: conception and assent (*taṣawwur* and *taṣdīq*).

Maʿnā helps us realize how a revolutionary theory of poetic affect could be constructed from Aristotelian logic and Arabic grammar. Al-Ǧurǧānī's literary criticism enabled *ḥaqīqah* to operate in a make-believe world of imagery, where it helped audiences feel the power of metaphor.

Maʿnā is the stuff of human cognition. *Ḥaqīqah* is the word for accurate connections between that stuff of cognition and language, or between that stuff of cognition and God, or between that stuff of cognition and the reality of the extramental world. *Maʿnā* is what we use when we think about what we can see, or feel, or know. *Ḥaqīqah* is when we get that right.

It has not been my intention in this book to argue that readers should join me in invariably translating *maʿnā* as "mental content" or *ḥaqīqah* as "accuracy." That has been a thought experiment, in which every time I have written "mental content" in English, the Arabic word has been *maʿnā,* and every time I have written "accuracy," "accurate," or "accurately," the Arabic word has been *ḥaqīqah.* What I have tried to do is advocate for the invariable understanding of *maʿnā* as a stable and useful category located in the mind. In the lexicon, *maʿānī* are connected with vocal forms. In theology, Ibn Fūrak used *maʿānī* as conceptual pigeonholes for the correct alignment of God, world, and theologians. In logic, Ibn Sīnā used *maʿānī* as the Arabic core of universal thought. In poetics, al-Ǧurǧānī used *maʿānī* in bundles to explain how poets manipulated the accuracy of the lexicographers. The *maʿānī* of poetry are not, of course, identical to the *maʿānī* of theology, but just as in English one can play tag in the morning, play chess in the afternoon, play Hamlet in the evening, and play the fool at night, all the while using "play" as a stable and useful piece of vocabulary, so too was *maʿnā* a stable and useful word in eleventh-century Arabic. The only reason I have invariably translated *maʿnā* as "mental content" is to ensure that I can advance this thesis: *maʿnā* was a stable and meaningful piece of core conceptual vocabulary. It was not a homonym, nor was it vague or ambiguous.

Translating *maʿnā* in exactly the same way wherever it appears is a methodology by which we can engage with the scope of usage in the texts. "Mental content" does a passable job as a translation; it produces some unidiomatic awkwardness, but that is to be expected—because the extent of the work that *maʿnā* did in eleventh-century Arabic cannot be replicated by any one word in English. Nor is this a matter of a single Arabic word being equivalent, in its various usages, to multiple words in English. That is the methodology that I enlist Kuhn to argue against: if we turn *maʿnā* into a set of mutually incompatible English words, we have domesticated it in a different conceptual vocabulary. The alternative strategy that is available for philologists trying to make sense of eleventh-century Arabic texts is to use an invariable translation. In my case, "mental content" helps English readers see the difference between the way Arabic uses *maʿnā* and the way English uses its own conceptual vocabulary of meaning, signification, and so forth. We are dealing with two core conceptual vocabularies, each of which carves reality at different joints. Domestication of the source vocabulary in the target vocabulary is a problem because it obscures this fact. There is a difference between *maʿnā* and meaning. In order to make sense of the theories that Arabic scholars wrote using *maʿnā,* we need to be constantly aware of that difference. Richard Frank was aware of it. My use of the invariable translation "mental content" is only useful insofar as it highlights this difference.

It is worth repeating that I make no claim for the necessity of an invariable translation of *maʿnā* as "mental content" in future work. Once we know that *maʿnā* was invariably a stable word for content in the mind, we can start to experiment with more idiomatic renderings in English and other European languages. Phrases containing the word *maʿnā* could be translated as "we think of this as," or "the concept here is," or "there is a certain content to that argument," or "this fits into the mental pigeonhole of," or "this word calls up a bundle of ideas." All these translation choices are idiomatic English ways of saying "mental content"; they depend on and posit the existence of stable mental contents.

My translation of *ḥaqīqah* as "accurate," "accurate account," or "accuracy" goes some way in the same direction. The Arabic word is used in ways that would in English be nominal or adjectival, and I have alternated between the three options above in order to ensure the stability and familiarity of my English syntax. But the core claim I make stands: *ḥaqīqah* can invariably be understood as the claim that something is correct, accurate, or an accurate account. We do not use a word in English that makes the claims about the relationship of mind to world and language that *ḥaqīqah* makes in Arabic. But we do have a lemma, "accuracy," that captures the claim that *ḥaqīqah* makes in Arabic about those relationships. *Maʿnā* and *ḥaqīqah* are equally foreign to English; the gap between the conceptual vocabulary that they constitute and Anglophone or European conceptual vocabulary is substantial. The difference between *maʿnā* and *ḥaqīqah* lies solely in the disparate availability in English of words that can represent the roles they play in Arabic.

This book has been written to establish a set of connected arguments. The first is that *maʿnā* and *ḥaqīqah* functioned as core conceptual vocabulary in the eleventh-century texts that I have read. The second is that this vocabulary was shared across the four scholarly disciplines of lexicography, theology, logic, and poetics. *Maʿnā* and *ḥaqīqah* were tools used by all scholars. In this book, we have seen four scholars do four different things with the same tools. The scholars were in constant and productive conversation with each other. Ibn Fūrak's theology engaged with ar-Rāġib's lexicon, as did Ibn Sīnā's logic (which gestured toward Ibn Fūrak's theology), and al-Ǧurǧānī's poetics built on Ibn Sīnā's theories of essence and cognitive process. Ibn Sīnā called his *maʿnā*-based account of cognition "logic," and al-Ǧurǧānī called his *maʿnā*-based account of poetic cognition "grammar." These were very different projects, but they started from a shared conceptual base and used a single conceptual vocabulary.

This observation has repercussions for how we look at the scholarly disciplines of eleventh-century Arabic. Thinking about *ḥaqīqah* in theology, logic, and poetics helps us see how fundamental lexicography was to all scholarship in Arabic in the eleventh century and beyond. In theology, the benefit derived from reading Ibn Fūrak with a focus on *maʿnā* and *ḥaqīqah* has been to resolve the apparent blurring of the relationships between language, epistemology, and ontology. The discipline of Islamic theology contained a theoretical assumption about the structure and operation of human cognition that ordered the nexus of language, mind, and reality as follows: *maʿānī* are stable pigeonholes of mental content, and *ḥaqīqah* is always the moment when those *maʿānī* accurately connect to words, the world, or God. The potential of these pigeonholes was realized in the Arabic logic of Ibn Sīnā, where *maʿnā* was the core cognitive building block. Human beings conceived of mental contents and then manipulated those mental contents according to logical rules in philosophical endeavors. Adamson has credited Ibn Sīnā with the discovery of mental existence,[1] and my work in this book goes some small way toward locating that development in the usage of *maʿnā* during the eleventh century and earlier, when the word was already a stable term for what existed in the mind. Theology had also shown how *maʿnā* could be used for qualities and attributes, things that do of course exist extramentally as well as in the mind. Ibn Sīnā took an existing piece of Arabic core conceptual vocabulary found everywhere from grammar to literary criticism via theology, brought it into Aristotelian philosophy and logic, and integrated it into his accounts of existence.

Ibn Sīnā's resolutions of questions of epistemology and ontology are useful for us and make sense to us because he was motivated by his work in the philhellenic Aristotelian tradition to establish clear boundaries between language, mind, and reality. For contingent reasons of history and geography, European and Anglophone philosophy and theology have also worked, for at least the last millennium, in that same Greek tradition. But the Islamic theologians who were talking about *maʿānī* in the eleventh century and earlier did not necessarily care so much about the division of language, mind, and reality made by Aristotle at the start of *De Interpretatione*. *Maʿnā* was at the core of their assumption about this nexus, and they wanted to align their *maʿānī* with God, not Greeks. Reading for *maʿnā* rather than looking for strictly ontological accounts or fearing linguistic relativism can help us appreciate Ibn Fūrak's physics and cosmology. Today's European and Anglophone conceptual vocabulary shares a genealogical connection to Ibn Sīnā; we all read Aristotle. But we share no such assumptions or vocabulary with Ibn Fūrak, a fact that heightens both the epistemological need and the hermeneutical rewards for reading his theology with close attention to *maʿnā*.

My arguments have some ramifications that extend beyond the scope of this book. The first is that this same Arabic core conceptual vocabulary can also be found across disciplines that appear in this book in passing, most notably grammar

1. Adamson (2017), cf. Panaccio (2017, 95).

and legal theory, but also in exegesis, mysticism (*taṣawwuf*), ethics, and *adab*. I am comfortable advancing this observation despite having not documented it sufficiently. The second is that use of this same core conceptual vocabulary extended well beyond the eleventh century. I have not attempted to document this; chapter 2, on "Precedents," did show that eleventh-century conceptual vocabulary was consistent with the previous four centuries of Arabic, but I have only briefly gestured toward the centuries of power and progress that followed. It is my contention that the conclusions reached in this book about *maʿnā* and *ḥaqīqah* could be profitably applied to and tested against the vast scholarly projects written in Arabic from the twelfth through the nineteenth century. The "science of lexical placement" founded by al-Īǧī in the fourteenth century is just the most obvious example.

Reading for *maʿnā* also helps us deal with the looming presence of the English word "meaning," a word that seems to occupy much of the same space as *maʿnā* without ever doing exactly the same work. Using examples from ordinary language, we may quickly observe the difference between *maʿnā* and "meaning" in two phrases: "the meaning of life" in English and *maʿnā al-ḥayāh* in Arabic. In eleventh-century Arabic, "the *maʿnā* of life," would simply describe the mental content lexically connected to the vocal form "life." (For Ibn Fāris, that was "the opposite of death"; for Ibn Fūrak and ar-Rāġib it was also a chance to parse the implications of the word's application to human beings and to God.)[2] But the English phrase "the meaning of life" comprises everything from divine cosmology to personal destiny. The Arabic genre of *adab* dealt with everything from cosmology to destiny via irony, politics, and rhetoric. *Adab* is therefore about meaning in the English sense. But *adab* is not about *maʿnā*, or at least not to the extent that Classical Arabic literary criticism, eleventh-century Islamic theology, and Arabic logic are about *maʿnā*. This leads us to the observation that although eleventh-century Arabic culture turned to *adab* when faced with the ironies of life or power, it turned to *maʿnā* when faced with truth or beauty. The question of aesthetics was approached via *maʿnā* and *ḥaqīqah* in a theoretical engagement that dealt with mental processes catalyzed by syntax, manipulated by reason, and operating with a grammar and a logic that the poets (and God in his Quran) used to deliver affect.

When I presented a very early version of some of the ideas in this book at Georgetown University in 2015, Jaroslav Stetkevych complained that it was a presentation of theories that missed out everything beyond the spinning circularity of words and word games. This is, I think, true. The meaning that Stetkevych was looking for, and finds, in Classical Arabic poetry is not in play in the disciplines considered in this book. Stetkevych calls much Arabic poetics "uninspired postulations

2. Ibn Fāris (1946–52, 2:122.6f), Ibn Fūrak (1987, 257), ar-Rāġib (1992), 268f.

of the chief problem of all aesthetic thinking."[3] How might al-Ǧurǧānī answer such a challenge? It is possible that he would accept the justice of the observation: Classical Arabic literary theory, the sort of poetics he wrote, was just one of the arenas in which poetry met with critical engagement. Classical Arabic poetry was widely performed in politics and society, and it was performed as constitutive of both politics and society. This was recorded and evaluated in *adab*, and in histories, biographies, and works of ethical and religious devotion. All these performances and records dealt with the meaning sought by Stetkevych. But al-Ǧurǧānī's poetics was a different way of dealing with poetry. (Lexicography, where poetry was a proof text for lexical precedent, was different again.) In al-Ǧurǧānī's poetics, logical grammar and syntax structured the catalytic creativity of poetry's vocal forms. It was a rational cognitive world of word games built, with a logic developed by Ibn Sīnā from Aristotle, on top of a theology of mental content and a lexicography of static reference. This poetics identified the chief problem of aesthetic thinking as formal structures of metaphor or syntax that empowered imagination and affect.

Reading for *maʿnā* enables us to thread our way through the tight and technical formal discussions of lexical reference, divine ontology, logical truth, and poetic structure. It gives us accounts of mental content that are tied closely to the vocal forms of words. But at the same time *maʿnā*, accompanied by the value of *ḥaqīqah*, can take us beyond lexical precedent into new logical conclusions, beyond text into the divine realm of God himself, or beyond simple comparison into make-believe imagery. *Maʿnā* was shared between God and the poets. *Maʿnā* was the interaction between human minds and the world.

3. Stetkevych (1979–80, 775).

REFERENCES

ʿAbbās, Iḥsān. 1971. *Tārīḫ an-Naqd al-Adabī ʿinda al-ʿArab.* Beirut: Dār al-Amānah.

Abu Deeb, Kamal. 1979. *Al-Jurjānī's Theory of Poetic Imagery.* Warminster: Aris & Phillips.

———. 1990. "Literary Criticism." In J. Ashtiany, T. M. Johnstone, J. D. Latham, and R. B. Serjeant, eds., *Abbasid Belles Lettres.* Cambridge: Cambridge University Press.

Abū Farağ al-Iṣfahānī. 1964–74. *Kitāb al-Aġānī.* Ed. Muḥammad Abū al-Faḍl Ibrāhīm. 24 vols. Cairo: Wizārat aṯ-Ṯaqāfah wa-l-Iršād al-Qawmī (Dār al-Kutub / Lağnah).

Abū Hilāl, al-Ḥasan b. ʿAbdallāh al-ʿAskarī. 2006. *Al-Furūq al-Luġawīyah.* Beirut: Dār al-Kutub al-ʿIlmīyah.

Abū Tammām, Ḥabīb b. Aws aṭ-Ṭāʾī, and Yaḥyā b. ʿAlī al-Ḫaṭīb at-Tabrīzī. 1994. *Šarḥ Dīwān Abī Tammām.* Ed. Rāğī Asmar. Beirut: Dār al-Kitāb al-ʿArabī.

Abū ʿUbaydah, Maʿmar b. al-Muṯannā. 1954. *Mağāz al-Qurʾān.* Ed. Fuat Sezgin. 2 vols. Cairo: Maktabat al-Ḫānğī.

———. 1998. *Kitāb an-Naqāʾiḍ: Naqāʾiḍ Ğarīr wa-l-Farazdaq.* Ed. Ḫalīl ʿImrān al-Manṣūr. 2 vols. Beirut: Dār al-Kutub al-ʿIlmīyah.

Abū Zayd, Naṣr Ḥāmid. 2005. *Iškālīyāt al-Qirāʾah wa-Ālīyāt at-Taʾwīl.* Beirut: al-Markaz aṯ-Ṯaqāfī al-ʿArabī.

Adamson, Peter. 2007. *Al-Kindī.* New York: Oxford University Press.

———. 2013. *Interpreting Avicenna: Critical Essays.* Cambridge: Cambridge University Press.

———. 2017. "Existence in Philosophy and Theology." In G. Krämer, D. Matringe, J. Nawas, and E. Rowson, eds., *Encyclopaedia of Islam, THREE.* Brill Online.

Adem, Rodrigo. 2017. "Classical Naṣṣ Doctrines in Imāmī Shīʿism: On the Usage of an Expository Term." *Shii Studies Review,* 42–71.

Ademollo, Francesco. 2015. "Names, Verbs, and Sentences in Ancient Greek Philosophy." In M. Cameron and R. J. Stainton, eds., *Linguistic Content: New Essays on the History of Philosophy of Language.* Oxford: Oxford University Press.

Ahmed, Asad Q. 2008. "The *Jiha/Tropos-Mādda/Hulē* Distinction in Arabic Logic and Its Significance for Avicenna's Modals." In S. Rahman, T. Street, and H. Tahiri, eds., *The Unity of Science in the Arabic Tradition: Science, Logic, Epistemology and Their Interactions.* Dordrecht: Springer.

Ali, Mohamed M. Yunis. 2000. *Medieval Islamic Pragmatics: Sunni Legal Theorists' Models of Textual Communication.* London: Routledge.

Al-Jallad, Ahmad. 2018. "The Earliest Stages of Arabic and Its Linguistic Classification." In A. Benmamoun and R. Bassiouney, eds., *Routledge Handbook of Arabic Linguistics,* 315–31. New York: Routledge.

Allard, Michel. 1965. *Le problème des attributs divins dans la doctrine d'al-Aš'arī et de ses premiers grands disciples.* Beirut: Imprimerie Catholique.

Al-'Āmirī, Abū al-Ḥasan Muḥammad ibn Yūsuf, and Everett Rowson. 1988. *A Muslim Philosopher on the Soul and Its Fate: Al-'Āmirī's Kitāb al-Amad 'alā l-Abad.* New Haven: American Oriental Society.

Al-Andalusī, Abū 'Abdallāh Ǧamāl ad-Dīn Muḥammad b. Aḥmad. 1987. *Al-Mi'yār fī Naqd al-Aš'ār.* Ed. 'Abdallāh Muḥammad Sulaymān Hindāwī. Cairo: Maṭba'at al-Amānah.

Andreas, Holger. 2017. "Theoretical Terms in Science." In E. N. Zalta, ed., *The Stanford Encyclopedia of Philosophy,* fall edition. https://plato.stanford.edu/archives/fall2017/entries/theoretical-terms-science/.

Aouad, Maroun. 2009. "Al-Fārābī critique des traditions non aristotéliciennes de la rhétorique." In F. Woerther, ed., *Literary and Philosophical Rhetoric in the Greek, Roman, Syriac and Arabic Worlds.* Hildesheim: Georg Olms.

Aristotle. 1938a. *Categories.* In volume 1 of *Aristotle.* The Loeb Classical Library, vol. 325. Cambridge, Mass.: Harvard University Press.

———. 1938b. *On Interpretation.* In volume 1 of *Aristotle.* The Loeb Classical Library, vol. 325. Cambridge, Mass.: Harvard University Press.

———. 1948. *Organon Aristotelis in Versione Arabica Antiqua / Manṭiq Aristū.* Ed. 'Abd ar-Raḥmān Badawī. 3 vols. Cairo: Dār al-Kutub al-Miṣrīyah. [Reprint, Kuwait/Beirut: Wakālat al-Maṭbū'āt / Dār al-Qalam, 1980.]

———. 1953. *Fann aš-Ši'r [Poetics]: Ma' at-tarǧamah al-'Arabīyah al-qadīmah wa-šurūḥ al-Fārābī wa-Ibn Sīnā wa-Ibn Rušd.* Ed. 'Abd ar-Raḥmān Badawī. Cairo: Maktabat an-Naḥḍah.

———. 1963. *"Categories" and "De Interpretatione."* Trans. and ed. J. L. Ackrill. Oxford: Clarendon Press.

———. 1964. *Aṭ-Ṭabī'ah.* Ed. 'Abd ar-Raḥmān Badawī. 2 vols. Cairo: al-Maktabah al-'Arabīyah.

———. 1982. *Aristotle's "Ars Rhetorica": The Arabic Version.* Ed. M. C. Lyons. 2 vols. Cambridge: Pembroke Arabic Texts.

———. 2002. *Nicomachean Ethics.* Trans. Christopher Rowe and Sarah Broadie. Oxford: Oxford University Press.

Aristotle et al. [Aristotle, Anna Akasoy, Alexander Fidora, and D. M. Dunlop.] 2005. *The Arabic Version of the Nicomachean Ethics.* Leiden: E. J. Brill.

Arkoun, M., and eds. 2009. "Miskawayh." In P. Bearman, T. Bianquis, C. E. Bosworth, E. van Donzel, and W. P. Heinrichs, eds., *Encyclopaedia of Islam,* 2nd ed. Brill Online.

Al-Aš'arī, Abū al-Ḥasan 'Alī b. Ismā'īl. 1929–33. *Kitāb Maqālāt al-Islāmīyīn wa-Iḫtilāf al-Muṣallīn.* Ed. Helmut Ritter. Istanbul: Deutsche Morgenländische Gesellschaft / F.A. Brockhaus. [Reprint, Wiesbaden: Steiner, 1980.]

———. 1953. *The Theology of al-Ash'arī: The Arabic Texts of al-Ash'arī's Kitāb al-luma' and Risālat istiḥsān al-khawḍ fī 'ilm al-kalām, with Briefly Annotated Translations, and Appendices Containing Material Pertinent to the Study of al-Ash'arī.* Trans. and ed. Richard Joseph McCarthy. Beirut: Imprimerie Catholique.

———. 1955. *Kitāb al-Luma'.* Ed. Ḥammūdah Ġurābah. Cairo: Maṭba'at Miṣr.

Azarnoosh, Azartash, and Farzin Negahban. 2008. "Abū Hilāl al-'Askarī." In W. Madelung and F. Daftary, eds. *Encyclopaedia Islamica.* Brill Online.

Baalbaki, Ramzi. 1983. "The Relation between *Naḥw* and *Balāġa:* A Comparative Study of the Methods of Sībawayh and Ǧurǧānī." *Zeitschrift für Arabische Linguistik* 11: 7–23.

———. 2014. *The Arabic Lexicographical Tradition: From the 2nd/8th to the 12th/18th Century.* Leiden: E.J. Brill.

Bäck, Allan. 1987. "Avicenna on Existence." *Journal of the History of Philosophy,* 25: 351–67.

———. 2008. "Avicenna the Commentator." In L.A. Newton, ed., *Medieval Commentaries on Aristotle's "Categories."* Leiden: E.J. Brill.

Al-Bāḫarzī, 'Alī b. Ḥasan. 1993. *Dumyat al-Qaṣr wa-'Uṣrat Ahl al-'Aṣr.* Ed. Muḥammad at-Tūnǧī. 3 vols. Beirut: Dār al-Ǧīl.

Al-Bāqillānī, Abū Bakr Muḥammad b. aṭ-Ṭayyib. 1957. *Kitāb at-Tamhīd.* Ed. R.J. McCarthy. Beirut: al-Maktabah aš-Šarqīyah.

———. 1963. *Al-Inṣāf fī Mā Yaǧib I'tiqāduhū wa-Lā Yaǧūz al-Ǧahl bih.* Ed. Muḥammad Zāhid al-Kawṯarī. Cairo: Mu'assasat al-Ḫānǧī. [Reprints, Cairo: Mu'assasat al-Ḫānǧī, 1963; and al-Maktabah al-Azharīyah li-t-Turāṯ, 2000.]

———. 1998. *At-Taqrīb wa-l-Iršād.* Ed. 'Abd al-Ḥamīd b. 'Alī Abū Zunayd. 3 vols. Beirut: Mu'assasat ar-Risālah.

Baššār b. Burd. 1976. *Dīwān Baššār b. Burd.* Ed. Muḥammad aṭ-Ṭāhir b. 'Āšūr. 4 vols. Tunis: aš-Širkah at-Tūnisīyah li-t-Tawzī'. [Reprint: Algiers, 2007.]

Al-Bayhaqī, Abū al-Ḥasan 'Alī b. Zayd. 1946. *Tārīḫ Ḥukamā' al-Islām.* [*Tatimmat Ṣiwān al-Ḥikmah.*] Ed. Muḥammad Kurd 'Alī. Damascus: Maṭbū'āt al-Maǧma' al-'Ilmī al-'Arabī.

Behzadi, Lale. 2009. *Sprache und Verstehen: Al-Ǧāḥiẓ über die Vollkommenheit des Ausdrucks.* Wiesbaden: Harrassowitz.

Benjamin, Walter. 1996. "The Task of the Translator." In M.P. Bullock and M.W. Jennings, eds., *Selected Writings.* Cambridge, Mass.: Belknap Press.

Bennett, David. 2017. "The *ma'nā* in Pre-Avicennian Thought." In *Intention and Signification: Philosophy of Language across Islamic Disciplines, 800–1200.* Albert Ludwig University, Freiburg. [Unpublished.]

Bernards, Monique. 1997. *Changing Traditions: Al-Mubarrad's Refutation of Sībawayh and the Subsequent Reception of the Kitāb.* Leiden: E.J. Brill.

Bertolacci, Amos. 2006. *The Reception of Aristotle's Metaphysics in Avicenna's Kitāb al-Šifā': A Milestone of Western Metaphysical Thought.* Leiden: E.J. Brill.

———. 2011. "A Community of Translators: The Latin Medieval Versions of Avicenna's *Book of the Cure.*" In C.J. Mews and J.N. Crossley, eds., *Communities of Learning: Networks and the Shaping of Intellectual Identity in Europe, 1100–1500.* Turnhout: Brepols.

Bettini, Lidia. 2011. "On *lafḏ* and *ma'nā* Again." In G. Lancioni and L. Bettini, eds., *The Word in Arabic.* Leiden: E.J. Brill.

Biesterfeldt, Hans Hinrich. 2017. "Ibn Farīghūn." In G. Krämer, D. Matringe, J. Nawas and E. Rowson, eds., *Encyclopaedia of Islam, THREE.* Brill Online.

Bird, Alexander. 2014. *Thomas Kuhn.* Durham: Routledge.

Black, Deborah L. 1990. *Logic and Aristotle's "Rhetoric" and "Poetics" in Medieval Arabic Philosophy.* Leiden: E.J. Brill.

———. 1999. "Mental Existence in Thomas Aquinas and Avicenna." *Mediaeval Studies* 61: 45–79.

———. 2010. "Intentionality in Medieval Arabic Philosophy." *Quaestio* 10: 65–81.

Boethius. 2010. *Boethius on Aristotle, "On Interpretation" 1–3.* Trans. Andrew Smith. London: Duckworth.

Brockelmann, Carl. 1996a. *Geschichte der arabischen Litteratur.* [*GAL.*] Leiden / New York: E.J. Brill.

———. 1996b. *Geschichte der arabischen Litteratur: Supplementband.* [*GALS.*] Leiden / New York: E.J. Brill.

Brodersen, Angelika. 2014. *Der unbekannte kalām.* Berlin: Lit Verlag.

Al-Buḥturī, Abū 'Ubādah al-Walīd. 1963–. *Dīwān.* Ed. Ḥasan Kāmil aṣ-Ṣayrafī. Cairo: Dār al-Ma'ārif.

de Callataÿ, Godefroid. 2005. *Ikhwan al-Safa': A Brotherhood of Idealists on the Fringe of Orthodox Islam.* Oxford: Oneworld.

Campbell, Donald T. 1958. "Common Fate, Similarity, and Other Indices of the Status of Aggregates of Persons as Social Entities." *Systems Research and Behavioural Science* 3: 14–25.

Cavell, Stanley. 2002. *Must We Mean What We Say? A Book of Essays.* Cambridge: Cambridge University Press.

Cesalli, Laurent, and Nadja Germann. 2008. "Signification and Truth Epistemology at the Crossroads of Semantics and Ontology in Augustine's Early Philosophical Writings." *Vivarium* 46: 123–54.

Cohen, S. Marc. 2016. "Aristotle's *Metaphysics.*" In E.N. Zalta, ed., *The Stanford Encyclopedia of Philosophy,* winter edition. https://plato.stanford.edu/archives/win2016/entries/aristotle-metaphysics/.

Coleridge, Samuel Taylor. 1816. *The Statesman's Manual.* London: Gale and Fenner.

Copeland, Rita, and Ineke Sluiter. 2012. *Medieval Grammar and Rhetoric: Language Arts and Literary Theory, AD 300–1475.* Oxford: Oxford University Press.

Creswell, Robyn S. 2009. "Abū l-'Atāhiya." In G. Krämer, D. Matringe, J. Nawas, and E. Rowson, eds., *Encyclopaedia of Islam, THREE.* Brill Online.

———. 2016. "Is Arabic Untranslatable?" *Public Culture* 28: 447–56.

Crivelli, Paolo. 2004. *Aristotle on Truth.* Cambridge: Cambridge University Press.

Crone, Patricia. 2009. "Atheism (Pre-modern)." In G. Krämer, D. Matringe, J. Nawas, and E. Rowson, eds., *Encyclopaedia of Islam, THREE.* Brill Online.

———. 2012. "Dahrīs." In G. Krämer, D. Matringe, J. Nawas, and E. Rowson, eds., *Encyclopaedia of Islam, THREE.* Brill Online.

Cross, Richard. 2009. "Some Varieties of Semantic Externalism in Duns Scotus's Cognitive Psychology." In D. Perler, ed., *Transformations of the Soul: Aristotelian Psychology, 1250–1650.* Leiden: E.J. Brill.

Aḏ-Ḏahabī, Šams ad-Dīn Muḥammad b. Aḥmad. 1985. *Siyar Aʿlām an-Nubalāʾ*. Ed. Šuʿayb al-Arnaʾūṭ. 23 vols. Beirut: Muʾassasat ar-Risālah.

———. 1990–2001. *Tārīḫ al-Islām wa-Wafayāt al-Mašāhīr wa-l-Aʿlām*. Ed. ʿUmar Tadmurī. 53 vols. Beirut: Dār al-Kitāb al-ʿArabī.

———. 2004. *Siyar Aʿlām an-Nubalāʾ*. Ed. Muṣṭafā ʿAbd al-Qādir ʿAṭāʾ. 16 vols. Beirut: Dār al-Kutub al-ʿIlmīyah.

Daiber, Hans. 1975. *Das theologisch-philosophische System des Muʿammar ibn ʿAbbād as-Sulamī (gest. 830 n. Chr.)*. Wiesbaden: Orient-Institut der Deutschen Morgenländischen Gesellschaft.

———. 2015. "Muʿammar b. ʿAbbād." In P. Bearman, T. Bianquis, C. E. Bosworth, E. van Donzel, and W. P. Heinrichs, eds., *Encyclopaedia of Islam,* 2nd ed. Brill Online.

D'Ancona, Cristina. 2013. "Greek Sources in Arabic and Islamic Philosophy." In E. N. Zalta, ed., *The Stanford Encyclopedia of Philosophy,* summer edition. http://plato.stanford.edu/.

Ad-Dārimī, Abū Saʿīd ʿUṯmān. 2007. "Kitāb Radd al-Imām ad-Dārimī ʿUṯmān b. Saʿīd ʿalā al-Marīsī al-ʿAnīd." In ʿ. S. An-Naššār and ʿ. aṭ-Ṭālibī, eds., *ʿAqāʾid as-Salaf.* Cairo: Dār as-Salām.

Davidson, Donald. 2006. "Pursuit of the Concept of Truth." In *The Philosophical Essays of Donald Davidson,* electronic edition. Charlottesville: InteLex Corp.

Davidson, Herbert A. 1969. "John Philoponus as a Source of Medieval Islamic and Jewish Proofs of Creation." *Journal of the American Oriental Society* 89: 357–91.

———. 1987. *Proofs for Eternity, Creation, and the Existence of God in Medieval Islamic and Jewish Philosophy.* New York: Oxford University Press.

Dhanani, Alnoor. 1994. *The Physical Theory of Kalām: Atoms, Space, and Void in Basrian Muʿtazilī Cosmology.* Leiden: E. J. Brill.

———. 2015. "The Impact of Ibn Sīnā's Critique of Atomism on Subsequent *Kalām* Discussions of Atomism." *Arabic Sciences and Philosophy* 25: 79–104.

Eichner, Heidrun. 2010. "Das avicennische Corpus Aristotelicum: Zur Virtualisierung des Aristotelestextes in der postavicennischen Tradition." In R. Goulet and U. Rudolph, eds., *Entre orient et occident: La philosophie et la science gréco-romaines dans le monde arabe.* Geneva: Vandœuvres.

El-Cheikh, Nadia Maria. 2002. "Women's History: A Study of Al-Tanūkhī." In M. Marín and R. Deguilhem, eds., *Writing the Feminine: Women in Arab Sources.* London: I. B. Tauris.

———. 2005. "Revisiting the Abbasid Harems." *Journal of Middle East Women's Studies* 1: 1–19.

———. 2015. *Women, Islam, and Abbasid Identity.* Cambridge, Mass.: Harvard University Press.

El Ferrane, Mohamed Ait. 1990. *Die Maʿnā-Theorie bei ʿAbdalqāhir al-Ǧurǧānī (gestorben 471/1079): Versuch einer Analyse der poetischen Sprache.* Frankfurt: Peter Lang.

El-Rouayheb, Khaled. 2006. "Opening the Gate of Verification: The Forgotten Arab-Islamic Florescence of the 17th Century." *International Journal of Middle East Studies* 38: 263–81.

———. 2010. *Relational Syllogisms and the History of Arabic Logic, 900–1900.* Leiden: E. J. Brill.

———. 2012. "Post-Avicennan Logicians on the Subject Matter of Logic: Some Thirteenth- and Fourteenth-Century Discussions." *Arabic Science and Philosophy* 22: 69–90.

———. 2015. *Islamic Intellectual History in the Seventeenth Century: Scholarly Currents in the Ottoman Empire and the Maghreb.* New York: Cambridge University Press.

Encyclopedia of Arabic Literature. 1998. London / New York: Routledge.

Endress, Gerhard. 1986. "Grammatik und Logik: Arabische Philologie und griechische Philosophie im Widerstreit." In B. Mojsisch, ed., *Sprachphilosophie in Antike und Mittelalter.* Amsterdam: Grüner.

———. 1987. "Die wissenschaftliche Literatur." In H. Gätje, ed., *Grundriss der arabischen Philologie.* Volume 2, *Literaturwissenschaft.* Wiesbaden: Dr. Ludwig Reichert.

———. 1989. "Die griechisch-arabischen Übersetzungen und die Sprache der arabischen Wissenschaften." In Gerhard Endress and Marita Schmeink, eds., *Symposium Graeco-Arabicum,* vol. 2, *Akten des Zweiten Symposium Graeco-Arabicum, Ruhr-Universität Bochum, 3.–5. März 1987.* Amsterdam: Grüner.

———. 2002. "The Language of Demonstration: Translating Science and the Formation of Terminology in Arabic Philosophy and Science." *Early Science and Medicine* 7: 231–54.

van Ess, Josef. 1966. *Die Erkenntnislehre des ʿAḍudaddīn al-Īcī: Übersetzung und Kommentar des 1. Buches seiner Mawāqif.* Wiesbaden: Steiner.

———. 1991–95. *Theologie und Gesellschaft im 2. und 3. Jahrhundert Hidschra.* Berlin: De Gruyter.

Al-Fārābī, Abū Naṣr Muḥammad. 1972. *Kitāb fī al-Manṭiq: Al-ʿIbārah.* Ed. Muḥammad Salīm Sālim. Cairo: Dār al-Kutub.

———. 1986a. *Risālatān Falsafiyatān.* Ed. Ǧaʿfar Āl Yāsīn. Beirut: Dār al-Manāhil.

———. 1986b. *Šarḥ al-Fārābī li-Kitāb Arisṭūṭālīs fī l-ʿIbārah.* Ed. Wilhelm Kutsch and Stanley Marrow. Beirut: Dār al-Mašriq.

Farahat, Omar. 2016. "Commands as Divine Attributes: Islamic Jurisprudence and the *Euthyphro* Question." *Journal of Religious Ethics* 44: 581–605.

Al-Farazdaq, Hammām b. Ġālib. 1987. *Dīwān.* Ed. ʿAlī Fāʿūr. Beirut: Dār al-Kutub al-ʿIlmīyah.

Al-Farrāʾ, Yaḥyā b. Ziyād. 1960. *Maʿānī al-Qurʾān.* Ed. Aḥmad Yūsuf Naǧātī, Muḥammad ʿAlī Naǧǧār, ʿAbd al-Fattāḥ Ismāʿīl Šalabī, and ʿAlī al-Naǧdī Nāṣif. 3 vols. Cairo: Al-Hayʾah al-Miṣrīyah al-ʿĀmmah li-l-Kitāb. [Reprint, Beirut: ʿĀlam al-Kutub, 1983.]

Farrin, Raymond. 2011. *Abundance from the Desert: Classical Arabic Poetry.* Syracuse: Syracuse University Press.

Frank, Richard M. 1967. "*Al-maʿnà:* Some Reflections on the Technical Meanings of the Term in the *Kalām* and Its Use in the Physics of Muʿammar." *Journal of the American Oriental Society* 87: 248–59.

———. 1968. "The *Kalâm,* an Art of Contradiction-Making or Theological Science? Some Remarks on the Question." *Journal of the American Oriental Society* 88: 295–309. [Review of *Le problème des attributs divins dans la doctrine d'al-Ašʿarî et de ses premiers grands disciples,* by Michel Allard.]

———. 1969. "The Divine Attributes according to the Teaching of Abū l-Hudhayl al-ʿAllāf." *Le Muséon: Revue d'Études Orientales* 82: 451–506. [Reprinted in Frank, *Texts and Studies on the Development and History of Kalām,* ed. Dimitri Gutas, vol. 2, *Early Islamic Theology: The Muʿtazilites and al-Ashʿarī.* Aldershot: Ashgate, 2007.]

———. 1978. *Beings and Their Attributes: The Teaching of the Basrian School of the Muʿtazila in the Classical Period.* Albany: State University of New York Press.

———. 1981. "Meanings Are Spoken of in Many Ways: The Earlier Arab Grammarians." *Le Muséon: Revue d'Études Orientales* 94: 259–319. [Reprinted in Frank, *Texts and Studies on the Development and History of Kalām*, ed. Dimitri Gutas, vol. 1, *Philosophy, Theology and Mysticism in Medieval Islam*. Aldershot: Ashgate, 2005.]

———. 1982. "Attribute, Attribution, and Being: Three Islamic Views." In P. Morewedge, ed., *Philosophies of Existence Ancient and Medieval*. New York: Fordham University Press. [Reprinted in Frank, *Texts and Studies on the Development and History of Kalām*, ed. Dimitri Gutas, vol. 3, *Classical Islamic Theology: The Ash'arites*. Aldershot: Ashgate, 2008.]

———. 1983. "Moral Obligation in Classical Muslim Theology." *Journal of Religious Ethics* 11: 204–23. [Reprinted in Frank, *Texts and Studies on the Development and History of Kalām*, ed. Dimitri Gutas, vol. 3, *Classical Islamic Theology: The Ash'arites*. Aldershot: Ashgate, 2008.]

———. 1984. "Bodies and Atoms: The Ash'arite Analysis." In M. E. Marmura, ed., *Islamic Theology and Philosophy: Studies in Honor of George F. Hourani*. Albany: State University of New York Press. [Reprinted in Frank, *Texts and Studies on the Development and History of Kalām*, ed. Dimitri Gutas, vol. 3, *Classical Islamic Theology: The Ash'arites*. Aldershot: Ashgate, 2008.]

———. 1989. "Knowledge and *Taqlīd*: The Foundations of Religious Belief in Classical Ash'arism." *Journal of the American Oriental Society* 109: 37–62. [Reprinted in Frank, *Texts and Studies on the Development and History of Kalām*, ed. Dimitri Gutas, vol. 3, *Classical Islamic Theology: The Ash'arites*. Aldershot: Ashgate, 2008.]

———. 1996. "Hearing and Saying What Was Said." *Journal of the American Oriental Society* 116: 611–18. [Reprinted in Frank, *Texts and Studies on the Development and History of Kalām*, ed. Dimitri Gutas, vol. 3, *Classical Islamic Theology: The Ash'arites*. Aldershot: Ashgate, 2008.]

———. 1999. "The Aš'arite Ontology, I: Primary Entities." *Arabic Sciences and Philosophy* 9: 163–231. [Reprinted in Frank, *Texts and Studies on the Development and History of Kalām*, ed. Dimitri Gutas, vol. 3, *Classical Islamic Theology: The Ash'arites*. Aldershot: Ashgate, 2008.]

———. 2000. "The Non-Existent and the Possible in Classical Ash'arite Teaching." *MIDEO* 24: 1–37. [Reprinted in Frank, *Texts and Studies on the Development and History of Kalām*, ed. Dimitri Gutas, vol. 3, *Classical Islamic Theology: The Ash'arites*. Aldershot: Ashgate, 2008.]

———. 2004. "Al-Aḥkām in Classical Aš'arite Teaching." In R. G. Morelon and A. Hasnawi, eds., *De Zénon d'Élée à Poincaré: Recueil d'études en hommage à Roshdi Rashed*. Paris: Peeters. [Reprinted in Frank, *Texts and Studies on the Development and History of Kalām*, ed. Dimitri Gutas, vol. 3, *Classical Islamic Theology: The Ash'arites*. Aldershot: Ashgate, 2008.]

Friedman, Rachel Ann. 2015. "Clarity, Communication, and Understandability: Theorizing Language in al-Bāqillānī's I'jāz al-Qur'ān and Uṣūl al-Fiqh Texts." Ph.D. dissertation, University of California, Berkeley.

Al-Ǧāḥiẓ, Abū 'Uṯmān 'Amr b. Baḥr. 1960. *Al-Bayān wa-t-Tabyīn*. Ed. 'Abd as-Salām Muḥammad Hārūn. 4 vols. Cairo: Maktabat al-Ḫānǧī.

———. 1965a. "Ar-Radd 'alā an-Naṣārā." In '. A.-S. M. Hārūn, ed., *Rasā'il al-Ǧāḥiẓ*. Cairo: Maktabat al-Ḫānǧī.

———. 1965b. "Risālah fī l-Ǧidd wa-l-Hazl." In ʿ. A.-S. M. Hārūn, ed., *Rasāʾil al-Ǧāḥiẓ*. Cairo: Maktabat al-Ḫānǧī.

———. 1966–69. *Kitāb al-Ḥayawān*. Ed. ʿAbd as-Salām Muḥammad Hārūn. Cairo: Muṣṭafā al-Bābī al-Ḥalabī.

Galen. 1821–33. *Claudii Galeni Opera Omnia*. Ed. Karl Gottlob Kühn. 20 vols. Leipzig: Prostat in Officina Libraria Car. Cnoblochii.

———. 1976. *Galen on the Affected Parts: Translation from the Greek Text with Explanatory Notes*. Basel: S. Karger.

Gaon, Saadiya Ben Joseph. 1880. *Kitāb al-Amānāt wa-l-Iʿtiqād*. Ed. S. Landauer. Leiden: E. J. Brill.

———. 1948. *The Book of Beliefs and Opinions*. Trans. Samuel Rosenblatt. New Haven: Yale University Press.

Garofalo, Ivan. 1997. "La traduzione araba del 'De Locis Affectis' di Galeno." *Studi Classici e Orientali* 45: 13–63.

Al-Ǧawharǧī, Muḥammad ʿAdnān. 1986. "Raʾy fī Taḥdīd ʿAṣr ar-Rāġib al-Iṣfahānī." *Maǧallat Maǧmaʿ al-Luġah al-ʿArabīyah bi-Dimašq* 61: 191–200.

Al-Ġazālī, Abū Ḥāmid. 1986. *Al-Maqṣad al-Asnā fī Šarḥ Maʿānī Asmāʾ Allāh al-Ḥusnā*. Ed. Fadlou A. Shehadi. Beirut: Dār al-Mašriq.

van Gelder, Geert Jan H. 1982. *Beyond the Line: Classical Arabic Literary Critics on the Coherence and Unity of the Poem*. Leiden: E. J. Brill.

van Gelder, Geert Jan H., and Marlé Hammond. 2008. *Takhyīl: The Imaginary in Classical Arabic Poetics*. Cambridge: Gibb Memorial Trust.

Georr, Khalil. 1948. *Les «Catégories» d'Aristote dans leurs versions Syro-Arabes*. Beirut: Institut Français de Damas.

Germann, Nadja. 2008. "Logik zwischen 'Kunst' und 'Wissenschaft': Avicenna zum Status der Logik in seiner *Isagoge*." *Recherches de Théologie et Philosophie Médiévales* 75: 1–32.

Ghersetti, Antonella. 2011. "'Word' in the Linguistic Thinking of ʿAbd al-Qāhir al-Jurjānī." In G. Lancioni and L. Bettini, eds., *The Word in Arabic*. Leiden: E. J. Brill.

Gilliot, Claude and Pierre Larcher. 2016. "Language and Style of the Qurʾān." In J. D. McAuliffe, ed., *Encyclopaedia of the Qurʾān*. Brill Online.

Gimaret, Daniel 1985. "Un document majeur pour l'histoire du *kalām:* Le *Muǧarrad Maqālāt al-Ašʿarī* d'ibn Fūrak." *Arabica* 32: 185–218.

———. 1988. *Les noms divins en islam: Exégèse lexicographique et théologique*. Paris: Cerf.

———. 1990. *La doctrine d'al-Ashʿarī*. Paris: Cerf.

Gleave, Robert. 2012. *Islam and Literalism: Literal Meaning and Interpretation in Islamic Legal Theory*. Edinburgh: Edinburgh University Press.

Greene, Roland. 2013. *Five Words: Critical Semantics in the Age of Shakespeare and Cervantes*. Chicago: University of Chicago Press.

Gregory of Nazianzus. 2001. *Sancti Gregorii Nazianzeni Opera: Versio Arabica Antiqua; Orationes I, XLV, XLIV*. Ed. Laurence Tuerlinckx. Turnhout: Brepols.

Griffel, Frank. 2017. "Contradictions and Lots of Ambiguity: Two New Perspectives on Premodern (and Postclassical) Islamic Societies." *Bustan: The Middle East Book Review* 8(1): 1–21.

Gruendler, Beatrice. 2005. "Motif vs. Genre: Reflections on the *Dīwān al-Maʿānī* of Abū Hilāl al-ʿAskarī." In T. Bauer and A. Neuwirth, eds., *Ghazal as World Literature*. Volume 1, *Transformations of a Literary Genre*. Beirut/Stuttgart: Ergon-Verlag.

———. 2007. "Al-ʿAskarī, Abū Hilāl." In G. Krämer, D. Matringe, J. Nawas, and E. Rowson, eds., *Encyclopaedia of Islam, THREE.* Brill Online.

Al-Ǧurǧānī, ʿAbd al-Qāhir b. ʿAbd ar-Raḥmān. 1172/77. *Dalāʾil al-Iʿǧāz.* MS Hüseyin Çelebi 913. Bursa: İnebey Yazma Eser Kütüphanesi.

———. 1952. *Dalāʾil al-Iʿǧāz.* Ed. Rašīd Riḍā. Cairo: Dār al-Manār.

———. 1954. *Asrār al-Balāġah: The Mysteries of Eloquence.* Ed. Helmut Ritter. Istanbul: Government Press.

———. 1959a. *Die Geheimnisse der Wortkunst (Asrār al-Balāġa).* Trans. Helmut Ritter. Wiesbaden: Steiner.

———. 1959b. "Ar-Risālah aš-Šāfiyah." In M. Ḫ. Allāh, ed., *Ṯalāṯ Rasāʾil fī Iʿǧāz al-Qurʾān.* Cairo: Dār al-Maʿārif.

———. 196-. *Šarḥ Miʾat ʿĀmil.* Delhi: Kitābḫānah-e Rāšidīyah.

———. 1972. *Al-Ǧumal.* Ed. ʿAlī Ḥaydar. Damascus: Maǧmaʿ al-Luġah al-ʿArabīyah.

———. 1978. *Dalāʾil al-Iʿǧāz.* Ed. Muḥammad Maḥmūd aš-Šinqīṭī. Beirut: Dār al-Maʿrifah. [Reprint: 1987.]

———. 1982. *Al-Muqtaṣid fī Šarḥ al-Īḍāḥ.* Ed. Kāẓim Baḥr al-Marǧān. 2 vols. Baghdad: Manšūrāt Wizārat aṯ-Ṯaqāfah wa-l-Aʿlām.

———. 1987. *Kitāb al-Miftāḥ fī aṣ-Ṣarf.* Ed. ʿAlī Tawfīq al-Ḥamd. Irbid: Muʾassasat ar-Risālah.

———. 1988. *Kitāb fī at-Taṣrīf.* Ed. Muḥsin Sālim al-ʿUmayrī. Mecca: Maktabat at-Turāṯ.

———. 1990. *Kitāb al-Ǧumal fī n-Naḥw.* Ed. Yusrī ʿAbd al-Ġanī ʿAbdallāh. Beirut: Dār al-Kutub al-ʿIlmīyah.

———. 1992a. *Dalāʾil al-Iʿǧāz.* Ed. Maḥmūd Muḥammad Šākir. Cairo: Dār al-Madanī.

———. 1992b. "Ar-Risālah aš-Šāfiyah." In M. M. Šākir, ed., *Dalāʾil al-Iʿǧāz.* Cairo: Dār al-Madanī.

———. 2006. *Les signes d'inimitabilite en grammaire de l'expression.* [*Dalāʾil al-Iʿǧāz.*] Trans. Hrazem Rachad. Tangier: Université Abdelmalik Essaâdi, École Supérieure Roi Fahd de Traduction.

———. 2007. *Al-Muqtaṣid fī Šarḥ at-Takmilah.* Ed. Aḥmad b. ʿAbdallāh ad-Dawīš. 3 vols. Riyadh: Ǧāmiʿat al-Imām Muḥammad b. Suʿūd.

Gutas, Dimitri. 1983. "Paul the Persian on the Classification of the Parts of Aristotle's Philosophy: A Milestone between Alexandria and Bagdad." *Der Islam* 60: 231–67.

———. 1988. *Avicenna and the Aristotelian Tradition: Introduction to Reading Avicenna's Philosophical Works.* Leiden: E. J. Brill.

———. 1998. *Greek Thought, Arabic Culture: The Graeco-Arabic Translation Movement in Baghdad and Early ʿAbbāsid Society (2nd–4th/8th–10th Centuries).* London: Routledge.

———. 2004. "Geometry and the Rebirth of Philosophy in Arabic with al-Kindī." In G. Endress, R. Arnzen, and J. Thielmann, eds., *Words, Texts, and Concepts Cruising the Mediterranean Sea: Studies on the Sources, Contents and Influences of Islamic Civilization and Arabic Philosophy and Science Dedicated to Gerhard Endress on His Sixty-Fifth Birthday.* Leuven: Peeters.

———. 2005. "The Logic of Theology (*kalām*) in Avicenna." In D. Perler and U. Rudolph, eds., *Logik und Theologie: Das Organon im arabischen und im lateinischen Mittelalter.* Leiden: E. J. Brill.

———. 2010a. "Greek Philosophical Works Translated into Arabic." In R. Pasnau and C. van Dyke, eds., *The Cambridge History of Medieval Philosophy.* Cambridge: Cambridge University Press.

———. 2010b. "Origins in Baghdad." In R. Pasnau and C. van Dyke, eds., *The Cambridge History of Medieval Philosophy.* Cambridge: Cambridge University Press.

———. 2012. "The Empiricism of Avicenna." *Oriens* 40(2): 391–436.

———. 2016. "Ibn Sina [Avicenna]." In E.N. Zalta, ed., *The Stanford Encyclopedia of Philosophy,* fall edition. https://plato.stanford.edu/archives/fall2016/entries/ibn-sina/.

Al-Ǧuwaynī, Imām al-Ḥaramayn ʿAbd al-Malik. 1979. *Al-Burhān fī Uṣūl al-Fiqh.* Ed. ʿAbd al-ʿAẓīm ad-Dīb. 2 vols. Qatar: Kullīyat aš-Šarīʿah Ǧāmiʿat Qaṭar.

Gyekye, Kwame. 1971. "The Terms 'Prima Intentio' and 'Secunda Intentio' in Arabic Logic." *Speculum* 46: 32–38.

Ḫalafallāh, Muḥammad. 1944. "Naẓarīyat ʿAbd al-Qāhir al-Ǧurǧānī fī Asrār al-Balāġah." *Maǧallat Kullīyat al-Ādāb (Ǧāmiʿat al-Iskandarīyah)* 2: 14–84.

Al-Ḫalīl b. Aḥmad. 1980. *Kitāb al-ʿAyn.* Ed. Mahdī al-Maḫzūmī and Ibrāhīm Sāmarrāʾī. 8 vols. in 4. Baghdad: Wizārat aṯ-Ṯaqāfah wa-l-Iʿlām.

Hamori, Andras. 1974. *On the Art of Medieval Arabic Literature.* Princeton: Princeton University Press.

Harb, Lara. 2013. "Poetic Marvels: Wonder and Aesthetic Experience in Medieval Arabic Literary Theory." Ph.D. dissertation, New York University.

———. 2015. "Form, Content, and the Inimitability of the Qurʾān in ʿAbd al-Qāhir al-Jurjānī's Works." *Middle Eastern Literatures* 18: 301–21.

———. 2017. "Al-Jurjānī, ʿAbd al-Qāhir." In G. Krämer, D. Matringe, J. Nawas, and E. Rowson, eds., *Encyclopaedia of Islam, THREE.* Brill Online.

Harb, Lara, and Alexander Key. Forthcoming. "Introduction." In Alexander Key ed., *Journal of Abbasid Studies* 5(1–2), special issue: *ʿAbd al-Qāhir al-Jurjānī.*

Al-Ḫaṭṭābī, Abū Sulaymān Ḥamd b. Muḥammad. 1959. "Bayān Iʿǧāz al-Qurʾān." In M.Ḫ. Allāh, ed., *Ṯalāṯ Rasāʾil fī Iʿǧāz al-Qurʾān.* Cairo: Dār al-Maʿārif.

Al-Ḫayyāṭ, ʿAbd ar-Raḥīm b. Muḥammad. 1957. *Kitāb al-Intiṣār wa-r-Radd ʿalā Ibn ar-Rāwandī al-Mulḥid.* Trans. and ed. Albert N. Nādir. Beirut: al-Maṭbaʿah al-Kāṯūlīkīyah.

Heemskerk, Margaretha T. 2000. *Suffering in the Muʿtazilite Theology: ʿAbd al-Jabbār's Teaching on Pain and Divine Justice.* Leiden: E.J. Brill.

———. 2007. "ʿAbd al-Jabbār b. Aḥmad al-Hamadhānī." In G. Krämer, D. Matringe, J. Nawas, and E. Rowson, eds., *Encyclopaedia of Islam, THREE.* Brill Online

Heinen, A. 2011. "Ašʿarīya." In E. Yarshater, ed., *Encyclopaedia Iranica.* Iranicaonline.

Heinrichs, Wolfhart. 1969. *Arabische Dichtung und griechische Poetik: Ḥāzim al-Qarṭāǧannīs Grundlegung der Poetik mit Hilfe aristotelischer Begriffe.* Beirut/Wiesbaden: Deutsche Morgenländische Gesellschaft / Steiner.

———. 1977. *The Hand of the Northwind: Opinions on Metaphor and the Early Meaning of istiʿāra in Arabic Poetics.* Wiesbaden: Deutsche Morgenländische Gesellschaft.

———. 1984. "On the Genesis of the *ḥaqīqa-majāz* Dichotomy." *Studia Islamica* 59: 111–40.

———. 1991/92. "Contacts between Scriptural Hermeneutics and Literary Theory in Islam: The Case of *majāz.*" *Zeitschrift für Geschichte der Arabisch-Islamischen Wissenschaften* 7: 253–84.

———. 1995. "The Classification of the Sciences and the Consolidation of Philology in Classical Islam." In J.W. Drijvers and A.A. MacDonald, eds., *Centres of Learning: Learning and Location in Pre-Modern Europe and the Near East.* Leiden / New York: E.J. Brill.

———. 1998. "*Lafẓ* and *maʿnā.*" In J.S. Meisami and P. Starkey, eds., *Encyclopedia of Arabic Literature.* London / New York: Routledge.

———. 2008. "*Takhyīl:* Make-Believe and Image Creation in Arabic Literary Theory." In G. J. H. van Gelder and M. Hammond, eds., *Takhyīl: The Imaginary in Classical Arabic Poetics.* Cambridge: Gibb Memorial Trust.

———. 2016. "On the Figurative (*majāz*) in Muslim Interpretation and Legal Hermeneutics." In M. Z. Cohen, ed., *Interpreting Scriptures in Judaism, Christianity, and Islam: Overlapping Inquiries.* Cambridge: Cambridge University Press.

Hildebrandt, Thomas. 2007. "Between Muʿtazilism and Mysticism: How Much of a Muʿtazilite Is Naṣr Ḥāmid Abū Zayd?" In C. Adang, S. Schmidtke, and D. Sklare, eds., *A Common Rationality: Muʿtazilism in Islam and Judaism.* Würzburg: Ergon-Verlag.

Hodges, Wilfred. 2011. *A Note: Ibn Sīnā on the Subject of Logic.* http://wilfridhodges.co.uk/arabic14.pdf. [Accessed 6 September 2017.]

———. 2012. *What Would Count as Ibn Sīnā (11th-Century Persia) Having First-Order Logic?* http://wilfridhodges.co.uk/arabic17.pdf. [Accessed 6 September 2017.]

———. 2016. *Ibn Sīnā on the Definition of Logic.* http://wilfridhodges.co.uk/arabic41.pdf. [Draft; accessed 6 September 2017.]

Al-Ḫwānsārī, Muḥammad Bāqir b. Zayn al-ʿĀbidīn. 1991. *Rawḍāt al-Ğannāt fī Aḥwāl al-ʿUlamāʾ wa-s-Sādāt.* 8 vols. Beirut: ad-Dār al-Islāmīyah.

Ibn Abī Ṭāhir Ṭayfūr, Aḥmad. 1949. *Sechster Band des Kitâb Baġdâd, von Aḥmad ibn Abî Ṭâhir Ṭaifûr.* Trans. and ed. Hans Keller. 2 vols. in 1. Cairo: ʿIzzat al-ʿAṭṭār al-Ḥusaynī.

Ibn Abī Uṣaybiʿah, Aḥmad b. al-Qāsim. 1884. *Kitāb fī Ṭabaqāt al-Aṭibbāʾ.* Ed. August Müller. 2 vols. in 1. Königsberg/Cairo: Selbstverlag.

Ibn al-Anbārī, Abū al-Barakāt ʿAbd ar-Raḥmān. 1970. *Nuzhat al-Alibbāʾ fī Ṭabaqāt al-Udabāʾ.* Ed. Ibrāhīm as-Sāmarrāʾī. Baghdad: Maktabat al-Andalus.

Ibn ʿAsākir, Abū al-Qāsim ʿAlī. 1928. *Tabyīn Kaḏib al-Muftarī.* Ed. al-Qudsī. Damascus: Maktabat at-Tawfīq.

Ibn Fāris, Abū al-Ḥusayn Aḥmad al-Qazwīnī. 1946–52. *Muʿğam Maqāyīs al-Luġah.* Ed. ʿAbd as-Salām Muḥammad Hārūn. Cairo: ʿĪsā al-Bābī al-Ḥalabī.

Ibn Farīʿūn, M.[?] 1985. *Jawāmiʿ al-ʿUlūm.* Frankfurt: Johann Wolfgang Goethe University, Institute for the History of Arabic-Islamic Science.

Ibn Fūrak, Abū Bakr Muḥammad. 1906. "Muqaddimah fī Nukat min Uṣūl al-Fiqh." In M. A. Sulaymānī, ed., *Mağmūʿ Rasāʾil fī Uṣūl al-Fiqh.* Beirut: al-Maṭbaʿah al-Ahlīyah.

———. 1987. *Muğarrad Maqālāt al-Ašʿarī.* Ed. Daniel Gimaret. Beirut: Dār al-Mašriq.

———. 1999. *Kitāb al-Ḥudūd fī al-Uṣūl: Al-ḥudūd wa-al-muwāḍaʿāt.* Ed. Muḥammad Sulaymānī. Beirut: Dār al-Ġarb al-Islāmī.

———. 2003. *Kitāb Muškil al-Ḥadīṯ aw Taʾwīl al-Aḫbār al-Mutašābihah.* Ed. Daniel Gimaret. Damascus: Institut Français de Damas.

———. 2009a. *Tafsīr al-Qurʾān al-ʿAẓīm.* Ed. ʿIlāl ʿAbd al-Qādir Bandwīš. M.A. thesis, Ğāmiʿat Umm al-Qurā, Mecca. [Quran 23:1–32:73.]

———. 2009b. *Tafsīr al-Qurʾān al-ʿAẓīm.* Ed. ʿĀṭif b. Kāmil b. Ṣāliḥ Buḫārī. M.A. thesis, Ğāmiʿat Umm al-Qurā, Mecca. [Quran 33:1–40:85.]

———. 2009c. *Tafsīr al-Qurʾān al-ʿAẓīm.* Ed. Sahīmat Bint Muḥammad Saʿīd Muḥammad Aḥmad Buḫārī. M.A. thesis, Ğāmiʿat Umm al-Qurā, Mecca. [Quran 71:1–114:6.]

Ibn al-Ğawzī, Abū al-Farağ ʿAbd ar-Raḥmān. 1983. *Talbīs Iblīs.* Beirut: Dār al-Qalam. [Reprint, Beirut: Dār Ṣādir, 1968.]

Ibn Ğinnī, Abū Fatḥ ʿUṯmān. 1952–56. *Al-Ḫaṣāʾiṣ.* Cairo: Dār al-Kutub al-Miṣrīyah.

———. 2004. *Al-Fasr: Šarḥ Ibn Ǧinnī al-Kabīr ʿalā Dīwān al-Mutanabbī.* Ed. Riḍā Raǧab. 5 vols. Damascus: Dār al-Yanābīʿ.

Ibn Ḫālawayh, Ḥusayn b. Aḥmad. 2017. *Al-Ḥusayn ibn Aḥmad ibn Khālawayh's Names of the Lion.* Trans. David Larsen. Seattle: Wave Books.

Ibn Ḫallikān, Abū al-ʿAbbās Šams ad-Dīn. 1948. *Wafayāt al-Aʿyān wa-Anbāʾ Abnāʾ az-Zamān.* Ed. Muḥammad Muḥyī ad-Dīn ʿAbd al-Ḥamīd. 6 vols. Cairo: Maktabat an-Nahḍah al-Miṣrīyah.

Ibn Ḥazm, Abū Muḥammad ʿAlī b. Aḥmad. 1899–1903. *Kitāb al-Faṣl fī l-Milal wa-l-Ahwāʾ wa-n-Niḥal.* 5 vols. in 2. Cairo: al-Maṭbaʿah al-Adabīyah.

Ibn Mattawayh, Abū Muḥammad al-Ḥasan. 1975. *At-Taḏkirah fī Aḥkām al-Ǧawāhir wa-l-Aʿrāḍ.* Ed. Sāmī Naṣr Luṭf and Fayṣal Badr ʿAwn. Cairo: Dār aṯ-Ṯaqāfah.

———. 2006. *An Anonymous Commentary on Kitāb al-Tadhkira by Ibn Mattawayh: Facsimile Edition of Mahdavi Codex 514 (6th/12th Century).* Ed. Sabine Schmidtke. Tehran: Iranian Institute of Philosophy; and Institute of Islamic Studies, Free University of Berlin.

———. 2009. *At-Taḏkirah fī Aḥkām al-Ǧawāhir wa-l-Aʿrāḍ.* Ed. Daniel Gimaret. 2 vols. Cairo: al-Maʿhad al-ʿIlmī al-Firansī.

Ibn al-Muqaffaʿ. 1978. "Al-Manṭiq." In M. T. Dānešpažūh, ed., *Al-Manṭiq li-Ibn al-Muqaffaʿ wa-Ḥudūd al-Manṭiq li-Ibn al-Bihrīz.* Tehran: Anǧumān-e Šāhanšāhī-ye Falsafah-ye Īrān.

Ibn al-Muʿtazz, ʿAbdallāh. 1961. *Dīwān.* Ed. Karim al-Bustānī. Beirut: Dār Ṣādir.

Ibn Qutaybah, Abū Muḥammad ʿAbdallāh. 1984. *Kitāb al-Maʿānī al-Kabīr.* [Ed. F. Krenkow.] 3 vols. Beirut: Dār al-Kutub al-ʿIlmīyah.

Ibn Rušd, Abū al-Walīd Muḥammad b. Aḥmad, and Aristotle. 1938–52. *Tafsīr Mā Baʿd aṭ-Ṭabīʿah.* Ed. Maurice Bouyges. 4 vols. Beirut: Imprimerie Catholique.

Ibn aṣ-Ṣalāḥ, Taqī ad-Dīn Abū ʿUmar ʿUṯmān. 1992. *Ṭabaqāt al-Fuqahāʾ aš-Šāfiʿīyah.* Ed. Muḥyī ad-Dīn ʿAlī Naǧīb. 2 vols. Beirut: Dār al-Bašāʾir al-Islāmīyah.

Ibn Sīnā, Abū ʿAlī al-Ḥusayn. 1508. "Logica." Trans. Dominicus Gundisalvus and Joannes Hispalensis. In C. Fabrianensis, ed., *Opera,* fol. 2–12. Venice: Per Bonetum Locatellum Bergomensem. [Reprint, Frankfurt: Minerva, 1961.]

———. 1938. *An-Naǧāh fī l-Ḥikmah al-Manṭiqīyah wa-t-Ṭabīʿīyah wa-l-Ilāhīyah.* Cairo: Muḥyī ad-Dīn Ṣabrī al-Kurdī.

———. 1952a. *Risālah-ye Manṭiq: Dānišnāmah-ye ʿAlāʾī.* Ed. Muḥammad Muʿīn and Muḥammad Miškāt. Tehran: Intišārāt-e Anǧumān-e Āṯār-e Millī.

———. 1952b. "Risālah fī l-Kalām ʿalā an-Nafs an-Nāṭiqah." In A. F. al-Ahwānī, ed., *Aḥwāl an-Nafs.* Cairo: Dār Iḥyāʾ al-Kutub al-ʿArabīyah. [Reprint, Paris: Dar Byblion, 2007.]

———. 1952c. "Aš-Šifāʾ: Al-Manṭiq, I (al-Madḫal)." In I. Madkūr, ed., *Aš-Šifāʾ.* Cairo: Wizārat al-Maʿārif al-ʿUmūmīyah.

———. 1956a. *Psychologie d'Ibn Sina (Avicenne) d'après son œuvre aš-Šifāʾ.* [*Aš-Šifāʾ: Aṭ-Ṭabīʿīyāt (an-Nafs).*] Trans. and ed. Ján Bakoš. 2 vols. Prague: Editions de l'Académie Tchécoslovaque des Sciences.

———. 1956b. "Aš-Šifāʾ: Al-Manṭiq, V (al-Burhān)." In I. Madkūr and A. A.-ʿ. ʿAfīfī, eds., *Aš-Šifāʾ.* Cairo: al-Hayʾah al-ʿĀmmah li-Šuʾūn al-Maṭābiʿ al-Amīrīyah.

———. 1959a. *Avicenna's "De Anima," Being the Psychological Part of Kitāb al-Shifāʾ.* Ed. Fazlur Rahman. London: Oxford University Press.

———. 1959b. "Aš-Šifāʾ: Al-Manṭiq, II (al-Maqūlāt)." In I. Madkūr, ed., *Aš-Šifāʾ.* Cairo: Wizārat aṯ-Ṯaqāfah wa-l-Iršād al-Qawmī.

———. 1970a. "Aš-Šifā': Al-Ilāhīyāt." In I. Madkūr, ed., *Aš-Šifā'*. Cairo: Dār al-Kātib al-'Arabī.

———. 1970b. "Aš-Šifā': Al-Manṭiq, III (al-'Ibārah)." In I. Madkūr, ed., *Aš-Šifā'*. Cairo: Dār al-Kātib al-'Arabī.

———. 1982. *Manṭiq al-Mašriqīyīn*. Ed. Šukrī an-Naǧǧār. Beirut: Dār al-Ḥadāṯah.

———. 2004. *The Metaphysics of the Healing: A Parallel English-Arabic Text*. Trans. Michael E. Marmura. Provo: Brigham Young University Press.

———. 2010. *The Deliverance: Logic*. Trans. Asad Q. Ahmed. Karachi: Oxford University Press.

Ibn Sīnā, Abū 'Alī al-Ḥusayn, and Naṣīr ad-Dīn aṭ-Ṭūsī. 1983–94. *Al-Išārāt wa-t-at-Tanbīhāt*. Cairo: Dār al-Ma'ārif.

Ibrahim, Bilal. 2013. "Faḫr ad-Dīn ar-Rāzī, Ibn al-Hayṯam and Aristotelian Science: Essentialism versus Phenomenalism in Post-Classical Islamic Thought." *Oriens* 41(3–4): 379–431.

Al-Īǧī, 'Aḍud ad-Dīn 'Abd ar-Raḥmān. 2010. "Risālat al-Waḍ'." In 'U. A. ar-Rāwī, ed., *Ḥāšiyah 'alā Šarḥ Risālat al-Waḍ'*. Beirut: Dār al-Kutub al-'Ilmīyah.

Iḫwān aṣ-Ṣafā'. 1957. *Rasā'il Iḫwān aṣ-Ṣafā' wa-Ḫullān al-Wafā'*. 4 vols. Beirut: Dār Ṣādir.

———. 2010–. *Rasā'il Iḫwān aṣ-Ṣafā' wa-Ḫullān al-Wafā'*. Oxford: Oxford University Press in association with the Institute of Ismaili Studies. [Critical edition and English translation: https://iis.ac.uk/series/Epistles-of-the-Brethren-of-Purity.]

Iványi, Tamás. 2015. "Luġa." In K. Versteegh, L. Edzard, and R. D. Jong, eds., *Encyclopedia of Arabic Language and Linguistics*. Brill Online.

Ivry, Alfred. 2012. "Arabic and Islamic Psychology and Philosophy of Mind." In E. N. Zalta, ed., *The Stanford Encyclopedia of Philosophy*, summer edition. https://plato.stanford.edu/archives/sum2012/entries/arabic-islamic-mind/.

Janssens, Jules. 2003. "Al-Ghazzâlî and His Use of Avicennian Texts." In M. Maróth, ed., *Problems in Arabic Philosophy*. Piliscsaba: Avicenna Institute of Middle East Studies.

Javadi, Mohsen. 2013. "Aristotle and Farabi on the Definition and Priority of Substance." In C. Kanzian and M. Legenhausen, eds., *Substance and Attribute: Western and Islamic Traditions in Dialogue*. Berlin: De Gruyter.

Al-Ka'bī, Abū Qāsim al-Balḫī. 1974. "Maqālāt al-Islāmīyīn." In F. Sayyid, ed., *Faḍl al-I'tizāl wa-Ṭabaqāt al-Mu'tazilah*. Tunis: ad-Dār at-Tūnisīyah li-n-Našr.

Kalbarczyk, Alexander. 2012. "A Hitherto Unknown Source for Studying Ibn Sīnā's Reception of Aristotle's *Categories*." *Oriens* 40: 305–54.

Kanazi, George J. 1989. *Studies in the Kitāb aṣ-Ṣinā'atayn of Abū Hilāl al-'Askarī*. Leiden: E. J. Brill.

Kant, Immanuel. 1987. *Critique of Judgment*. Indianapolis: Hackett.

Keegan, Matthew. Forthcoming. "Throwing the Reins to the Reader: Hierarchy, Jurjānian Poetics, and Al-Muṭarrizī's Commentary on the *Maqāmāt*." In Alexander Key ed., *Journal of Abbasid Studies* 5(1–2), special issue: *'Abd al-Qāhir al-Jurjānī*.

Kelsey, Sean. 2015. "Aristotle on Interpreting Nature." In M. Leunissen, ed., *Aristotle's Physics: A Critical Guide*. Cambridge: Cambridge University Press.

Key, Alexander. 2010. "Language and Literature in al-Rāġib al-Iṣfahānī." In *Reflections on Language and Knowledge in Middle Eastern Societies*. Cambridge: Cambridge Scholars Publishing.

———. 2011. "Al-Rāghib al-Iṣfahānī." In M. St. Germain and T. De Young, eds., *Essays in Arabic Literary Biography*, vol. 1. Wiesbaden: Harrassowitz.

———. 2012. "A Linguistic Frame of Mind: Ar-Rāġib al-Iṣfahānī and What It Meant to Be Ambiguous." Ph.D. dissertation, Harvard University.

———. 2015. Review of *Islam and Literalism: Literal Meaning and Interpretation in Islamic Legal Theory*, by Robert Gleave. *Journal of Near Eastern Studies* 74: 179–84.

———. Forthcoming. "Translation of Poetry from Persian to Arabic: ʿAbd al-Qāhir al-Jurjānī and Others." In Alexander Key ed., *Journal of Abbasid Studies* 5(1–2), special issue: *ʿAbd al-Qāhir al-Jurjānī*.

Key, Alexander, and Peter Adamson. 2015. "Philosophy of Language in the Medieval Arabic Tradition." In M. Cameron and R. J. Stainton, eds., *Linguistic Content: New Essays on the History of Philosophy of Language*. Oxford: Oxford University Press.

Khalfallah, Nejmeddine. 2014. *La théorie sémantique de ʿAbd al-Qāhir al-Jurjānī (m. 1078)*. Paris: L'Harmattan.

Al-Kindī, Abū Yūsuf Yaʿqūb. 1950. *Rasāʾil al-Kindī al-Falsafīyah*. Ed. Muḥammad ʿAbd al-Hādī Abū Rīdah. 2 vols. Cairo: Dār al-Fikr al-ʿArabī.

Klima, Gyula. 2013. "The Medieval Problem of Universals." In E. N. Zalta, ed., *The Stanford Encyclopedia of Philosophy*, fall edition. http://plato.stanford.edu/archives/fall2008/entries/arabic-islamic-language/.

Kneale, William, and Martha Kneale. 1962. *The Development of Logic*. Oxford: Clarendon Press.

König, Daniel G. 2013. "Augustine and Islam." In K. Pollmann and W. Otten, eds., *The Oxford Guide to the Historical Reception of Augustine*. Oxford: Oxford University Press.

Korta, Kepa, and John Perry. 2015. "Pragmatics." In E. N. Zalta, ed., *The Stanford Encyclopedia of Philosophy*, winter edition. https://plato.stanford.edu/archives/win2015/entries/pragmatics/.

Kouloughli, Djamel Eddine. 2016a. "Lafḏ." In K. Versteegh, L. Edzard, and R. D. Jong, eds., *Encyclopedia of Arabic Language and Linguistics*. Brill Online.

———. 2016b. "Maʿnā." In K. Versteegh, L. Edzard, and R. D. Jong, eds., *Encyclopedia of Arabic Language and Linguistics*. Brill Online.

Kraemer, Joel L. 1986. *Philosophy in the Renaissance of Islam: Abū Sulaymān al-Sijistānī and His Circle*. Leiden: E. J. Brill.

Kuhn, Thomas S. 2000. *The Road since Structure: Philosophical Essays, 1970–1993, with an Autobiographical Interview*. Chicago: University of Chicago Press.

———. 2009. "On Incommensurability and Translation." In M. Baker, ed., *Translation Studies*. New York: Routledge.

Lane, Edward William. 1863–93. *Arabic-English Lexicon*. London: Williams & Norgate.

Larkin, Margaret. 1995. *The Theology of Meaning: ʿAbd al-Qāhir al-Jurjānī's Theory of Discourse*. New Haven: American Oriental Society.

Larsen, David. 2007. "Means of Intelligibility." Ph.D. dissertation, University of California, Berkeley.

———. Forthcoming. "Captivity and Meaning in Classical Arabic Philology." In Alexander Key ed., *Journal of Abbasid Studies* 5(1–2), special issue: *ʿAbd al-Qāhir al-Jurjānī*.

Lawlor, Leonard. 2016. "Jacques Derrida." In E. N. Zalta, ed., *The Stanford Encyclopedia of Philosophy*, winter edition. https://plato.stanford.edu/archives/win2016/entries/derrida/.

Leezenberg, Michiel. 2001. *Contexts of Metaphor*. Amsterdam: Elsevier.

Lewin, B. 2012. "Ibn al-Muʿtazz." In P. Bearman, T. Bianquis, C. E. Bosworth, E. van Donzel, and W. P. Heinrichs, eds., *Encyclopaedia of Islam*, 2nd ed. Brill Online.

Liddell, H.G., and R. Scott. 1968. *A Greek-English Lexicon.* 9th ed. Rev. H. Stuart Jones. Oxford: Clarendon Press.

Liu, Lydia He. 1995. *Translingual Practice: Literature, National Culture, and Translated Modernity—China, 1900–1937.* Stanford: Stanford University Press.

Lizzini, Olga. 2016. "Ibn Sina's Metaphysics." In E.N. Zalta, ed., *The Stanford Encyclopedia of Philosophy,* fall edition. https://plato.stanford.edu/archives/fall2016/entries/ibn-sina-metaphysics/.

López-Farjeat, Luís Xavier. 2016. "Avicenna on Non-Conceptual Content and Self-Awareness in Non-Human Animals." In J. Kaukua and T. Ekenberg, eds., *Subjectivity and Selfhood in Medieval and Early Modern Philosophy.* New York: Springer.

Lowry, Joseph E. 2004. "The Legal Hermeneutics of al-Shāfiʿī and Ibn Qutayba: A Reconsideration." *Islamic Law and Society* 11: 1–41.

———. 2007. *Early Islamic Legal Theory: The Risāla of Muḥammad ibn Idrīs al-Shāfiʿī.* Leiden: E.J. Brill.

Lyons, John. 1977. *Semantics.* Cambridge: Cambridge University Press.

Madelung, Wilferd. 1974. "Ar-Rāġib al-Iṣfahānī und die Ethik al-Ġazālīs." In R. Gramlich, ed., *Islamwissenschaftliche Abhandlungen: Fritz Meier zum sechzigsten Geburtstag.* Wiesbaden: Steiner.

de Man, Paul. 1983. "The Rhetoric of Temporality." In *Blindness and Insight: Essays in the Rhetoric of Contemporary Criticism.* Minneapolis: University of Minnesota Press.

Marenbon, John. 2010. "The Emergence of Medieval Latin Philosophy." In R. Pasnau and C. van Dyke, eds., *The Cambridge History of Medieval Philosophy.* Cambridge: Cambridge University Press.

———. 2013. *Abelard in Four Dimensions: A Twelfth-Century Philosopher in His Context and Ours.* Notre Dame: University of Notre Dame Press.

Marmura, Michael. 1980. "Avicenna's Proof from Contingency for God's Existence in His Metaphysics of the *Shifāʾ.*" *Mediaeval Studies* 42: 337–52.

Al-Marzūqī, Abū ʿAlī al-Iṣfahānī, and Ḥabīb b. Aws aṭ-Ṭāʾī Abū Tammām. 1991. *Šarḥ Dīwān al-Ḥamāsah.* Ed. Aḥmad Amīn and ʿAbd as-Salām Muḥammad Hārūn. 4 vols. in 2. Beirut: Dār al-Ǧīl.

Massignon, Louis. 1982. *The Passion of al-Hallāj: Mystic and Martyr of Islam.* Princeton: Princeton University Press.

Mavroudi, Maria. 2015. "Greek Language and Education under Early Islam." In B. Sadeghi, A.Q. Ahmed, A.J. Silverstein, and R.G. Hoyland, eds., *Islamic Cultures, Islamic Contexts: Essays in Honor of Professor Patricia Crone.* Leiden: E.J. Brill.

McGinnis, Jon. 2008. "Avicenna's Naturalized Epistemology and Scientific Method." In S. Rahman, T. Street, and H. Tahiri, eds., *The Unity of Science in the Arabic Tradition: Science, Logic, Epistemology and Their Interactions.* Dordrecht: Springer.

———. 2010. *Avicenna.* Oxford: Oxford University Press.

McGinnis, Jon, and David C. Reisman. 2004. *Interpreting Avicenna: Science and Philosophy in Medieval Islam; Proceedings of the Second Conference of the Avicenna Study Group.* Leiden: E.J. Brill.

Melchert, Christopher. 2011. "Education, IV: The Medieval Madrasa." In E. Yarshater, ed., *Encyclopaedia Iranica.* Iranicaonline.

Meyerhof, Max. 1948. "ʿAli al-Bayhaqi's *Tatimmat Siwan al-Hikma:* A Biographical Work on Learned Men of Islam." *Osiris* 8: 122–217.

Miller, Jeannie. 2013. "More than the Sum of Its Parts: Animal Categories and Accretive Logic in Volume One of al-Jāḥiẓ's *Kitāb al-Ḥayawān*." Ph.D. dissertation, New York University.

———. 2016a. Review of *Al-Jāḥiẓ: In Praise of Books*, by James E. Montgomery. *Journal of Near Eastern Studies* 75: 196–98.

———. 2016b. "What It Means to Be a Son: Adam, Language, and Theodicy in a Ninth-Century Dispute." *Journal of the Canadian Society for Syriac Studies* 16: 60–79.

———. Forthcoming. "Bayān, Genre, and Gesture: Al-Jurjānī's Self-Positioning." In Alexander Key ed., *Journal of Abbasid Studies* 5(1–2), special issue: *ʿAbd al-Qāhir al-Jurjānī.*

Moi, Toril. 2017. *Revolution of the Ordinary: Literary Studies after Wittgenstein, Austin, and Cavell.* Chicago: University of Chicago Press.

Montgomery, James E. 2006. "The Empty Ḥijāz." In J. E. Montgomery, ed., *Arabic Theology, Arabic Philosophy: From the Many to the One; Essays in Celebration of Richard M. Frank.* Leuven: Peeters.

Moutaouakil, Ahmed. 1982. *Réflexions sur la théorie de la signification dans la pensée linguistique arabe.* Rabat: Faculté des Lettres et des Sciences Humaines de Rabat.

An-Naḥḥās, Abū Ǧaʿfar Aḥmad. 1988. *Maʿānī al-Qurʾān.* Ed. Muḥammad ʿAlī aṣ-Ṣābūnī. 6 vols. Mecca: Ǧāmiʿat Umm al-Qurā.

Netton, Ian Richard. 2002. *Muslim Neoplatonists: An Introduction to the Thought of the Brethren of Purity (Ikhwān al-Ṣafāʾ).* London / New York: Routledge/Curzon.

Noy, Avigail S. 2016. "The Emergence of ʿIlm al-Bayān: Classical Arabic Literary Theory in the Arabic East in the 7th/13th Century." Ph.D. dissertation, Harvard University.

———. Forthcoming. "The Legacy of ʿAbd al-Qāhir al-Jurjānī in the Arabic East before al-Qazwīnī's *Talkhīṣ al-Miftāḥ*." In Alexander Key ed., *Journal of Abbasid Studies* 5(1–2), special issue: *ʿAbd al-Qāhir al-Jurjānī.*

Nwyia, Paul. 1970. *Exégèse coranique et langage mystique: Nouvel essai sur le lexique technique des mystiques musulmans.* Beirut: Dār al-Mašriq.

Ouyang, Wen-chin. 1997. *Literary Criticism in Medieval Arabic-Islamic Culture: The Making of a Tradition.* Edinburgh: Edinburgh University Press.

Panaccio, Claude. 2017. *Mental Language: From Plato to William of Ockham.* Trans. Joshua P. Hochschild and Meredith K. Ziebart. New York: Fordham University Press.

Peacock, A. C. S. 2015. *The Great Seljuk Empire.* Edinburgh: Edinburgh University Press.

Perseus Digital Library. http://www.perseus.tufts.edu. [Accessed 2016.]

Peters, Johannes Reinier Theodorus Maria. 1976. *God's Created Speech: A Study in the Speculative Theology of the Muʿtazilī Qāḍī l-Quḍāt Abū l-Ḥasan ʿAbd al-Jabbār bn Aḥmad al-Hamadānī.* Leiden: E. J. Brill.

Pollock, Sheldon I. 2014. "Introduction." In S. I. Pollock, B. A. Elman, and K.-M. K. Chang, eds., *World Philology.* Cambridge, Mass.: Harvard University Press.

Pormann, Peter E. 2013. "Avicenna on Medical Practice, Epistemology, and the Physiology of the Inner Senses." In P. Adamson, ed., *Interpreting Avicenna: Critical Essays.* Cambridge: Cambridge University Press.

Porphyry. 2003. *Porphyry: Introduction.* Trans. Jonathan Barnes. Oxford: Clarendon Press.

Al-Qāḍī ʿAbd al-Ǧabbār, Ibn Aḥmad al-Asadābādī. 1965–74. *Al-Muġnī fī Abwāb at-Tawḥīd wa-l-ʿAdl.* Ed. Ṭāhā Ḥusayn. 14 vols. Cairo: ad-Dār al-Miṣrīyah li-t-Taʾlīf wa-n-Našr.

Al-Qāḍī al-Ǧurǧānī, ʿAlī b. ʿAbd al-ʿAzīz. 1966. *Al-Wasāṭah bayn al-Mutanabbī wa-Ḫuṣūmih.* Ed. ʿAlī Muḥammad Baǧǧāwī. Cairo: ʿĪsā al-Bābī al-Ḥalabī.

Al-Qifṭī, ʿAlī b. Yūsuf. 2009. *Inbāh ar-Ruwāh ʿalā Anbāh an-Nuḥāh*. Ed. Muḥammad Abū al-Fāḍl Ibrāhīm. Beirut/Cairo: Muʾassasat al-Kutub aṯ-Ṯaqāfīyah / Dār al-Fikr al-ʿArabī.

Quine, Willard Van Orman. 1986. *Philosophy of Logic*. Cambridge, Mass.: Harvard University Press.

———. 2004. "Meaning and Translation." In L. Venuti, ed., *The Translation Studies Reader*. New York: Routledge.

Al-Qušayrī, Abū Qāsim ʿAbd al-Karīm. 1966. *Ar-Risālah al-Qušayrīyah*. Ed. ʿAbd al-Karīm Maḥmūd and Maḥmūd Ibn aš-Šarīf. 2 vols. Cairo: Dār al-Kutub al-Ḥadīṯah.

———. 2000. *Laṭāʾif al-Išārāt*. Ed. Ibrāhīm Basyūnī. 3 vols. Cairo: al-Hayʾah al-Maṣrīyah al-ʿĀmmah li-l-Kitāb.

———. 2007. *Al-Qushayri's Epistle on Sufism: Al-Risala al-qushayriyya fi ʿilm al-tasawwuf*. Ed. Muhammad S. Eissa. Trans. Alexander D. Knysh. Reading: Garnet.

Ar-Rāġib, Abū al-Qāsim al-Ḥusayn b. Muḥammad al-Iṣfahānī. 409/1018. *Mufradāt Ġarīb al-Qurʾān al-Karīm*. [*Quranic Glossary*.] Manuscript. Library of Muḥammad Luṭfī al-Ḫaṭīb, London. [Private collection.]

———. 1280. *Al-Iʿtiqādāt*. MS 56. Āstān-e Quds-e Rażāvī, Mashhad.

———. (Ca. 14th century.) *Kitāb min Kalām ar-Rāġib fī l-Badīʿ (Afānīn al-Balāġah)*. MS 165. Landberg Collection, Beinecke Rare Book and Manuscript Library, Yale University.

———. 1554. *Al-Iʿtiqādāt*. MS Sehid Ali 382. Süleymaniye, Istanbul.

———. 1680. *Al-Iʿtiqādāt*. MS Feyzullah Efendi 2141. Süleymaniye, Istanbul.

———. 1984. *Muqaddimat Jāmiʿ at-Tafāsīr maʿ Tafsīr al-Fātiḥah wa Maṭāliʿ al-Baqarah*. Ed. Aḥmad Ḥasan Farḥāt. Kuwait: Dār ad-Daʿwah.

———. 1986. *Maǧmaʿ al-Balāġah*. Ed. ʿUmar ʿAbd ar-Raḥmān as-Sārīsī. 2 vols. Amman: Maktabat al-Aqṣā.

———. 1988a. *Al-Iʿtiqādāt*. Ed. Šamrān al-ʿAǧalī. Beirut: Muʾassasat al-Ašraf.

———. 1988b. *Tafṣīl an-Našʾatayn wa Taḥṣīl as-Saʿādatayn*. Ed. Asʿad as-Saḥmarānī. Beirut: Dār an-Nafāʾis.

———. 1992. *Mufradāt Alfāẓ al-Qurʾān al-Karīm*. Ed. Ṣafwān ʿAdnān Dāwūdī. Beirut/Damascus: Dār al-Qalam / Dār aš-Šāmīyah. [Reprint, Qum: Ṭalīʿat an-Nūr, 2006.]

———. 2001. *Tafsīr ar-Rāġib al-Iṣfahānī: Dirāsah wa-taḥqīq min sūrat an-nisāʾ āyat 114 wa-ḥattā nihāyat sūrat al-māʾidah*. [*Quran 4:114–5:120*.] Ed. Hind Bint Muḥammad b. Zāhid Sardār. 2 vols. M.A. thesis, Ǧāmiʿat Umm al-Qurā, Mecca.

———. 2003. *Tafsīr ar-Rāġib al-Iṣfahānī: Min awwal sūrat āl ʿimrān wa-ḥattā nihāyat al-āyah min sūrat an-nisāʾ*. [*Quran 3:1–4:113*.] Ed. ʿĀdil b. ʿAlī aš-Šidī. 2 vols. Riyadh: Madār al-Waṭan li-n-Našr.

———. 2005a. *Rasāʾil ar-Rāġib al-Iṣfahānī*. Ed. ʿUmar ʿAbd ar-Raḥmān as-Sārīsī. Irbid: ʿĀlam al-Kutub al-Ḥadīṯ.

———. 2005b. "Risālah fī Marātib al-ʿUlūm wa-l-Aʿmāl ad-Dunyawīyah." In ʿ.ʿ. A. R. As-Sārīsī, ed., *Rasāʾil ar-Rāġib al-Iṣfahānī*. Irbid: ʿĀlam al-Kutub al-Ḥadīṯ.

———. 2006. *Muḥāḍarāt al-Udabāʾ wa-Muḥāwarāt aš-Šuʿarāʾ wa-l-Bulaġāʾ*. Ed. Riyāḍ ʿAbd al-Ḥamīd Murād. 5 vols. Beirut: Dār Ṣādir.

———. 2007. *Kitāb aḏ-Ḏarīʿah ilā Makārim aš-Šarīʿah*. Ed. Abū al-Yazīd al-ʿAǧamī. Cairo: Dār as-Salām.

———. N.d. *Tafsīr*. MS Carullah 84. Süleymaniye, Istanbul. [Methodological introduction plus exegesis of Quran 1:1–5:120.]

———. N.d.(2). *Al-Iʿtiqādāt*. MS AR 5277. Chester Beatty Library, Dublin.

———. N.d.(3). *Tafsīr.* MS Ayasofya 212. Süleymaniye, Istanbul. [Quran 1:1–2:223.]

Ransom, John Crowe. 1979. *The New Criticism.* Westport: Greenwood Press.

Ar-Rāzī, Faḫr ad-Dīn. 1992. *Nihāyat al-Īǧāz fī Dirāyat al-Iʿǧāz.* Ed. Aḥmad Ḥiǧāzī Aḥmad as-Saqqā. Beirut/Cairo: Dār al-Ǧīl / al-Maktab aṯ-Ṯaqāfī.

Reisman, David C., and Ahmed H. al-Rahim. 2003. *Before and after Avicenna: Proceedings of the First Conference of the Avicenna Study Group.* Leiden: E. J. Brill.

Rippin, Andrew. 2015. "Al-Mubarrad (d. 285/898) and Polysemy in the Qurʾān." In A. Rippin and R. Tottoli, eds., *Books and Written Culture of the Islamic World: Studies Presented to Claude Gilliot on the Occasion of His 75th Birthday.* Leiden: E. J. Brill.

———. 2016. "Foreign Vocabulary." In J. D. McAuliffe, ed., *Encyclopaedia of the Qurʾān.* Brill Online.

Rowson, Everett K., and Abū al-Ḥasan Muḥammad b. Yūsuf al-ʿĀmirī. 1988. *A Muslim Philosopher on the Soul and Its Fate: Al-ʿĀmirī's Kitāb al-Amad ʿalā l-Abad.* New Haven: American Oriental Society.

Rudolph, Ulrich. 2017. "Abū Naṣr al-Fārābī." In U. Rudolph, R. Hansberger, and P. Adamson, eds., *Philosophy in the Islamic World.* Leiden: E. J. Brill.

Ar-Rummānī, ʿAlī b. ʿĪsā. 1993–94. "Šarḥ Kitāb Sībawayh." Ed. Muḥammad Ibrāhīm Yūsuf Šaybah. Ph.D. dissertation, Ǧāmiʿat Umm al-Qurā, Mecca.

Sabra, A. I. 1980. "Avicenna on the Subject Matter of Logic." *The Journal of Philosophy* 77: 746–64.

———. 2006. "*Kalām* Atomism as an Alternative Philosophy to Hellenizing *Falsafa.*" In J. E. Montgomery, ed., *Arabic Theology, Arabic Philosophy: From the Many to the One; Essays in Celebration of Richard M. Frank.* Dudley: Peeters.

———. 2009. "The Simple Ontology of *Kalām* Atomism: An Outline." *Early Science and Medicine* 14: 68–78.

Sadan, Joseph. 1991. "Maidens' Hair and Starry Skies: Imagery System and *maʿānī* Guides: The Practical Side of Arabic Poetics as Demonstrated in Two Manuscripts." In S. Somekh, ed., *Studies in Medieval Arabic and Hebrew Poetics.* Leiden: E. J. Brill.

Sadeghi, Behnam. 2013. *The Logic of Law-making in Islam: Women and Prayer in the Legal Tradition.* Cambridge: Cambridge University Press.

As-Samarqandī, ʿAlī b. Yaḥyā. 2010. "Šarḥ ʿalā Risālat al-Waḍʿ." In ʿ. A. ar-Rāwī, ed., *Ḥāšiyah ʿalā Šarḥ Risālat al-Waḍʿ.* Beirut: Dār al-Kutub al-ʿIlmīyah.

Aṣ-Ṣarīfīnī, Taqī ad-Dīn Abū Isḥāq Ibrāhīm. 1989. *Al-Muntaḫab min as-Siyāq li-Tārīḫ Nīsabūr.* Ed. Muḥammad Aḥmad ʿAbd al-ʿAzīz Zaydān. Beirut: Dār al-Kutub al-ʿIlmīyah.

Schmidtke, Sabine. 2008. "Theological Rationalism in the Medieval Islamic World." *Al-ʿUṣūr al-Wusṭā: The Bulletin of Middle East Medievalists* 20: 17–30.

Sennet, Adam. 2015. "Ambiguity." In E. N. Zalta, ed., *The Stanford Encyclopedia of Philosophy,* spring edition. http://plato.stanford.edu/archives/spr2015/entries/ambiguity/.

Sezgin, Fuat. 1967–. *Geschichte des arabischen Schrifttums.* Leiden/Frankfurt: E. J. Brill / Institut für Geschichte der Arabisch-Islamischen Wissenschaften.

Sharlet, Jocelyn. 2015. Review of *Abundance from the Desert: Classical Arabic Poetry,* by Raymond Farrin. *Journal of Near Eastern Studies* 74: 184–87.

Shields, Christopher. 2016. "Aristotle's Psychology." In E. N. Zalta, ed., *The Stanford Encyclopedia of Philosophy,* winter edition. https://plato.stanford.edu/archives/win2016/entries/aristotle-psychology/.

Sībawayh, Abū Bišr ʿAmr b. ʿUṯmān. 1966. *Al-Kitāb.* Ed. ʿAbd as-Salām Muḥammad Hārūn. 5 vols. Cairo: Dār al-Qalam.

Aš-Šidyāq, Aḥmad Fāris. 2013. *Leg over Leg; or, The Turtle in the Tree: Concerning the Fāriyāq, What Manner of Creature Might He Be.* New York: New York University Press.

Simplicius. 2003. *On Aristotle's "Categories" 1–4.* Trans. Michael Chase. Ithaca: Cornell University Press.

As-Sīrāfī, Abū Saʿīd. 2008. "Šarḥ Kitāb Sībawayh." In A.Ḥ. Mahdalī and ʿA.S. ʿAlī, eds., *Šarḥ Kitāb Sībawayh.* Beirut: Dār al-Kutub al-ʿIlmīyah.

Skinner, Quentin. 2002. *Visions of Politics.* Volume 1, *Regarding Method.* Cambridge: Cambridge University Press.

Smyth, William Earl. 1986. "Persian and Arabic Theories of Literature: A Comparative Study of al-Sakkâkî's *Miftâḥ al-ʿulûm* and Shams-i Qays' *Al-Muʿjam fî maʿâyîr ashʿâr al-ʿajam.*" Ph.D. dissertation, New York University.

Sontag, Susan. 1966. *Against Interpretation, and Other Essays.* New York: Farrar, Straus, and Giroux.

Sorabji, Richard. 2005. *The Philosophy of the Commentators, 200–600 AD: A Sourcebook.* Volume 3, *Logic and Metaphysics.* Ithaca: Cornell University Press.

Sperl, Stefan. 1989. *Mannerism in Arabic Poetry: A Structural Analysis of Selected Texts, Third Century AH/Ninth Century AD–Fifth Century AH/Eleventh Century AD.* Cambridge: Cambridge University Press.

Stephanus of Alexandria. 2000. *"Philoponus" on Aristotle's "On the Soul" 3.9–13, with Stephanus on Aristotle, "On Interpretation."* Trans. William Charlton. Ithaca: Cornell University Press.

Stetkevych, Jaroslav. 1979–80. "The Arabic Qaṣīdah: From Form and Content to Mood and Meaning." In *Eucharisterion: Essays Presented to Omeljan Pritsak on His Sixtieth Birthday by His Colleagues and Students,* Harvard Ukrainian Studies 3–4, part 2: 774–85. Cambridge, Mass.: Ukrainian Research Institute.

Strauss, Leo. 1989. "How to Begin to Study Medieval Philosophy." In L. Strauss and T.L. Pangle, eds., *The Rebirth of Classical Political Rationalism: An Introduction to the Thought of Leo Strauss.* Chicago: University of Chicago Press.

Street, Tony. 2004. "Arabic Logic." In D.M. Gabbay, J. Woods, and A. Kanamori, eds., *Handbook of the History of Logic.* Amsterdam/Boston: Elsevier.

———. 2015. "Arabic and Islamic Philosophy of Language and Logic." In E.N. Zalta, ed., *The Stanford Encyclopedia of Philosophy,* spring edition. http://plato.stanford.edu/archives/fall2008/entries/arabic-islamic-language/.

Strobino, Riccardo. 2016. "Per Se, Inseparability, Containment and Implication: Bridging the Gap between Avicenna's Theory of Demonstration and Logic of the Predicables." *Oriens* 44: 181–266.

As-Subkī, Tāǧ ad-Dīn ʿAbd al-Wahhāb. 1964–. *Ṭabaqāt aš-Šāfiʿīyah al-Kubrā.* Ed. ʿAbd al-Fattāḥ Muḥammad al-Ḥulw and Maḥmūd Muḥammad aṭ-Ṭanāḥī. 9 vols. Cairo: ʿĪsā al-Bābī al-Ḥalabī.

Aṣ-Ṣūlī, Ibrāhīm b. al-ʿAbbās. 1937. "Šiʿr al-Kātib aš-Šāʿir al-Maṭbūʿ Ibrāhīm b. al-ʿAbbās aṣ-Ṣūlī." In ʿAbd al-ʿA. al-Maymanī, ed., *Aṭ-Ṭarāʾif al-Adabīyah.* Cairo: Laǧnat at-Taʾlīf wa-t-Tarǧamah wa-n-Našr.

As-Suyūṭī, Ǧalāl ad-Dīn. 1979. *Buġyat al-Wuʿāh fī Ṭabaqāt al-Luġawīyīn wa-n-Nuḥāh.* Ed. Muḥammad Abū al-Faḍl Ibrāhīm. 2 vols. Beirut: Dār al-Fikr.

Aṯ-Ṯaʿālibī, Abū Manṣūr ʿAbd al-Malik. 1983. *Yatīmat ad-Dahr fī Maḥāsin Ahl al-Aṣr.* Ed. Mufīd Muḥammad Qamīḥah. 5 vols. Beirut: Dār al-Kutub al-ʿIlmīyah.

Aṭ-Ṭaḥāwī, Aḥmad b. Muḥammad. 1994. *Šarḥ Maʿānī al-Āṯār.* Ed. Muḥammad Zahrī an-Naǧǧār and Muḥammad Sayyid Ǧād al-Ḥaqq. 5 vols. Beirut: ʿĀlam al-Kutub.

At-Tawḥīdī, Abū Ḥayyān. 1970. *Al-Muqābasāt.* Ed. Muḥammad Tawfīq Ḥusayn. Baghdad: Maṭbaʿat al-Iršād.

Thiele, Jan. 2016a. "Between Cordoba and Nīsābūr: The Emergence and Consolidation of Ashʿarism (Fourth–Fifth/Tenth–Eleventh Century)." In S. Schmidtke, ed., *The Oxford Handbook of Islamic Theology.* Oxford: Oxford University Press.

———. 2016b. "Conceptions of Self-Determination in Fourth-/Tenth-Century Muslim Theology: Al-Bāqillānī's Theory of Human Acts in Its Historical Context." *Arabic Sciences and Philosophy* 26(2): 245–69.

Thom, Paul. 2008. "Logic and Metaphysics in Avicenna's Modal Syllogistic." In S. Rahman, T. Street, and H. Tahiri, eds., *The Unity of Science in the Arabic Tradition: Science, Logic, Epistemology and Their Interactions.* Dordrecht: Springer.

———. 2016. "On Logics of Genus and Differentia in the Aristotelian Tradition." *Documenti e Studi sulla Tradizione Filosofica Medievale* 27: 131–62.

Thomas, Stephanie Bowie. 2000. "The Concept of Muḥāḍara in the *Adab* Anthology, with Special Reference to al-Rāghib al-Iṣfahānī's *Muḥāḍarāt al-Udabāʾ.*" Ph.D. dissertation, Harvard University.

Toorawa, Shawkat M. 2005. *Ibn Abī Ṭāhir Ṭayfūr and Arabic Writerly Culture: A Ninth-Century Bookman in Baghdad.* London: Routledge.

Treiger, Alexander. 2012. "Avicenna's Notion of Transcendental Modulation of Existence (*taškīk al-wuǧūd, analogia entis*) and Its Greek and Arabic Sources." In F. M. M. Opwis and D. Reisman, eds., *Islamic Philosophy, Science, Culture, and Religion: Studies in Honor of Dimitri Gutas.* Leiden: E. J. Brill.

———. 2016. "Origins of *Kalām.*" In S. Schmidtke, ed., *The Oxford Handbook of Islamic Theology.* Oxford: Oxford University Press.

Ullmann, Manfred. 2002–7. *Wörterbuch zu den griechisch-arabischen Übersetzungen des 9. Jahrhunderts.* Wiesbaden: Harrassowitz. [Including supplementary volumes.]

Vagelpohl, Uwe. 2008. *Aristotle's "Rhetoric" in the East: The Syriac and Arabic Translation and Commentary Tradition.* Leiden: E. J. Brill.

———. 2010. "The ʿAbbasid Translation Movement in Context: Contemporary Voices on Translation." In J. Nawas, ed., *ʿAbbasid Studies,* vol. 2, *Occasional Papers of the School of ʿAbbasid Studies, Leuven, 28 June–1 July 2004.* Leuven: Peeters.

———. 2015. "The *Rhetoric* and *Poetics* in the Islamic World." In A. Alwishah and J. Hayes, eds., *Aristotle and the Arabic Tradition.* Cambridge: Cambridge University Press.

Vasalou, Sophia. 2009. "'Their Intention Was Shown by Their Bodily Movements': The Basran Muʿtazilites on the Institution of Language." *Journal of the History of Philosophy* 47: 201–21.

Versteegh, Kees. 1992. "Grammar and Rhetoric: Ǧurǧānī on the Verbs of Admiration." *Jerusalem Studies of Arabic and Islam* 15: 113–33.

Vishanoff, David R. 2011. *The Formation of Islamic Hermeneutics: How Sunni Legal Theorists Imagined a Revealed Law.* New Haven: American Oriental Society.

Wakelnig, Elvira. 2014. *A Philosophy Reader from the Circle of Miskawayh.* Cambridge: Cambridge University Press.

Wansborough, John. 1967. "A Note on Arabic Rhetoric." In H. Meller and H.J. Zimmermann, eds., *Lebende Antike: Symposium für Rudolf Sühnel.* Berlin: Schmidt.

———. 1970. "*Majāz al-qurʾān:* Periphrastic Exegesis." *Bulletin of the School of Oriental and African Studies* 33: 247–66.

———. 1984. Review of *Aristotle's "Ars Rhetorica": The Arabic Version; A New Edition with Commentary and Glossary,* by M.C. Lyons. *Bulletin of the School of Oriental and African Studies* 47: 550–51.

Weipert, Reinhard. 2007. "Abū ʿUbayda." In G. Krämer, D. Matringe, J. Nawas, and E. Rowson, eds., *Encyclopaedia of Islam, THREE.* Brill Online.

Weiss, Bernard. 2014. "Waḍʿ al-Luġa." In K. Versteegh, L. Edzard, and R.D. Jong, eds., *Encyclopedia of Arabic Language and Linguistics.* Brill Online.

Williams, Thomas. 2003. *The Cambridge Companion to Duns Scotus.* Cambridge: Cambridge University Press.

Wisnovsky, Robert. 2003. *Avicenna's Metaphysics in Context.* London: Duckworth.

———. 2004a. "The Nature and Scope of Arabic Philosophical Commentary in Post-Classical (ca. 1100–1900 AD) Islamic Intellectual History: Some Preliminary Observations." In P. Adamson, H. Baltussen, and M.W.F. Stone, eds., *Philosophy, Science and Exegesis in Greek, Arabic and Latin Commentaries,* vol. 2. Bulletin of the Institute of Classical Studies, Supplement 83(2). London: Institute of Classical Studies.

———. 2004b. "One Aspect of the Avicennian Turn in Sunni Theology." *Arabic Science and Philosophy* 14: 65–100.

Wittgenstein, Ludwig. 2006. *Philosophical Investigations: The German Text, with a Revised English Translation.* Trans. G.E.M. Anscombe. Oxford: Blackwell.

Wolfson, Harry Austryn. 1956. "The Muslim Attributes and the Christian Trinity." *The Harvard Theological Review* 49: 1–18.

———. 1965. "Muʿammar's Theory of Maʿnā." In G. Makdisi, ed., *Arabic and Islamic Studies in Honor of Hamilton A.R. Gibb.* Cambridge, Mass.: Department of Near Eastern Languages and Literatures of Harvard University.

———. 1976. *The Philosophy of the Kalam.* Cambridge, Mass.: Harvard University Press.

Wright, William. 1898. *A Grammar of the Arabic Language.* Cambridge: Cambridge University Press.

Al-Yamānī, ʿAbd al-Bāqī b. ʿAbd al-Maǧīd. 1986. *Išārat at-Taʿyīn fī Tarāǧim an-Nuḥāh wa-l-Luġawīyīn.* Ed. ʿAbd al-Maǧīd Diyāb. Riyadh: Markaz al-Malik Fayṣal li-l-Buḥūṯ wa-d-Dirāsāt al-Islāmīyah.

Az-Zaǧǧāǧī, Abū al-Qāsim ʿAbd ar-Raḥmān b. Isḥāq. 1959. *Al-Īḍāḥ fī ʿIlal an-Naḥw.* Ed. Māzin al-Mubārak. Cairo: Dār al-ʿUrūbah.

———. 1984. *Kitāb Ḥurūf al-Maʿānī.* Ed. ʿAlī Tawfīq al-Ḥamad. Beirut: Muʾassasat ar-Risālah.

Zemánek, Petr. 2015. "Root." In K. Versteegh, L. Edzard, and R.D. Jong, eds., *Encyclopedia of Arabic Language and Linguistics.* Brill Online.

Zimmermann, F.W. 1981. *Al-Farabi's Commentary and Short Treatise on Aristotle's "De Interpretatione."* Oxford: Oxford University Press for the British Academy.

Zysow, Aron. 2013. *The Economy of Certainty: An Introduction to the Typology of Islamic Legal Theory.* Atlanta: Lockwood Press.

INDEX OF NAMES AND SUBJECTS

فهرس المصطلحات العربية الموجودة في الحواشي

فهرس القوافي

فهرس صدور الأبيات

CPSIA information can be obtained
at www.ICGtesting.com
Printed in the USA
LVHW03s0739080818
586192LV00002B/2/P

9 780520 298019